如发现印、装质量问题，影响阅读，请与出版社联系调换。

(联系地址：北京市方庄小区芳城园三区 13 号楼　邮编：100078)

中国教育统计年鉴

EDUCATIONAL STATISTICS YEARBOOK OF CHINA

1999

中华人民共和国
教育部发展规划司
DEPARTMENT OF DEVELOPMENT & PLANNING
MINISTRY OF EDUCATION
THE PEOPLE'S REPUBLIC OF CHINA

图书在版编目（CIP）数据

中国教育统计年鉴．1999/教育部发展规划司编．
北京：人民教育出版社，2000
ISBN 7-107-13874-X

Ⅰ．中...
Ⅱ．教...
Ⅲ．教育事业-统计资料-中国-1999-年鉴．
Ⅳ．G526．6-66

中国版本图书馆 CIP 数据核字（2000）第 39000 号

*

人民教育出版社出版发行
（北京沙滩后街 55 号　邮编：100009）
网址：http://www.pep.com.cn
人民教育出版社印刷厂印装　全国新华书店经销
2000 年 9 月第 1 版　　2000 年 9 月第 1 次印刷
开本：787 毫米×1 092 毫米　1/16　印张：25.75
字数：560 千字　印数：0 001～2 600 册
定价：60.00 元

说　明

《中国教育统计年鉴》(1999)是一本全面反映中华人民共和国教育事业发展情况的资料性年鉴，是由教育部发展规划司根据全国各省、自治区、直辖市教育委员会、高教局、教育厅(局)填报的学校基层报表数字整理汇编而成的。教育部教育管理信息中心承担了数据的计算机处理汇总工作。

本年鉴包括以下部分:综合部分、高等教育、中等教育、初等教育幼儿教育、特殊教育、成人教育、各级各类学校的分布情况、办学条件、科学研究等。

本年鉴是各有关部门研究教育改革和发展的必备资料工具书,是教育界各机关、学校指导部门制定教育计划、指导教育改革必不可少的依据。

本年鉴所列资料，暂缺台湾省的数字;凡未注明年份的均为 1999 年的数字。

Notes from the Compiler

The Educational Statistics Yearbook of China for 1999 is an informational yearbook comprehensively reflecting the development of the educational undertaking of the People's Republic of China, and it was compiled by the Department of Development and Planning of Ministry of Education, based on the synthetic statistical returns relating to schools of various types and levels completed by the Educational Commissions (or the Bureaus of Education and Higher Education) of the provincial governments and the goverments of various autonomous regions and municipalities directly under the State Council. All data were processed and calculated using Computers by the Educational Management Information Center of Ministry of Education.

The yearbook is composed of the following parts: summary tables, higher education, secondary education, primary education, special education, re-primary education, adult education, geographical distribution of schools by type and level, Physical Facilities, Scientific Research Activities.

The yearbook is a requisite reference for all departments concerned with the study of educational reform and development, and provides indispensable factual information to the educational community (circles), the state organs, and all supervisory bodies of education (schools) engaged in curricular development and the guidance of educational reform.

The yearbook lacks the data of Taiwan Province. Data in tables are for 1999, unless otherwise notified.

目　录

第一部分　教育事业发展

一、综合部分

全国各级各类学校基本情况 …… 2
全国各级普通学校基本情况 …… 2
全国各级成人学校基本情况 …… 3
全国各级自学考试基本情况 …… 4
各级普通学校校数 …… 8
各级普通学校学生数 …… 9
各级普通学校招生数 …… 10
各级普通学校教职工数 …… 11
各级普通学校专任教师数 …… 12
高级中等学校学生数的构成 …… 13
教育规模 …… 14
小学学龄儿童净入学率 …… 14
各级普通教育毛入学率 …… 15
各级普通教育毕业生升学率 …… 15
每十万人口各级学校平均在校生数 …… 16
各级普通学校生师比 …… 16
普通高等学校校均规模 …… 16
各级普通学校女学生和女教职工数 …… 17
各级普通学校少数民族学生和少数民族教职工数 …… 18

二、普通教育

(一) 高等教育

普通高等学校校数 …… 20
普通高等学校规模 …… 20
普通高等学校设置专业数 …… 21
普通高等学校工科分大类学生数 …… 21
普通高等学校基本情况 …… 22
普通高等学校本专科学生数 …… 24
普通高等学校学生数补充资料 …… 24
普通高等学校分科学生数 …… 26
普通高等学校函授部、夜大学、成人脱产班分科学生数 …… 28
普通高等学校学生数变动情况 …… 28
普通高等学校分科专任教师数 …… 30
专任教师中本学年内不担任教学工作的人数 …… 31
非教学人员中有教师职称的人数 …… 31
普通高等学校专任教师学历情况 …… 32
普通高等学校专任教师年龄情况 …… 32
普通高等学校教职工数补充资料 …… 32
普通高等学校专任教师变动情况 …… 34

普通高等学校校舍情况 ……34
社会力量举办的非学历高等教育机构基本情况 ……36

研究生

全国研究生基本情况 ……38
高等学校研究生基本情况 ……40
科研机构研究生基本情况 ……42
全国研究生指导教师情况 ……44
普通高等学校研究生指导教师情况 ……45
科研机构研究生指导教师情况 ……46

(二) 中等教育

1、中等专业学校

中等专业学校分类别情况 ……48
中等专业学校学生数变动情况 ……48
中等专业学校分科学生数 ……50
中等专业学校学生数补充资料 ……50
中等专业学校专任教师年龄情况 ……51
中等专业学校分课程专任教师数 ……52
中等专业学校分中央部门、地方学校基本情况 ……52
中等专业学校女学生和女教职工数 ……52
中等专业学校专任教师变动情况 ……54
中等专业学校专任教师学历情况 ……54
中等专业学校校舍情况 ……54
中等专业学校其他情况 ……55

2、普通中学

普通中学校数、班数 ……57
普通中学学生数 ……58
普通中学教职工数 ……60
普通中学分课程专任教师学历情况 ……62
普通中学专任教师专业技术职务、年龄结构情况 ……64
普通中学校舍情况 ……66
普通初中班额情况 ……66

3、职业中学

职业中学校数、班数、毕业生数和招生数 ……68
职业中学在校学生数和毕业班学生数 ……70
职业中学高中阶段分科学生数 ……72
职业中学教职工数 ……72
职业中学专任教师学历情况 ……74
职业中学专任教师专业技术职务、年龄结构情况 ……76
职业中学校舍情况 ……78

(三) 初等教育(小学)

小学校数、班数和学生数 ……80
小学教职工数 ……82
小学专任教师专业技术职务、年龄结构情况 ……84

学龄儿童入学率 ……86
小学专任教师学历情况 ……86
小学校舍情况 ……87
小学班额情况 ……87
(四) 特殊教育
特殊教育学校基本情况 ……90
(五) 幼儿教育
幼儿教育基本情况 ……94
园长、专任教师学历情况 ……94

三、成人教育

(一) 高等教育
成人高等学校基本情况 ……96
成人高等学校分本专科学生数 ……98
成人高等学校分科学生数 ……100
成人高等学校其他学生数 ……100
成人高等学校专任教师学历情况 ……102
成人高等学校在校学生、教职工的政治及其他情况 ……102
成人高等学校专任教师年龄情况 ……104
成人高等学校学生数变动情况 ……104
成人高等学校固定资产情况及其他 ……106
成人高等学校校舍情况 ……106
(二) 成人中、初等教育
1、成人中等专业学校
成人中等专业学校分类别情况 ……110
成人中等专业学校教职工数 ……112
成人中等专业学校校舍情况 ……112
2、成人中学
成人中学基本情况 ……114
3、成人小学
成人小学基本情况 ……114
4、成人技术培训教育
成人技术培训学校基本情况 ……116
5、全国农业广播电视学校
全国农业广播电视学校基本情况 ……118
全国农业广播电视学校分年度学生数 ……118

四、各级各类学校分布情况

普通高等学校基本情况（总计） ……120
职业技术学院基本情况 ……122
综合大学基本情况 ……124
高等理工院校基本情况 ……126
高等农业院校基本情况 ……128
高等林业院校基本情况 ……130
高等医药院校基本情况 ……132

高等师范院校基本情况 ……134
高等语文院校基本情况 ……136
高等财经院校基本情况 ……138
高等政法院校基本情况 ……140
高等体育院校基本情况 ……142
高等艺术院校基本情况 ……144
高等民族院校基本情况 ……146
普通高等学校女学生和女教职工数 ……148
中等专业学校基本情况 ……150
中等技术学校基本情况 ……152
中等工业学校基本情况 ……154
中等农业学校基本情况 ……156
中等林业学校基本情况 ……158
中等医药学校基本情况 ……160
中等财经学校基本情况 ……162
中等政法学校基本情况 ……164
中等体育学校基本情况 ……166
中等艺术学校基本情况 ……168
其他中等技术学校基本情况 ……170
中等师范学校基本情况 ……172
中等师范学校中幼儿师范学校基本情况 ……174
中等专业学校女学生和女教职工数 ……176
普通中学校数、班数（总计） ……178
普通中学校数、班数（城市） ……180
普通中学校数、班数（县镇） ……182
普通中学校数、班数（农村） ……184
普通中学毕业生数、招生数、毕业班学生数（总计） ……186
普通中学毕业生数、招生数、毕业班学生数（城市） ……187
普通中学毕业生数、招生数、毕业班学生数（县镇） ……188
普通中学毕业生数、招生数、毕业班学生数（农村） ……189
普通中学在校学生数（总计） ……190
普通中学在校学生数（城市） ……192
普通中学在校学生数（县镇） ……194
普通中学在校学生数（农村） ……196
普通中学学生总数中女学生数 ……198
普通中学教职工数（总计） ……200
普通中学教职工数（城市） ……202
普通中学教职工数（县镇） ……204
普通中学教职工数（农村） ……206
普通中学教职工总数中民办教职工数 ……208
普通中学教职工总数中女教职工数 ……210
职业中学校数、班数、毕业生数和招生数（总计） ……212
职业中学校数、班数、毕业生数和招生数（城市） ……214
职业中学校数、班数、毕业生数和招生数（县镇） ……216
职业中学校数、班数、毕业生数和招生数（农村） ……218
职业中学在校学生数、毕业班学生数（总计） ……220

职业中学在校学生数、毕业班学生数（城市）……222
职业中学在校学生数、毕业班学生数（县镇）……224
职业中学在校学生数、毕业班学生数（农村）……226
职业中学学生总数中女学生数……228
职业中学教职工数（总计）……230
职业中学教职工数（城市）……232
职业中学教职工数（县镇）……234
职业中学教职工数（农村）……236
职业中学教职工总数中女教职工数……238
小学校数、班数、招生数、毕业生数（总计）……240
小学校数、班数、招生数、毕业生数（城市）……242
小学校数、班数、招生数、毕业生数（县镇）……244
小学校数、班数、招生数、毕业生数（农村）……246
六年制小学校数、班数、招生数、毕业生数……248
小学在校学生数和毕业班学生数（总计）……250
小学在校学生数和毕业班学生数（城市）……252
小学在校学生数和毕业班学生数（县镇）……254
小学在校学生数和毕业班学生数（农村）……256
六年制小学在校学生数和毕业班学生数……258
小学在校学生数和毕业班学生总数中女生数……260
小学教职工数（总计）……262
小学教职工数（城市）……264
小学教职工数（县镇）……266
小学教职工数（农村）……268
小学教职工总数中民办教职工数……270
小学教职工总数中女教职工数……272
小学学龄儿童入学率情况……274
小学女学龄儿童入学率情况……276
特殊教育学校基本情况（包括盲聋哑学校及弱智儿童辅读学校）……278
特殊教育学校中盲聋哑学校基本情况……280
幼儿园基本情况（总计）……282
成人高等学校基本情况（总计）（不包括普通高等学校函授部、夜大学）……284
成人高等学校本、专科学生数（总计）（不包括普通高等学校函授部、夜大学）……286
广播电视大学基本情况……288
广播电视大学本、专科学生数……290
职工高等学校基本情况……292
职工高等学校本、专科学生数……294
农民高等学校基本情况……296
独立函授学院基本情况……296
独立函授学院本、专科学生数……296
教育学院基本情况……298
教育学院本、专科学生数……300
管理干部学院基本情况……302
管理干部学院本、专科学生数……304
普通高等学校举办函授部、夜大学、成人脱产班分本专科学生数……306
成人高等学校其他学生数（总计）……308

成人中等专业学校基本情况（总计）（列入计划，学制两年以上）……310
广播电视中等专业学校基本情况（列入计划，学制两年以上）……312
职工中等专业学校基本情况（列入计划，学制两年以上）……314
农民中等专业学校基本情况（列入计划，学制两年以上）……316
教师进修学校基本情况（列入计划，学制两年以上）……318
干部中等专业学校基本情况（列入计划，学制两年以上）……320
成人中学基本情况（总计）……322
职工中学基本情况……324
农民中学基本情况……326
成人技术培训学校基本情况（总计）……328
职工技术培训学校基本情况……330
农民技术培训学校基本情况……332
成人小学基本情况……334
职工小学基本情况……336
农民小学基本情况……338
农民小学中扫盲班基本情况……340
全国农业广播电视学校基本情况……342

第二部分　办学条件

一、教育经费

全国教育经费来源和支出情况……346
各地区教育经费来源和支出情况(1998年)……347
各类学校教育经费来源和支出情况(1998年)……348

二、教育基本建设投资

教育基本建设投资完成情况(1999年)……350
教育基本建设投资分省完成情况(1999年)……352

三、仪器设备

教育、科研仪器设备分省情况(1998年)……356
教育、科研仪器设备分省情况(1999年)……357

第三部分　科学研究活动及其他

一、自然科学与技术

全国普通高等学校科技人力情况(1998年)……360
全国普通高等学校科技人力中科学家和工程师技术职务(职称)情况(1998年)……361
全国普通高等学校科技经费情况(1998年)……362
全国普通高等学校研究与发展课题、成果情况(1998年)……363

二、社会科学

全国普通高等学校人文、社会科学人力情况(1998年)……366
全国普通高等学校人文、社会科学研究与发展经费情况(1998年)……368
全国普通高等学校人文、社会科学研究与发展课题、成果情况(1998年)……370

普通高等学校招生报名情况 (1998 年)······372
普通高等学校招生报名情况(一) (1999 年)······374
普通高等学校招生报名情况(二) (1999 年)······376

附表:

国内生产总值······380
各地区国内生产总值(1998 年)······381
国家财政收支总额及增长速度······382
中央财政和地方财政收支总额······383
人口数及构成······384
各地区总人口和出生率、死亡率、自然增长率(1998 年)······385
各地区按性别和受教育程度分的人口······386
各地区分性别的 15 岁及 15 岁以上文盲、半文盲人口······388

CONTENTS

PART Ⅰ

THE DEVELOPMENT OF THE EDUCATIONAL UNDERTAKING

SUMMARY TABLES

Basic Statistics of Regular and Adult Schools in China by Level & Type (2)
Basic Statistics of Regular Schools in China by Level & Type (2)
Basic Statistics of Adult Schools in China by Level & Type (3)
Basic Statistics of Applicants for State-administered Examination for Self-learners by Level (4)
Number of Regular Schools by Level & Type (8)
Enrolment of Regular Schools by Level & Type (9)
Number of Regular School Entrants by Level & Type (10)
Number of Regular School Teachers, Staff & Workers by Level & Type (11)
Number of Regular School Full-time Teachers by Level & Type (12)
Composition of Students in Regular Secondary Schools (13)
Size of Education (14)
Net Enrolment Rate of School-age Children & Annual Retention Rate of Enrolment in Primary Schools (14)
Gross Enrolment Rate of Regular School by Level (15)
Promotion Rate of Regular School by Level & Type Gradutes (15)
Number of Students per 100,000 Inhabitants by level (16)
Pupil-Teacher Ratio of Regular Education by level (16)
Average Size of Regular Inst. of Higher Education (16)
Number of Female Students, Teachers, Staff & Workers by Level & Type of Regular Schools (17)
Number of Minority Students Enrolled, Teachers, Staff & Workers in Regular Schools at Various Levels (18)

REGULAR EDUCATION

HIGHER EDUCATION

Number of Regular Higher Educational Institutions (20)
Breakdown of Regular Higher Educational Institutions by Size of Enrolments (20)
Number of Specialities and Number of Educational Programmes Established by Field of Study in Regular Higher Educational Institutions (21)
Breakdown of Engineering Students by Subfield of Study in Regular Higher Educational Institutions (21)
Basic Statistics of Regular Higher Educational Institutions (22)
Number of Undergraduate Students by Type of Courses in Regular Higher Educational Institution (24)
Supplementary Data for Speical Categories of Undergraduate Students (24)
Number of Students by Field of Study in Regular Higher Educational Institutions (26)
Number of Students Enrolled in Correspondence Divisions、Evening Schools & Short-cycle Courses for Cadres Attached to Regular Institutions of Higher Education (28)
Changes in Undergraduate Enrolment (28)

Number of Full－time Teachers by Field of Study in Regular Higher Educational Institutions (30)
Number of Full－time Teachers Carrying No Teaching Load (31)
Breakdown of Non－Teaching Staff with Academic Ranks (31)
Breakdown of Full－time Teachers by Academic Qualifications in Regular Higher Educational Institutions (32)
Breakdown of Full－time Teachers by Age in Regular Higher Educational Institutions (32)
Supplementary Data for Teachers, Staff & Workers in Regular HEIs (32)
Changes of Full－time Teachers in Regular Higher Educational Institutions (34)
Condition of School Buildings in Regular Higher Educational Institutions (34)
Basic Conditions of In－formal Schooling at Non－State Higher Education Institutions (36)

GRADUATE EDUCATION
Basic Statistics of Graduate Education in China (38)
Basic Statistics of Graduate Education in Regular Higher Educational Institutions (40)
Basic Statistics of Graduate Education in Research Organizations (42)
Basic Data on Supervisors of Postgraduate Programmes in China (44)
Basic Data on Supervisors of Postgraduate Programmes in Regular Higher Educational Institutions (45)
Basic Data on Supervisors of Postgraduate Programmes in Research Organizations (46)

SECONDARY EDUCATION
SPECIALIZED SECONDARY SCHOOLS
Basic Statistics of Specialized Secondary Schools by Field of Study (48)
Changes in Enrolment of Specialized Sec.Schools (48)
Number of Students by Field of Study in Specialized Secondary Schools (50)
Supplementary Data for Total Enrolment of Specialized Secondary Schools (50)
Breakdown of Full－time Teachers by Age in Specialized Secondary Schools (51)
Number of Full－time Teachers of Specialized Secondary Schools by Subject Taught (52)
Basic Statistics of Specialized Secondary Schools by Control (52)
Number of Female Students, Teachers,Staff & Workers in Specialized Secondary Schools (52)
Changes of Full－time Teachers in Specialized Sec. Schools (54)
Breakdown of Full－time Teachers by Educational Attainment in Specialized Sec. Schools (54)
Condition of School Buildings in Specialized Sec. Schools (54)
Supplementary Data on Specialized Sec。Schools (55)

GENERAL SECONDARY SCHOOLS
Number of General Secondary Schools and Classes (57)
Number of Students in General Secondary Schools (58)
Number of Teachers, Staff & Workers in General Secondary Schools (60)
Number of Full－time General Secondary School Teachers by Subject Taught & Educational Attainment (62)
Full－time Teachers in General Secondary Schools Broken Down by Rank and Age (64)
Condition of School Buildings in General Secondary Schools (66)
Size of Junior Secondary Classes (66)

VOCATIONAL SCHOOLS

Number of Schools, Classes, Graduates & Students Admitted in vocational Schools (68)
Enrolment of Vocational Schools and Graduates for Next Year (70)
Number of Senior Level Students in Vocational Schools by Field of Study (72)
Number of Teachers, Staff & Workers in Vocational Schools (72)
Number of Full−time Vocational School Teachers by Educational Attainment (74)
Full−time Teachers in Vocational Schools Broken Down by Rank and Age (76)
Condition of School Buildings in Vocational Schools (78)

PRIMARY EDUCATION (PRIMARY SCHOOLS)

Number of Schools, Classes & Students in Primary Schools (80)
Number of Teachers, Staff & Workers in Primary schools (82)
Full−time Primary School Teachers Broak Down by Rank and Age (84)
Net Enrolment Rate of School−age Children (86)
Breakdown of Full−time Primary School Teachers by Educational Attainment (86)
Condition of School Buildings in Primary Schools (87)
Size of Primary School Classes (87)

SPECIAL EDUCATION

Basic Statistics of Speical Education Schools (90)

PRE−PRIMARY EDUCATION

Basic Statistics of Pre−primary Education (94)
Breakdown of Kindergarten Heads and Teachers by Educational Attainment (94)

ADULT EDUCATION

HIGHER EDUCATION

Basic Statistics for Adult Higher Educational Institutions (96)
Number of Students by Type of Schools in all Adult Higher Education Institutions (98)
Number of Students by Field of Study in Adult Higher Educational Institutions (100)
Number of Other Students in Adult Higher Educational Institutions (100)
Breakdown of Full−time Teachers by Academic Qualifications in Adult Higher Educational Institutions (102)
Supplementary Information on Students and Staff & Workers of Adult Higher Educational Institutions (102)
Breakdown of Full−time Teachers by Age in Adult Higher Educational Institutions (104)
Changes in Enrolment of Adult Higher Educational Institutions (104)
Condition of Fixed Assets and Teaching Resources in Adult Higher Educational Institutions (106)
Condition of School Buildings in Adult Higher Educational Institutions (106)

SECONDARY EDUCATION AND PRIMARY EDUCATION

Basic Statistics of Adult Specialized Secondary Schools by Field of Study (110)
Number of Teachers, Staff & Workers in Adult Specialized Secondary Schools (112)
Condition of School Buildings in Adult Specialized Secondary Schools (112)

Basic Statistics of Adult Secondary Schools (114)
Basic Statistics of Adult Primary Schools (114)
Basic Statistics of Adult Technical Training Schools (116)
Basic Data on National Agric. Broadcasting and T.V. Schools (118)
Number of Students on National Agric. Broadcasting and T.V. Schools (118)

GEOGRAPHICAL DISTRIBUTION OF SCHOOLS BY TYPE AND LEVEL

Basic Statistics of Regular Higher Educational Institutions (Regional Aggregates) (120)
Basic Statistics of Short-cycle Vocational Colleges (122)
Basic Statistics of Comprehensive Universities (124)
Basic Statistics of Institutions of Science & Technology (126)
Basic Statistics of Institutions of Agriculture (128)
Basic Statistics of Institutions of Forestry (130)
Basic Statistics of Institutions of Medicine & Pharmacy (132)
Basic Statistics of Teachers Colleges (134)
Basic Statistics of Institutions of Languages & Literatures (136)
Basic Statistics of Institutions of Finance & Economics (138)
Basic Statistics of Institutions of Political Science & Law (140)
Basic Statistics of Institutions of Physical Culture (142)
Basic Statistics of Institutions of Art (144)
Basic Statistics of Institutions of Nationalities (146)
Number of Female Students, Teachers, Staff & Workers in Regular Higher Educational Institutions (148)
Basic Statistics of Specialized Secondary Schools (150)
Basic Statistics of Secondary Technical Schools (152)
Basic Statistics of Secondary Industrial Schools (154)
Basic Statistics of Secondary Agricultural Schools (156)
Basic Statistics of Secondary Forestry Schools (158)
Basic Statistics of Secondary Health Schools (160)
Basic Statistics of Secondary Finance & Economics Schools (162)
Basic Statistics of Secondary Politics & Law Schools (164)
Basic Statistics of Secondary Physical Culture Schools (166)
Basic Statistics of Secondary Art Schools (168)
Basic Statistics of Other Secondary Technical Schools (170)
Basic Statistics of Teacher Training Schools (172)
Basic Statistics of Pre-primary Teacher Training Schools (174)
Number of Female Students, Teachers, Staff & Workers in Speicalized Secondary Schools (176)
Number of General Secondary Schools and Classes (Regional Aggregates) (178)
Number of General Secondary Schools and Classes (Urban) (180)
Number of General Secondary Schools and Classes (County Seats & Towns) (182)
Number of General Secondary Schools and Classes (Rural) (184)
Number of Graduates, Entrants & Graduates for Next Year in General Secondary Schools (Regional Aggregates) (186)

Number of Graduates, Entrants & Graduates for Next Year in General Secondary Schools (Urban) (187)
Number of Graduates, Entrants & Graduates for Next Year in General Secondary Schools (County Seats & Towns) (188)
Number of Graduates, Entrants & Graduates for Next Year in General Secondary Schools (Rural) (189)
Enrolment of General Secondary Schools (Regional Aggregates) (190)
Enrolment of General Secondary Schools (Urban) (192)
Enrolment of General Secondary Schools (County Seats & Towns) (194)
Enrolment of General Secondary Schools (Rural) (196)
Number of Female Students in General Secondary Schools (198)
Number of Teachers, Staff & Workers in General Secondary Schools (Regional Aggregates) (200)
Number of Teachers, Staff & Workers in General Secondary Schools (Urban) (202)
Number of Teachers, Staff & Workers in General Secondary Schools (County Seats & Towns)(204)
Number of Teachers, Staff & Workers in General Secondary Schools (Rural) (206)
Number of General Secondary School Teachers, Staff & Workers Maintained by the Communities (208)
Number of Female Teachers, Staff & Workers in General Secondary Schools (210)
Number of Schools, Classes, Graduates & Students Admitted in Vocational Schools (Regional Aggregates) (212)
Number of Schools, Classes, Graduates & Students Admitted in Vocational Schools (Urban) (214)
Number of Schools, Classes, Graduates & Students Admitted in Vocational Schools (County Seats & Towns) (216)
Number of Schools, Classes, Graduates & Students Admitted in Vocational Schools (Rural) (218)
Enrolment and Number of Graduates for Next Year in Vocational Schools (Regional Aggregates) (220)
Enrolment and Number of Graduates for Next Year in Vocational Schools (Urban) (222)
Enrolment and Number of Graduates for Next Year in Vocational Schools (County Seats & Towns) (224)
Enrolment and Number of Graduates for Next Year in Vocational Schools (Rural) (226)
Number of Female Students in Vocational Schools (228)
Number of Teachers, Staff & Workers in Vocational Schools (Regional Aggregates) (230)
Number of Teachers, Staff & Workers in Vocational Schools (Urban) (232)
Number of Teachers, Staff & Workers in Vocational Schools (County Seats & Towns) (234)
Number of Teachers, Staff & Workers in Vocational Schools (Rural) (236)
Number of Female Teachers, Staff & Workers in Vocational Schools (238)
Number of Schools, Classes, Graduates & Students Admitted in Primary Schools (Regional Aggregates) (240)
Number of Schools, Classes, Graduates & Students Admitted in Primary Schools (Urban) (242)
Number of Schools, Classes Graduates & Students Admitted in Primary Schools (County Seats & Towns) (244)
Number of Schools, Classes, Graduates & Students Admitted in Primary Schools (Rural) (246)
Number of Schools, Classes, Students Admitted & Graduates in 6－year Primary Schools (248)

Enrolment and Number of Graduates for Next Year in Primary Schools (Regional Aggregates)(250)
Enrolment and Number of Graduates for Next Year in Primary schools (Urban) (252)
Enrolment and Number of Graduates for Next Year in Primary Schools (County Seats & Towns) (254)
Enrolment and Number of Graduates for Next Year in Primary Schools (Rural) (256)
Enrolment and Number of Graduates for Next Year in 6-year Primary Schools (258)
Number of Female Students in Primary Schools (260)
Number of Teachers, Staff & Workers in Primary Schools (Regional Aggregates) (262)
Number of Teachers, Staff & Workers in Primary Schools (Urban) (264)
Number of Teachers, Staff & Workers in Primary Schools (County Seats & Towns) (266)
Number of Teachers, Staff & Workers in Primary Schools (Rural) (268)
Number of Primary School Teachers, Staff & Workers Maintained by the Communities (270)
Number of Female Teachers, Staff & Workers in Primary Schools (272)
Net Enrolment Rate of School-age Children in Primary Schools (274)
Net Enrolment Rate of Female School-age Children in Primary Schools (276)
Basic Statistics of Special Education Schools (Including Schools for the Blind, the Deaf-mute & the Retarded) (278)
Basic Statistics of Schools for the Blind & the Deaf-mute (280)
Basic Statistics of Kindergartens (Regional Aggregates) (282)
Basic Statistics of Adult Higher Educational Institutions (Regional Aggregates) (Evening Schools & Divisions of Correspondence run by Regular Institutions of Higher Education are not Included in Aggregates) (284)
Number of Students in Adult Higher Educational Institutions by Type of Courses (Regional Aggregates) (Evening Schools & Divisions of Correspondence run by Institutions of Higher Education are not Included in Aggregates) (286)
Basic Statistics of Radio/TV Universities (288)
Number of Students in Radio/TV Universities by Type of Courses (290)
Basic Statistics of Workers' Colleges (292)
Number of Students in Workers' Colleges by Type of Courses (294)
Basic Statistics of Peasants' Colleges (296)
Basic Statistics of Independent Correspondence Colleges (296)
Number of Students in Independent Correspondence Colleges by Type of Courses (296)
Basic Statistics of Educational Colleges (298)
Number of Students in Educational Colleges by Type of Courses (300)
Basic Statistics of Institutes for Administration (302)
Number of Students in Institutes for Administration by Type of Courses (304)
Number of Students by Type of Courses in Correspondence Divisions, Evening Schools & Short-cycle Courses for Adults run by Regular Institutions of Higher Education (306)
Number of Other Students in Adult Higher Educational Institutions (Regional Aggregates) (308)
Basic Statistics of Adult Specialized Secondary Schools (Regional Aggregates) (Limited to State-planned Enrolment and Courses Lasting 2 Years and Over) (310)
Basic Statistics of Radio/TV Specialized Secondary Schools (Limited to State-planned Enrolment and Courses Lasting 2 Years and Over) (312)

Basic Statistics of Specialized Secondary Schools for Staff & Workers (Limited to State-planned Enrolment and Courses Lasting 2 Years and Over) (314)
Basic Statistics of Specialized Secondary Schools for Peasants (Limited to State-planned Enrolment and Courses Lasting 2 Years and Over) (316)
Basic Statistics of In-service Teacher Training Schools (Limited to State-planned Enrolment and Courses Lasting 2 Years and Over) (318)
Basic Statistics of Specialized Secondary Schools for Cadres (Limited to State-planned Enrolment and Courses Lasting 2 Years and Over) (320)
Basic Statistics of General Secondary Schools for Adults (Regional Aggregates) (322)
Basic Statistics of General Secondary Schools for Staff & Workers (324)
Basic Statistics of General Secondary Schools for Peasants (326)
Basic Statistics of Technical Training Schools for Adults (Regional Aggregates) (328)
Basic Statistics of Technical Training Schools for Staff & Workers (330)
Basic Statistics of Technical Training Schools for Peasants (332)
Basic Statistics of Adults Primary Schools (334)
Basic Statistics of Worker Primary Schools (336)
Basic Statistics of Peasant Primary Schools (338)
Basic Statistics of Literacy Classes in Peasant Primary Schools (340)
Basic Data on National Agric. Broadcasting and T.V. Schools (342)

PART Ⅱ PHYSICAL FACILITIES

PUBLIC EXPENDITURE ON EDUCATION

Sources of Educational Fund and Expenditure for Education (346)
Sources of Educational Fund and Expenditure for Education by Region(1998) (347)
Sources of Educational Fund and Expenditure for Education in Various Schools (1998) (348)

CAPITAL CONSTRUCTION INVESTMENT IN THE EDUCATIONAL SECTOR

Data on the Completion of Capital Construction Investment in the Educational Sector (1999) (350)
Data on the Completion of Capital Construction Investment in the Educational Sector (Regional Aggregatates) (1999) (352)

INSTRUMENT AND EQUIPMENT

Classification of Instruments and Equipment for Instruction and Scientific Research by Province (1998) (356)
Classification of Instruments and Equipment for Instruction and Scientific Research by Province (1999) (357)

PART Ⅲ SCIENTIFIC RESEARCH ACTIVITES & OTHER

NATURAL SCIENCE AND TECHNOLOGY

Scientific and Technical Manpower in Regular HEIs(1998) (360)
Statistics of Scientists and Engineer Among S&T Manpower in Regular HEIs by Level of Post (1998)(361)
S & T Expenditure in Regular HEIs(1998) (362)
Statistics of R & D Projects and Achievements in Regular HEIs(1998) (363)

SOCIAL SCIENCE

Professional Manpower in Regular HEIs in the Fields of the Humanities and Social Acience(1998) (366)
Humanities and Social Sciences R & D Expenditure in Regular HEIs(1998) (368)
Basic Statistics of Humunities and Social Sciences R & D Project and Achievements in Regular HEIs (1998) (370)
Recruitment of Student for Regular Higher Educational Institutions(1998) (372)
Recruitment of Student for Regular Higher Educational Institutions (1) (1999) (374)
Recruitment of Student for Regular Higher Educational Institutions (2) (1999) (376)

APPENDIXES

Gross Domestic Product (380)
Gross Domestic Product by Region(1998) (381)
Total Government Revenue and Expenditures and Their Increase Rate (382)
Total Revenue and Expenditures of Central and Local Governments (383)
Population and its Composition (384)
Total Population and Birth Rate, Death Rate and Natural Growth Rate by Region(1998) (385)
Population by Sex, Educational Level and Region (386)
Illiterate and Semi-Literate Population Aged 15 and over by Sex and Region (388)
TRANSLATOR'S NOTES (389)

第一部分

Part I

教育事业发展

The Development of the Educational Undertaking

一、综合部分

SUMMARY TABLES

全国各级各类学校基本情况

Basic Statistics of Regular and Adult Schools in China by Level & Type

单位：万人 in 10 thousand

	学校数(所) Schools	毕业生数 Graduates	招生数 Entrants	在校学生数 Enrolment	教职工数 Teachers, Staff & Workers 计 Total	其中：专任教师 of which: Full-time Teachers
总计 Total	1586640	15609.33	16440.71	32671.86	1596.04	1228.35
一、高等学校 Higher Educational Institutions	1942	179.05	284.68	742.27	126.51	52.33
二、中等学校 Reg. Secondary Schools	639648	12554.58	11984.26	15481.39	683.10	493.85
三、初等学校 Primary Schools	762394	2871.88	2549.23	14084.78	666.09	591.79
四、特殊教育学校 Special Education Schools	1520	3.81	5.01	37.16	4.51	3.14
五、幼儿园 Kindergartens	181136		1617.54	2326.26	115.83	87.24

全国各级普通学校基本情况

Basic Statistics of Regular Schools in China by Level & Type

单位：万人 in 10 thousand

	学校数(所) Schools	毕业生数 Graduates	招生数 Entrants	在校学生数 Enrolment	教职工数 Teachers, Staff & Workers 计 Total	其中：专任教师 Of which: Full-time Teachers
总计 Total	861009	4635.06	6776.45	24325.62	1476.67	1179.15
一、研究生 Graduate Education	775	5.47	9.22	23.36		
1. 高等学校 Inst. of Higher Education	446	5.08	8.68	21.87		
2. 科研机构 Research Organizations	329	0.39	0.54	1.49		
二、普通高等学校本专科 Reg. Inst. of Higher Edu. Undergraduates	1071	84.76	159.68	413.42	106.51	42.57
本科院校 University	597	62.30	111.84	314.93	87.37	33.58
专科院校 Non-university Tertiary	474	21.01	40.21	87.83	18.81	8.82
分校、大专班及其他 Undergraduate Classes Branch and others		1.45	7.63	10.66	0.33	0.17
三、普通中等学校 Reg. Secondary Schools	94991	2227.28	2955.47	7977.45	602.71	460.16
1. 中等专业学校 Specialized Sec. Schools	3962	140.15	163.37	515.50	52.86	27.37
中等技术学校 Sec. Technical Schools	3147	109.25	134.25	424.98	42.14	21.18
中等师范学校 Teacher Training Schools	815	30.90	29.12	90.52	10.72	6.19
2. 技工学校 Skilled Worker Schools	4098	66.25	51.55	156.05	26.98	15.03
3. 普通中学 General Sec. Schools	77213	1852.71	2546.00	6771.28	475.36	384.05
高中 Senior	14127	262.91	396.32	1049.71		69.24
初中 Junior	63086	1589.80	2149.68	5721.57		314.81
4. 职业中学 Vocational Schools	9636	167.83	194.14	533.92	47.23	33.55
高中 Senior	8317	143.69	160.38	443.84		29.61
初中 Junior	1319	24.14	33.76	90.08		3.94
5. 工读学校 Correctional Work-study Schools	82	0.34	0.41	0.71	0.28	0.16
四、小学 Primary Schools	582291	2313.74	2029.53	13547.96	647.12	586.05
五、特殊教育学校 Special Education Schools	1520	3.81	5.01	37.16	4.51	3.14
六、幼儿园 Kindergartens	181136		1617.54	2326.26	115.83	87.24

注："普通高等学校本专科"学生数中包含有在成人高等学校中举办的"新高职"学生数。

全国各级成人学校基本情况

Basic Statistics of Adult Schools in China by Level & Type

单位:万人
in 10 thousand

	学校数(所) Schools	毕业生数 Graduates	招生数 Entrants	在校学生数 Enrolment	教职工数 Teachers, Staff & Workers 计 Total	其中:专任教师 of which: Full-time Teachers
总 计 Total	725631	10974.27	9664.26	8316.24	119.37	49.20
一、成人高等学校 Higher Educational Institutions for Adults	871	88.82	115.77	305.49	20.01	9.76
1. 广播电视大学 Radio/TV Universities	45	17.02	19.38	48.68	5.32	2.57
2. 职工高等学校 Workers' Colleges	507	10.17	14.40	32.80	8.15	4.11
3. 农民高等学校 Peasants' Colleges	3	0.05	0.04	0.10	0.02	0.01
4. 管理干部学院 Institutes for Administration	146	6.63	7.19	17.10	3.21	1.34
5. 教育学院 Educational Colleges	166	6.86	9.61	22.73	3.22	1.68
6. 独立函授学院 Independent Correspondence Colleges	4	0.44	0.40	1.22	0.09	0.05
7. 普通高等学校举办: Run by Reg. Inst. of HEIs	0	47.65	66.74	182.84	0.00	0.00
函授部 Divisions of Correspondence		26.88	37.72	105.99		
夜大学 Evening Schools		9.90	13.27	40.09		
成人脱产班 Short-cycle Courses for Adults		10.87	15.75	35.76		
合计中:电大、普通专科班(A)		7.22	8.14	19.77		
二、成人中等学校 Sec. Education for Adults	544657	10327.30	9028.79	7503.93	80.39	33.70
1. 成人中等专业学校 Specialized Sec. Schools for Adults	5165	118.81	97.97	302.12	23.22	13.07
广播电视中等专业学校 Radio/TV Specialized Sec. Schools	151	21.42	18.77	62.54	1.83	0.90
职工中等专业学校 Specialized Sec. Schools for Staff & Workers	2093	29.13	25.24	80.89	8.83	4.78
干部中等专业学校 Specialized Sec. Schools for Cadres	290	5.09	4.12	11.98	1.55	0.78
农民中等专业学校 Specialized Sec. Schools for Peasants	440	8.28	7.34	21.93	2.09	1.35
函授中等专业学校 Correspondence Specialized Sec. Schools	62	6.78	4.91	13.70	1.00	0.48
教师进修学校 In-service Teacher Training Schools	2129	16.56	9.37	27.18	7.92	4.78
其他类学校举办 Run by Other Type School		31.55	28.22	83.90		
2. 成人中学 General Sec. Schools for Adults	5277	51.61	54.29	65.18	3.46	2.05
职工中学 General Sec. Schools for Staff & Workers	1655	22.99	29.79	32.58	2.01	1.13
农民中学 General Sec. Schools for Peasants	3622	28.62	24.50	32.60	1.45	0.92
3. 成人技术培训学校 Technical Training Schools for Adults	534215	10156.88	8876.53	7136.63	53.71	18.58
职工技术培训学校 Technical Training Schools for Staff & Workers	11326	609.23	599.11	386.40	9.00	4.71
农民技术培训学校 Technical Training Schools for Peasants	522889	9547.65	8277.42	6750.23	44.71	13.87
三、成人初等学校 Adult Primary Schools	180103	558.15	519.70	536.82	18.97	5.74
1. 职工初等学校 Worker Primary Schools	964	15.54	19.45	19.75	0.34	0.18
2. 农民初等学校 Peasant Primary Schools	179139	542.61	500.25	517.07	18.63	5.56
其中: 扫盲班 of which: Literacy Classes	128668	299.27	255.78	283.19	13.64	3.74

注:成人中等专业学校中"其他类学校举办"是指:在成人高等学校和普通中等专业学校中招收的成人中专学生数。
(A): Of the total: The Regular Short-cycle Courses in Radio/TV Universities, for graduates from higher Schools.

全国各级自学

Basic Statistics of Applicants for State－administered

	1983－1999 合计 Total	1983 上半年 First half year	1983 下半年 Second half year	1984 上半年 First half year	1984 下半年 Second half year	1985 上半年 First half year	1985 下半年 Second half year
毕业生人数 Gradutes							
本科 Nonmal course	210939					14	12
专科 Short－cycle course	2375963			133	1345	2060	6565
中专 Specialized Secondary	394987					20481	58
单科合格科次数 Passed Main－courses							
本科 Nonmal course	10201378	422	697	796	991	1459	1051
专科 Short－cycle course	73983762	38845	183048	333081	604054	737796	1083782
中专 Specialized Secondary	4910756	697	2347	3531	7418	306865	126506
报考人数 Applicants							
计 Total							
本科 Nonmal course	10904361	884	1217	1639	2305	2871	2298
专科 Short－cycle course	109216270	63873	262022	622088	848654	1075594	1421211
中专 Specialized Secondary	5475832		3424	5033	6541	173459	92108
首次报考人数 First Time							
本科 Nonmal course	3768604	27	229	134	542	437	260
专科 Short－cycle course	29285975	155490	179385	395455	506255	451823	659196
中专 Specialized Secondary	1431526		3424	1726	1628	77273	36963
报考科次 Main－courses to be Examined							
本科 Nonmal course	35155549	2002	2691	3655	5030	6163	4907
专科 Short－cycle course	217353816	122070	493654	1200947	1773843	2348639	2810102
中专 Specialized Secondary	9839287		6519	10760	15748	412224	114254
实考人数 Actural Examined							
本科 Nonmal course	7841662	764	1015	1159	1680	2144	1339
专科 Short－cycle course	74115961	51302	184494	467105	646309	773841	1103508
中专 Specialized Secondary	3464846		2739	4026	5232	141533	74167
实考科次 Actural Main－courses Examined							
本科 Nonmal course	18116580	1345	2252	2608	3632	4522	3054
专科 Short－cycle course	158797543	89637	379350	881387	1338541	1662720	2145185
中专 Specialized Secondary	7913471		5540	8276	13466	364624	178952
在档考生人数 Exmainees on File							
累计数 Sum.							
本科 Nonmal course	13496410	32	138	200	314	445	532
专科 Short－cycle course	148569950	12133	87335	223148	420059	612138	941438
中专 Specialized Secondary	10715409		2191	3651	4406	110901	77402
其中：新生数 of Which: Curent session							
本科 Nonmal course	2299796	5	106	62	114	131	87
专科 Short－cycle course	140662838	9650	75202	135813	207389	199941	330492
中专 Specialized Secondary	958261		2191	1460	755	106495	14983

考试基本情况

Examination for Self－learners by Level

1986		1987		1988		1989		1990	
上半年 First half year	下半年 Second half year	上半年 First half year	下半年 Second half year	上半年 First half year	下半年 Second half year	上半年 First half year	下半年 Second half year	上半年 First half year	下半年 Second half year
11	14	47	51	110	297	569	475	968	996
29693	43189	35358	44585	62168	61371	65231	68691	55900	62165
40872	26354	36235	6458	24353	7018	22541	13650	22421	19232
2209	3909	20393	26218	26032	37060	39168	64327	78114	81320
1070299	1215432	1123822	1284691	1137868	1094216	1198715	1191751	12192921	384306
327902	182631	316528	267492	370725	292607	364207	250955	288846	229963
3055	5183	26519	30260	36623	44275	57221	722553	94678	100954
1346466	1573841	1644984	1672448	1720821	1437775	1583220	15505211	17430211	967666
25701	205532	306449	288042	337384	285974	311221	236820	244444	211646
908	1076	22193	13077	18657	22046	28295	35163	42355	30534
372588	468172	4325534	455694	458736	422219	488568	477809	563357	560707
128020	72036	145919	107781	155492	99285	93647	52421	52835	54243
6760	12395	61389	74391	86939	111530	123281	162051	223191	226670
3029215	3608182	3715386	3930776	3933345	3262016	3575839	3321740	39265904	429172
649167	449848	703118	642607	802734	630291	722308	525811	528329	453117
2184	3614	19106	22508	25306	32639	38411	54234	68138	74413
1065145	1226720	1271532	1312029	1282150	1148626	1179460	1176964	13142811	527055
203477	161941	241953	225098	268656	221898	251625	188288	195981	169272
4950	9037	43809	53187	57371	65374	76907	113512	151073	153152
2298087	2673822	2748537	2910030	2711644	2262622	2484042	2469332	26100463	166408
503119	347333	533521	501135	616610	475617	578516	413627	425431	366461
995	1569	9969	16639	24326	34070	46679	66738	86317	91789
1089218	1285689	1448597	1643128	1789585	1942242	2098872	2299196	25394802	802246
139667	151457	225168	279959	389175	428824	479678	496265	520414	536915
463	574	8318	6689	7689	9806	12783	20192	21338	16678
196752	222011	204010	231031	194104	192385	215460	254243	282812	304963
53713	42049	61600	52382	90641	55804	53868	40255	29821	39219

全国各级自学

Basic Statistics of Applicants for State-administered

	1991		1992		1993	
	上半年 First half year	下半年 Second half year	上半年 First half year	下半年 Second half year	上半年 First half year	下半年 Second half year
毕业生人数 Gradutes						
本科 Nonmal course	1493	2097	1882	2335	3131	4405
专科 Short－cycle course	50873	57261	56544	68783	64314	79240
中专 Specialized Secondary	27747	17188	12116	15385	7727	11518
单科合格科次数 Passed Main－courses						
本科 Nonmal course	91453	92914	101001	83496	89330	120632
专科 Short－cycle course	1541534	1409168	1724308	1712135	1892727	1932457
中专 Specialized Secondary	229039	122986	125314	123432	84250	94233
报考人数 Applicants						
计 Total						
本科 Nonmal course	107773	119108	144169	131202	130662	149559
专科 Short－cycle course	2317126	2452597	2747837	2555932	2448307	2282192
中专 Specialized Secondary	201985	1556631	134711	136804	85942	77898
首次报考人数 First Time						
本科 Nonmal course	39122	36192	51494	44324	40888	66450
专科 Short－cycle course	785899	699302	767826	698494	746191	585416
中专 Specialized Secondary	58508	44063	28003	29684	26066	19355
报考科次 Main－courses to be Examined						
本科 Nonmal course	261323	275544	321831	281634	269341	329869
专科 Short－cycle course	5251674	5466671	6347546	5628587	5523236	5083088
中专 Specialized Secondary	457455	310859	303599	298516	188349	175525
实考人数 Actural Examined						
本科 Nonmal course	80177	89894	108670	85516	87518	109209
专科 Short－cycle course	1709769	1879978	2019650	1823672	1800286	1809209
中专 Specialized Secondary	164397	117728	104537	99785	62300	61176
实考科次 Actural Main－courses Examined						
本科 Nonmal course	170282	190586	218633	170168	167123	215850
专科 Short－cycle course	3594482	3818644	4218246	3798290	3852910	3783069
中专 Specialized Secondary	363477	229198	230898	222968	136876	138481
在档考生人数 Exmainees on File						
累计数 Sum.						
本科 Nonmal course	122406	139306	161447	178047	191352	220839
专科 Short－cycle course	3144251	3943844	3765591	4100882	4318000	4598507
中专 Specialized Secondary	545690	540773	555862	572808	575283	577479
其中:新生数 of Which: Curent session						
本科 Nonmal course	21969	19320	24748	19405	14282	33806
专科 Short－cycle course	388122	352568	363639	373677	376662	465778
中专 Specialized Secondary	26654	24870	19542	15873	15433	14283

考试基本情况(续)

Examination for Self－learners by Level

1994		1995		1996		1997		1998		1999	
上半年 First half year	下半年 Second half year	上半年 First half year	下半年 Second half year	上半年 First half year	下半年 Second half year	上半年 First half year	下半年 Second half year	上半年 First half year	下半年 Second half year	上半年 First half year	下半年 Second half year
2926	3189	4038	5356	6367	10542	11968	14397	20995	26883	35649	49722
61573	71139	93512	94441	111174	132161	120143	142260	142959	154532	162957	173643
3703	5289	6509	6998	5192	3539	4644	7494	3897	4881	4913	6574
129329	158578	254752	309574	475722	1109072	766218	889266	1060654	1203668	1320084	1561469
1523309	1811068	2446593	2679101	3254101	4228469	3699496	3716269	3815468	3625667	4075143	4022122
48341	82260	99495	48173	76389	52094	80439	73433	63766	47858	71544	48490
146231	181233	266767	319935	473368	563962	764068	858627	1085391	1285720	1419295	1624756
1961769	2101827	2690697	2972271	3697085	3847639	4254102	4266257	4700993	4735980	4987845	5019729
33286	49597	69959	36144	56749	38723	56493	50900	43814	37126	42653	32639
57200	65373	98559	124282	191034	207316	311324	313261	460927	476071	493832	475022
643421	592417	846470	983974	1242201	1174411	1377656	1240486	1707067	1525575	1520849	1207332
5978	12951	19723	10909	19391	11357	8327	12679	10312	11272	11323	8932
302314	391276	630083	794966	11555214	1551981	1865408	2147826	2603249	3151309	3413241	3896095
4094754	4503667	6287980	7148558	8821241	9288200	10261520	10232875	11293634	11114518	12271102	11914135
85108	137956	185242	107238	157664	99076	144500	129130	116865	89191	110630	75549
95629	129937	19665	250499	368030	439792	611844	698959	896439	1020578	1136176	1264476
1396486	1508963	2110719	2403378	2949857	3025277	3564459	3590675	3966594	3883557	4084862	4029519
32900	50784	61053	39468	49581	32042	49926	45363	38989	33388	38918	26625
216800	278165	453270	575933	841700	1158977	1388387	1605291	1972423	2319280	2541013	2886914
3033011	3367729	4930802	5505422	6774769	7135008	8059057	7915029	8881093	8547288	9118389	9142498
73259	122654	163501	93965	134506	86619	127671	111046	101827	76808	99004	68485
179567	244819	320303	408028	510616	742738	876431	1237555	1487435	1857008	2048267	2189494
2930253	3678144	4582744	4906938	6288806	6516221	7281740	7951516	8864050	9397127	9982109	10229401
204775	267577	279226	230057	259359	250632	312656	341143	247502	365202	371406	371906
36576	33358	45182	61209	101294	169958	180815	174282	262682	390717	306769	298389
298456	293360	362996	396765	642875	693354	1180048	706471	959792	1504782	803393	643842
6875	10550	13420	6776	13974	11039	61742	15329	14581	17210	15525	9349

各级普通学校校数

Number of Regular Schools by Level & Type

单位：所
Unit:Number of Sohools

	1949	1965	1978	1980	1985	1998	1999
普通高等学校 Reg. Inst. of Higher Education	205	434	598	675	1016	1022	1071
普通中等学校 Reg. Secondary Schools	5219	81274	167118	128065	108494	96548	95255
中等专业学校 Specialized Sec. Schools	1171	1265	2760	3069	3557	4109	3962
中等技术学校 Sec. Technical Schools	561	871	1714	2052	2529	3234	3147
中等师范学校 Teachers Training Schools	610	394	1046	1017	1028	875	815
技工学校 Skilled Worker Schools	3	281	2013	3305	3548	4362	4098
普通中学 General Sec. Schools	4045	18102	162345	118377	93221	77888	77213
高中 Senior	1597	4112	49215	31300	17318	13948	14127
初中 Junior	2448	13990	113130	87077	75903	63940	63086
职业中学 Vocational Schools	–	61626	...	3314	8070	10074	9636
工读学校 Correctional Work－study Schools	–	–	–	...	98	82	82
小学 Primary Schools	346769	1681939	949323	917316	832309	609626	582291
特殊教育学校 Special Education Schools	...	266	292	292	375	1535	1520
幼儿园 Kindergartens	...	19226	163952	170419	172262	181368	181136

各级普通学校学生数

Enrolment of Regular Schools by Level & Type

单位:万人
in 10 thousand

	1949	1965	1978	1980	1985	1998	1999
研究生 (人) Graduate Education(Person)	629	4546	10934	21604	87331	198885	233513
普通高等学校本专科 Undergraduate Education	11.65	67.44	85.63	114.37	170.31	340.88	413.42
普通中等学校 Reg. Secondary Schools	127.05	1441.97	6675.37	5747.83	5167.46	7533.83	7977.45
中等专业学校 Specialized Sec. Schools	22.88	54.74	88.92	124.34	157.11	498.08	515.50
中等技术学校 Sec. Technical Schools	7.71	39.24	52.93	76.13	101.29	405.97	424.98
中等师范学校 Teacher Training Schools	15.17	15.50	35.99	48.21	55.82	92.11	90.52
技工学校 Skilled Worker Schools	0.27	10.10	38.20	70.04	74.17	181.30	156.05
普通中学 General Sec. Schools	103.90	933.79	6548.25	5508.08	4705.96	6301.03	6771.28
高中 Senior	20.72	130.82	1553.08	969.79	741.13	938.00	1049.71
初中 Junior	83.18	802.97	4995.17	4538.29	3964.83	5363.03	5721.57
职业中学 Vocational Schools	–	443.34	–	45.37	229.57	541.62	533.92
高中 Senior	–	77.50	–	31.92	184.34	454.92	443.84
初中 Junior	–	365.84	–	13.45	45.23	86.70	90.08
工读学校 Correctional Work-study Schools	–	–	–	–	0.65	0.61	0.71
小学 Primary Schools	2439.10	11620.90	14624.00	14627.00	13370.20	13953.80	13547.96
特殊教育学校 Special Education Schools	–	2.29	3.09	3.31	4.17	35.84	37.16
幼儿园 Kindergartens	–	171.30	787.70	1150.80	1479.70	2403.03	2326.26

各级普通学校招生数

Number of Regular School Entrants by Level & Type

单位:万人
in 10 thousand

	1949	1965	1978	1980	1985	1998	1999
研究生 (人) Graduate Education(Person)	242	1456	10708	3616	46871	72508	92225
普通高等学校本专科 Undergraduate Education	3.06	16.42	40.15	28.12	61.92	108.36	159.68
普通中等学校 Reg. Secondary Schools	50.97	673.11	2769.29	2044.92	1825.70	2764.71	2955.47
中等专业学校 Specialized Sec. Schools	9.74	20.85	44.70	46.76	66.83	166.83	163.37
中等技术学校 Sec. Technical Schools	4.28	14.64	26.79	25.29	45.36	134.89	134.25
中等师范学校 Teacher Training Schools	5.46	6.21	17.91	21.47	21.47	31.94	29.12
技工学校 Skilled Worker Schools	...	...	25.70	33.13	35.54	59.40	51.55
普通中学 General Sec. Schools	41.23	345.78	2698.89	1934.31	1606.91	2320.91	2546.00
高中 Senior	7.11	45.89	692.91	383.40	257.51	359.55	396.32
初中 Junior	34.12	299.89	2005.98	1550.91	1349.40	1961.36	2149.68
职业中学 Vocational Schools	–	306.48	–	30.72	116.10	217.57	194.14
高中 Senior	–	55.67	–	24.06	98.49	182.68	160.38
初中 Junior	–	250.81	–	6.66	17.61	34.89	33.76
工读学校 Correctional Work-study Schools	–	–	–		0.32	0.30	0.41
小学 Primary Schools	680.00	3296.02	3315.36	2942.34	2298.17	2201.38	2029.53
特殊教育学校 Special Education Schools	–	–	0.59	0.59	0.92	4.91	5.01
幼儿园 Kindergartens	–	–	–	–	–	1719.96	1617.54

各级普通学校教职工数

Number of Regular School Teachers, Staff & Workers by Level & Type

单位: 万人
in 10 thousand

	1949	1965	1978	1980	1985	1998	1999
总计 **Total**	102.30	567.87	1083.45	1167.61	1209.56	1463.00	1480.70
普通高等学校本专科 Undergraduate Education	4.60	33.30	51.80	63.20	87.06	102.96	106.51
普通中等学校 Reg. Secondary Schools	12.80	110.50	422.06	437.21	439.45	595.56	602.71
中等专业学校 Specialized Sec. Schools	2.40	12.20	23.70	29.80	40.32	54.65	52.86
中等技术学校 Sec. Technical Schools	1.10	10.10	17.60	22.30	31.31	43.50	42.14
中等师范学校 Teacher Training Schools	1.30	2.10	6.10	7.50	9.01	11.15	10.72
技工学校 Skilled Worker Schools	–	–	6.66	13.61	21.53	31.00	26.98
普通中学 General Sec. Schools	10.40	67.70	391.70	389.70	355.69	462.13	475.36
职业中学 Vocational Schools	–	30.60	–	4.10	21.59	47.78	47.23
工读学校 Correctional Work-study Schools	–	–	–	–	0.32	0.27	0.28
小学 Primary Schools	84.90	407.50	562.00	605.40	602.10	644.56	647.12
特殊教育学校 Special Education Schools	–	0.37	0.69	0.80	1.15	4.16	4.51
幼儿园 Kindergartens	–	16.20	46.90	61.00	79.80	115.76	115.83

各级普通学校专任教师数

Number of Regular School Full－time Teachers by Level & Type

单位:万人
in 10 thousand

	1949	1965	1978	1980	1985	1998	1999
总计 **Total**	93.43	476.89	902.31	939.48	933.48	1158.83	1178.63
普通高等学校本专科 Undergraduate Education	1.61	13.81	20.63	24.69	34.43	40.73	42.57
普通中等学校 Reg. Secondary Schools	8.22	70.93	330.96	323.30	305.65	445.63	460.16
中等专业学校 Specialized Sec. Schools	1.56	5.51	9.96	12.87	17.40	27.85	27.37
中等技术学校 Sec. Technical Schools	0.66	4.37	6.93	9.10	12.80	21.50	21.18
中等师范学校 Teacher Training Schools	0.90	1.14	3.03	3.77	4.60	6.35	6.19
技工学校 Skilled Worker Schools	–	–	2.80	6.14	8.89	14.50	15.03
普通中学 General Sec. Schools	6.66	45.71	318.20	301.97	265.16	369.71	384.05
高中 Senior	1.40	7.79	74.13	57.07	49.17	64.24	69.24
初中 Junior	5.26	37.92	244.07	244.90	215.99	305.47	314.81
职业中学 Vocational Schools	–	19.71	–	2.32	14.07	33.57	33.55
高中 Senior	–	5.29	–	1.65	11.58	29.61	29.61
初中 Junior	–	14.42	–	0.67	2.49	3.96	3.94
工读学校 Correctional Work－study Schools	–	–	–	–	0.13	0.15	0.16
小学 Primary Schools	83.60	385.71	522.55	549.94	537.68	581.94	586.05
特殊教育学校 Special Education Schools	–	0.26	0.42	0.48	0.73	2.99	3.14
幼儿园 Kindergartens	–	6.18	27.75	41.07	54.99	87.54	87.24

高级普通中等学校学生数的构成

Composition of Students in Regular Secondary Schools

	合 计 Total	普通高中 Senior General Secondary Schools	中等职业技术学校 Secondary Vocational－technical Schools			
			小 计 Subtotal	中等专业学校 Specialized Sec. Schools	技工学校 Skilled Worker Schools	职业中学 Vocational Schools
学生数(万人) No. of Students (in 10 thousand)						
1965	271.1	130.8	140.3	52.7	10.1	77.5
1980	1196.0	969.8	226.2	124.3	70.0	31.9
1985	1156.7	741.1	415.6	157.1	74.2	184.3
1990	1322.0	717.3	604.7	224.4	133.2	247.1
1997	1939.6	850.1	1089.5	465.4	193.1	431.0
1998	2084.1	938.0	1146.1	498.1	193.1	454.9
1999	2190.3	1049.7	1115.4	515.5	156.1	443.8
比重(%) Percentage						
1965	100	48.2	51.8	19.5	3.7	28.6
1980	100	81.1	18.9	10.4	5.8	2.7
1985	100	64.1	35.9	13.6	6.4	15.9
1990	100	54.3	45.7	17.0	10.0	18.7
1997	100	43.8	56.2	24.0	10.0	22.2
1998	100	45.0	55.0	23.9	9.3	21.8
1999	100	48.5	51.5	23.8	7.2	20.5

教育规模

Size of Education

单位:万人

Unit: in 10 Thousand persons

年份 Year	学校数(万所) Schools (in 10 Thousand)	学生数 Enrolment	教职工数 Teachers Staff & Workers	教育人口* Educational Population	教育人口比重(%) Propotion of Education Population
1985	144	21753	1261	23014	22.0
1990	136	23654	1432	25086	22.2
1996	155	30401	1549	31950	26.2
1997	157	31076	1577	32653	26.7
1998	155	31809	1580	33389	27.0
1999	159	32672	1596	34268	27.5

* 教育人口为学生数与教职工数之和;

小学学龄儿童净入学率

Net Enrolment Rate of School－age Children & Annual Retention Rate of Enrolment in Primary Schools

单位:%

Unit: %

年份	按7－11周岁计算 the age 7－11	按各地相应学龄、学制计算 According to Provincial entrance Age Primary Sohooling years			
		小计 Total	男 Male	女 Female	性别差 Gencler Gap
1990	97.8	96.3	－	－	－
1991	97.9	96.8	－	－	－
1992	98.0	97.2	98.2	96.1	2.1
1993	98.3	97.7	98.5	96.8	1.7
1994	98.7	98.4	99.0	97.7	1.3
1995	98.7	98.5	98.9	98.2	0.7
1996	99.1	98.8	99.0	98.6	0.4
1997	99.2	98.9	99.0	98.8	0.2
1998	99.3	98.9	99.0	98.9	0.1
1999	99.5	99.1	99.1	99.0	0.1

注: 1992年以前的入学率是按7－11周岁统一计算的。

从1992年起入学率是按各地不同入学年龄和学制分别计算的。

Note: Net Enrolment Rate of school－age chidren before year 1992 was calculated during the age of 7～ 11.

Since 1992, the rate varies according to provincial entrance age and primary schooling years.

各级普通教育毛入学率①

Gross Enrolment Rate of Regular Schools by Level

单位：%
Unit: %

年份 Year	小学 Primary 按各地相应学龄计算 According to provincial entrant age primary Schools years	初中② Junior 12－14周岁 the age of 12－14	高中阶段③ Senior 15－17周岁 the age of 15－17		高等教育④ IHEs 18－22周岁 the age of 18－22
			职前	全口径	
1990	111.0	66.7	21.9	26.0	3.4
1991	109.5	69.7	23.9	28.4	3.5
1992	109.4	71.8	22.6	26.0	3.9
1993	107.3	73.1	24.1	28.4	5.0
1994	108.7	73.8	26.2	30.7	6.0
1995	106.6	78.4	28.8	33.6	7.2
1996	105.7	82.4	31.4	38.0	8.3
1997	104.9	87.1	33.8	40.6	9.1
1998	104.3	87.3	34.4	40.7	9.8
1999	104.3	88.6	35.8	41.0	10.5

注：① 毛入学率指该级教育在校学生总数与政府规定的该级学龄段人口总数的百分比。

② 初中包括普通初中和职业初中。

③ 高中阶段教育(全口径)包括：普通高中、职业高中、成人高中、普通中专、成人中专和技工学校；职前高中教育阶段包括：普通高中、职业高中、技工学校和普通中专。

④ 高等教育包括研究生、普通高校本专科、成人高校本专科、军事院校本专科、学历文凭考试专科、电大注册视听生专科、高等教育自学考试本专科等形式教育。计算口径为：

$$\text{高等教育毛入学率}=\frac{\text{研究生}+\text{普通高等本专科}+\text{成人高校本专科}+\text{军事院校}+\text{学历文凭考试}+\text{电大注册视听生注册人数}\times 0.3+\text{高等教育自学考试毕业生}\times 5}{18-22\text{岁年龄组人口数}}\times 100\%$$

各级普通学校毕业生升学率

Promotion Rate of Regular School by Level & Type Graduates

单位：%
Unit: %

年份 Year	小学升学率 Promotion Rate of Primary School Graduates			初中升学率① Promotion Rate of Junior Sec.School Graduates			高中升学率② Promotion Rate of Senior School Graduates		
	小学毕业生数 No. of Primary School Graduates	初级中等学校招生数 No. of Junior Sec. School Entrants	升学率(%) Promotion Rate (%)	初中毕业生数 No. of Junior Sec. School Graduates	高级中等学校招生数 No. of Senior Sec. School Entrants	升学率(%) Promotion Rate (%)	普通高中毕业生数 No. of Senior Sec. School Graduates	普通高等学校招生数 No. of Regular IHEs Entrants	升学率(%) Promotion Rate (%)
1990	1863.1	1389.2	74.6	1109.1	450.4	40.6	233.0	63.7	27.3
1991	1846.7	1435.1	77.7	1085.5	462.9	42.6	223.0	63.9	28.7
1992	1872.4	1491.7	79.7	1102.4	478.1	43.4	226.1	79.0	34.9
1993	1841.5	1505.6	81.8	1134.2	500.5	44.1	231.7	100.3	43.3
1994	1899.6	1644.9	86.6	1166.4	541.1	46.4	209.3	97.7	46.7
1995	1961.5	1781.1	90.8	1244.3	601.6	48.3	201.6	100.7	49.9
1996	1934.1	1791.4	92.6	1297.8	633.4	48.8	204.9	104.6	51.0
1997	1960.1	1836.5	93.7	1463.3	753.6	51.5	221.7	107.8	48.6
1998	2117.4	1996.3	94.3	1603.1	812.2	50.7	251.8	116.0	46.1
1999	2313.7	2183.4	94.4	1613.9	798.5	49.5	262.9	167.8	63.8

注：① 1993年以前(含1993年)初中毕业生数中不含职业初中毕业生数，1993年以后初中毕业生数为普通初中和职业初中毕业生数之和。

② 高中升学率为普通高校招生数(含电大普通班)与普通高中毕业生数之比。

每十万人口各级学校平均在校生数

Number of Students per 100,000 Inhabitants by level

单位:人

年　份	高等学校① Higher Education	高中阶段② Senior	初中阶段③ Junior	小　学 Primary	幼儿园 Kindergratens
1990	326	1337	3426	10707	1725
1991	304	1355	3465	10502	1907
1992	313	1365	3518	10413	2072
1993	376	1448	3599	10656	2190
1994	433	1293	3681	10819	2219
1995	457	1610	3945	11010	2262
1996	470	1780	4180	11273	2208
1997	482	1905	4289	11435	2058
1998	504	1978	4408	11287	1944
1999	594	2032	4656	10855	1864

注: ① 高等学校仅含普通高校和成人高校。

② 高中阶段(全口径)包括:普通高中、职业高中、普通中专、技工学校、成人中专和成人高中。

③ 初中阶段包括:普通初中和职业初中。

各级普通学校生师比

Pupil－Teacher Ratio of Regular Education by level

单位:%
Unit: %

年　份 Year	小学 Primary	普通初中 Junior	普通高中 Senior	职业中学 Vacational Secondary Schools	普通中专 Regular Secondary Schools	普通高校 Regular Inst. of Higher Educations		
						全　国 Total	本科院校 University	专科院校 non－university tertiry
1992	22.07	15.85	12.24	13.82	14.60	6.83	6.63	7.30
1993	22.37	15.65	14.96	13.86	14.55	8.00	7.82	8.61
1994	22.85	16.07	12.16	14.66	15.07	9.25	9.00	10.10
1995	23.30	16.73	12.95	15.35	15.95	9.83	9.71	10.16
1996	23.73	17.18	13.45	15.38	16.43	10.36	10.32	10.20
1997	24.16	17.33	14.05	15.88	16.71	10.87	10.80	10.85
1998	23.98	17.56	14.60	16.13	17.82	11.62	11.63	11.09
1999	23.12	18.17	15.16	15.91	17.88	13.37	13.37	13.09

注:普通高校"生师比"中所用学生数为折合数。折合系数分别为:留学生×3, 研究生×2, 进修生×1.5 专业证书班学生数×1.5, 本专科学生数×1, 预科班学生数×1,函授生×0.2, 夜大学生数×0.5 成人脱产班学生数×1

普通高等学校校均规模

Average Size of Regular Inst. of Highter Education

单位:人

	1992	1993	1994	1995	1996	1997	1998	1999
全　国 Total	2074	2381	2591	2758	2927	3112	3335	3815
本科院校 University	2676	3094	3418	3632	3857	4062	4418	5275
专科院校 non－university tertiry	1051	1235	1338	1405	1466	1594	1701	1975

注:校均规模是指全日制本、专科在校生平均规模。

各级普通学校女学生和女教职工数

Number of Female Students, Teachers, Staff & Workers by Level & Type of Regular Schools

单位:万人
in 10 thousand

	女学生 Female Students		女教职工 Female Teachers, Staff & Workers		女专任教师 Female Full－time Teachers	
	人数 Number	占学生总数的比重(%) Percentage	人数 Number	占教职工总数的比重(%) Percentage	人数 Number	占专任教师总数的比重(%) Percentage
普通高等学校 Regular IHEs	162.06	39.66	43.81	41.14	15.90	37.35
中等技术学校 Sec. Technical Schools	227.80	53.60	18.36	43.56	9.58	45.24
中等师范学校 Teacher Training Schools	59.65	65.89	4.39	40.96	2.60	42.00
普通中学 General Sec. Schools	3109.24	45.92	182.71	38.44	155.03	40.37
职业中学 Vocational Schools	254.73	47.71	18.80	39.81	14.15	42.17
工读学校 Correctional Work－study Schools	0.06	8.32	0.08	29.25	0.04	27.89
小学 Primary Schools	6454.87	47.64	308.79	47.72	290.97	49.65
特殊教育学校 Special Education Schools	13.09	35.22	2.69	59.60	2.04	65.05
幼儿园 Kindergartens	1071.36	46.06	107.80	93.06	81.70	93.64

各级普通学校少数民族学生和少数民族教职工数

Number of Minority Students Enrolled, Teachers, Staff & Workers in Regular Schools at Various Levels

单位: 万人
in 10 thousand

	少数民族学生 Minority Students		少数民族教职工 Minority Teachers ,Staff & Workers		少数民族专任教师 Minority Full-time Teacher	
	人 数 Number	占学生总数的比重(%) Percentage	人 数 Number	占教职工总数的比重(%) Percentage	人 数 Number	占专任教师总数的比重(%) Percentage
普通高等学校 Regular IHEs	24.77	6.06	5.40	5.07	2.33	5.46
中等技术学校 Sec. Technical Schools	27.96	6.58	2.29	5.43	1.25	5.91
中等师范学校 Teacher Training Schools	9.71	10.72	0.98	9.10	0.61	9.89
普通中学 General Sec. Schools	463.29	6.84	33.89	7.13	27.14	7.07
职业中学 Vocational Schools	24.15	4.52	2.37	5.01	1.68	5.02
工读学校 Correctional Work-study Schools	.01	1.45	0.01	1.95	0.01	2.51
小 学 Primary Schools	1214.18	8.96	61.79	9.55	54.51	9.30
特殊教育学校 Special Education Schools	1.17	3.15	0.22	4.81	0.16	5.06
幼 儿 园 Kindergartens	81.85	3.52	4.19	3.62	3.23	3.70

二、普通教育

REGULAR EDUCATION

(一) 高等教育

HIGHER EDUCATION

普通高等学校校数

Number of Regular Higher Educational Institutions

单位: 所

	合　计 Total	大学、专门学院 Universities & Colleges	专科学校 Short-Cycle Colleges	职业技术学院 Short-Cycle Vocational Colleges
总　　计 Total	1071	597	313	161
综合大学 Comprehensive University	74	60	14	–
理工院校 Natural Sciences & Technology	268	192	76	–
农业院校 Agriculture	47	38	9	–
林业院校 Forestry	7	7	0	–
医药院校 Medicine & Pharmacy	118	97	21	–
师范院校 Teacher Training	227	87	140	–
语文院校 Language & Literature	15	12	3	–
财经院校 Finance & Economics	74	39	35	–
政法院校 Political Science & Law	25	11	14	–
体育院校 Physical Culture	14	13	1	–
艺术院校 Art	29	29	0	–
其他院校 Others	173	12	0	161

普通高等学校规模

Breakdown of Regular Higher Educational Institutions by Size of Enrolments

单位: 所

	学校数 Institutions	300人及以下 300 and under	301～500人 301 to 500	501～1000人 501 to 1000	1001～1500人 1001 to 1500	1501～2000人 1501 to 2000	2001～3000人 2001 to 3000	3001～4000人 3001 to 4000	4001～5000人 4001 to 5000	5001人及以上 5001 and over
总　　计 Total	1071	26	23	71	115	121	232	126	104	253
综合大学 Comprehensive University	74	0	0	1	7	1	4	0	7	54
理工院校 Natural Sciences & Technology	268	1	1	7	7	15	51	31	43	112
农业院校 Agriculture	47	0	0	1	4	3	9	4	9	17
林业院校 Forestry	7	0	0	0	0	0	2	1	3	1
医药院校 Medicine & Pharmacy	118	2	0	8	19	16	37	21	13	2
师范院校 Teacher Training	227	1	1	4	21	39	64	38	13	46
语文院校 Language & Literature	15	1	0	2	1	1	5	4	0	1
财经院校 Finance & Economics	74	1	0	2	9	4	23	11	11	13
政法院校 Political Science & Law	25	1	0	2	5	7	4	1	2	3
体育院校 Physical Culture	14	0	0	2	3	2	7	0	0	0
艺术院校 Art	29	0	5	14	10	0	0	0	0	0
其他院校 Others	173	19	16	28	29	33	26	15	3	4

普通高等学校设置专业数

Number of Specialities and Number of Educational Programmes Estabished by Field of Study in Regular Higher Educational Institutions

	合计 Total	哲学 Philosophy	经济 Economics	法学 Law	教育 Education	文学 Literature	历史 History	理学 Science	工学 Engineering	农学 Agriculture	医学 Medicine
种数 No. of Sp.	781	12	35	26	19	109	16	74	378	54	58
点数 No. of Ed. Prog.	22940	58	3546	838	859	3569	380	2500	9180	1017	993

普通高等学校工科分大类学生数

Breakdown of Engineering Students by Subfield of Study in Regular Higher Educational Institutions

单位:人

	毕业生数 Graduates	招生数 Entrants	在校学生数 Enrolment
总　计 Total	326180	607597	1613300
地　矿 Applied Geology	5892	8071	25091
材　料 Materials Science	13268	22989	68911
机　械 Mechanical Engineering	59000	92223	270506
仪器仪表 Instrument & Meter	6611	9962	27370
热能核能 Thermal & Nuclear Energy	6508	9787	28734
电　工 Electrical Engineering	34317	61072	165300
电子与信息 Electronics & Information	81392	201359	462252
土　建 Civil Engineering & Architcture	42067	72413	200362
水　利 Hydraulics	4368	7661	21337
测　绘 Survey & Measure	1514	3857	9217
环　境 Environment	3425	11119	23902
化工与制药 Chernical Engineering & Pharmaceutics	18018	26197	80559
轻工粮食食品 Grain & Food	10020	16514	46007
农业工程 Agriculture Engineering	4440	7515	21234
林业工程 Forestry Engineering	1507	2802	7813
纺　织 Textile	5257	7458	20760
交通运输 Transportation	7280	12373	34949
航空航天 Aeronautics & Astronautics	1243	2561	7303
兵　器 Weaponry	362	361	1277
公安技术 Public Security Technology	1014	1543	4970
工程力学 Engineering Mechanics	620	1047	3423
管理工程 Management Engineering	18057	28713	82023

普 通 高 等 学

Basic Statistics of Regular Higher

	学 校 数(所) Institutions		本 专 科 学 生 数 Undergraduate Students						
	计 Total	其中:中央部门所属学校数 Of Which Inst. under Central Ministries & Agencies	毕业生数 Graduates	招生数* Students Admitted	在校学生数* Enrolment	合计 Total	计 Subtotal	计 Subtotal	教授 Professors
总 计 Total	1071	248	847617	1548554	4085874	1065093	881068	425682	39359
其中:女 of which: Female	0	0	323238	625400	1620554	438130	358489	158974	5933
本科院校 University	597	207	623017	1118444	3149273	873670	706592	335771	37481
专科院校 Non-university Tertiry	474	41	210083	402116	878253	188078	171237	88206	1852
分校、大专班 Undergraduate Classes Branch Sohools	0	0	14517	27994	58348	3345	3239	1705	26
综合大学 Comprehensive Universities	74	15	130492	209769	617269	167943	135646	65307	7935
理工院校 Natural Sciences & Tech.	268	115	291018	517656	1415858	378948	293351	141156	14765
农业院校 Agriculture	47	11	40795	78120	200589	57274	44442	20721	1957
林业院校 Forestry	7	5	5242	10720	27618	7921	6185	3047	372
医药院校 Medicine & Pharmacy	118	18	56460	98712	300821	115718	95182	41166	5152
师范院校 Teacher Training	227	9	192556	344177	845354	174505	157962	81419	5106
语文院校 Language & Literature	15	8	7561	15048	37924	11926	10265	4961	421
财经院校 Finance & Economics	74	28	52921	92867	249073	48988	45142	21024	1549
政法院校 Political Science & Law	25	11	12315	24690	65196	15154	14437	5824	392
体育院校 Physical Culture	14	6	4957	9336	24809	7008	6492	3225	237
艺术院校 Art	29	10	4563	9190	24368	11770	10965	5744	590
民族院校 Nationalities	12	6	8597	14891	42751	10621	9485	4780	292
职业技术学院 Shore-cycle Vocational Colleges	161	6	40140	123378	234244	57317	51514	27308	591
总计中 of the total	248	248	259356	422565	1242943	428293	327031	150776	21276
中央部委所属院校 Inst. under Central Ministries & Agencies	46	46	94055	140288	444669	170074	121656	58671	10482
其中: of which:									
教育部所属院校 Inst.under MOE	202	202	165301	282277	798274	258219	205375	92105	10794
地方所属院校 Inst.under Local Auth.	823	0	588261	1125989	2842931	636800	554037	274906	18083

* 表中招生数和在校学生数不包括 1999 年成人高校举办的新高职学生数。

校基本情况

Educational Institutions

单位：人

教职工数 Teachers, Staff & Workers									
校本部教职工 Teachers, Staff & Workers in the College or Uni. Proper							科研机构人员 Personnel in Affiliated Research Org.	校办工厂、农场职工 Employees in School-run Factories, Farms	附设机构人员 Personnel in Other Subsidiary Units
专任教师 Full-time Teachers				教辅人员 Supporting Staff	行政人员 Adm. Personnel	工勤人员 Workers			
副教授 Asso. Professors	讲师 Lecturers	助教 Assistants	教员 Instructors						
125900	156390	83196	20837	131531	179630	144225	49536	57770	76719
37896	65359	39855	9931	69874	73423	56218	17592	19608	42441
105107	117555	60358	15270	110513	142339	117969	48302	48739	70037
20463	38070	22370	5451	20596	36691	25744	1198	9020	6623
330	765	468	116	422	600	512	36	11	59
21053	23141	10381	2797	20769	27554	22016	10718	6744	14835
43800	50372	25842	6377	47347	57117	47731	21802	27915	35880
6177	7199	4373	1015	6205	8810	8706	1852	7418	3562
914	997	632	132	991	1185	962	326	723	687
11916	13763	8327	2008	20342	18547	15127	10717	3723	6096
22730	31033	17946	4604	19527	31799	25217	2331	4640	9572
1399	1939	953	249	1370	2013	1921	182	385	1094
6206	8751	3536	982	4739	11050	8329	562	1570	1714
1499	2479	1191	263	1490	4641	2482	198	63	456
912	1279	684	113	549	1495	1223	71	38	407
1682	1984	1150	338	1004	2659	1558	208	233	364
1333	2045	833	277	1092	2060	1553	222	139	775
6279	11408	7348	1682	6106	10700	7400	347	4179	1277
49063	51546	23488	5403	57866	63077	55312	37434	22521	41307
20520	18580	7223	1866	22575	20880	19530	19005	10132	19281
28543	32966	16265	3537	35291	42197	35782	18429	12389	22026
76837	104844	59708	15434	73665	116553	88913	12102	35249	35412

普通高等学校

Number of Undergraduate Students by Type of

	毕业生数 Graduates			招生数* Students Admitted	
	计 Total	本科 Normal Courses	专科 Short-cycle Courses	计 Total	本科 Normal Courses
总计 Total	847617	440935	406682	1548554	936690
国家任务 Students Enrolled according to State Plan	706825	398424	308401	1383030	935458
委托培养 Students Enrolled by Contract	66899	16044	50855	0	0
自费生 Tuition-paying Students	71607	24932	46675	0	0
新职高	0	0	0	163885	0
教师本专科 In-service Teacher Training Courses	2286	1535	751	1639	1232
中央部委所属学校 Inst. under Central Ministries & Agencies	259356	195764	63592	422565	343286
其中: of which: 教育部所属学校 Inst. under MOE of Education	94055	80270	13785	140288	124808
地方所属学校 Inst. under Local Aut	588261	245171	343090	1125989	593404

* 同第 22 页。

普通高等学校

Supplementary Data for Special Categories

	学生总数中 Of Total Enrolment		成人第二专科学历 Students for secend diplomas	预科班 Pre-university Courses
	第二学士学位 Second Bachelor's Degrees	走读生 Students Who Not Live in Campus		
毕(结)业生数 Graduates	2408	27419	20119	8897
招生数 Students Admitted	1989	52681	48548	13092
在校学生数 Enrolment	4408	127596	100921	14193
毕(结)业班学生数 Graduates for Next Year	2212	27663	25850	8480

本专科学生数

Courses in Regular Higher Educational Institutions

单位:人

专科 Short-cycle Courses	在校学生数* Enrolment 计 Total	本科 Normal Courses	专科 Short-cycle Courses	毕业班学生数 Graduates for Next year 计 Total	本科 Normal Courses	专科 Short-cycle Courses
611864	4085874	2724421	1361453	894911	503159	391752
447572	3888523	2698101	1190422	867752	481568	386184
0	11217	8441	2776	9416	7155	2261
0	17008	14180	2828	15663	13008	2655
163885	163885	0	163885	0	0	0
407	5241	3699	1542	2080	1428	652
79279	1242943	1073438	169505	269661	217462	52199
15480	444669	410816	33853	99170	87988	11182
532585	2842931	1650983	1191948	625250	285697	339553

学生数补充资料

of Undergraduate Students

单位:人

外国留学生 Foreign Students	自考助学班 Tutored students for Self-exam	另有其他学生数 Students in Different Duration 三个月以下 Under 3 mouths	三个月至一年以内 3 Mouths -one year	一年及以上 Over one year
10911	81314	155242	75464	63357
14758	143525	79633	59151	59921
25749	335847	37051	66975	133496
8864	94842	27563	26859	54292

普通高等学校

Number of Students by Field of Study in

	毕业生数 Graduates			招生 Students	
	计 Total	本科 Normal Courses	专科 Short－cycle Courses	计 Total	本科 Normal Courses
总计 Total	847617	440935	406682	1548554	936690
哲学 Philosophy	1067	852	215	1763	1386
经济学 Economics	134258	67611	66647	237129	131459
法学 Law	31500	16363	15137	69048	42765
教育学 Education	40271	15479	24792	67257	35163
文学 Literature	120957	44285	76672	230175	117599
历史学 History	13374	6097	7277	19070	11043
理学 Science	90395	42351	48044	155880	99870
工学 Engineering	326180	195354	130826	607597	386458
农学 Agriculture	28070	17453	10617	52251	35834
医学 Medicine	61545	35090	26455	108384	75113
总计中：师范 of the Total: Teacher Training	147281	46424	100857	234674	105732

* 同第 22 页。

分科学生数

Rrgular Higher Educational Institutions

单位:人

数* Admitted	在校学生数* Enrolment			毕业班学生数 Graduates for Next Year		
专科 Short－cycle Courses	计 Total	本科 Normal Courses	专科 Short－cycle Courses	计 Total	本科 Normal Courses	专科 Short－cycle Courses
611864	4085874	2724421	1361453	894911	503159	391752
377	4892	4272	620	953	835	118
105670	614028	385525	228503	142445	77732	64713
26283	174496	115687	58809	36892	20217	16675
32094	167145	97316	69829	41718	18025	23693
112576	563698	307059	256639	130503	53944	76559
8027	55652	35055	20597	13805	6916	6889
56010	421048	278259	142789	94719	49537	45182
221139	1613300	1144396	468904	343970	219906	124064
16417	142415	105486	36929	30481	19266	11215
33271	329200	251366	77834	59425	36781	22644
128942	620438	305499	314939	154170	55620	98550

普通高等学校函授部、

Number of Students Enrolled in Correspondence Divisions、Evening Schools and Short－

	函授部、夜大学 Correspondence Divisions and Evening Schools							
	毕业生数 Graduates			招生数 Students Admitted			在校 Enrolment	
	计 Total	本科 Normal Courses	专科 Short－cycle Courses	计 Total	本科 Normal Courses	专科 Short－cycle Courses	计 Total	本科 Normal Courses
总计 Total	367825	80581	287244	509865	145661	364204	1470727	355886
哲学 Philosophy	54	10	44	109	0	109	288	11
经济学 Economics	134827	19202	115625	140676	29832	110844	426034	76984
法学 Law	21078	6744	14334	32796	12043	20753	86632	27981
教育学 Education	21029	8776	12253	38372	15554	22818	93966	35535
文学 Literature	1405	15771	45634	98878	29883	68995	252487	67646
历史学 History	3801	1770	2031	5028	3042	1986	13623	7467
理学 Science	16488	9539	6949	25309	17076	8233	63873	38937
工学 Engineering	77198	15521	61677	116253	29034	87219	371014	79859
农学 Agriculture	7363	577	6786	10860	1230	9630	29177	3042
医学 Medicine	24582	2671	21911	41584	7967	33617	133633	18424
总计中：师范 of the Total: Teacher Training	57247	22876	34371	100075	42758	57317	245092	96247

普通高等学校学

Changes in

	上学年初报表在校学生数 Total enrolment at beginning of previous academic year	增加学生数 Factors of Increase					
		计 **Total**	招生数 No.of Students Admitted	复学 Students Resuming Studies	其他学校转入 Transfers from Other Inst.	其他 Others	计 **Total**
本专科学生 Undergraduate Students	3404374	1569946	1548554	4670	6360	10362	888446

夜大学、成人脱产班分科学生数

cycle Courses for Cadres Attached to Regular Institutions of Higher Education

单位:人

学生数	成人脱产班 Short－cycle Courses for Cadres								
	毕业生数 Graduates			招生数 Students Admitted			在校学生数 Enrolment		
专科 Short－cycle Courses	计 Total	本科 Normal Courses	专科 Short－cycle Courses	计 Total	本科 Normal Courses	专科 Short－cycle Courses	计 Total	本科 Normal Courses	专科 Short－cycle Courses
1114841	108717	5978	102739	157465	28819	128646	357635	52424	305211
277	12	0	12	0	0	0	0	0	0
349050	37593	653	36940	41404	5321	36083	92621	9795	82826
58651	5471	205	5266	9225	1837	7388	16927	3205	13722
58431	1751	269	1482	1186	174	1012	2805	440	2365
184841	13385	1017	12368	22607	4134	18473	42478	5910	36568
6156	396	0	396	332	11	321	704	13	691
24936	2532	159	2373	1991	406	1585	4568	634	3934
291155	32984	2386	30598	55924	12393	43531	139176	24538	114638
26135	1551	0	1551	2050	254	1796	4021	318	3703
115209	13042	1289	11753	22746	4289	18457	54335	7571	46764
148845	7337	890	6447	7998	1728	6270	16216	2660	13556

生数变动情况

Undergraduate Enrolment

单位:人

减少学生数 Factors of Decrease								本学年初报表在校学生数
毕业生 Graduates	结业生 Completers of Courses without formal awards	休学 Suspended	退学 Quitting	开除 Expelled	死亡 Dead	转到其他学校 Transfers to Other Inst.	其他 Others	Total enrolment at beginning of current academic year
847617	6282	6154	11140	690	465	5812	10286	4085874

普通高等学校分科专任教师数

Number of Full－time Teachers by Field of Study in Regular Higher Educational Institutions

单位:人

	合计 Total	教授 Prof.	副教授 Asso.Prof.	讲师 Lecturers	助教 Assistants	教员 Instructors	合计中公共课教师 Faculty Members Teaching Basic Courses
总计 Total	425682	39359	125900	156390	83196	20837	84311
其中：女 Of which: Female	158974	5933	37896	65359	39855	9931	32253
哲学 Philosophy	14263	1166	4371	5920	2333	473	7518
经济学 Economics	33785	2576	9184	13602	6846	1577	3301
法学 Law	11637	882	2839	4941	2348	627	2461
教育学 Education	38246	1519	9327	16205	9109	2086	19961
文学 Literature	74725	4632	18643	28020	18361	5069	21997
历史学 History	8074	962	2489	3144	1183	296	1610
理学 Science	76095	7850	25912	26708	12524	3101	18689
工学 Engineering	117940	12886	37579	41378	20938	5159	6646
农学 Agriculture	14959	1902	4805	5141	2481	630	268
医学 Medicine	35958	4984	10751	11331	7073	1819	1860

专任教师中本学年内不担任教学工作的人数

Number of Full－time Teachers Carrying No Teaching Load

单位：人

	合计 Total	教授 Prof.	副教授 Asso. Prof.	讲师 Lecturers	助教 Assistants	教员 Instructors
总计 Total	30099	2093	7164	12797	7122	923
脱产进修 On Leave for Upgrading	16930	508	3657	7951	4488	326
科学研究 Scientific Research	4762	1088	1884	1363	402	25
外借人员 Working for other Institutions or Org.	656	54	195	249	132	26
因病休养 Convalescents	845	73	207	361	180	24
其他 Others	6906	370	1221	2873	1920	522

非教学人员中有教师职称的人数

Breakdown of Non－Teaching Staff with Academic Ranks

单位：人

	合计 Total	教授 Prof.	副教授 Asso. Prof.	讲师 Lecturers	助教 Assistants
总计 Total	48276	4995	12379	19729	11173
行政人员中 Adm. Personnel	26108	1965	6612	11057	6474
科研机构人员中 Personnel in Research Org.	12745	2689	4021	4311	1724
教辅人员中 Supporting Staff	5436	159	910	2359	2008
校办厂、场职工中 Employees in School－run Factories & Farms	814	41	199	463	111
附设机构人员中 Personnel in Subsidiary Units	3173	141	637	1539	856

普通高等学校专

Breakdown of Full-time Teachers by Academic

	合 计 Total	研 究 生 毕 业 Completion of Postgraduate Courses		
		博 士 Doctor's Degrees	硕 士 Master's Degrees	未授博士、硕士学位的 Without advanced higher degrees
总 计 Total	425682	23136	100492	8479
其中:女教师 of which: Female Teachers	158974	3246	33001	2604
教授 Prof.	39359	6331	7158	1577
副教授 Asso. Prof.	125900	10500	30864	2631
讲师 Lecturers	156390	5351	44339	3156
助教 Assistants	83196	508	13964	962
教员 Instructors	20837	446	4167	153

普通高等学校专

Breakdown of Full-time Teachers by Age

	合 计 Total	30岁及以下 30 years & under	31～35岁 31～35years
总 计 Total	425682	117406	94150
其中:女教师 of which: Female Teachers	158974	57877	38232
教授 Prof.	39359	17	773
副教授 Asso. Prof.	125900	415	15153
讲师 Lecturers	156390	26877	68713
助教 Assistants	83196	70813	8556
教员 Instructors	20837	19284	955

普通高等学校教

Supplementary Data for Teachers,

	教 职 工 总 数 中 Of the Total Number of Staff and Workers				
	函授部、夜大学教职工 Teachers, Staff & Workers in Correspondence Divisions, & Evening Schools		思想政治教育教师 Political Teachers	兼 任 教 师 Part-time Teachers	编制外招聘教师数 Number of teachers recruited beyond authorized strength or size of Staff
	计 Total	其中:专任教师 of which: Full-time Teachers			
人 数 Number	21190	8461	26231	18788	5777

任教师学历情况

Qualifications in Regular Higher Educational Institutions

单位:人

高等学校本科毕业 Completion of Normal Undergraduate Courses			高等学校专科毕业及本专科肄业二年以上 Completion of Short-cycle Courses or at least two years of undergraduate courses	高等学校本专科肄业未满两年及以下 Attendance in undergraduate Courses less than 2 years
学士 With Bachelor's Degrees	研究生肄业 Having Some Postgraduate Training	未授学士学位的 Without Bachelor's Degrees		
217694	847	54979	18345	1710
95334	304	17284	6628	573
10113	107	13187	791	95
47390	250	27444	6391	430
84811	361	10499	7114	759
61314	113	2970	3061	304
14066	16	879	988	122

任教师年龄情况

in Regular Higher Educational Institutions

单位:人

36～40岁 36～40 years	41～45岁 41～45 years	46～50岁 46～50 years	51～55岁 51～55years	56～60岁 56～60 years	61岁及以上 61 years & over
72324	45161	25496	28818	32095	10232
24632	14277	7737	8311	6490	1418
3099	4786	3352	6191	11960	9181
30372	26462	16083	18446	17976	993
36018	12894	5702	4043	2109	34
2544	866	291	96	26	4
291	153	68	42	24	20

职工数补充资料

Staff & Workers in Regular HEIs

单位:人

另有其他人员 Employees not elsewhere clossified					
聘期一年以上的外国专家、教授 Foreign experts with a term of one year and over	附属中学教职工 Staff & Workers in Attached Sec. Schools	附属小学教职工 Staff & Workers in Attached Primary Schools	现有离退休人员 Number of People on Pension	服务公司等集体所有制人员 Employees of Collective owned Units (Labour Service Co., etc.)	停薪留职人员 Personnel with pay temporarily suspended
1830	18237	7068	362685	31002	5161

普通高等学校专

Changes of Full－time Teachers in Regular

	上学年初报表专任教师数 Total number of full－time teachers at beginning of previous academic year	增加专 Factors				
		合 计 Total	当年分配毕业生 New recruits from current year graduates			
			计 Total	其中：博士、硕士毕业 Of which: completing doc. & mas. deg. prog.	其中：本科毕业 Of which: completing 1st degree courses	计 Total
专任教师 Full－time Teachers	407922	44187	19241	7834	11110	17330

普 通 高 等 学

Condition of School Buildings in Regular

	合 计 Total	教学及辅助用房 Teaching & Administritive					
		计 Subtotal	教 室 Classroom	图书馆 Library	实验实习场附属用房 Lab. and Supplementary building	体育馆 Gymnasium	会 堂 Hall
校舍建筑总面积 Total Floor Space	175247930	55716277	20820141	7464558	23949659	2049696	1432223
其中：外单位借用面积 of which: Under lease by other units	909213	33209	12348	800	18568	0	1493
危房面积 Floor space of dilapidated buildings	3555109	927482	358464	69158	422864	43208	33788
当年新增面积 New floor space added in current year	13203023	3423595	1581530	328379	1308823	174056	30807
正在施工面积 Floor space under construction	15215354	4601697	1908226	666567	1632993	315592	78319
借租用校舍面积 Leased Floorspace	900426	283042	209057	12403	48041	8876	4665

任教师变动情况

Higher Educational Institutions

单位：人

任教师数 of Increase				减少专任教师数 Factors of Decrease			本学年初报表专任教师数 Total number of full-time teachers at beginning of current academic year
外单位教师调入 Teachers recruited form other units	校内、外非教师调入 Non-teaching personnel changed into teachers		合计 total	上学年离退休人员 Retired from their posts during previcus academic year	调离教师岗位人员 Transferred from teaching to non-teaching posts	其他 Others	
其中：普通高校调入 of which: from reg. HEIs	计 Total	其中：本校职工转为教师 Of which: with change of status in their own institutions					
6417	7616	4491	26427	11619	5728	9080	425682

校校舍情况

Higher Educational Institutions

单位：m²

行政办公用房 Adm. Buildings	生活用房 Residential Building						
	计 Subtotal	学生宿舍 Students' Dormitories	学生食堂 Students' Dining Halls	教工单身宿舍 Apartments for Single	教工及家属住宅 Residences for Teachers & Workers	教工食堂 Halls for Staff & Workers	福利及附属用房 Welfare anxiliary Buildings
8043390	111488263	28158463	5273630	3200165	58339024	932186	15584795
30730	845274	40199	1923	12532	641264	385	148971
198883	2428744	452164	64696	160910	1307906	24001	419067
379111	9400317	2717420	393735	252338	5407799	19259	609766
294164	10319493	2318492	401129	363028	6700652	116665	419527
42147	575237	421819	35593	13431	79670	409	24315

社会力量举办的非学历高等教育机构基本情况

Basic Conditions of In-formal Schooling at Non-State Higher Education Institutions

单位：人

	机构数(个) Ins. No	结业生数 No. of Completers		招生数 Entrants		注册学生数 Enrollmant		专职教职工数 Teachers, Staff & Workers			兼职教师 Part-time Teachers
		计 Sub-total	其中：of which: 学历文凭 With Diplomas	计 Sub-total	其中：of which: 学历文凭 With Diplomas	计 Sub-total	其中：of which: 学历文凭 With Diplomas	计 Sub-total	其中：of which: 教师 Teachers	行政人员 Adm. personnel	
总计 Total	1240	778318	44759	903862	129082	1184371	258103	50384	24723	22562	54770
其中：女 of which: female		355132	23645	416065	59961	547124	119343	19166	9265	9127	18106

研　究　生

GRADUATE　EDUCATION

全国研究生

Basic Statistics of Graduate

	合计 Total			攻读博士学位 Candidates for Doctor's	
	毕业生数 Graduates	招生数 Entrants	在学研究生数 Enrolment	毕业生数 Graduates	招生数 Entrants
总计 Total	54670	92225	233513	10320	19915
其中:女 of which: Female	17049	31233	75720	2054	4892
委托培养 Students enrolled by contract	8068	15673	37410	1380	3511
哲学 Philosophy	649	1301	3079	180	356
经济学 Economics	6302	10828	27763	717	1546
法学 Law	3257	5583	14581	343	807
教育学 Education	1008	2455	5499	149	295
其中:体育学 of which: Science of Physical Culture & Sports	235	429	1053	27	44
文学 Literature	3310	5454	13671	358	759
其中:艺术学 of which: Science of Art	366	794	1752	30	87
历史学 History	970	1553	3927	227	438
理学 Sciences	8251	13182	33413	2411	3853
工学 Engineering	23369	39068	99211	4039	8567
其中:力学 of which: Mechanics	688	955	2651	208	310
农学 Agriculture	1949	3450	8856	460	887
其中:林学 of which: Forestry	225	427	1093	44	91
医学 Medicine	5605	9351	23513	1436	2407

基本情况

Education in China

单位: 人

研究生 Degrees	攻读硕士学位研究生 Candidates for Master's Degrees			研究生班研究生 Students Enrolled in Postgraduate Courses not Awarding Degrees		
在学研究生数 Enrolment	毕业生数 Graduates	招生数 Entrants	在学研究生数 Enrolment	毕业生数 Graduates	招生数 Entrants	在学研究生数 Enrolment
54038	44189	71847	178525	161	463	950
11945	14934	26214	63492	61	127	283
8013	6632	12065	29160	56	97	237
869	469	945	2210	0	0	0
3600	5554	9224	23985	31	58	178
1842	2914	4776	12739	0	0	0
713	859	2160	4786	0	0	0
117	208	385	936	0	0	0
1804	2903	4670	11739	49	25	128
194	287	682	1430	49	25	128
1076	743	1115	2851	0	0	0
10411	5834	9329	23002	6	0	0
25494	19285	30151	73132	45	350	585
1049	480	645	1602	0	0	0
2277	1489	2563	6579	0	0	0
239	181	336	854	0	0	0
5952	4139	6914	17502	30	30	59

高等学校研究生

Basic Statistics of Graduate Education in

	合　　计 Total			攻读博士学位 Candidates for Doctor's	
	毕业生数 Graduates	招生数 Entrants	在学研究生数 Enrolment	毕业生数 Graduates	招生数 Entrants
总　计 **Total**	50753	86778	218650	8749	17724
其中:女 of which: Female	16118	29771	71976	1756	4373
委托培养 Students enrolled by contract	7895	15507	36890	1245	3370
哲　学 Philosophy	620	1250	2924	165	329
经济学 Economics	6046	10521	26928	618	1402
法　学 Law	3152	5416	14131	307	734
教育学 Education	984	2427	5416	134	280
其中:体育学 of which: Science of Physical Culture & Sports	235	429	1053	27	44
文　学 Literature	3276	5407	13543	348	740
其中:艺术学 of which: Science of Art	361	781	1717	30	80
历史学 History	955	1530	3856	221	426
理　学 Sciences	6570	10725	26686	1514	2678
工　学 Engineering	21922	37134	94012	3642	7992
其中:力学 of which: Mechanics	624	860	2381	182	267
农　学 Agriculture	1858	3312	8448	423	816
其中:林学 of which: Forestry	216	412	1055	44	83
医　学 Medicine	5370	9056	22706	1377	2327

基本情况

Regular Higher Educational Institutions

单位: 人

研究生 Degrees	攻读硕士学位研究生 Candidates for Master's Degrees			研究生班研究生 Students Enrolled in Postgraduate Courses not Awarding Degrees		
在学研究生数 Enrolment	毕业生数 Graduates	招生数 Entrants	在学研究生数 Enrolment	毕业生数 Graduates	招生数 Entrants	在学研究生数 Enrolment
47649	41843	68591	170051	161	463	950
10583	14301	25271	61110	61	127	283
7564	6594	12040	29089	56	97	237
788	455	921	2136			
3204	5397	9061	23546	31	58	178
1646	2845	4682	12485			
670	850	2147	4746			
117	208	385	936			
1753	2879	4642	11662	49	25	128
173	282	676	1416	49	25	128
1045	734	1104	2811			
6916	5050	8047	19770	6	0	0
23814	18235	28792	69613	45	350	585
906	442	593	1475			
2080	1435	2496	6368			
221	172	329	834			
5733	3963	6699	16914	30	30	59

	合计 Total			攻读博士学位 Candidates for Doctor's	
	毕业生数 Graduates	招生数 Entrants	在学研究生数 Enrolment	毕业生数 Graduates	招生数 Entrants
总　计 Total	3917	5447	14863	1571	2191
其中:女 of which: Female	931	1462	3744	298	519
委托培养 Students enrolled by contract	173	166	520	135	141
哲　学 Philosophy	29	51	155	15	27
经济学 Economics	256	307	835	99	144
法　学 Law	105	167	450	36	73
教育学 Education	24	28	83	15	15
其中:体育学 of which: Science of Physical Culture & Sports	0	0	0		
文　学 Literature	34	47	128	10	19
其中:艺术学 of which: Science of Art	5	13	35	0	7
历史学 History	15	23	71	6	12
理　学 Sciences	1681	2457	6727	897	1175
工　学 Engineering	1447	1934	5199	397	575
其中:力学 of which: Mechanics	64	95	270	26	43
农　学 Agriculture	91	138	408	37	71
其中:林学 of which: Forestry	9	15	38	0	8
医　学 Medicine	235	295	807	59	80

基本情况

in Research Organizations

单位: 人

研究生 Degrees	攻读硕士学位研究生 Candidates for Master's Degrees			研究生班研究生 Students Enrolled in Postgraduate Courses not Awarding Degrees		
在学研究生数 Enrolment	毕业生数 Graduates	招生数 Entrants	在学研究生数 Enrolment	毕业生数 Graduates	招生数 Entrants	在学研究生数 Enrolment
6389	2346	3256	8474	–	–	
1362	633	943	2382	–	–	
449	38	25	71	–	–	
81	14	24	74	–	–	–
396	157	163	439	–	–	
196	69	94	254	–		
43	9	13	40	–	–	
51	24	28	77	–	–	–
21	5	6	14	–	–	–
31	9	11	40	–	–	–
3495	784	1282	3232	–	–	
1680	1050	1359	3519	–	–	
143	38	52	127	–	–	–
197	54	67	211	–	–	
18	9	7	20	–	–	–
219	176	215	588	–	–	–

全国研究生指导教师情况

Basic Data on Supervisors of Postgraduate Programmes in China

单位：人

	合计 Total	30岁及以下 30 years and under	31－35	36－40	41－45	46－50	51－55	56－60	61岁及以上 61 years and over
总　计 Total	80813	319	6894	13090	12741	8871	12151	15523	11224
其中：女 of which: Female	13026	38	886	1917	2113	1624	2327	2680	1441
一、分职称 By academic rank									
教授 Professors	35913	11	906	2973	3963	3207	5668	9638	9547
副教授 Asso. Professors	35967	262	5149	8729	7594	4735	5115	3771	612
其他高级职称 with other adv. titles	8933	46	839	1388	1184	929	1368	2114	1065
二、分指导关系 By supervisory function									
博士导师 Supervisors of doctoral programmes	5611	2	94	244	373	294	529	1293	2782
硕士导师 Supervisors of master's degree prog.	65157	311	6518	11993	11234	7825	10163	11878	5235
博士、硕士导师 Supervisors of doc. & mas. degree programmes	10045	6	282	853	1134	752	1459	2352	3207

普通高等学校研究生指导教师情况

Basic Data on Supervisors of Postgraduate Programmes in Regular Higher Educational Institutions

单位：人

	合计 Total	30岁及以下 30 years and under	31－35	36－40	41－45	46－50	51－55	56－60	61岁及以上 61 years and over
总　计 Total	71860	276	6090	11734	11742	8171	11149	13093	9605
其中：女 of which: Female	12093	35	833	1821	1982	1507	2184	2428	1303
一、分职称 By academic rank									
教授 Professors	32371	9	745	2638	3684	2995	5279	8548	8473
副教授 Asso. Professors	34559	241	4896	8365	7370	4566	4986	3570	565
其他高级职称 with other adv. titles	4930	26	449	731	688	610	884	975	567
二、分指导关系 By supervisory function									
博士导师 Supervisors of doctoral programmes	3880	0	56	171	285	232	370	767	1999
硕士导师 Supervisors of master's degree prog.	59130	273	5813	10821	10452	7256	9454	10390	4671
博士、硕士导师 Supervisors of doc. & mas. degree programmes	8850	3	221	742	1005	683	1325	1936	2935

科研机构研究生指导教师情况

Basic Data on Supervisors of Postgraduate Programmes in Research Organizations

单位：人

	合计 Total	30岁及以下 30 years and under	31-35	36-40	41-45	46-50	51-55	56-60	61岁及以上 61 years and over
总 计 Total	8953	43	804	1356	999	700	1002	2430	1619
其中：女 of which: Female	933	3	53	96	131	117	143	252	138
一、分职称 By academic rank									
教授 Professors	3542	2	161	335	279	212	389	1090	1074
副教授 Asso. Professors	1408	21	253	364	224	169	129	201	47
其他高级职称 with other adv. titles	4003	20	390	657	496	319	484	1139	498
二、分指导关系 By supervisory function									
博士导师 Supervisors of doctoral programmes	1731	2	38	73	88	62	159	526	783
硕士导师 Supervisors of master's degree prog.	6027	38	705	1172	782	569	709	1488	564
博士、硕士导师 Supervisors of doc. & mas. degree programmes	1195	3	61	111	129	69	134	416	272

(二) 中等教育

SECONDARY EDUCATION

1. 中等专业学校

SPECIALIZED SECONDARY SCHOOLS

中等专业学校

Basic Statistics of Specialized Secondary

	学校数(所) Schools	毕业生数 Graduates	招生数 Entrants			在校学生数 Enrolments			
			计 Total	招高中毕业生数 Graduates From Senior Sec. School	招初中毕业生数 Graduates From Junior Sec. School		合计 Total	计 Subtotal	计 Subtotal
总 计 Total	3962	1401451	1633761	114271	1519490	5154984	528636	498781	273645
中等技术学校 Sec. Technical Schools	3147	1092478	1342516	88854	1253662	4249768	421445	394665	211778
工业学校 Industry	1022	462262	555803	25717	530086	1886145	167458	154386	82194
农业学校 Agriculture	335	133848	157890	6608	151282	496859	49727	46443	24558
林业学校 Forestry	52	17804	25648	1752	23896	78012	8682	8209	4180
医药学校 Health	525	137255	175854	4853	171001	534161	67752	60799	31793
财经学校 Finance & Economics	573	200701	251834	18864	232970	756852	66465	64715	34874
政法学校 Politics&Law	142	41098	49979	24812	25167	115064	14869	14757	6752
体育学校 PhysicalCulture	181	22063	28145	111	28034	81936	15059	14551	8074
艺术学校 Art	168	24822	37182	1207	35975	118270	17103	16786	11007
其他学校 Others	149	52625	60181	4930	55251	182469	14330	14019	8346
中等师范学校 Teacher Training Schools	815	308973	291245	25417	265828	905216	107191	104116	61867
其中: of which:									
幼儿师范学校 Pre-Primary Teacher Training Schools	61	18604	18900	268	18632	59823	7858	7312	4296

中等专业学校学

Changes in Enrolment of

	上学年初报表在校学生数 Total enrolment at beginning of previous academic year	增加学生数 Factors of Increase					
		计 Total	本学年初招生数 No. of Students Admitted	复学 Students Resuming Studies	其他学校转入 Transfers from Other Schools	其他 Others	计 Total
总 计 Total	4981540	1684941	1633761	1243	9265	40672	1511497
中等技术学校 Sec. Technical Schools	4060689	1382645	1342516	1064	7041	32024	1193566
中等师范学校 Teacher Training Schools	920851	302296	291245	179	2224	8648	317931

分类别情况

Schools by Field of Study

单位:人

教职工数 Teachers, Staff & Workers									兼任教师 Part-time Teachers
校本部教职工 Employees in the School Proper							校办厂、场职工 Employees in School-run Factories & Farms	附设机构人员 Employees in Subsidiary Units	
专任教师 Full-time Teachers				教辅人员 Supporting Staff	行政人员 Adm. Personnel	工勤人员 Workers			
高级讲师 Senior Lecturers	讲师 Lecturers	助理讲师 Assistant Lecturers	教员 Instructors						
48736	119881	94479	10549	47066	96118	81952	17814	12041	11321
39269	94869	70148	7492	38629	78872	65386	15773	11007	11046
15506	37188	26597	2903	15712	30387	26093	9339	3733	5017
4045	10435	9200	878	5051	7764	9070	2665	619	791
916	1882	1304	78	848	1487	1694	330	143	85
7136	14681	9283	693	7626	11432	9948	1846	5107	1690
6177	16212	11403	1082	5103	14497	10241	1082	668	1370
1018	2871	2495	368	1258	4738	2009	32	80	113
1357	3864	2575	278	891	3044	2542	31	477	153
1948	4433	3919	707	1205	2698	1876	197	120	852
1166	3303	3372	505	935	2825	1913	251	60	975
9467	25012	24331	3057	8437	17246	16566	2041	1034	275
767	1720	1597	212	555	1467	994	127	419	1

生数变动情况

Specialized Sec. Schools

单位:人

上学年毕业生数 Graduates	上学年结业生数 Completers of Courses without formal award	减少学生数 Factors of Decrease						本学年初报表在校学生数 Total enrolment at beginning of current academic year
		休学 Suspended	退学 Quitting	开除 Expelled	死亡 Dead	转到其他学校 Transfers to Other Schools	其他 Others	
1401451	4314	3863	26147	1230	474	13925	60093	5154984
1092478	4048	3639	25213	1133	363	11860	54832	4249768
308973	266	224	934	97	111	2065	5261	905216

中等专业学校分科学生数

Number of Students by Field of Study in Specialized Secondary Schools

单位：人

	毕业生数 Graduates	招生数 Entrants			在校学生数 Enrolment	毕业班学生数 Graduates for Next Year
		计 Total	招高中毕业生数 Graduates from Senior Sec. School	招初中毕业生数 Graduates From Junior Sec. School		
总　计　Total	1401451	1633761	114271	1519490	5154984	1511882
工　科　Industry	406832	543010	22190	520820	1797589	461779
农　科　Agriculture	50926	68168	3041	65127	207115	58390
林　科　Forestry	11732	17305	1539	15766	52455	14187
医药卫生科　Health	135794	173754	4357	169397	526507	131161
财　经　Finance & Economics	211571	182290	15519	166771	621729	218714
管　理　Administration	153615	190723	11995	178728	578299	168399
政　法　Politics & Law	45197	62311	26371	35940	141755	46177
艺　术　Art	45132	78782	3255	75527	231419	57907
体　育　Physical Culture	19125	26712	111	26601	75160	21269
师　范　Teachier Training	321527	290706	25893	264813	922956	333899
其中：of which:						
幼儿师范专业 For Pre－Primary Teacher	27495	27027	0	27027	86611	29445
特教师范专业 For Special Education	2211	2526	289	2237	7492	2168

中等专业学校学生数补充资料

Supplementary Data for Total Enrolment of Specialized Secondary Schools

单位：人

	成人中专学生数 Students in Adult Spec. Sec. Schools				另有其他学生数 Additional categories of students		
	干部中专班 SSS Classes for Cadres	职工中专班 SSS Classes for Workers	农村中专班 SSS Classes for Peasants	函授 Correspondence	进修班 Refresher Courses	培训班 Training Courses	其他 Others
毕业生数 Graduates	202610		89087	54296	163528	30090	32907
招生数 Entrants	192933		99693	54714	78700	21923	52140
在校生数 Enrolment	547183		263105	150089	32376	21143	111355

中等专业学校专任教师年龄情况

Breakdown of Full－time Teachers by Age in Specialized Secondary Schools

单位:人

	合 计 Total		30岁以下 30 years and under	31－35	36－40	41－45	46－50	51－55	56－60	61岁以上 61 years and over
	计 Total	其中:女 of Which: Female								
总 计 Total	273645	121792	88541	69080	40742	28041	18419	17044	11332	446
高级讲师 Senior Lecturers	48736	17008	90	2214	7413	10177	8532	10810	9096	404
讲 师 Lecturers	119881	53940	11986	47330	28026	15763	8989	5703	2052	32
助理讲师 Assistant Lecturers	94479	45634	66969	19023	5105	1952	822	466	136	6
教 员 Instructors	10549	5210	9496	513	198	149	76	65	48	4
中等技术学校 Technical Schools	211778	95808	65642	52631	32153	22925	15081	13830	9099	417
高级讲师 Senior Lecturers	39269	14216	80	1776	6025	8239	6871	8666	7231	381
讲 师 Lecturers	94869	43926	9479	36566	21978	12989	7432	4691	1703	31
助理讲师 Assistant Lecturers	70148	34068	49456	13892	3984	1570	706	416	120	4
教 员 Instructors	7492	3598	6627	397	166	127	72	57	45	1
中等师范学校 Teacher Training Schools	61867	25984	22899	16449	8589	5116	3338	3214	2233	29
高级讲师 Senior Lecturers	9467	2792	10	438	1388	1938	1661	2144	1865	23
讲 师 Lecturers	25012	10014	2507	10764	6048	2774	1557	1012	349	1
助理讲师 Assistant Lecturers	24331	11566	17513	5131	1121	382	116	50	16	2
教 员 Instructors	3057	1612	2869	116	32	22	4	8	3	3

中等专业学校分课

Number of Full－time Teachers of Specialized

	合计 Total	普通课 General Educational Subjects	专 Special			
			工 科 Industry	农 科 Agriculture	林 科 Forestry	医药卫生科 Health
总 计 Total	273645	92648	39947	8317	1912	18545
中等技术学校 Sec. Technical Schools	211778	65493	39554	8288	1904	18503
中等师范学校 Teacher Training Schools	61867	27155	393	29	8	42

中等专业学校分中央部

Basic Statistics of Specialized

	学校数（所） Schools	毕业生数 Graduates	招 生 数 Entrants			在 校 学 生 数 Enrolment	毕业班 学生数 Graduates for Next Year	合 计 Total		
			计 Total	招高中毕业生数 Graduates From Senior Sec. School	招初中毕业生数 Graduates From Junior Sec. School				计 Subtotal	
										计 Subtotal
总 计 Total	3962	1401451	1633761	114271	1519490	5154984	1511882	528636	498781	273645
中央部委所属学校 Run by Contral Ministries & Agencies	301	109788	120256	11292	108964	400814	107997	52594	47771	22892
地方所属学校 Run by Local Authorities	3661	1291663	1513505	102979	1410526	4754170	1403885	476042	451010	250753

中等专业学校女学

Number of Female Students, Teachers, Staff &

	女 学 生 数 Female Students						合 计 Total		
	毕业生数 Graduates	招 生 数 Entrants			在校学生数 Enrolmen	毕业班学生数 Graduates for Next Year		计 Subtotal	
		计 Total	招高中毕业生数 Graduates From Senior Sec. School	招初中毕业生数 Graduates From Junior Sec. School					计 Subtotal
总 计 Total	731473	917006	48914	868092	2874488	790741	227468	214546	121792
中等技术学校 Sec. Technical Schools	538176	727959	35766	692193	2277997	588809	183567	172386	95808
中等师范学校 Teacher Training Schools	193297	189047	13148	175899	596491	201932	43901	42160	25984

程专任教师数

Secondary Schools by Subject Taught

单位：人

业 课 Subjects						技术基础课 Basic Technical Subjects	实习指导课 Practice Course
财经科 Finance & Economics	管理科 Administration	政法科 Politics & Law	艺术科 Art	体育科 Physical Culture	师范科 Teacher Training		
19033	7673	6449	15607	10774	28633	18801	5306
18992	7547	6234	10883	8698	2690	17784	5208
41	126	215	4724	2076	25943	1017	98

门、地方学校基本情况

Secondary Schools by Control

单位：人

教 职 工 数 Teachers, Staff & Workers									兼任教师（不在教工数中） Part-time Teachers
校本部教职工 Employees in the School Proper							校办厂、场职工 Employees in School-run Factories & Farms	附设机构人员 Employees in Subsidiary Units	
专任教师 Full-time Teachers				教辅人员 Supporting Staff	行政人员 Adm. Personnel	工勤人员 Workers			
高级讲师 Senior Lecturers	讲师 Lecturers	助理讲师 Assistant Lecturers	教员 Instructors						
48736	119881	94479	10549	47066	96118	81952	17814	12041	11321
5073	10903	6330	586	5564	10518	8797	2484	2339	903
43663	108978	88149	9963	41502	85600	73155	15330	9702	10418

生和女教职工数

Workers in Specialized Secondary Schools

单位：人

女教职工数 Female Teachers, Staff & Workers									兼任教师（不在教工数中） Part-time Teachers
校本部女教职工 Female Employees in the School Proper							校办厂、场职工 Employees in School-run Factories & Farms	附设机构人员 Employees in Subsidiary Units	
专任女教师 Female Full-time Teachers				教辅人员 Supporting Staff	行政人员 Adm. Personnel	工勤人员 Workers			
高级讲师 Senior Lecturers	讲师 Lecturers	助理讲师 Assistant Lecturers	教员 Instructors						
17008	53940	45634	5210	26888	36719	29147	6363	6559	3950
14216	43926	34068	3598	21914	31187	23477	5397	5784	3872
2792	10014	11566	1612	4974	5532	5670	966	775	78

中等专业学校专

Changes of Full－time Teachers

	上学年初报表在校学生数 Number of total full－time teachers at beginning of previous academic year	增加专任教 Factors of						
		合计 Total	当年分配毕业生 New recruits from current year graduates					其他校 Teachers from
			计 Total	研究生 Completing postgraduate courses	本科生 Completing 1st degree courses	专科生 Completing short－cycle courses	中专生 Completing SSS courses	计 Total
总计 Total	276412	20109	8317	192	6305	1578	242	7090
中等技术学校 Sec. Technical Schools	213268	16083	6221	162	4720	1147	192	5772
中等师范学校 Teacher Training Schools	63144	4026	2096	30	1585	431	50	1318

中等专业学校专任教师学历情况

Breakdown of Full－time Teachers by Educational Attainment in Specialized Sec.Schools

单位:人

	合计 Total	高等学校本科毕业及以上 Completion of Normal Courses in IHEs	高等学校专科毕业及本专科肄业两年以上 Completion of Short－cycle Courses or at least 2 years of Undergraduate Courses	高等学校本专科肄业未满两年 Less than 2 years attendance at IHEs	中专、高中毕业及以下 Completion of Specialized or General Sec.Ed. & Lower
总计 Total	273645	195626.00	62412.00	1666	13941
中等技术学校 Sec.Technical Schools	211778	148087.00	49801.00	1384	12506
中等师范学校 Teacher Training Schools	61867	47539.00	12611.00	282	1435

中等专业学

Condition of School Buildings

	合计 Total				
	计 Total	教学辅助用房 Teaching & assistant building	行政办公用房 Administritive	生活福利用房 Residential and Welfare	计 Total
校舍建筑面积 Floor Space	108475370	39124327	6647398	62703645	87830617
其中:被外单位借占面积 of which: Under long－term lease or occupation by other units	347829	139338	20311	188180	322374
危房面积 Floor space of dilapidated buildings	984251	196752	32602	754897	810706
当年新增面积 New floor space added in current year	5428194	1942488	200735	3284971	4516635
正在施工面积 Floor space under construction	3767001	1477541	196018	2093442	2992790
借、租用校舍面积 Leased floor space	923696	432499	57633	433564	903657

任教师变动情况

in Specialized Sec. Schools

单位: 人

师 数 Increase				减 少 专 任 教 师 Factors of Decrease				本学年初报表专任教师数 Total number of full-time teachers at beginning of current academic year
教师调入 recruited other units	非教师调入 Non-teaching personnel changed into teachers			合 计 Total	上学年内离退休人数 Retired from their posts during previous academic year	调离教师岗位人员 Transferred from teaching to non-teaching posts	其 他 Others	
其中: 中等专业学校调入 of which: from other SSSs	计 Total	其中: 本校职工转为教师 of which: change of status in their own institutions						
3606	4702	3810		22876	4293	4633	13950	273645
2955	4090	3239		17573	3374	3605	10594	211778
651	612	571		5303	919	1028	3356	61867

中等专业学校其他情况

Supplementary Data on Specialized Sec. Schools

	学校占地面积(平方米) Area of school site (m^2)	学校藏书(万册) Library collections (in 10000 volumes)	固定资产总额(万元) Fixed assets (in 10000 yuan)	科研仪器设备值(万元) Equipments & Instruments for Teaching and Research (in 10000 yuan)	生产实习设备值(万元) Equipments for Production and Practive (in 10000 yuan)
总 计 Total	292787914	23779.91	25002474.87	1088719	367513
中等技术学校 Sec. Technical Schools	237832951	18693.51	14562764.33	916602	322386
中等师范学校 Teacher Training Schools	54954963	5086.40	10439710.54	172117	45127

校校舍情况

in Specialized Sec. Schools

单位: m^2

中等技术学校 Secondary Technical Schools			中等师范学校 Teacher Training Schools			
教学辅助用房 Teaching & assistant building	行政办公用房 Administritive	生活福利用房 Residential and Welfare	计 Total	教学辅助用房 Teaching & assistant building	行政办公用房 Administritive	生活福利用房 Residential and Welfare
31424622	5367514	51038481	20644753	7699705	1279884	11665164
133706	16801	171867	25455	5632	3510	16313
164908	22460	623338	173545	31844	10142	131559
1625057	172380	2719198	911559	317431	28355	565773
1163766	174639	1654385	774211	313775	21379	439057
426796	57238	419623	20039	5703	395	13941

2. 普通中学

GENERAL SECONDARY SCHOOLS

普通中学校数、班数

Number of General Secondary Schools and Classes

	学校数（所）Schools				班数（个）Classes	
	计 Total	初级中学 Junior Sec. Schools	高级中学 Senior Sec. Schools	完全中学 Complete Sec. Schools	初中 Junior Sec. Schools	高中 Senior Sec. Schools
总计 Total	77213	63086	4270	9857	1044904	194823
教育部门和集体办 Run by Ed. Dept. & Communities	68493	57429	3504	7560	977287	171322
其他部门办 Run by Non-ed. Dept.	6127	4241	255	1631	52565	15443
民办 Run by private and other social sources	2593	1416	511	666	15052	8058
城市 Urban	14223	8702	1496	4025	185213	77521
教育部门和集体办 Run by Ed. Dept. & Communities	9221	5690	989	2542	143562	61071
其他部门办 Run by Non-ed. Dept.	3527	2375	155	997	32730	10727
民办 Run by private and other social sources	1475	637	352	486	8921	5723
县镇 County Seats & Towns	19905	13963	1918	4024	277666	90580
教育部门和集体办 Run by Ed. Dept. & Communities	18020	12765	1720	3535	265363	85900
其他部门办 Run by Non-ed. Dept.	1138	736	60	342	8225	2700
民办 Run by private and other social sources	747	462	138	147	4078	1980
农村 Rural	43085	40421	856	1808	582025	26722
教育部门和集体办 Run by Ed. Dept. & Communities	41252	38974	795	1483	568362	24351
其他部门办 Run by Non-ed. Dept.	1462	1130	40	292	11610	2016
民办 Run by private and other social sources	371	317	21	33	2053	355
总计中 Of the total 四年制初中 4-year junior sec. Schools	3902	3822	0	80	72566	0
小学附设初中班 Junior Sec. Classes attached to primary schools	0	0	0	0	26236	0

普 通 中 学

Number of Students in

	毕业生数 Graduates		招生数 Students Admitted		初 Junior	
	初中 Junior Sec. Schools	高中 Senior Sec. Schools	初中 Junior Sec. Schools	高中 Senior Sec. Schools	计 Total	一年级 Grade 1
总计 Total	15898024	2629091	21496821	3963239	57215671	21556031
教育部门和集体办 Run by Ed. Dept. & Communities	15139487	2405085	20363256	3539327	54271742	20420953
其他部门办 Run by Non-ed. Dept.	624086	180483	824120	253765	2235397	825360
民办 Run by private and other social sources	134451	43523	309445	170147	708532	309718
城市 Urban	2743332	989019	3453372	1519240	9394809	3461014
教育部门和集体办 Run by Ed. Dept. & Communities	2257808	833693	2775681	1224888	7588561	2781958
其他部门办 Run by Non-ed. Dept.	406623	126217	513132	180539	1418521	513694
民办 Run by private and other social sources	78901	29109	164559	113813	387727	165362
县镇 County Seats & Towns	4241585	1282215	5689309	1892528	15123148	5703313
教育部门和集体办 Run by Ed. Dept. & Communities	4109729	1238159	5460262	1803129	14571170	5474336
其他部门办 Run by Non-ed. Dept.	93275	30504	130871	42225	336595	131541
民办 Run by private and other social sources	38581	13552	98176	47174	215383	97436
农村 Rural	8913107	357857	12354140	551471	32697714	12391704
教育部门和集体办 Run by Ed. Dept. & Communities	8771950	333233	12127313	511310	32112011	12164659
其他部门办 Run by Non-ed. Dept.	124188	23762	180117	31001	480281	180125
民办 Run by private and other social sources	16969	862	46710	9160	105422	46920
总计中 Of the total						
四年制初中 4-year junior sec. Schools	636665	0	1382277	0	3876882	1402578
小学附设初中班 Junior Sec. Classes attached to primary schools	278394	0	513395	0	1197696	515576
女学生 Female Students	7402804	1071021	10086690	1645542	26765358	10111133

学 生 数

General Secondary Schools

单位:人

中 Sec.Schools			在校学生数 Enrolments 高中 Senior Sec.Schools			
二年级 Grade 2	三年级 Grade 3	四年级 Grade 4	计 Total	一年级 Grade 1	二年级 Grade 2	三年级 Grade 3
18710291	16317095	632254	10497078	3972694	3468491	3055893
17749425	15526554	574810	9443222	3547379	3120334	2775509
734145	619480	56412	690616	254694	228499	207423
226721	171061	1032	363240	170621	119658	72961
3071777	2709810	152208	4060943	1522348	1355906	1182689
2486108	2213021	107474	3318847	1226996	1108040	983811
461038	399859	43930	494188	181058	164775	148355
124631	96930	804	247908	114294	83091	50523
4965180	4357056	97599	5017292	1899040	1650105	1468147
4784719	4217770	94345	4806236	1809379	1582020	1414837
111823	89994	3237	112138	42478	36310	33350
68638	49292	17	98918	47183	31775	19960
10673334	9250229	382447	1418843	551306	462480	405057
10478598	9095763	372991	1318139	511004	430274	376861
161284	129627	9245	84290	31158	27414	25718
33452	24839	211	16414	9144	4792	2478
1106383	735667	632254	0	0	0	0
385837	286501	9782	0	0	0	0
8747206	7605134	301885	4327085	1653556	1426252	1247277

普通中学

Number of Teachers, Staff & Workers

教职

Teachers,

	合计 Total	专任教师 Full-time Teachers		
		计 Total	初中 Junior Sec. Schools	高中 Senior Sec. Schools
总计 Total	4753600	3840556	3148117	692439
教育部门办 Run by Ed. Dept.	4297242	3514486	2896363	618123
其他部门办 Run by Non-ed.Dept.	322556	238508	181578	56930
集体办 Communities	63852	41171	40928	243
民办 Run by private and other social sources	69950	46391	29248	17143
城市 Urban	1203374	898508	629000	269508
教育部门办 Run by Ed. Dept.	944547	712720	494911	217809
其他部门办 Run by Non-ed.Dept.	206789	155425	116450	38975
集体办 Communities	6503	651	591	60
民办 Run by private and other social sources	45535	29712	17048	12664
县镇 County Seats & Towns	1485485	1179747	856280	323467
教育部门办 Run by Ed. Dept.	1407029	1124413	815023	309390
其他部门办 Run by Non-ed.Dept	52226	38985	28702	10283
集体办 Communities	8550	4325	4190	135
民办 Run by private and other social sources	17680	12024	8365	3659
农村 Rural	2064741	1762301	1662837	99464
教育部门办 Run by Ed. Dept.	1945666	1677353	1586429	90924
其他部门办 Run by Non-ed.Dept.	63541	44098	36426	7672
集体办 Communities	48799	36195	36147	48
民办 Run by private and other social sources	6735	4655	3835	820
总计中:女教职工 Of the total Female Teachers, Staff & Workers	1827092	1550341	1308691	241650

教 职 工 数

in General Secondary Schools

单位: 人

工数 Staff & Workers				代课教师 Substitute Teachers	临时工 Temporary Workers	兼任教师 Part-time Teachers
行政人员 Adm. Personnel	工勤人员 Workers	校办工厂、农场职工 Employees in School-run Factories & Farms				
		计 Total	其中:由厂、场收入支付工资的职工 Employees maintained by income of school-run businesses			
473446	402649	36949	17110	112872	102061	21819
419915	335464	27377	9778	79203	76209	8874
42288	38650	3110	1573	2787	2098	1582
1542	15073	6066	5543	23748	19170	281
9701	13462	396	216	7134	4584	11082
179347	102788	22731	12534	13731	19478	12736
143427	73172	15228	6732	7512	14188	3458
28992	20120	2252	983	1550	1491	1239
95	817	4940	4673	398	893	16
6833	8679	311	146	4271	2906	8023
146675	148650	10413	3212	26294	36966	5866
137793	135507	9316	2423	19754	29209	2814
6440	6491	310	152	305	198	240
255	3202	768	625	4489	6291	77
2187	3450	19	12	1746	1268	2735
147424	151211	3805	1364	72847	45617	3217
138695	126785	2833	623	51937	32812	2602
6856	12039	548	438	932	409	103
1192	11054	358	245	18861	11986	188
681	1333	66	58	1117	410	324
121910	140803	14038	7673	51920	43095	6605

普通中学分课程专
Number of Full－time General Secondary School Teachers

	合计 Total	初中 Junior Sec. Schools			
		计 Total	大学本科毕业及以上 Completion of Normal Courses in IHEs	大学专科毕业 Completion of Short－cycle Courses in IHEs	中专毕业 Complete Specialized Sec. Education
总计 Total	3840556	3148117	391751	2304064	373534
政治 Politics	283575	233512	35005	167869	24652
语文 Language & Literature	749178	639610	86343	482616	61568
数学 Math.	708643	599561	71244	451745	65218
物理 Physics	313772	236514	30833	180963	20306
化学 Chemistry	225514	151434	22263	115168	11464
生物 Biology	146322	122138	20034	81213	16732
地理 Geography	142600	118825	16350	79542	18009
历史 History	182951	141834	21333	97628	18146
英语 English	547401	450421	40645	366479	35358
俄语 Russian	3164	2067	254	1503	209
日语 Japanese	1527	989	248	615	99
体育 Physical Culture	191352	152850	18813	98240	29727
生理卫生 Physiology & Hygiene	14877	14343	903	8376	4123
音乐 Music	73409	67385	3906	41122	20095
美术 Fine Arts	70567	64462	4048	42392	15730
计算机课 Computer Literacy	29523	20815	3985	14247	2293
职业劳动 Vocational Practice	35654	32700	2424	18996	7880
其他课 Others	27915	23152	2909	13782	4804
不任课 No Teaching Load	92612	75505	10211	41568	17121

任教师学历情况

by Subject Taught & Educational Attainment

单位:人

高中毕业及以下的 Complete Sec. Education & Lower	高中 Senior Sec. Schools				
	计 Total	大学本科毕业及以上 Completion of Normal Courses in IHEs	大学专科毕业 Completion of Short-cycle Courses in IHEs	中专毕业 Complete Specialized Sec. Education	高中毕业及以下的 Complete Sec. Education & Lower
78768	692439	455989	224768	8749	2933
5986	50063	34968	14400	520	175
9083	109568	77188	31336	807	237
11354	109082	79317	28980	493	292
4412	77258	54099	22456	454	249
2539	74080	52158	21231	450	241
4159	24184	17000	6892	235	57
4924	23775	15972	7426	284	93
4727	41117	28660	12130	238	89
7939	96980	55127	41010	617	226
101	1097	687	385	15	10
27	538	344	174	18	2
6070	38502	19421	16959	1721	401
941	534	190	264	74	6
2262	6024	1761	3733	475	55
2292	6105	1950	3785	324	46
290	8708	4769	3759	157	23
3400	2954	1128	1387	301	138
1657	4763	2089	2081	441	152
6605	17107	9161	6380	1125	441

普通中学专任教师专业

Full－time Teachers in General Secondary

	合　计 Total	25岁及以下 25 years and under	26－30	31－35
合　计 Total	3840556	820324	931848	775872
初中：小计 Junior Sec. Schools Subtotal	3148117	714951	774386	603803
其中：女 of which: Female	1308691	358199	353803	254700
高　级 Senior	94979	28	185	1830
一　级 1st grade	822787	2053	47091	174020
二　级 2nd grade	1374344	121218	533064	385520
三　级 3rd grade	414690	230852	134443	30594
未评级 Rank undecided	441317	360800	59603	11839
高中：小计 Senior Sec. Schools Subtotal	692439	105373	157462	172069
其中：女 of which: Female	241650	51670	64871	59654
高　级 Senior	111085	39	205	4664
一　级 1st grade	258279	863	26044	102602
二　级 2nd grade	232660	33828	114717	62739
三　级 3rd grade	27101	15971	9025	1429
未评级 Rank undecided	63314	54672	7471	635

技术职务、年龄结构情况

Schools Broken Down by Rank and Age

单位：人

Unit: person

36－40	41－45	46－50	51－55	56－60	61岁及以上 61 years and over	总计中：女 Of the total female
421009	324552	233272	219537	109253	4889	1550341
330758	272784	196224	172250	80853	2108	1308691
120673	95221	69727	51294	4784	290	0
5999	13003	21469	32882	18378	1205	40750
153338	157938	125397	110713	51532	705	308919
157666	94700	45828	26367	9871	110	564075
9860	4967	2223	1222	513	16	180690
3895	2176	1307	1066	559	72	214257
90251	51768	37048	47287	28400	2781	241650
26216	14713	9970	12147	2167	242	0
12650	16757	17863	32950	23371	2586	28030
62927	30460	17285	13260	4672	166	84084
14099	4275	1759	944	285	14	88888
374	170	66	52	13	1	10627
201	106	75	81	59	14	30021

普通中学校舍情况

Condition of School Buildings in General Secondary Schools

	总计 Total	城市 Urban	县镇 County Seats & Towns	农村 Rural
教学及辅助用房(平方米) Teaching & assistant buildings	208656087	57269303	63351204	88035580
行政办工用房(平方米) Administritive	50052724	15609466	15163932	19279326
生活用房(平方米) Residential and Welfare	194861802	45514497	67719974	81627331
校舍建筑面积(平方米) Floor Space	453570613	118393266	146235110	188942237
其中: of which:				
当年新增面积(平方米) New floor space added in current year	23816524	6300669	8804707	8711148
危险房屋面积(平方米) Floor space of dilapidated buildings	3171673	613271	918709	1639693

普通初中班额情况

Size of Junior Secondary Classes

	班数(个) No. of Classes	班额(班) Size of Classes					
		25人及以下 25 and under	26－35	36－45	46－55	56－65	66人及以上 66 and over
总计 Total	1044904	14046	53068	189224	376946	267195	144425
城市 Urban	185213	4300	13926	41146	65614	40979	19248
县镇 County Seats & Towns	277666	2799	10751	46532	105307	72034	40243
农村 Rural	582025	6947	28391	101546	206025	154182	84934

3. 职业中学

VOCATIONAL SCHOOLS

职业中学校数、

Number of Schools, Classes, Graduates

	学校数(所) Schools			
	计 Total	初中 Junior Sec. Schools	高中 Senior Sec. Schools	初、高中合设 Junior & Senior Sec. Schools
总计 Total	9636	1319	7828	489
教育部门和集体办 Run by Ed. Dept. & Communities	6966	1300	5239	427
其他部门办 Run by Non-ed. Dept.	1720	6	1686	28
民办 Run by private and other social sources	950	13	903	34
城市 Urban	3763	30	3615	118
教育部门和集体办 Run by Ed. Dept. & Communities	1848	28	1747	73
其他部门办 Run by Non-ed. Dept.	1172	1	1150	21
民办 Run by private and other social sources	743	1	718	24
县镇 County Seats & Towns	3206	173	2821	212
教育部门和集体办 Run by Ed. Dept. & Communities	2592	164	2228	200
其他部门办 Run by Non-ed. Dept.	439	3	432	4
民办 Run by private and other social sources	175	6	161	8
农村 Rural	2667	1116	1392	159
教育部门和集体办 Run by Ed. Dept. & Communities	2526	1108	1264	154
其他部门办 Run by Non-ed. Dept.	109	2	104	3
民办 Run by private and other social sources	32	6	24	2
总计中 of the total				
教育部门其他部门联办 Run by Ed. Dept. & Non-ed. Dept.	326	6	303	17
其他学校附设 Attached to other schools	0	0	0	0
女学生 Female Students	0	0	0	0

班数、毕业生数和招生数

& Students Admitted in Vocational Schools

班数（个） Classes		毕业生数（人） Graduates		招生数（人） Students Admitted	
初中 Junior	高中 Senior	初中 Junior	高中 Senior	初中 Junior	高中 Senior
16500	104427	241425	1436865	337591	1603783
16207	83089	238223	1132010	332960	1266934
112	15391	1001	236539	1142	232182
181	5947	2201	68316	3489	104667
555	52807	7730	696479	8723	749175
383	36528	6586	477299	7022	498104
89	11579	711	168544	704	170127
83	4700	433	50636	997	80944
3084	37096	41852	530359	60164	612065
3032	32841	40926	455112	59199	537088
12	3186	149	59899	221	53799
40	1069	777	15348	744	21178
12861	14524	191843	210027	268704	242543
12792	13720	190711	199599	266739	231742
11	626	141	8096	217	8256
58	178	991	2332	1748	2545
130	5334	728	66753	2253	72522
1192	6466	9005	100158	29215	88559
0	0	104918	676093	151795	735720

职业中学在校学

Enrolment of Vocational

	在校学生数 Enrolments					
		初中 Junior				
	合计 Total	计 Total	一年级 Grade 1	二年级 Grade 2	三年级 Grade 3	计 Total
总计 Total	5339170	900751	339306	300519	260926	4438419
教育部门和集体办 Run by Ed. Dept. & Communities	4363080	889075	334643	296684	257748	3474005
其他部门办 Run by Non-ed. Dept.	702670	3047	1174	977	896	699623
民办 Run by private and other social sources	273420	8629	3489	2858	2282	264791
城市 Urban	2259771	21636	9166	6658	5812	2238135
教育部门和集体办 Run by Ed. Dept. & Communities	1528268	16495	7433	4946	4116	1511773
其他部门办 Run by Non-ed. Dept.	518863	2082	736	616	730	516781
民办 Run by private and other social sources	212640	3059	997	1096	966	209581
县镇 County Seats & Towns	1738468	156817	60193	49773	46851	1581651
教育部门和集体办 Run by Ed. Dept. & Communities	1531398	154848	59228	49192	46428	1376550
其他部门办 Run by Non-ed. Dept.	157877	326	221	92	13	157551
民办 Run by private and other social sources	49193	1643	744	489	410	47550
农村 Rural	1340931	722298	269947	244088	208263	618633
教育部门和集体办 Run by Ed. Dept. & Communities	1303414	717732	267982	242546	207204	585682
其他部门办 Run by Non-ed. Dept.	25930	639	217	269	153	25291
民办 Run by private and other social sources	11587	3927	1748	1273	906	7660
总计中 of the total						
教育部门其他部门联办 Run by Ed. Dept. & Non-ed. Dept.	225555	8505	2455	4075	1975	217050
其他学校附设 Attached to other schools	345970	62421	29864	19426	13131	283549
女学生 Female Students	2547269	407583	153465	137055	117063	2139686

生数和毕业班学生数

Schools and Graduates for Next Year

单位:人

高中 Senior						毕业班学生数 Graduates for Next Year	
二年制 2-year		三年制 3-year			四年制 4-year	初中 Junior	高中 Senior
一年级 Grade 1	二年级 Grade 2	一年级 Grade 1	二年级 Grade 2	三年级 Grade 3			
306708	288179	1274898	1293088	1192346	83200	263967	1506104
239857	224379	1008092	1002669	932715	66293	260789	1178392
38954	35386	191676	218861	205020	9726	896	243360
27897	28414	75130	71558	54611	7181	2282	84352
86458	89853	643270	696070	651182	71302	6468	759943
46455	51742	436081	470549	451315	55631	4772	518361
22761	20161	145196	165858	154142	8663	730	176624
17242	17950	61993	59663	45725	7008	966	64958
156821	139425	452784	432188	390792	9641	49707	534292
131722	116625	402217	377171	339943	8872	49284	460020
15215	13226	39254	45277	43810	769	13	57659
9884	9574	11313	9740	7039	0	410	16613
63429	58901	178844	164830	150372	2257	207792	211869
61680	56012	169794	154949	141457	1790	206733	200011
978	1999	7226	7726	7068	294	153	9077
771	890	1824	2155	1847	173	906	2781
10203	10665	58022	59602	60435	18123	1745	74825
14677	16624	74760	88731	84241	4516	16187	103637
126700	119838	604126	638818	605126	45078	117556	737871

职业中学高中
Number of Senior Level Students in

	合计 Total	工科 Industry	农科 Agriculture	林科 Forestry	医药卫生科 Health
毕业生数 Graduates	1436865	499736	122398	25963	106949
招生数 Students Admitted	1603783	619864	143330	33088	128188
在校学生数 Enrolment	4438419	1624428	354200	79451	384565
毕业班学生数 Graduates for Next Year	1506104	535028	114987	25625	119256

职业中学
Number of Teachers, Staff

	教职 Teachers, Staff					
	合计 Total	专任教师 Full-time Teachers			行政人员 Adm. Personnel	工勤人员 Workers
		计 Total	初中 Junior	高中 Senior		
总计 Total	472254	335501	39420	296081	68158	56163
教育部门办 Run by Ed. Dept.	396376	289836	38310	251526	54513	44035
其他部门办 Run by Non-ed. Dept.	56133	34440	233	34207	10159	8633
集体办 Run by Communities	3819	1235	598	637	218	950
民办 Run by private & other Social Sources	15926	9990	279	9711	3268	2545
城市 Urban	205524	137522	1513	136009	37867	22993
教育部门办 Run by Ed. Dept.	151351	104573	1190	103383	27115	15370
其他部门办 Run by Non-ed. Dept.	40874	25438	172	25266	7966	5681
集体办 Run by Communities	1372	152	2	150	113	117
民办 Run by private & other Social Sources	11927	7359	149	7210	2673	1825
县镇 County Seats & Towns	171676	123305	8169	115136	21307	23363
教育部门办 Run by Ed. Dept.	155110	113479	7994	105485	18885	19914
其他部门办 Run by Non-ed. Dept.	12230	7382	15	7367	1855	2516
集体办 Run by Communities	978	248	75	173	42	314
民办 Run by private & other Social Sources	3358	2196	85	2111	525	619
农村 Rural	95054	74674	29738	44936	8984	9807
教育部门办 Run by Ed. Dept.	89915	71784	29126	42658	8513	8751
其他部门办 Run by Non-ed. Dept.	3029	1620	46	1574	338	436
集体办 Run by Communities	1469	835	521	314	63	519
民办 Run by private & other Social Sources	641	435	45	390	70	101
总计中 of the total 女教职工 Female Teachers, Staff & Workers	187984	141465	12640	128825	21144	20529

阶段分科学生数

Vocational Schools by Field of Study

单位:人

财经科 Finance & Economics	管理科 Administration	政法 Politics & Law	艺术 Art	体育 Physical Culture	师范 Teacher Training
274848	183829	36263	76137	20295	90447
224450	209280	38284	95293	25905	86101
709963	600658	106445	262195	64654	251860
269251	204011	39779	84913	22281	90973

教职工数

& Workers in Vocational Schools

单位:人

工数 & Workers		代课教师 Substitute Teachers	临时工 Temporary Workers	兼任教师 Part－time Teachers
校办工厂、农场职工 Employees in School－run Factories & Farms				
计 Total	其中：由厂、场收入支付工资的职工 Employees maintained by income of school－run businesses			
12432	6447	13065	15459	26159
7992	3588	7400	10972	9697
2901	1489	1645	1540	9087
1416	1299	1470	1806	671
123	71	2550	1141	6704
7142	3678	5171	5629	16838
4293	2058	1852	3489	3888
1789	652	1160	1126	6724
990	942	35	283	326
70	26	2124	731	5900
3701	1740	5190	6942	6283
2832	1159	3906	5550	3322
477	236	435	362	2015
374	332	470	685	204
18	13	379	345	742
1589	1029	2704	2888	3038
867	371	1642	1933	2487
635	601	50	52	348
52	25	965	838	141
35	32	47	65	62
4846	2881	4328	5351	7655

职业中学专

Number of Full－time Vocational

	合　计 Total	初　中 Junior Sec. Schools			
		计 Total	大学本科毕业及以上 Completion of Normal Courses in IHEs	大学专科毕　业 Completion of Short－cycle Courses in IHEs	中专毕业 Complete Specialized Sec. Education
总　　计 **Total**	335501	39420	2563	26561	8989
文　化　课 Cultural Subjects					
专　业　课 Special Subjects	175065	34350	2256	23672	7400
工科 Industry	52956	318	34	196	80
农科 Agriculture	13760	1656	101	971	493
林科 Forestry	2706	386	15	254	100
医药卫生科 Health	8106	75	5	43	23
财经科 Finance & Economics	21487	84	6	60	14
管理科 Administration	12322	89	13	49	21
政法 Politics & Law	3255	138	15	97	22
艺术 Arts	13207	456	24	226	188
体育 Physical Culture	8611	962	33	503	351
师范 Teacher Training	7882	209	14	110	80
实习指导课 Practice Course	7968	145	14	66	53
不任课 No Teaching Load	8176	552	33	314	164

任教师学历情况

School Teachers by Educational Attainment

单位: 人

高中毕业及以下 Complete General Sec. Education & Lower	高中 Senior Sec. Schools 计 Total	大学本科毕业及以上 Completion of Normal Courses in IHEs	大学专科毕业 Completion of Short-cycle Courses in IHEs	中专毕业 Complete Specialized Sec. Education	高中毕业及以下 Complete General Sec. Education & Lower
1307	296081	119994	150515	20428	5144
1022	140715	63185	69577	6420	1533
8	52638	22001	27080	2865	692
91	12104	4472	6502	983	147
17	2320	972	1154	165	29
4	8031	2711	3712	1476	132
4	21403	8154	11704	1330	215
6	12233	4919	6335	761	218
4	3117	1314	1590	167	46
18	12751	3182	7583	1702	284
75	7649	2540	3985	883	241
5	7673	2610	3984	959	120
12	7823	1709	3647	1488	979
41	7624	2225	3662	1229	508

职业中学专任教师专业

Full－time Teachers in Vocational

	合　计 Total	25岁及以下 25 years and under	26－30	31－35
合　计 Total	335501	64496	85286	68752
初中：小计 Junior Sec. Schools Subtotal	39422	9235	9855	7692
其中：女 of which: Female	12640	4083	3670	2486
高　级 Senior	434	0	0	10
一　级 1st grade	7111	29	235	1186
二　级 2nd grade	18087	1007	5918	5405
三　级 3rd grade	7105	3062	2634	841
未评级 Rank undecided	6685	5137	1068	250
高中：小计 Senior Sec. Schools Subtotal	296079	55261	75431	61060
其中：女 of which: Female	128825	30045	36747	26537
高　级 Senior	24352	22	104	541
一　级 1st grade	93238	420	7236	26342
二　级 2nd grade	118821	15400	54035	31140
三　级 3rd grade	25248	13635	8624	1782
未评级 Rank undecided	34420	25784	5432	1255

技术职务、年龄结构情况

Schools Broken Down by Rank and Age

单位：人
Unit: person

36－40	41－45	46－50	51－55	56－60	61岁及以上 61 years and over	总计中：女 of the total female
36145	27147	20511	20918	11011	1235	141465
4459	3499	2047	1691	904	40	12640
1099	726	353	191	28	4	0
24	45	94	141	112	8	78
1301	1542	1108	1061	625	24	1415
2721	1715	741	429	145	6	5786
291	153	80	32	12	0	2490
122	44	24	28	10	2	2871
31686	23648	18464	19227	10107	1195	128825
12048	8988	7068	6314	898	180	0
1556	3132	4545	8036	5596	820	7902
19387	15116	11174	9449	3835	279	37415
9546	4521	2245	1379	506	49	54238
542	338	169	123	31	4	11902
655	541	331	240	139	43	17368

职业中学校舍情况

Condition of School Buildings in Vocational Schools

	总计 Total	城市 Urban	县镇 County Seats & Towns	农村 Rural
教学及辅助用房(平方米) Teaching & Assistant Buildings	25662199	11692061	9005659	4964479
行政办公用房(平方米) Administritive	6292427	2937627	2171346	1183454
生活福利用房(平方米) Residential and Welfare	26223289	10237990	10597491	5387808
校舍建筑面积(平方米) Floor Space	58177915	24867678	21774496	11535741
其中: of which:				
当年新增面积 (平方米) New floor space added in current year	2753339	1264804	1099349	389186
危险房屋面积 (平方米) Floor space of dilapidated buildings	404848	120379	158142	126327

（三）初等教育(小学)

PRIMARY EDUCATION
(PRIMARY SCHOOLS)

小学校数、班

Number of Schools, Classes &

	学校数(所) Schools	教学点数(个) External teaching sites	班　数(个) Classes	毕业生数(人) Graduates	招生数(人) Students Admitted
总　计　Total	582291	186065	3967402	23137366	20295337
教育部门和集体办 Run by Ed. Dept. & Communities	567222	179404	3805147	22151895	19293751
其他部门办 Run by Non－ed. Dept.	11805	4276	134125	890074	811937
民办 Run by private & other social scouces	3264	2385	28130	95397	189649
城　市　Urban	32602	5939	406866	3292056	2798203
教育部门和集体办 Run by Ed. Dept. & Communities	26468	4250	323357	2697244	2231100
其他部门办 Run by Non－ed. Dept.	5134	1583	71748	547044	484199
民办 Run by private & other social scouces	1000	106	11761	47768	82904
县　镇　County Seats & Towns	81162	14752	661794	4616602	3966688
教育部门和集体办 Run by Ed. Dept. & Communities	78660	14155	637327	4469528	3823077
其他部门办 Run by Non－ed. Dept.	1928	389	19912	132030	114513
民办 Run by private & other social scouces	574	208	4555	15044	29098
农　村　Rural					
教育部门和集体办 Run by Ed. Dept. & Communities	468527	165374	2898742	15228708	13530446
其他部门办 Run by Non－ed. Dept.	462094	160999	2844463	14985123	13239574
民办 Run by private & other social scouces	4743	2304	42465	211000	213225
总　计　中　Of the total	1690	2071	11814	32585	77647
六年制　6－year Schools	370317	124784	2689058	14325089	13184354
女学生　Female Students	0	0	0	11027229	9666388

数和学生数

Students in Primary Schools

在校学生数（人） Enrolments						
合计 Total	一年级 Grade 1	二年级 Grade 2	三年级 Grade 3	四年级 Grade 4	五年级 Grade 5	六年级 Grade 6
135479642	20900537	22801386	25338360	25737577	25097535	15604247
129459894	19891988	21797182	24266033	24634946	24010361	14859384
5042886	817123	825768	895841	936431	936586	631137
976862	191426	178436	176486	166200	150588	113726
18377600	2809608	2842118	3174356	3395633	3471658	2684227
14915633	2241130	2286489	2571018	2755667	2828920	2232409
3041066	485504	482651	529160	567086	577791	398874
420901	82974	72978	74178	72880	64947	52944
26360773	4030543	4322982	4853832	4991326	4939136	3222954
25485821	3886072	4179171	4698165	4830549	4778660	3113204
708569	115155	114754	125763	131004	132670	89223
166383	29316	29057	29904	29773	27806	20527
90741269	14060386	15636286	17310172	17350618	16686741	9697066
89058440	13764786	15331522	16996850	17048730	16402781	9513771
1293251	216464	228363	240918	238341	226125	143040
389578	79136	76401	72404	63547	57835	40255
92283826	13629075	14517623	16002087	16379485	16151309	15604247
64548651	9937953	10867208	12072020	12283684	11976936	7410850

小 学 教

Number of Teachers, Staff &

	教 职 Teachers, Staff			
	合 计 Total	专 任 教 师 Full－time Teachers	行 政 人 员 adm. Personnel	工 勤 人 员 Workers
总 计 **Total**	6471159	5860455	430146	169427
教育部门办 Run by Ed. Dept.	5556634	5038106	389490	119689
其他部门办 Run by Non－ed. Dept.	341536	288057	28342	24369
集体办 Run by Communities	519420	496643	8035	13753
民办 Run by private & other social sources	53569	37649	4279	11616
城市 Urban	1070312	918705	99123	47499
教育部门办 Run by Ed. Dept.	827176	718475	78484	26248
其他部门办 Run by Non－ed. Dept.	196773	167553	17099	11678
集体办 Run by Communities	13939	12395	334	659
民办 Run by private & other social sources	32424	20282	3206	8914
县镇 County Seats & Towns	1332805	1194309	91031	43590
教育部门办 Run by Ed. Dept.	1225880	1100561	85231	36538
其他部门办 Run by Non－ed. Dept.	52295	44018	4498	3617
集体办 Run by Communities	45813	43422	608	1621
民办 Run by private & other social sources	8817	6308	694	1814
农村 Rural	4068042	3747441	239992	78338
教育部门办 Run by Ed. Dept.	3503578	3219070	225775	56903
其他部门办 Run by Non－ed. Dept.	92468	76486	6745	9074
集体办 Run by Communities	459668	440826	7093	11473
民办 Run by private & other social sources	12328	11059	379	888
总计中：女教职工 of the tatol Female Teachers, Staff & Workers	3087871	2909652	102162	72650

职 工 数

Workers in Primary Schools

单位：人

工数 & Workers		代课教师 Subtitute Teachers	临时工 Temporary Workers
校办工厂、农场职工 Employees in School-run Factories & Farms			
计 Total	其中:由厂、场收入支付工资的职工 Of which: Employees maintained by income of school-run businesses		
11131	2681	706535	92125
9349	1684	395229	54860
768	277	7870	1656
989	705	293433	32570
25	15	10003	3039
4985	1425	28450	12631
3969	831	17721	9989
443	110	2554	738
551	469	6549	801
22	15	1626	1103
3875	715	81370	16603
3550	518	43802	10139
162	73	792	302
162	124	35765	5782
1	0	1011	380
2271	541	596715	62891
1830	335	333706	34732
163	94	4524	616
276	112	251119	25987
2	0	7366	1556
3407	1035	403713	49294

小学专任教师专业

Full－time Primary School Teachers

	合　计 Total	25岁及以下 25 years and under	26－30	31－35	36－40
合　计 Total	5860455	1142025	865961	792958	753906
其中：女 of which: Female	2909652	714629	518033	432751	366813
中教高级 Senior secondary	6115	45	121	273	454
小教高级 Senior primary	1489690	2345	32743	102605	186121
小教一级 1st grade primary	2738706	172781	548045	536823	478160
小教二级 2nd grade primary	971018	503405	198907	107518	64315
小教三级 3rd grade primary	70908	26635	15506	10439	6723
未评级 Rank undecided	584018	436814	70639	35300	18133

技术职务、年龄结构情况

Broken Down by Rank and Age

单位：人
Unit: person

41－45	46－50	51－55	56－60	61岁及以上 61 years and over	总计中：女 of the total female
887159	679905	518848	216791	2902	2909652
385087	285712	189233	17004	390	0
789	1150	1840	1338	105	2757
354830	356816	314750	138093	1387	696419
470745	285325	178339	67521	967	1310845
44906	27332	17634	6820	181	525030
5022	3291	2188	1054	50	32107
10867	5991	4097	1965	212	342494

学龄儿童入学率

Net Enrolment Rate of School－age Children

单位: 人

	学龄儿童总数 Total School- age Children	已入学的学龄儿童数 School-age Children Enrolled	学龄儿童入学率 Net Enrolment Rate (%)
总　计 Total	129913742	128727848	99.09
城　市 Urban	17552470	17474359	99.55
县　镇 County Seats & Towns	25151330	24994791	99.38
农　村 Rural	87209942	86258698	98.91
总计中：女儿童 of the total girls	62131991	61538530	99.04

小学专任教师学历情况

Breakdown of Full－time Primary School Teachers by Educational Attainment

单位: 人

	合 计 Total	大学本科毕业及以上 Completion of Normal Courses in IHEs	大学专科毕业 Completion of Short－cycle Courses in IHEs	中专毕业 Complete Specialized Sec. Education in IHEs	高中毕业 Complete General Sec. Education	高中毕业以下的 Complete Sec. Education & Lower
人数 Number	5860455	43110	909654	4271889	395324	240478
%	100.00	0.74	15.52	72.89	6.75	4.10

小学校舍情况

Condition of School Buildings in Primary Schools

	总计 Total	城市 Urban	县镇 County Seats & Towns	农村 Rural
教学及辅助用房(平方米) Teaching & Assistant Buildings	396205337	54688824	75503509	266013004
行政办公及房(平方米) Administritive	61142713	10410440	12177982	38554291
生活福利用房 Residential and Welfare	129778849	18732661	28189469	82856719
校舍建筑面积(平方米) Floor Space	587126899	83831925	115870960	387424014
其中: of which:				
当年新增面积(平方米) New floor space added in current year	17424785	3114051	4093725	10217009
危险房屋面积(平方米) Floor space of dilapidated buildings	4242063	290016	520921	3431126

小学班额情况

Size of Primary Classes

	班数(个) No. of Classes	班额(班) Size of Classes					
		10人及以下 10 and under	11－20	21－30	31－40	41－50	50人及以上 50 and over
总计 **Total**	3967402	161724	547497	860661	1002648	784344	610528
城市 Urban	406866	3544	15627	40175	86476	116946	144098
县镇 County Seats & Towns	661794	12355	53113	106204	160157	160441	169524
农村 Rural	2898742	145825	478757	714282	756015	506957	296906

(四) 特殊教育

SPECIAL EDUCATION

特 殊 教 育 学

Basic Statistics of

	学校数(所) Schools	班数(个) Classes		毕业生数 Graduates		
		小 学 Primary Sch.	初 中 Junior Sec. Sch.	计 Total	小 学 Primary Sch.	初 中 Junior Sec. Sch.
总 计 **Total**	1520	19959	2028	38143	31434	6709
盲聋哑学校合计 Total Number of Schools for the Blind & the Deaf-mute	1102	7827	971	10502	7619	2883
盲聋哑学校 Schools for the Blind & the Deaf-mute	185	1336	259	2064	1369	695
盲生部 Blind	0	200	46	241	137	104
聋哑生部 Deaf-mute	0	1136	213	1823	1232	591
聋哑学校 Schools for the Deaf-mute	888	5134	591	6415	4666	1749
盲 校 Schools for the Blind	29	165	91	444	227	217
普通学校附设及随班就读 Attached to Regular Schools	0	1192	30	1579	1357	222
盲生 Blind	0	380	6	368	300	68
聋哑生 Deaf-mute	0	812	24	1211	1057	154
合计中:女生、女教职工数 of the Total: Female Students, Teachers, Staff & Workers	0	0	0	3402	2361	1041
弱智儿童校、(班)合计 Total No. of Schools for Retarded Children	418	12132	1057	27641	23815	3826
弱智儿童辅读校(班) Schools for Reguarded Children	418	2817	151	3106	2488	618
普通学校附设及随班就读 Attached to Regular Schools	0	9315	906	24535	21327	3208
合计中:女生、女教职工数 of the Total: Female Students Teachers, Staff & Workers	0	0	0	9961	8634	1327

校基本情况

Special Education Schools

单位:人

招生数 Students Admitted			在校学生数 Enrolments			教职工数 Teachers, Staff & Workers	
计 Total	小学 Primary Sch.	初中 Junior Sec. Sch.	计 Total	小学 Primary Sch.	初中 Junior Sec. Sch.	计 Total	其中:专任教师 of which: Full-time Teachers
50074	40484	9590	371625	336651	34974	45119	31377
17464	14405	3059	101108	89505	11603	31490	22097
3644	2927	717	18470	16047	2423	5903	4259
546	378	168	2148	1682	466	837	628
3098	2549	549	16322	14365	1957	5066	3631
10509	8904	1605	60229	53717	6512	23118	16229
599	314	285	2634	1653	981	1403	901
2712	2260	452	19775	18088	1687	1066	708
647	481	166	5088	4507	581	396	298
2065	1779	286	14687	13581	1106	670	410
5828	4725	1103	33960	29981	3979	17605	13617
32610	26079	6531	270517	247146	23371	13629	9280
5317	5077	240	34144	32038	2106	7102	5767
27293	21002	6291	236373	215108	21265	6527	3513
11055	8829	2226	96939	89003	7936	9285	6794

（五）幼儿教育

PRE－PRIMARY EDUCATION

幼儿教育基本情况

Basic Statistics of Pre－primary Education

	园数(所) Kindergartens	班数(个) Classes	在园幼儿数(人) Children Enrolled	教职工数(人) Teachers, Staff & Workers 计 Total	其中: of which: 园长 Kindergarten Heads	教师 Teachers	保健员 Health Nurses
总计 Total	181136	781450	23262588	1158302	85479	872422	63211
按办别分: By Category of Maintenance:							
教育部门办 Run by Ed.Dept.	35710	281028	9246571	338625	20302	271112	16081
其他部门办 Run by Non－ed.Dept.	17427	86277	2729662	283346	20880	161656	25404
集体办 Run by Communities	90979	328075	9062073	390873	23064	338968	10533
民办 Run by private & other social sources	37020	86070	2224282	145458	21233	100686	11193
按城乡分: By Location							
城市 Urban	37301	160103	5104824	454107	38353	272745	35795
县镇 County Seats & Towns	41939	172369	5566255	289227	22324	228671	18349
农村 Rural	101896	448978	12591509	414968	24802	371006	9067
总计中: 女幼儿、女教职工 of the Total: Girls & Female Teachers' Staff & Workers	0	0	10713648	1077963	79966	816956	56905

园长、专任教师学历情况

Breakdown of Kindergarten Heads and Teachers by Educational Attainment

单位:人

	合计 Total	师范院校本专科毕业 A	中师毕业 B	职业高中幼教专业毕业 C	非师范专业毕业 D 高中毕业及以上 E	非师范专业毕业 D 初中毕业及以下 F	合计中: 取得"专业合格证书"的 G
总计 Total	957901	87752	419228	149695	187700	113526	108241
园长 Kindergarten Heads	85479	17163	39312	10306	13999	4699	7692
教师 Teachers	872422	70589	379916	139389	173701	108827	100549

A. Graduates of teachers colleges.

B. Graduates of sec. teachers training schools.

C. Graduates of pre－school education programmes in vocational schools.

D. Graduates from non－teacher training institutions.

E. Graduates of senior secondary schools and those with higher qualifications.

F. Graduates of junior secondary schools and those with lower qualifications.

G. Of the total: Those awarded "teaching certificates".

三、成人教育

ADULT EDUCATION

（一）高等教育

HIGHER EDUCATION

成人高等学校

Baisc Statistics of Adult Higher

	学校数(所) Institutions		本专科学生 Normal & Short-cycle						
	计 Total	其中中央所属院校 of which: Inst Under Central Ministries & Agencies	毕业生数 Graduates	招生数 Entrants	在校生数 Enrolment	合计 Total	计 Total	计 Total	教授 Professors
总计 Total	871	119	411687	538654	1274789	200054	192068	97644	1726
其中:女 of which: Female	0	0	192726	255388	602795	84070	80926	40764	311
广播电视大学 Radio/TV Universities	45	1	170210	196230	489155	53177	51684	25687	178
职工高等学校 Workers' Colleges	507	73	101741	143953	348215	81469	77262	41096	676
农民高等学校 Peasants' Colleges	3	0	481	428	953	206	205	127	0
管理干部学院 Institutes for Administration	146	41	66259	90274	189336	32135	30763	13371	493
教育学院 Educational Colleges	166	3	68624	103568	234735	32201	31298	16843	354
独立函授学院 Independent Correspondence Colleges	4	1	4372	4201	12395	866	856	520	25

单位:人

教职工数 Teachers Staff & Workers										兼任教师 Part-time Teachers
校本部教职工数 Employees in the School Proper							科研机构人员 Personnel in Affiliated Research Org.	校办工厂、农场人员 Personnel in School-run Factories, Farms	附设机构人员 Personnel in Other Subsidiary Units	
专任教师数 Full-time Teachers				教辅人员 Supporting Staff	行政人员 Adm. Personnel	工勤人员 Workers				
副教授 Asso. Prof.	讲师 Lecturers	助教 Assistants	教员 Instructors							
23244	45870	22223	4581	23870	44321	26233	1079	3690	3217	35291
7470	20271	10598	2114	12294	18200	9668	328	1278	1538	10065
4555	11819	7575	1560	7313	13158	5526	157	393	943	19450
9906	20236	8481	1797	9125	16017	11024	452	2201	1554	11367
10	54	58	5	7	44	27	0	1	0	9
3840	6015	2638	385	3903	8179	5310	217	775	380	2167
4780	7483	3409	817	3385	6779	4291	249	317	337	1167
153	263	62	17	137	144	55	4	3	3	1131

成人高等学校分

Number of Students by Type of Schools

	毕业生数 Graduates		
	计 Total	本科 Normal Courses	专科 Short－cycle Courses
总计 Total	888229	105924	782305
一、成人高等学校 Adult Higher Educational Institutions	411687	19365	392322
其中:全脱产 of which: Full－time	168713	5712	163001
新高职	0	0	0
广播电视大学 Radio/TV Universities	170210	1104	169106
其中:全脱产 of which: Full－time	33849	0	33849
普通专科班 Regular Short－cycle Courses	72163	0	72163
职工高等学校 Workers' Colleges	101741	1012	100729
其中:全脱产 of which: Full－time	52470	492	51978
农民高等学校 Peasants' Colleges	481	0	481
其中:全脱产 of which: Full－time	481	0	481
管理干部学院 Institutes for Administration	66259	2013	64246
其中:全脱产 of which: Full－time	50023	1416	48607
教育学院 Educational Colleges	68624	15212	53412
其中:全脱产 Of which: Full－time	31853	3804	28049
独立函授学院 Independent Correspondence Colleges	4372	24	4348
其中:全脱产 of which: Full－time	37	0	37
二、普通高等学校举办 Run by Regular IHEs	476542	86559	389983
函授部 Divisions of Correspondence	268841	61844	206997
夜大学 Evening Schools	98984	18737	80247
成人脱产班 Short－cycle Courses for Adult	108717	5978	102739

＊招生数和在校生数包括 1999 年在成人高校中举办的新高职学生数。

本专科学生数

in all Adult Higher Education Institutions

单位:人

招生数* Entrants			在校学生数* Enrolments		
计 Total	本科 Normal Courses	专科 Short-cycle Courses	计 Total	本科 Normal Courses	专科 Short-cycle Courses
1205984	207508	998476	3103151	484049	2619102
538654	33028	505626	1274789	75739	1199050
207782	10305	197477	442360	18424	423936
48294	0	48294	48294	0	48294
196230	1128	195102	489155	3295	485860
46147	0	46147	93523	0	93523
81433	0	81433	197688	0	197688
143953	2302	141651	348215	4609	343606
72924	1603	71321	160671	2797	157874
428	0	428	953	0	953
428	0	428	953	0	953
90274	3459	86815	189336	7901	181435
52926	2535	50391	116969	5282	111687
103568	26051	77517	234735	59610	175125
33961	6167	27794	68549	10345	58204
4201	88	4113	12395	324	12071
1396	0	1396	1695	0	1695
667330	174480	492850	1828362	408310	1420052
377198	110352	266846	1069861	270129	799732
132667	35309	97358	400866	85757	315109
157465	28819	128646	357635	52424	305211

成人高等学校

Number of Students by Field of Study in

	毕业生数 Graduates		
	计 Total	本科 Normal Courses	专科 Short－cycle Courses
总计 Total	411687	19365	392322
哲学 Philosophy	28	0	28
经济学 Economics	168191	1190	167001
法学 Law	44076	2250	41826
教育学 Education	16157	4301	11856
文学 Literature	74967	6403	68564
历史学 History	2838	355	2483
理学 Science	15391	3609	11782
工学 Engineering	69663	898	68765
农学 Agriculture	1970	0	1970
医学 Medicine	18406	359	18047
总计中：师范类 Of the ToTal: Teacher Training	42808	12101	30707

注:本表不包括普通高等学校举办的函授部、夜大学和成人脱产班的学生数。

Note: Numbers of Students in Correspondenes Divisions、Evening Schools & Short－cycle courses of Adult run by Regular Institutions of Education are not included.

* 同第 98 页

成人高等学校

Number of Other Students in Adult

	学历教育学生总数中 Of total formal students			第二学历 Students for second diploma	预科班
	高中起点本科	高中起点专科	专升本		
毕(结)业生数 Graduates	10917	367295	20943	11800	12072
招生数 Entrants	16051	469127	32842	27327	12783
在校生数 Enrolment	37771	1102808	72771	56349	12151
毕(结)业班学生数 Graduates for Next Year	11775	380233	25340	12634	6622

分科学生数

Adult Higher Educational Institutions

单位:人

招生数* Students Admitted			在校学生数* Enrolment		
计 Total	本科 Normal Courses	专科 Short－cycle Courses	计 Total	本科 Normal Courses	专科 Short－cycle Courses
538654	33028	505626	1274789	75739	1199050
67	0	67	126	0	126
168252	2963	165289	414700	6154	408546
57322	2126	55196	130539	5888	124651
27626	6664	20962	64892	17287	47605
114610	12413	102197	249561	25676	223885
2714	699	2015	6402	1579	4823
18664	5814	12850	43127	13669	29458
117077	1856	115221	284251	4303	279948
3059	0	3059	5302	0	5302
29263	493	28770	75889	1183	74706
66283	20778	45505	153255	47761	105494

其他学生数

Higher Educational Institutions

单位:人

证书教育 Job－specific training		岗位培训 Job－specific training		成人中专班 Spec.Sec.classes foradult	电大注册视听生	其他 Others
单科班 Single subject courses	专业证书班 lasses for certifite-oriented traine	资格培训 Qualifications－oriented training	适应培训 Adaptation training			
73315	127532	1018433	1014183	112883	19010	88645
90690	66465	365927	723807	89221	126899	57272
55664	110501	175885	155724	291834	284946	99216
14920	52903	60127	82780	113156	58245	26138

成人高等学校专

Breakdown of Full－time Teachers by Academic Qualifications

	合计 Total		研究生毕业 Completion of Postgraduate Courses			
	计 Total	其中：女 Of which Female	计 Total	博士 Doctor's Degrees	硕士 Master's Degrees	未授博士、硕士学位的 Without advanced degrees
总计 Total	97644	40764	5648	256	4525	867
其中：女 of which Female	40764	0	1918	49	1598	271
教授 Professors	1726	311	291	51	180	60
副教授 Asso. Professors	23244	7470	1905	132	1459	314
讲师 Lecturers	45870	20271	2712	69	2204	439
助教 Assistants	22223	10598	546	3	496	47
教员 Instructors	4581	2114	194	1	186	7

成人高等学校在校学生、教

Supplementary Information on Students and Staff

	在校学生总数中 Of Total Enrolment						教职工总 Of Teachers, Staff	
	共产党员 Member of C.P.C.	共青团员 Member of C.Y.L.	民主党派 Member of Dem. Parties	华侨 Overseas Chinese	港澳	少数民族 Minorities	共产党员 Member of C.P.C.	共青团员 Member of C.Y.L.
总计 Total	50469	634091	2245	529	7161	50230	84833	20440
广播电视大学 Radio/TV Universities	19964	259931	2148	461	6471	18354	21279	7185
职工高等学校 Workers' Colleges	15230	183279	68	48	248	10424	32038	7824
农民高等学校 Peasants' Colleges	56	318	0	0	0	187	84	30
管理干部学院 Institutes for Administration	7027	97260	4	11	6	9284	16118	2315
教育学院 Educational Colleges	6409	85491	25	9	436	11711	14907	2966
独立函授学院 Independent Correspondence Colleges	1783	7812	0	0	0	270	407	120

任教师学历情况

in Adult Higher Educational Institutions

单位:人

高等学校本科毕业 Completion of Normal Undergraduate Courses				高等学校专科毕业及本专科肄业二年以上 Completion of Shore-cycle Courses or at least two years of undergraduate ed.	高等学校本专科肄业未满两年及以下 Attendance in undergraduate Courses less than 2 years
计 Total	学士 With Bachelor's Degrees	研究生肄业 Having Some Postgraduate Training	未获学士学位的 Without Bachelor's Degrees		
75837	55105	251	20481	14737	1422
32241	24717	69	7455	6093	512
1364	748	5	611	59	12
19342	11521	93	7728	1860	137
35671	26711	128	8832	6956	531
16420	13594	23	2803	4660	597
3040	2531	2	507	1202	145

职工的政治及其他情况

& Workers of Adult Higher Educational Institutions

单位:人

数中 & Workers				专任教师中 Of Full-time Teachers					
民主党派 Member of Dem. Parties	华侨 Overseas Chinese	港澳	少数民族 Minorities	共产党员 Member of C.P.C.	共青团员 Member of C.Y.L.	民主党派 Member of Dem. Parties	华侨 Overseas Chinese	港澳	少数民族 Minorities
4472	249	921	6734	37194	12027	3169	125	510	3383
933	45	440	1509	9124	4313	583	24	249	660
1424	61	212	1874	14880	4455	1005	27	138	925
0	0	0	63	47	27	0	0	0	37
609	34	38	1173	5865	1290	382	15	19	556
1499	109	231	2103	7033	1893	1194	59	104	1197
7	0	0	12	245	49	5	0	0	8

成人高等学校
Breakdown of Full-time Teachers by

	合 计 Total	30岁及以下 30 years and under	31－35	36－40
总 计 Total	97644	23350	21738	16738
其中：女 of which: female	40764	11890	10577	7331
教 授 Professors	1726	4	8	42
副教授 Asso. Professors	23244	32	1205	3522
讲 师 Lecturers	45870	4221	15742	11668
助 教 Assistants	22223	15377	4408	1331
无职称 Rank Undecided	4581	3716	375	175

成人高等学校学
Changes in Enrolment of

	上学年初报表在校学生数 Total enrolment at beginning of previous academic year	增加学生数 Factors of Increase						
		计 Total	本学年初招生数 No.of Students Admitted	复 学 Students Resuming Studies	其他学校转入 Transfers from Other Inst.	其他 Others	计 Total
总 计 Total	1186243	572651	538654	3766	6927	23304	484105
广播电视大学 Radio/TV Universities	484353	209176	196230	1338	2262	9346	204374
职工高等学校 Workers' Colleges	319205	150513	143953	948	1359	4253	121503
农民高等学校 Peasants' Colleges	878	607	428	0	179	0	532
管理干部学院 Institutes for Administration	168894	93577	90274	673	669	1961	73135
教育学院 Educational Colleges	200409	114039	103568	797	2378	7296	79713
独立函授学院 Independent Correspondence	12504	4739	4201	10	80	448	4848

专任教师年龄情况
Age in Adult Higher Educational Institutions

单位：人
Unit: person

41－45	46－50	51－55	56－60	61岁及以上 61 years and over
11680	7836	8742	6798	762
4696	2748	2619	817	86
119	135	349	782	287
4327	3585	5383	4789	401
6500	3756	2790	1130	63
606	295	156	47	3
128	65	64	50	8

生数变动情况
Adult Higher Educational Institutions

单位：人

上学年毕业生数 Graduates	上学年结业生数 Completers of Courses without formal award	减少学生数 Factors of Decrease: 休学 Suspended	退学 Quitting	开除 Expelled	死亡 Dead	转到其他学校 Transfers to Other Inst.	其他 Others	本学年初报表在校学生数 Total enrolment at beginning of current academic year
411687	11694	3550	13147	272	53	17264	26438	1274789
170210	8774	1693	7013	74	13	2003	14594	489155
101741	1039	1203	3798	80	23	7681	5938	348215
481	0	0	20	0	0	0	31	953
66259	1049	291	937	105	12	1947	2535	189336
68624	703	358	1172	13	5	5627	3211	234735
4372	129	5	207	0	0	6	129	12395

成人高等学校固定

Condition of Fixed Assets and

	固定资产值（万元） Fixed Assets (in 10000 yuan)	
	合 计 Total	其中：教仪设备 Of which: Teaching Equipment
		计 Total
总 计 Total	2224271.97	438535.11
广播电视大学 Radio/TV Universities	568463.39	133405.13
职工高等学校 Workers' Colleges	855985.73	187645.34
农民高等学校 Peasants' Colleges	3140.88	207.08
管理干部学院 Institutes for Administration	518287.57	65776.57
教育学院 Educational Colleges	259686.80	50430.99
独立函授学院 Independent Correspondence Colleges	18707.60	1070.00

成人高等学校

Condition of School Buildings in Adult

	校舍建筑总面积 Total Floor Space	校舍建 Of total
		被外单位借占用面积 Floor space hired by other schools or units
总 计 Total	35292343	116812
一、教学及辅助用房 Teaching & assistant buildings	13583000	34911
教室 Classroom	6985878	25167
图书馆 Library	1454574	1401
实验实习及辅助 Lab. and supplementary buildings	3111768	4543
体育馆 Gymnasium	1456445	3600
会堂 Hall	574335	200
二、行政办公用房 Administritive	2980121	22631
三、生活用房 Residential buildings	18729222	59270
学生宿舍 Students' dormitories	5888671	12558
学生食堂 Students' dining halls	1368050	2928
教工单身宿舍 Apartments for Single	471307	3626
生活福利及其他 Residential, welfare and others	8028847	18787
教工食堂 Dining halls for teachers, staff and workers	230644	425
生活福利及其他附属用 Residential, welfare and anxiliary buildings	2741703	20946

资产情况及其他

Teaching Resources in Adult Higher Educational Institutions

资产值 & Instruments	图书、音像资料情况 audio－visual ed. resources			学校占地面积 (平方米) Area of School sites (m²)
电教设备 Audio－visual media	图书资料 (万册) Book (in 10 thousand)	录音带 (盒) Recording cassettes	录像带 (盘) Video tape cassette	
197617.31	10650.34	2786389	2334298	74262984
81995.62	2478.79	1855228	1595918	19641609
67094.62	4052.97	590810	409022	28484610
136.08	317.50	306	175	468000
27508.51	1662.99	100947	88801	14650743
20301.68	2078.25	234936	230720	10611409
580.80	59.84	4162	9662	406613

校舍情况

Higher Educational Institutions

单位：平方米 Unit: m²

筑 总 面 积 中 Foolr Space		正在施工面积 Under Construction	借租用校舍面积 Buildings rent or leased
危 房 面 积 Dilapidated Buildings	当 年 新 增 面 积 Newly added in current year		
184020	2144160	1072718	493224
48872	988907	541946	272266
16405	524158	258767	205187
3156	67012	33858	18143
5741	307406	137708	25549
19473	55873	94886	16381
4097	34458	16727	7006
20573	116505	73929	30807
114575	1038748	456843	190151
30893	362393	122579	131725
3821	68577	23843	25576
7045	15695	18202	3806
43597	471648	266989	3232
313	11469	5250	490
28906	108966	19980	25322

（二）中、初等教育

SECONDARY EDUCATION AND PRIMARY EDUCATION

成人中等专业学校

Basic Statistics of Adult Specialized

	学校数(所) Schools	分 校(所) Branches	工作站(个) Working Stations	毕业生数 Graduates	招生数 Entrants		
					计 Total	招高中毕业生起点 Graduates From Senior Sec. School	招初中毕业生起点 Graduates From Junior Sec. School
合 计 Total	5165	1787	3305	872581	697535	207253	490282
其中：女 of which: Female	0	0	0	430462	326843	91078	235765
一、按部门分 By Control							
中央部门学校 Run by Central Ministries & Agencies	198	38	385	34103	30980	13560	17420
地方学校 Run by Local Authorities	4967	1749	2920	838478	666555	193693	472862
二、按类别分 By Field of Study							
广播电视中专 Radio/TV Specialized Sec. Schools	151	821	1153	214152	187732	54571	133161
职工中专 Specialized Sec. Schools for Staff & Workers	2093	231	378	291295	252361	39545	212816
干部中专 Specialized Sec. Schools for Cadres	290	115	48	50881	41157	10017	31140
农民中专 Specialized Sec. Schools for peasants	440	314	172	82847	73427	10685	62742
函授中专 Correspondence Specialized Sec. Schools	62	288	1333	67759	49134	32247	16887
教师进修学校 In-service Teacher Training Schools	2129	18	221	165647	93724	60188	33536

注：本表未包括普通中等专业学校举办的成人中专学生。

Note: Adult Student enroled in specialized Secondary Schools are not included.

分类别情况
Secondary Schools by Field of Study

单位: 人

在校学生数 Enrolments	毕业班学生数 Graduates for Next Year	教职工数 Teachers, Staff & Workers					兼任教师数 Part-time Teachers
		合计 Total	专任教师 Full-time Teachers	教辅人员 Supporting Staff	行政人员 Adm. Personnel	工勤人员 Workers	
2182112	857360	232255	130665	23592	43992	34006	61690
1038743	413119	93591	53486	11556	15023	13526	18172
100923	32239	9676	4281	1191	2403	1801	2692
2081189	825121	222579	126384	22401	41589	32205	58998
625419	237347	18266	9007	3589	3780	1890	23200
808863	300791	88289	47793	7762	18437	14297	20164
119759	48967	15504	7759	1490	3683	2572	3441
219316	85201	20949	13474	1703	2735	3037	3642
136962	57389	10029	4800	1899	2644	686	8753
271793	127665	79218	47832	7149	12713	11524	2490

成人中等专业

Number of Teachers, Staff & Workers in

	校本部 Employees	
	合计 Total	专任教师 Full－time Teachers
总计 Total	232255	130665
其中：女教职工 of which: Female	93591	53486
一、教师小计 Those with teaching rank	124986	100869
高级讲师 Senior Lectures	23308	17705
讲师 Lecturers	60817	49758
助理讲师 Assistant Lecturers	40861	33406
二、其他小计 Those with other professional ranks	58936	22940
副高级职称 Senior－level ones	7163	3195
中级职称 Middle－level ones	25928	10683
初级职称 Junior－level ones	25845	9062
三、无职称人数 Without professional titles	48333	6856

成人中等专业

Condition of School Buildings in Adult

	自有 Buildings owned by					
	校舍建筑面积 Floor Space	教学用房 Building for Inst. Purposes				
		计 Total	教室 Classrooms		实验室 Laboratories	图书馆 Libraries
			计 Total	其中：电化教室 of which: equipped with audio－visual media		
总计 Total	30946759	9732331	7274761	843819	1498096	959474
广播电视中等专业学校 Radio/TV Specialized Sec. Schools	1787923	617608	481791	79161	73700	62117
职工中等专业学校 Specialized Sec. Schools for Staff & Workers	13721190	4422191	3164571	326106	827453	430167
干部中等专业学校 Specialized Sec. Schools for Cadres	3063469	822105	639761	56577	71000	111344
农民中等专业学校 Specialized Sec. Schools for Peasants	3072206	973719	685477	68116	207555	80687
函授中等专业学校 Correspondence Specialized Sec. Schools	1127278	584917	459170	92706	65745	60002
教师进修学校 In－service Teacher Training Schools	8174693	2311791	1843991	221153	252643	215157

学校教职工数

Adult Specialized Secondary Schools

单位：人

Unit: in person

教职工数 in the School Proper			兼任教师数 Part－time Teachers
教辅人员 Supporting Staff	行政人员 Adm. Personnel	工勤人员 Workers	
23592	43992	34006	61690
11556	15023	13526	18172
7389	15364	1364	37557
716	4835	52	10014
3292	7409	358	20615
3381	3120	954	6928
10413	17897	7686	21531
742	2380	846	5061
4476	8149	2620	12381
5195	7368	4220	4089
5790	10731	24956	2602

学校校舍情况

Adult Specialized Secondary Schools

单位：平方米 Unit: m^2

校舍 the adult SSSs						租用校舍 Buildings rent or leased	兼用校舍 Buildings for multiple purposes
办公用房 Administritive	非教学用房 Building Not for Inst. Purposes			其他用房 Others	其中：新增校舍 Of which New floor space added		
	计 Total	其中 Of which					
		教职工宿舍 Residences for Staff & Workers	学生宿舍 Students' Dormitories				
3231935	12574023	5926721	5796147	5408470	1365985	1139552	2642532
224995	752710	313201	254273	192610	97250	76425	510308
1212732	5442563	2307149	2810490	2643704	613951	666550	1672593
270493	1401518	677969	691880	569353	126763	92265	172421
257942	1298685	613228	633791	541860	124818	113777	124699
106471	330530	122216	205614	105360	26839	103133	49772
1159302	3348017	1892958	1200099	1355583	376364	87402	112739

成 人 中 学

Basic Statistics of Adult

	学校数 (所) Schools	教学班 (点) (个) External Teaching Sites (Classes)	毕业生数 Graduates		招
			计 Total	其中：女生 of which Female	计 Total
成人中学 General Sec. Schools for Adults	5277	13103	516160	245106	542911
1. 职工中学 General Sec. Schools for Staff & Workers	1655	5976	229917	117167	297864
高中 Senior	1432	5256	207217	106842	270079
初中 Junior	223	720	22700	10325	27785
2. 农民中学 General Sec. Schools for Peasants	3622	7127	286243	127939	245047
高中 Senior	1459	2732	90254	37233	86600
初中 Junior	2163	4395	195989	90706	158447

成 人 小 学

Basic Statistics of Adult

	学校数 (所) Schools	教学班 (点) (个) External Teaching Sites (Classes)	毕业生数 Graduates		招
			计 Total	其中：女生 of which Female	计 Total
成人初等学校 Adult Primary Schools	180103	338963	5581463	3225131	5197010
1. 职工初等学校 Worker Primary Schools	964	4254	155382	75840	194467
2. 农民初等学校 Peasant Primary Schools	179139	334709	5426081	3149291	5002543
小学班 Primary Classes	50471	91842	2433353	1321596	2444759
扫盲班 Literacy Classes	128668	242867	2992728	1827695	2557784

基本情况
Secondary Schools

单位：人

生数 Entrants	在校学生数 Enrolment		教职工数 Teachers, Staff & Workers		兼任教师数 Part-time Teachers
其中：女生 of which: Female	计 Total	其中：女生 of which: Female	计 Total	其中专任教师 of which: Full-time Teachers	
261786	651874	301590	34578	20484	31609
149386	325835	155895	20083	11273	14376
136534	292887	141529	18958	10664	13406
12852	32948	14366	1125	609	970
112400	326039	145695	14495	9211	17233
34341	138637	56119	7713	5652	9566
78059	187402	89576	6782	3559	7667

基本情况
Primary Schools

单位：人

生数 Entrants	在校学生数 Enrolment		教职工数 Teachers, Staff & Workers		兼任教师数 Part-time Teachers
其中：女生 of which: Female	计 Total	其中：女生 of which: Female	计 Total	其中专任教师 of which: Full-time Teachers	
2986260	5368296	3107534	189698	57321	486295
90287	197549	89131	3434	1752	5118
2895973	5170747	3018403	186264	55569	481177
1318642	2338836	1243168	49856	18135	108873
1577331	2831911	1775235	136408	37434	372304

成人技术培训学

Basic Statistics of Adult

	学校数（所）Schools	教学班（点）（个）External Teaching Sites (Classes)	毕业生数 Graduates			
			计 Total	其中：of which:		计 Total
				长班 A	短班 B	
成人技术培训学校 Technical Training Schools for Adults	534215	1040913	101568857	7576207	93992650	88765294
其中：教育部门办 of which: Run by Ed. Dept.	454225	845899	83781958	5709829	78072129	73299933
其他部门办 Run by Non-ed. Dept.	79990	195014	17786899	1866378	15920521	15465361
一、职工技术培训学校 Technical Training Schools for Staff & Workers	11326	73399	6092314	1229185	4863129	5991137
其中：教育部门办 of which: Run by Ed. Dept.	3367	17036	1758902	338252	1420650	1801557
其他部门办 Run by Non-ed. Dept.	7959	56363	4333412	890933	3442479	4189580
二、农民技术培训学校 Technical Training Schools for Peasants	522889	967514	95476543	6347022	89129521	82774157
其中：教育部门办 of which: Run by Ed. Dept.	450858	828863	82023056	5371577	76651479	71498376
其他部门办 Run by Non-ed. Dept.	72031	138651	13453487	975445	12478042	11275781
其中：1. 县办农技 of which: County-run Agro-technical Schools	1976	8384	751996	151673	600323	736179
2. 乡办农技 Township-run Agro-technical Schools	42717	214445	31489446	3531398	27958048	27410269
3. 村办农技 Village-run Agro-technical Schools	478196	744685	63235101	2663951	60571150	54627709

A. Lengthy courses (total teaching time no less than 150 h.)

B. Short courses (total teaching time less than 150 h.)

校基本情况

Technical Training Schools

单位：人

招生数 Entrants 其中：of which: 长班 A	短班 B	在校学生数 Enrolment 计 Total	其中：of which 长班 A	短班 B	教职工数 Teachers, Staff & Workers 计 Total	其中专任教师 of which: Full－time Teachers	兼任教师数 Part－time Teachers
6877699	81887595	71366317	6064346	65301971	537128	185812	1104945
5050289	68249644	59699571	4796391	54903180	405189	129407	889931
1827410	13637951	11666746	1267955	10398791	131939	56405	215014
1343328	4647809	3863992	866392	2997600	90019	47091	80215
383046	1418511	1324091	274178	1049913	22956	12057	21905
960282	3229298	2539901	592214	1947687	67063	35034	58310
5534371	77239786	67502325	5197954	62304371	447109	138721	1024730
4667243	66831133	58375480	4522213	53853267	382233	117350	868026
867128	10408653	9126845	675741	8451104	64876	21371	156704
163811	572368	610668	161664	449004	14444	9313	10585
3228172	24182097	22618218	2954696	19663522	130271	68499	222691
2142388	52485321	44273439	2081594	42191845	302394	60909	791454

全国农业广播电视学校基本情况

Basic Data on National Agric. Broadcasting and T.V. Schools

单位：人

地 区	学校数(所) Schools	毕业生数 Graduates	招生数 Entrants	在校学生数 Enrollments	其他各类证书教育、技术培训毕(结)业学生数 No. of Grad. & Completers for Other Edu. Form and Tech. Traning	小计 Total	专任教师 Full-time Teachers	教辅人员 Supporting	行政人员 Adm. Personnel	工勤人员 Workers	兼职教师(不在教职工数中) Part-time Teachers
总 计 Total	39	149788	156237	497715	3473558	21467	10416	5211	3809	2031	25857

全国农业广播电视学校分年度学生数

Number of Students on National Agric. Broadcasting and T.V. Schools

单位：人

	1981	1984	1985	1987	1988	1989	1991	1992	1993	1994	1995	1996	1997	1998	1999	合计 Total
注册学生数 Enrollments	310764	477127	249451	369429	114281	100286	158136	245432	106016	142284	182922	223588	233856	191476	156237	3261285
毕业生数 Graduates	66133	145910	109122	183761	63401	67062	95345	154384	75855	104650	134859	149788				1350270

四、各级各类学校分布情况

GEOGRAPHICAL DISTRIBUTION OF SCHOOLS BY TYPE AND LEVEL

普通高等学校

Basic Statistics of Regular Higher

地区 Region	学校数(所) Institutions	本专科学生数 Undergraduate Students			教职 Teachers, Staff			
						校本部 Teachers, Staff & Workers		
							专任 Full-time	
		毕业生数 Graduates	招生数 Students Admitted	在校学生数 Enrolment	合计 Total	计 Subtotal	计 Subtotal	教授 Professors
总计 Total	1071	847617	1548554	4085874	1065093	881068	425682	39359
北京 Beijing	64	50307	78429	235140	108214	83006	35236	5700
天津 Tianjin	21	19292	31670	90450	25808	21001	9647	1285
河北 Hebei	48	39606	72856	176702	43218	36227	17263	1141
山西 Shanxi	23	19628	37897	94120	23632	20569	9547	733
内蒙古 Inner Mongolia	19	10911	18253	49732	16854	15096	7671	568
辽宁 Liaoning	64	49964	87851	235819	59590	51459	25179	2135
吉林 Jilin	40	30315	52553	139595	38283	32177	15166	1379
黑龙江 Heilongjiang	39	30218	62480	157063	42608	33396	15804	1803
上海 Shanghai	41	40316	63244	186307	60285	44358	20092	2565
江苏 Jiangsu	72	61499	127013	329825	74786	61425	30457	2798
浙江 Zhejiang	36	26750	52657	138564	30523	25487	13140	1150
安徽 Anhui	37	23101	51726	133025	27397	23650	12375	1051
福建 Fujian	30	20691	38710	102589	20972	17804	8853	643
江西 Jiangxi	34	25057	43586	110873	25481	20172	10147	824
山东 Shandong	52	49612	82410	213679	49624	42384	21252	2005
河南 Henan	56	39890	78805	185486	43365	37524	18776	1047
湖北 Hubei	57	49362	96375	257875	70404	56476	27858	2763
湖南 Hunan	51	39688	77237	193553	42409	35998	17990	1364
广东 Guangdong	50	47988	85341	220810	44645	37076	18489	1473
广西 Guangxi	29	19262	32596	90286	19090	16629	8651	555
海南 Hainan	5	3700	4903	14569	3607	3021	1436	62
重庆 Chongqing	23	20442	34374	96569	23824	19751	9987	859
四川 Sichuan	43	35465	65481	180256	45343	38835	17891	1488
贵州 Guizhou	20	10568	24810	56454	13133	12216	6050	379
云南 Yunnan	24	15757	27502	73902	18297	16637	8296	638
西藏 Tibet	4	1066	1657	4021	1736	1569	765	11
陕西 Shaanxi	43	36328	68034	179447	50819	40693	19750	1910
甘肃 Gansu	18	14007	23010	62637	16624	14068	6899	472
青海 Qinghai	6	2490	3172	9347	3454	3329	1711	51
宁夏 Ningxia	5	2680	4487	13121	3962	3640	1788	118
新疆 Xinjiang	17	11657	19435	54058	17106	15395	7516	389

基本情况(总计)

Educational Institutions (Regional Aggregates)

单位:人

工 数 & Workers									
教职工 in College or Uni.Proper							科研机构人员 Personnel in Affiliated Research Org.	校办工厂、农场职工 Employees in School-run Factories, Farms	附设机构人员 Personnel in Other Subsidiary Units
教师 Teachers				教辅人员 Supporting Staff	行政人员 Adm. Personnel	工勤人员 Workers			
副教授 Asso. Professors	讲师 Lecturers	助教 Assistants	教员 Instructors						
125900	156390	83196	20837	131531	179630	144225	49536	57770	76719
11523	12124	4724	1165	17908	15659	14203	13756	4865	6587
3282	3269	1302	509	3482	4421	3451	1589	1428	1790
4775	6274	3806	1267	4528	7576	6860	697	2967	3327
2370	3936	1999	509	2811	4416	3795	368	918	1777
2198	2978	1618	309	2348	3080	1997	191	1031	536
7856	9436	4830	922	7409	10883	7988	1810	2580	3741
4312	5396	3418	661	4876	6523	5612	1426	2127	2553
5298	5093	3035	575	4709	6838	6045	1466	3163	4583
6377	7876	2751	523	7720	8934	7612	4304	5044	6579
8896	10577	6400	1786	9089	12435	9444	3484	5065	4812
3802	5006	2446	736	3600	4953	3794	1374	1503	2159
3463	4416	2523	922	3047	4476	3752	1350	842	1555
2380	3041	2263	526	2332	4155	2464	683	1112	1373
2939	3405	2492	487	2586	4204	3235	267	3409	1633
6838	7447	4061	901	5327	9451	6354	1556	2560	3124
5178	7435	4131	985	4887	7569	6292	650	3082	2109
8498	9275	5377	1945	8219	11970	8429	3065	3389	7474
5471	6711	3237	1207	4432	7188	6388	1804	1963	2644
5793	7211	3513	499	6231	7922	4434	1943	1375	4251
2295	3396	1942	463	2236	3362	2380	313	1136	1012
411	575	346	42	395	645	545	98	259	229
3023	3854	1961	290	2910	3998	2856	1005	938	2130
5082	6720	3702	899	5861	7960	7123	2209	1604	2695
1647	2295	1365	364	1742	2634	1790	289	229	399
2513	3177	1549	419	2328	3516	2497	495	217	948
95	331	293	35	158	369	277	28	64	75
5284	7799	3932	825	5729	7442	7772	2469	2756	4901
1674	2761	1587	405	1978	2481	2710	686	1117	753
294	744	531	91	338	641	639	29	0	96
465	694	375	136	426	797	629	51	129	142
1868	3138	1687	434	1889	3132	2858	81	898	732

职业技术学

Basic Statistics of Short－

地区 Region	学校数(所) Institutions	本专科学生数 Undergraduate Students 毕业生数 Graduates	招生数 Students Admitted	在校学生数 Enrolment	教职 Teachers, Staff 合计 Total	校本部 Teachers, Staff & Workers 计 Subtotal	专任 Full－time 计 Subtotal	教授 Professors
总计 Total	161	40140	123378	234244	57317	51514	27308	591
北京 Beijing	4	981	3115	6327	1195	1091	542	4
天津 Tianjin	3	516	2082	3955	421	408	196	21
河北 Hebei	7	1821	6569	12324	2492	1976	1007	1
山西 Shanxi	3	767	2250	4112	1553	1449	682	4
内蒙古 Inner Mongolia	4	262	1321	1919	1300	1114	649	11
辽宁 Liaoning	9	1897	5072	9808	2593	2433	1274	20
吉林 Jilin	5	431	1267	2307	1208	1163	517	4
黑龙江 Heilongjiang	6	1115	3510	6558	1567	1509	812	53
上海 Shanghai	5	493	4078	5686	891	877	447	51
江苏 Jiangsu	16	5731	12253	27576	5167	4637	2657	57
浙江 Zhejiang	9	2314	9105	16376	2910	2821	1478	70
安徽 Anhui	7	1760	4541	9929	1658	1601	948	13
福建 Fujian	9	2782	6004	14439	1824	1783	926	7
江西 Jiangxi	4	630	2718	4088	1474	1108	582	4
山东 Shandong	5	1326	3283	5638	1537	1473	797	12
河南 Henan	14	4160	9965	19624	6819	6381	3556	41
湖北 Hubei	11	3968	11078	23124	7694	6501	3287	96
湖南 Hunan	8	1526	6368	11280	2896	2543	1480	4
广东 Guangdong	13	3041	14944	23864	3793	3658	1963	48
广西 Guangxi	5	801	2888	5983	1826	1466	738	11
海南 Hainan	0	0	0	0	0	0	0	0
重庆 Chongqing	1	0	333	333	359	349	206	2
四川 Sichuan	5	1881	3685	8246	2046	1857	947	21
贵州 Guizhou	1	194	478	1045	233	233	129	1
云南 Yunnan	1	387	1308	2045	330	320	161	1
西藏 Tibet	0	0	0	0	0	0	0	0
陕西 Shaanxi	3	261	2712	3358	2024	1330	596	19
甘肃 Gansu	2	478	1255	1726	827	777	323	2
青海 Qinghai	0	0	0	0	0	0	0	0
宁夏 Ningxia	0	0	0	0	0	0	0	0
新疆 Xinjiang	1	617	1196	2574	680	656	408	13

院基本情况

cycle Vocational Colleges

单位：人

工数 & Workers									
教职工 in College or Uni. Proper							科研机构人员 Personnel in Affiliated Research Org.	校办工厂、农场职工 Employees in School－run Factories, Farms	附设机构人员 Personnel in Other Subsidiary Units
教师 Teachers				教辅人员 Supporting Staff	行政人员 Adm. Personnel	工勤人员 Workers			
副教授 Asso. Professors	讲师 Lecturers	助教 Assistants	教员 Instructors						
6279	11408	7348	1682	6106	10700	7400	347	4179	1277
116	233	156	33	134	256	159	10	94	0
46	66	37	26	68	97	47	0	8	5
194	413	312	87	214	422	333	8	485	23
135	353	154	36	168	266	333	0	74	30
168	310	146	14	144	230	91	0	77	109
326	563	302	63	268	581	310	6	74	80
155	162	194	2	182	227	237	17	28	0
290	334	120	15	193	294	210	6	4	48
146	191	39	20	82	227	121	0	0	14
586	1024	854	136	547	853	580	44	474	12
232	666	426	84	294	521	528	31	28	30
243	418	218	56	145	344	164	8	5	44
150	351	330	88	209	431	217	19	2	20
121	231	200	26	127	227	172	23	154	189
184	332	182	87	130	326	220	3	12	49
720	1545	1012	238	691	1273	861	28	308	102
781	1246	851	313	856	1533	825	87	960	146
344	606	444	82	310	364	389	0	289	64
503	800	506	106	465	781	449	19	36	80
176	375	159	17	171	303	254	11	338	11
0	0	0	0	0	0	0	0	0	0
57	90	43	14	38	69	36	0	10	0
254	389	229	54	216	457	237	4	99	86
16	59	40	13	27	74	3	0	0	0
27	86	34	13	41	72	46	0	6	4
0	0	0	0	0	0	0	0	0	0
157	258	128	34	211	208	315	0	563	131
63	186	71	1	85	162	207	0	50	0
0	0	0	0	0	0	0	0	0	0
0	0	0	0	0	0	0	0	0	0
89	121	161	24	90	102	56	23	1	0

综合大学

Basic Statistics of

地区 Region	学校数(所) Institutions	本专科学生数 Undergraduate Students 毕业生数 Graduates	招生数 Students Admitted	在校学生数 Enrolment	教职 Teachers, Staff 合计 Total	校本部 Teachers, Staff & Workers 计 Subtotal	专任 Full-time 计 Subtotal	教授 Professors
总计 Total	74	130492	209769	617269	167943	135646	65307	7935
北京 Beijing	3	5885	9971	29647	13178	10417	4435	1011
天津 Tianjin	1	1698	2763	9000	4641	3420	1431	346
河北 Hebei	1	1779	3377	8935	2087	1773	854	84
山西 Shanxi	1	1546	2955	7730	2155	1777	810	106
内蒙古 Inner Mongolia	1	1223	1730	5493	1554	1387	679	94
辽宁 Liaoning	4	6782	11044	32701	6415	6177	2936	220
吉林 Jilin	4	7691	12515	35294	10603	8662	4024	332
黑龙江 Heilongjiang	4	5976	11300	29413	8790	6059	2697	227
上海 Shanghai	2	6869	8645	29362	10430	7525	3447	516
江苏 Jiangsu	5	11161	18624	56735	12300	10205	4890	619
浙江 Zhejiang	2	8469	11551	39593	11250	8323	4608	721
安徽 Anhui	1	1776	3228	9109	1998	1738	798	112
福建 Fujian	2	4181	6220	19764	4874	3630	1801	166
江西 Jiangxi	5	4407	7046	19634	3962	3571	1814	212
山东 Shandong	3	7583	11129	33239	7956	6649	3247	444
河南 Henan	2	4901	9714	27281	5639	4890	2488	284
湖北 Hubei	4	6073	10241	29097	8453	6401	3080	384
湖南 Hunan	2	2739	5560	14739	2882	2501	1254	135
广东 Guangdong	10	14516	21131	62106	14545	11235	5648	594
广西 Guangxi	1	3729	5104	16607	4101	3289	1723	178
海南 Hainan	1	909	1298	4014	860	719	349	20
重庆 Chongqing	2	1937	3569	9145	1441	1396	671	18
四川 Sichuan	2	4214	6084	19649	7267	5432	2762	344
贵州 Guizhou	1	1579	4506	9957	2849	2665	1191	99
云南 Yunnan	1	1964	2608	8402	2386	2174	994	165
西藏 Tibet	1	435	624	1434	581	534	271	2
陕西 Shaanxi	3	3329	6427	16765	4092	3719	1909	151
甘肃 Gansu	1	1760	2471	7830	2985	2333	1066	134
青海 Qinghai	1	774	871	2621	914	914	441	13
宁夏 Ningxia	1	1387	2205	6692	2075	1910	938	60
新疆 Xinjiang	2	3220	5258	15281	4680	4221	2051	144

基本情况

Comprehensive Universities

单位：人

工 数 & Workers									
教 职 工 in College or Uni. Proper							科研机构人员 Personnel in Affiliated Research Org.	校办工厂、农场职工 Employees in School-run Factories, Farms	附设机构人员 Personnel in Other Subsidiary Units
教 师 Teachers				教辅人员 Supporting Staff	行政人员 Adm. Personnel	工勤人员 Workers			
副教授 Asso. Professors	讲 师 Lecturers	助 教 Assistants	教 员 Instructors						
21053	23141	10381	2797	20769	27554	22016	10718	6744	14835
1523	1441	286	174	2181	1913	1888	1031	724	1006
553	351	101	80	682	708	599	431	0	790
258	304	104	104	280	310	329	112	55	147
201	276	102	125	220	412	335	78	31	269
200	219	148	18	268	283	157	107	18	42
1007	1189	503	17	725	1535	981	98	10	130
1040	1449	942	261	1074	1929	1635	699	300	942
920	816	583	151	666	1595	1101	114	501	2116
1219	1389	243	80	1223	1279	1576	1167	837	901
1496	1645	912	218	1524	2281	1510	880	750	465
1600	1461	595	231	1378	1420	917	1130	538	1259
259	261	77	89	157	371	412	62	52	146
619	600	313	103	472	965	392	308	276	660
567	581	352	102	535	652	570	60	49	282
1304	1050	281	168	916	1456	1030	337	235	735
743	865	562	34	618	963	821	158	392	199
989	1013	569	125	987	1182	1152	754	388	910
419	396	204	100	391	506	350	41	129	211
1849	2202	833	170	1767	2408	1412	845	570	1895
551	709	271	14	559	617	390	156	323	333
134	162	33	0	127	175	68	26	3	112
170	325	139	19	223	322	180	21	0	24
1035	977	378	28	938	1080	652	1127	295	413
392	463	232	5	518	389	567	94	36	54
368	309	138	14	399	433	348	90	38	84
22	107	140	0	54	144	65	10	0	37
460	830	421	47	522	526	762	300	14	59
235	459	161	77	492	346	429	417	81	154
82	177	148	21	100	133	240	0	0	0
248	364	178	88	178	459	335	42	45	78
590	751	432	134	595	762	813	23	54	382

高等理工院

Basic Statistics of Institutions

地区 Region	学校数(所) Institutions	本专科学生数 Undergraduate Students 毕业生数 Graduates	招生数 Students Admitted	在校学生数 Enrolments	教职 Teachers, Staff 合计 Total	校本部 Teachers, Staff & Workers 计 Subtotal	专任 Full-time 计 Subtotal	教授 Professors
总计 Total	268	291018	517656	1415858	378948	293351	141156	14765
北京 Beijing	20	23672	35384	107323	38425	27939	13236	2158
天津 Tianjin	6	8697	14138	41183	10959	8287	3993	521
河北 Hebei	16	14680	25904	66126	16225	13596	6433	470
山西 Shanxi	4	6463	10109	29309	7987	6357	2961	234
内蒙古 Inner Mongolia	2	1883	3368	10017	3362	2459	1236	90
辽宁 Liaoning	19	22437	38309	105525	27419	21534	10471	1087
吉林 Jilin	13	11258	20009	52215	13097	10799	5070	527
黑龙江 Heilongjiang	9	11559	22031	57918	15643	11928	5880	763
上海 Shanghai	15	19584	30503	90755	29198	20861	9249	1194
江苏 Jiangsu	25	27475	58232	145700	34785	26808	13205	1227
浙江 Zhejiang	6	4771	9401	26573	5522	4404	2130	116
安徽 Anhui	7	7680	14209	39661	10630	8414	4291	555
福建 Fujian	4	4378	8757	24508	4584	3786	1801	182
江西 Jiangxi	6	5038	10010	25497	5121	3910	1981	142
山东 Shandong	14	13928	24833	64669	16283	12736	6476	628
河南 Henan	14	11614	22754	58254	13611	10318	4779	269
湖北 Hubei	16	20676	38985	108793	31170	24049	12125	1448
湖南 Hunan	16	14787	25669	69674	16884	13183	6777	564
广东 Guangdong	5	7076	11530	33648	7915	5964	3136	269
广西 Guangxi	4	3698	5863	16422	2809	2462	1304	48
海南 Hainan	0	0	0	0	0	0	0	0
重庆 Chongqing	9	8702	13475	38302	10860	8247	4244	400
四川 Sichuan	12	12067	24332	66661	18017	15727	6187	562
贵州 Guizhou	1	1265	2355	6460	1649	1217	655	57
云南 Yunnan	2	3390	5481	15690	3806	3284	1658	130
西藏 Tibet	0	0	0	0	0	0	0	0
陕西 Shaanxi	17	20015	33962	93037	27053	20145	9608	999
甘肃 Gansu	3	2777	5452	14393	3378	2686	1306	86
青海 Qinghai	0	0	0	0	0	0	0	0
宁夏 Ningxia	0	0	0	0	0	0	0	0
新疆 Xinjiang	3	1448	2601	7545	2556	2251	964	39

校基本情况

of Science & Technology

单位：人

工数 & Workers — 教职工 in College or Uni. Proper — 教师 Teachers: 副教授 Asso. Professors	讲师 Lecturers	助教 Assistants	教员 Instructors	教辅人员 Supporting Staff	行政人员 Adm. Personnel	工勤人员 Workers	科研机构人员 Personnel in Affiliated Research Org.	校办工厂、农场职工 Employees in School-run Factories, Farms	附设机构人员 Personnel in Other Subsidiary Units
43800	50372	25842	6377	47347	57117	47731	21802	27915	35880
4381	4562	1837	298	4603	5485	4615	4346	2911	3229
1403	1323	502	244	1472	1485	1337	904	1188	580
1938	2284	1286	455	1853	2940	2370	257	1342	1030
690	1180	778	79	1024	1208	1164	235	611	784
368	394	298	86	378	508	337	36	777	90
3583	3513	1897	391	3888	4000	3175	1228	2105	2552
1658	1780	957	148	1825	2220	1684	455	834	1009
2029	1836	1115	137	1745	2303	2000	813	1073	1829
2981	3552	1412	110	4250	3725	3637	2392	2028	3917
3874	4873	2357	874	4457	5093	4053	2111	2664	3202
622	845	374	173	706	918	650	128	474	516
1332	1469	713	222	1398	1449	1276	989	547	680
566	598	396	59	571	877	537	165	346	287
601	616	532	90	536	854	539	68	717	426
2074	2306	1266	202	1735	2629	1896	676	1625	1246
1263	1861	1064	322	1682	1854	2003	330	1951	1012
3931	3795	2231	720	3557	4916	3451	1742	1332	4047
2041	2666	1078	428	1562	2493	2351	1285	916	1500
1041	1354	450	22	1136	1261	431	416	361	1174
264	511	354	127	314	470	374	28	170	149
0	0	0	0	0	0	0	0	0	0
1312	1608	825	99	1513	1542	948	675	640	1298
1766	2170	1324	365	2537	3338	3665	320	694	1276
207	188	115	88	111	203	248	99	120	213
555	606	240	127	528	692	406	177	92	253
0	0	0	0	0	0	0	0	0	0
2781	3516	1941	371	3261	3736	3540	1803	1761	3344
323	484	313	100	475	371	534	108	390	194
0	0	0	0	0	0	0	0	0	0
0	0	0	0	0	0	0	0	0	0
216	482	187	40	230	547	510	16	246	43

高等农业院

Basic Statistics of

地区 Region	学校数(所) Institutions	本专科学生数 Undergraduate Students: 毕业生数 Graduates	招生数 Students Admitted	在校学生数 Enrolments	教职 Teachers, Staff: 合计 Total	校本部 Teachers, Staff & Workers: 计 Subtotal	专任 Full-time: 计 Subtotal	教授 Professors
总计 Total	47	40795	78120	200589	57274	44442	20721	1957
北京 Beijing	2	2215	3381	9882	3459	2739	1263	200
天津 Tianjin	1	346	430	1249	374	356	175	14
河北 Hebei	3	2947	4518	12209	3225	2373	1168	98
山西 Shanxi	1	772	1796	4645	1395	1270	542	61
内蒙古 Inner Mongolia	2	1386	3173	8410	2840	2596	1219	119
辽宁 Liaoning	2	1840	3152	8352	2154	1995	898	80
吉林 Jilin	2	1145	2657	5833	2649	1908	789	60
黑龙江 Heilongjiang	2	1744	5450	11528	3595	2419	1111	150
上海 Shanghai	1	1119	1180	3648	797	682	316	30
江苏 Jiangsu	1	1488	2504	7073	2448	1872	748	111
浙江 Zhejiang	1	587	1261	2733	442	393	216	3
安徽 Anhui	1	886	1901	5228	1302	1044	586	64
福建 Fujian	1	704	1788	4252	1346	1006	468	58
江西 Jiangxi	2	1725	2943	7351	3276	1325	613	49
山东 Shandong	2	2483	5017	11879	2689	2097	989	123
河南 Henan	4	2047	4891	11288	2742	2299	1134	91
湖北 Hubei	2	1643	3871	10707	3039	2294	1108	99
湖南 Hunan	1	1367	2528	6622	1435	1250	578	57
广东 Guangdong	3	3511	6834	17219	3451	2849	1352	87
广西 Guangxi	0	0	0	0	0	0	0	0
海南 Hainan	1	954	1279	3890	1044	690	294	8
重庆 Chongqing	2	1814	3029	8219	2169	1715	882	59
四川 Sichuan	3	2305	4165	11098	2150	1607	839	53
贵州 Guizhou	0	0	0	0	0	0	0	0
云南 Yunnan	1	917	1550	4627	1211	1092	530	45
西藏 Tibet	1	169	272	749	458	389	204	3
陕西 Shaanxi	1	1719	3583	9065	2860	2399	1065	118
甘肃 Gansu	1	910	1610	4124	1317	1095	464	43
青海 Qinghai	0	0	0	0	0	0	0	0
宁夏 Ningxia	1	321	560	1837	634	511	247	17
新疆 Xinjiang	2	1731	2797	6872	2773	2177	923	57

校基本情况

Institutions of Agriculture

单位：人

工数 & Workers									
教职工 in College or Uni. Proper							科研机构人员 Personnel in Affiliated Research Org.	校办工厂、农场职工 Employees in School-run Factories, Farms	附设机构人员 Personnel in Other Subsidiary Units
教师 Teachers				教辅人员 Supporting Staff	行政人员 Adm. Personnel	工勤人员 Workers			
副教授 Asso. Professors	讲师 Lecturers	助教 Assistants	教员 Instructors						
6177	7199	4373	1015	6205	8810	8706	1852	7418	3562
514	384	148	17	411	679	386	154	217	349
51	84	26	0	31	73	77	0	12	6
376	378	234	82	255	488	462	106	671	75
146	209	103	23	82	246	400	0	63	62
371	394	283	52	391	561	425	26	89	129
267	306	239	6	235	414	448	56	15	88
145	311	242	31	355	264	500	129	598	14
304	418	192	47	367	375	566	120	893	163
95	130	61	0	98	150	118	23	74	18
262	190	154	31	328	318	478	0	407	169
50	91	63	9	47	65	65	9	15	25
186	206	103	27	144	205	109	29	65	164
158	123	108	21	114	184	240	65	171	104
148	174	212	30	187	266	259	30	1753	168
331	309	178	48	252	478	378	49	209	334
411	396	179	57	321	464	380	92	183	168
290	381	248	90	362	447	377	210	330	205
207	181	86	47	168	294	210	25	11	149
417	595	214	39	493	674	330	131	172	299
0	0	0	0	0	0	0	0	0	0
63	105	100	18	54	128	214	54	256	44
272	276	254	21	285	231	317	133	190	131
223	305	210	48	265	325	178	179	113	251
0	0	0	0	0	0	0	0	0	0
138	179	142	26	199	183	180	40	14	65
21	84	75	21	46	68	71	13	24	32
255	341	232	119	217	439	678	120	165	176
154	168	75	24	137	160	334	41	117	64
0	0	0	0	0	0	0	0	0	0
94	101	35	0	75	119	70	7	82	34
228	380	177	81	286	512	456	11	509	76

高等林业院

Basic Statistics of

地区 Region	学校数(所) Institutions	本专科学生数 Undergraduate Students 毕业生数 Graduates	招生数 Students Admitted	在校学生数 Enrolments	教职 Teachers, Staff 合计 Total	校本部 Teachers, Staff & Workers 计 Subtotal	专任 Full-time 计 Subtotal	教授 Professors
总计 Total	7	5242	10720	27618	7921	6185	3047	372
北京 Beijing	1	814	1840	4529	1283	829	439	96
天津 Tianjin	0	0	0	0	0	0	0	0
河北 Hebei	0	0	0	0	0	0	0	0
山西 Shanxi	0	0	0	0	0	0	0	0
内蒙古 Inner Mongolia	0	0	0	0	0	0	0	0
辽宁 Liaoning	0	0	0	0	0	0	0	0
吉林 Jilin	0	0	0	0	0	0	0	0
黑龙江 Heilongjiang	1	1288	2410	6521	2144	1637	744	100
上海 Shanghai	0	0	0	0	0	0	0	0
江苏 Jiangsu	1	949	1836	4644	1532	1183	662	74
浙江 Zhejiang	1	259	1136	2108	456	404	191	5
安徽 Anhui	0	0	0	0	0	0	0	0
福建 Fujian	1	647	1000	3161	775	591	269	23
江西 Jiangxi	0	0	0	0	0	0	0	0
山东 Shandong	0	0	0	0	0	0	0	0
河南 Henan	0	0	0	0	0	0	0	0
湖北 Hubei	0	0	0	0	0	0	0	0
湖南 Hunan	1	754	1598	4134	1103	975	455	51
广东 Guangdong	0	0	0	0	0	0	0	0
广西 Guangxi	0	0	0	0	0	0	0	0
海南 Hainan	0	0	0	0	0	0	0	0
重庆 Chongqing	0	0	0	0	0	0	0	0
四川 Sichuan	0	0	0	0	0	0	0	0
贵州 Guizhou	0	0	0	0	0	0	0	0
云南 Yunnan	1	531	900	2521	628	566	287	23
西藏 Tibet	0	0	0	0	0	0	0	0
陕西 Shaanxi	0	0	0	0	0	0	0	0
甘肃 Gansu	0	0	0	0	0	0	0	0
青海 Qinghai	0	0	0	0	0	0	0	0
宁夏 Ningxia	0	0	0	0	0	0	0	0
新疆 Xinjiang	0	0	0	0	0	0	0	0

校基本情况

Institutions of Forestry

单位：人

工数 & Workers									
教职工 in College or Uni. Proper							科研机构人员 Personnel in Affiliated Research Org.	校办工厂、农场职工 Employees in School-run Factories, Farms	附设机构人员 Personnel in Other Subsidiary Units
教师 Teachers				教辅人员 Supporting Staff	行政人员 Adm. Personnel	工勤人员 Workers			
副教授 Asso. Professors	讲师 Lecturers	助教 Assistants	教员 Instructors						
914	997	632	132	991	1185	962	326	723	687
156	125	56	6	94	213	83	130	66	258
0	0	0	0	0	0	0	0	0	0
0	0	0	0	0	0	0	0	0	0
0	0	0	0	0	0	0	0	0	0
0	0	0	0	0	0	0	0	0	0
0	0	0	0	0	0	0	0	0	0
0	0	0	0	0	0	0	0	0	0
220	248	143	33	415	188	290	54	352	101
0	0	0	0	0	0	0	0	0	0
181	218	181	8	129	263	129	87	122	140
40	84	38	24	47	88	78	4	6	42
0	0	0	0	0	0	0	0	0	0
71	81	77	17	79	132	111	7	111	66
0	0	0	0	0	0	0	0	0	0
0	0	0	0	0	0	0	0	0	0
0	0	0	0	0	0	0	0	0	0
0	0	0	0	0	0	0	0	0	0
147	135	91	31	146	186	188	44	66	18
0	0	0	0	0	0	0	0	0	0
0	0	0	0	0	0	0	0	0	0
0	0	0	0	0	0	0	0	0	0
0	0	0	0	0	0	0	0	0	0
0	0	0	0	0	0	0	0	0	0
0	0	0	0	0	0	0	0	0	0
99	106	46	13	81	115	83	0	0	62
0	0	0	0	0	0	0	0	0	0
0	0	0	0	0	0	0	0	0	0
0	0	0	0	0	0	0	0	0	0
0	0	0	0	0	0	0	0	0	0
0	0	0	0	0	0	0	0	0	0
0	0	0	0	0	0	0	0	0	0

高 等 医 药 院

Basic Statistics of

地 区 Region	学校数(所) Institutions	本专科学生数 Undergraduate Students			教职 Teachers, Staff			
						校本部 Teachers, Staff & Workers		
							专任 Full-time	
		毕业生数 Graduates	招生数 Students Admitted	在校学生数 Enrolments	合计 Total	计 Subtotal	计 Subtotal	教授 Professors
总 计 Total	118	56460	98712	300821	115718	95182	41166	5152
北 京 Beijing	6	2100	2482	9612	24506	16578	5140	928
天 津 Tianjin	2	1161	1508	5486	2373	1816	755	98
河 北 Hebei	5	3887	6253	18694	5427	4146	1794	193
山 西 Shanxi	4	1913	4494	10800	2673	2441	1141	123
内蒙古 Inner Mongolia	3	1285	1540	5338	1984	1910	905	93
辽 宁 Liaoning	6	2881	4773	15309	5486	4899	2096	264
吉 林 Jilin	3	1601	2202	7151	2393	1987	928	102
黑龙江 Heilongjiang	5	2092	4151	12237	3790	3116	1414	261
上 海 Shanghai	4	1814	2198	9179	4678	3422	1414	232
江 苏 Jiangsu	8	3888	6542	23029	7266	6201	2877	365
浙 江 Zhejiang	3	1226	1854	5746	1640	1509	705	51
安 徽 Anhui	4	1960	4372	12077	2727	2409	1135	126
福 建 Fujian	2	1074	2807	6987	1647	1438	700	56
江 西 Jiangxi	6	2502	4078	11597	3661	2853	1338	171
山 东 Shandong	8	4152	5804	19530	5625	4996	2511	301
河 南 Henan	5	2944	5036	12881	4176	3743	1611	132
湖 北 Hubei	6	2723	5287	16333	5509	5007	2011	246
湖 南 Hunan	6	2409	6100	15766	4332	3746	1666	154
广 东 Guangdong	5	2685	4958	15905	4574	3937	1612	166
广 西 Guangxi	4	1775	3997	11133	2492	2282	1112	126
海 南 Hainan	1	318	467	1198	379	362	134	10
重 庆 Chongqing	1	930	1149	4205	1299	1237	680	108
四 川 Sichuan	4	2558	4679	15017	5284	4233	1993	234
贵 州 Guizhou	4	1623	3704	9162	2405	2339	1250	109
云 南 Yunnan	3	1143	1953	6780	2277	1976	964	95
西 藏 Tibet	1	54	53	250	136	117	49	1
陕 西 Shaanxi	3	1279	2706	7656	3281	2878	1575	248
甘 肃 Gansu	2	1099	1432	4592	1267	1207	631	62
青 海 Qinghai	1	223	375	1226	428	428	204	6
宁 夏 Ningxia	1	304	492	1452	522	522	213	32
新 疆 Xinjiang	2	857	1266	4493	1481	1447	608	59

校基本情况

Institutions of Medicine & Pharmacy

单位：人

工数 & Workers 教职工 in College or Uni. Proper 教师 Teachers 副教授 Asso. Professors	讲师 Lecturers	助教 Assistants	教员 Instructors	教辅人员 Supporting Staff	行政人员 Adm. Personnel	工勤人员 Workers	科研机构人员 Personnel in Affiliated Research Org.	校办工厂、农场职工 Employees in School-run Factories, Farms	附设机构人员 Personnel in Other Subsidiary Units
11916	13763	8327	2008	20342	18547	15127	10717	3723	6096
1326	1625	1076	185	7329	1931	2178	7433	157	338
280	244	98	35	389	455	217	159	77	321
613	564	315	109	693	818	841	92	131	1058
301	447	185	85	397	549	354	10	79	143
275	349	157	31	433	314	258	1	26	47
567	767	431	67	861	1117	825	284	187	116
205	336	233	52	300	357	402	77	112	217
389	425	288	51	523	640	539	329	137	208
342	484	265	91	652	780	576	266	541	449
877	820	678	137	1066	1274	984	264	379	422
248	229	156	21	191	323	290	32	44	55
349	357	225	78	341	478	455	176	28	114
149	259	225	11	247	300	191	46	93	70
380	421	313	53	412	632	471	8	490	310
832	817	456	105	773	1031	681	209	114	306
554	561	300	64	481	908	743	27	147	259
595	587	367	216	944	1334	718	116	184	202
526	506	331	149	579	778	723	310	101	175
479	588	329	50	955	794	576	234	72	331
354	336	257	39	357	451	362	59	18	133
65	43	16	0	60	98	70	4	0	13
218	240	90	24	172	236	149	0	0	62
523	653	471	112	642	942	656	369	343	339
354	417	316	54	322	452	315	40	26	0
298	347	164	60	267	456	289	53	0	248
4	17	19	8	11	29	28	5	8	6
404	677	213	33	400	371	532	89	197	117
173	245	106	45	131	233	212	25	0	35
38	72	74	14	89	59	76	0	0	0
49	79	44	9	77	100	132	0	0	0
149	251	129	20	248	307	284	0	32	2

高等师范院

Basic Statistics of

地区 Region		学校数(所) Institutions	本专科学生数 Undergraduate Students			教职 Teachers, Staff			
						合计 Total	校本部 Teachers, Staff & Workers		
							计 Subtotal	专任 Full-time	
			毕业生数 Graduates	招生数 Students Admitted	在校学生数 Enrolments			计 Subtotal	教授 Professors
总计	**Total**	227	192556	344177	845354	174505	157962	81419	5106
北京	Beijing	3	3186	4617	14850	6269	5536	2470	387
天津	Tianjin	2	3365	4805	12622	3223	3046	1354	120
河北	Hebei	12	11509	21368	44372	9937	8954	4566	213
山西	Shanxi	8	5927	12485	27729	6139	5667	2554	126
内蒙古	Inner Mongolia	6	4067	5787	14753	4517	4377	2291	139
辽宁	Liaoning	13	8784	15031	36270	9216	8554	4702	202
吉林	Jilin	6	5893	9489	25258	5820	5188	2675	278
黑龙江	Heilongjiang	7	4111	8550	21250	4594	4317	2109	172
上海	Shanghai	2	4861	7476	21499	7054	5018	2534	307
江苏	Jiangsu	9	7754	21020	49732	8294	7758	4039	272
浙江	Zhejiang	7	5702	11559	29053	4927	4611	2444	114
安徽	Anhui	13	6634	18890	44447	7086	6543	3719	153
福建	Fujian	8	5852	10024	24719	5186	4857	2502	147
江西	Jiangxi	8	8418	12425	31820	5704	5342	2843	161
山东	Shandong	13	16615	24564	59879	11813	10947	5676	386
河南	Henan	13	11835	21650	44976	8401	7981	4235	188
湖北	Hubei	7	6834	14469	33608	7002	5446	2750	216
湖南	Hunan	12	12313	23452	55658	9662	8878	4480	328
广东	Guangdong	7	12693	17242	47127	6227	5539	2912	208
广西	Guangxi	9	6492	10034	27269	5454	4807	2553	137
海南	Hainan	2	1519	1859	5467	1324	1250	659	24
重庆	Chongqing	4	4612	8424	23076	4827	4219	2088	186
四川	Sichuan	12	9296	16540	42960	6891	6444	3391	124
贵州	Guizhou	10	4181	8662	19907	4155	4018	1936	72
云南	Yunnan	11	5393	9401	23055	4951	4689	2472	122
西藏	Tibet	0	0	0	0	0	0	0	0
陕西	Shaanxi	8	5481	10451	25859	5635	4768	2439	147
甘肃	Gansu	6	4965	7175	19879	4712	4011	2107	98
青海	Qinghai	3	1011	1315	3810	1558	1505	866	24
宁夏	Ningxia	1	265	343	872	235	235	142	3
新疆	Xinjiang	5	2988	5070	13578	3692	3457	1911	52

校基本情况

Teachers Colleges

单位：人

工数 & Workers									
教职工 in College or Uni. Proper							科研机构人员 Personnel in Affiliated Research Org.	校办工厂、农场职工 Employees in School-run Factories, Farms	附设机构人员 Personnel in Other Subsidiary Units
教师 Teachers				教辅人员 Supporting Staff	行政人员 Adm. Personnel	工勤人员 Workers			
副教授 Asso. Professors	讲师 Lecturers	助教 Assistants	教员 Instructors						
22730	31033	17946	4604	19527	31799	25217	2331	4640	9572
924	873	213	73	981	808	1277	346	185	202
447	550	221	16	519	669	504	46	72	59
1039	1786	1230	298	991	1820	1577	99	64	820
640	1114	549	125	737	1373	1003	45	58	369
667	1024	415	46	575	908	603	0	44	96
1289	1953	1013	245	917	1719	1216	90	172	400
775	911	587	124	861	870	782	36	248	348
768	620	444	105	409	857	942	2	203	72
903	929	297	98	764	1128	592	287	1079	670
1247	1296	914	310	786	1628	1305	30	158	348
600	1040	547	143	579	925	663	19	200	97
872	1330	1038	326	661	1155	1008	64	137	342
611	878	651	215	563	1072	720	71	109	149
831	1057	671	123	586	982	931	40	133	189
1621	1998	1405	266	1217	2441	1613	245	254	367
1236	1733	850	228	918	1553	1275	15	101	304
884	928	495	227	817	1051	828	85	119	1352
1400	1631	779	342	1031	1774	1593	67	225	492
946	987	714	57	817	1217	593	218	70	400
615	977	644	180	595	964	695	48	279	320
149	265	197	24	154	244	193	14	0	60
637	809	383	73	454	914	763	113	83	412
826	1429	754	258	779	1234	1040	125	25	297
441	770	481	172	619	956	507	22	37	78
659	1003	557	131	566	953	698	64	55	143
0	0	0	0	0	0	0	0	0	0
608	1048	495	141	632	894	803	71	3	793
497	767	637	108	516	728	660	61	471	169
138	418	247	39	98	306	235	0	0	53
38	42	37	22	23	40	30	0	0	0
422	867	481	89	362	616	568	8	56	171

高等语文院

Basic Statistics of

地区 Region		学校数(所) Institutions	本专科学生数 Undergraduate Students			教职 Teachers, Staff			
							校本部 Teachers, Staff & Workers		
								专任 Full-time	
			毕业生数 Graduates	招生数 Students Admitted	在校学生数 Enrolments	合计 Total	计 Subtotal	计 Subtotal	教授 Professors
总计	**Total**	15	7561	15048	37924	11926	10265	4961	421
北京	Beijing	7	2948	5535	13766	5629	4984	2338	270
天津	Tianjin	1	507	657	2106	524	509	275	19
河北	Hebei	0	0	0	0	0	0	0	0
山西	Shanxi	0	0	0	0	0	0	0	0
内蒙古	Inner Mongolia	0	63	217	372	197	191	113	4
辽宁	Liaoning	1	359	1194	2868	600	571	312	18
吉林	Jilin	0	0	0	0	0	0	0	0
黑龙江	Heilongjiang	0	0	0	0	0	0	0	0
上海	Shanghai	1	657	1307	3411	1452	827	411	42
江苏	Jiangsu	0	0	0	0	0	0	0	0
浙江	Zhejiang	1	253	295	833	153	150	60	1
安徽	Anhui	0	0	0	0	0	0	0	0
福建	Fujian	1	505	1060	2239	333	312	168	2
江西	Jiangxi	0	0	0	0	0	0	0	0
山东	Shandong	0	0	0	0	0	0	0	0
河南	Henan	0	0	0	0	0	0	0	0
湖北	Hubei	0	0	0	0	0	0	0	0
湖南	Hunan	0	0	0	0	0	0	0	0
广东	Guangdong	1	1204	2947	6630	1206	1131	500	21
广西	Guangxi	0	0	0	0	0	0	0	0
海南	Hainan	0	0	0	0	0	0	0	0
重庆	Chongqing	1	479	723	2609	798	707	349	15
四川	Sichuan	0	0	0	0	0	0	0	0
贵州	Guizhou	0	0	0	0	0	0	0	0
云南	Yunnan	0	0	0	0	0	0	0	0
西藏	Tibet	0	0	0	0	0	0	0	0
陕西	Shaanxi	1	586	1113	3090	1034	883	435	29
甘肃	Gansu	0	0	0	0	0	0	0	0
青海	Qinghai	0	0	0	0	0	0	0	0
宁夏	Ningxia	0	0	0	0	0	0	0	0
新疆	Xinjiang	0	0	0	0	0	0	0	0

校基本情况

Institutions of Languages & Literatures

单位：人

工数 & Workers 教职工 in College or Uni. Proper 教师 Teachers 副教授 Asso. Professors	讲师 Lecturers	助教 Assistants	教员 Instructors	教辅人员 Supporting Staff	行政人员 Adm. Personnel	工勤人员 Workers	科研机构人员 Personnel in Affiliated Research Org.	校办工厂、农场职工 Employees in School-run Factories, Farms	附设机构人员 Personnel in Other Subsidiary Units
1399	1939	953	249	1370	2013	1921	182	385	1094
772	844	329	123	635	872	1139	51	21	573
68	90	75	23	56	114	64	8	7	0
0	0	0	0	0	0	0	0	0	0
0	0	0	0	0	0	0	0	0	0
19	57	19	14	17	40	21	6	0	0
64	176	50	4	49	121	89	9	0	20
0	0	0	0	0	0	0	0	0	0
0	0	0	0	0	0	0	0	0	0
101	180	77	11	134	243	39	35	350	240
0	0	0	0	0	0	0	0	0	0
19	18	17	5	20	47	23	0	3	0
0	0	0	0	0	0	0	0	0	0
23	71	72	0	29	90	25	0	4	17
0	0	0	0	0	0	0	0	0	0
0	0	0	0	0	0	0	0	0	0
0	0	0	0	0	0	0	0	0	0
0	0	0	0	0	0	0	0	0	0
0	0	0	0	0	0	0	0	0	0
149	179	128	23	253	115	263	37	0	38
0	0	0	0	0	0	0	0	0	0
0	0	0	0	0	0	0	0	0	0
89	140	93	12	89	179	90	20	0	71
0	0	0	0	0	0	0	0	0	0
0	0	0	0	0	0	0	0	0	0
0	0	0	0	0	0	0	0	0	0
0	0	0	0	0	0	0	0	0	0
95	184	93	34	88	192	168	16	0	135
0	0	0	0	0	0	0	0	0	0
0	0	0	0	0	0	0	0	0	0
0	0	0	0	0	0	0	0	0	0
0	0	0	0	0	0	0	0	0	0

高等财经院

Basic Statistics of

地区 Region		学校数(所) Institutions	本专科学生数 Undergraduate Students			教职 Teachers, Staff			
							校本部 Teachers, Staff & Workers		
								专任 Full-time	
			毕业生数 Graduates	招生数 Students Admitted	在校学生数 Enrolments	合计 Total	计 Subtotal	计 Subtotal	教授 Professors
总计	**Total**	74	52921	92867	249073	48988	45142	21024	1549
北京	Beijing	5	3819	5187	17026	5172	4543	1979	220
天津	Tianjin	2	2480	4307	11799	2175	2087	902	82
河北	Hebei	2	2415	3881	11250	2257	1892	975	62
山西	Shanxi	2	2240	3808	9795	1730	1608	857	79
内蒙古	Inner Mongolia	1	654	996	2970	702	672	332	16
辽宁	Liaoning	4	3357	5274	14978	2768	2464	1148	129
吉林	Jilin	4	1643	3093	8312	1668	1645	717	30
黑龙江	Heilongjiang	4	1948	4248	9611	2120	2046	872	60
上海	Shanghai	6	3142	4978	14018	2977	2753	1193	102
江苏	Jiangsu	4	2163	4036	10427	1710	1545	795	36
浙江	Zhejiang	3	2669	4787	12516	2316	2007	893	36
安徽	Anhui	4	2405	4585	12574	1996	1901	898	28
福建	Fujian	1	268	700	1466	174	174	94	1
江西	Jiangxi	2	2086	3908	9718	1943	1728	852	85
山东	Shandong	3	2396	5208	13035	2247	2061	917	61
河南	Henan	3	2031	4039	9459	1675	1610	814	40
湖北	Hubei	4	2933	4512	12615	2655	2416	1143	110
湖南	Hunan	4	3326	4761	13237	2695	2416	1028	68
广东	Guangdong	2	1999	3099	8203	1208	1116	568	25
广西	Guangxi	3	1232	1918	5070	646	630	368	6
海南	Hainan	0	0	0	0	0	0	0	0
重庆	Chongqing	1	680	1173	3636	537	537	269	10
四川	Sichuan	2	1473	3235	8597	1626	1585	773	94
贵州	Guizhou	2	1108	3021	5676	962	919	440	18
云南	Yunnan	1	726	1458	3785	973	937	421	21
西藏	Tibet	0	0	0	0	0	0	0	0
陕西	Shaanxi	3	2136	3911	11714	2433	2330	1005	91
甘肃	Gansu	1	944	1600	4260	770	725	355	19
青海	Qinghai	0	0	0	0	0	0	0	0
宁夏	Ningxia	0	0	0	0	0	0	0	0
新疆	Xinjiang	1	648	1144	3326	853	795	416	20

校基本情况

Institutions of Finance & Economics

单位:人

工数 & Workers 教职工 in College or Uni. Proper 教师 Teachers 副教授 Asso. Professors	讲师 Lecturers	助教 Assistants	教员 Instructors	教辅人员 Supporting Staff	行政人员 Adm. Personnel	工勤人员 Workers	科研机构人员 Personnel in Affiliated Research Org.	校办工厂、农场职工 Employees in School-run Factories, Farms	附设机构人员 Personnel in Other Subsidiary Units
6206	8751	3536	982	4739	11050	8329	562	1570	1714
674	747	226	112	491	1114	959	105	295	229
286	335	130	69	203	550	432	29	53	6
253	370	221	69	159	386	372	13	180	172
257	357	128	36	183	362	206	0	2	120
100	126	68	22	93	160	87	7	0	23
357	445	153	64	222	555	539	33	17	254
195	302	178	12	181	480	267	5	7	11
312	344	120	36	357	480	337	28	0	46
305	540	205	41	267	726	567	58	89	77
208	305	220	26	153	314	283	31	99	35
280	419	114	44	254	402	458	17	193	99
222	375	149	124	201	474	328	22	8	65
12	35	35	11	24	26	30	0	0	0
268	282	165	52	178	452	246	38	113	64
294	395	156	11	197	634	313	22	89	75
222	409	113	30	155	453	188	0	0	65
392	398	122	121	224	651	398	6	57	176
330	485	118	27	210	617	561	32	226	21
184	196	153	10	147	242	159	0	92	0
72	170	102	18	53	122	87	0	8	8
0	0	0	0	0	0	0	0	0	0
76	125	58	0	4	185	79	0	0	0
185	365	129	0	265	189	358	29	12	0
125	189	88	20	81	324	74	25	10	8
131	202	67	0	101	213	202	10	0	26
0	0	0	0	0	0	0	0	0	0
256	485	169	4	236	556	533	41	20	42
90	153	82	11	45	188	137	11	0	34
0	0	0	0	0	0	0	0	0	0
0	0	0	0	0	0	0	0	0	0
120	197	67	12	55	195	129	0	0	58

高 等 政 法 院

Basic Statistics of

地　区 Region	学校数(所) Institutions	本专科学生数 Undergraduate Students 毕业生数 Graduates	招生数 Students Admitted	在校学生数 Enrolments	教职 Teachers, Staff 合　计 Total	校本部 Teachers, Staff & Workers 计 Subtotal	专任 Full-time 计 Subtotal	教授 Professors
总　计　**Total**	25	12315	24690	65196	15154	14437	5824	392
北　京　Beijing	4	2481	4019	12364	3798	3573	1223	152
天　津　Tianjin	0	0	0	0	0	0	0	0
河　北　Hebei	1	335	601	1804	1351	1302	364	13
山　西　Shanxi	0	0	0	0	0	0	0	0
内蒙古　Inner Mongolia	0	0	0	0	0	0	0	0
辽　宁　Liaoning	2	799	1576	4519	1095	1076	440	35
吉　林　Jilin	1	221	361	848	263	255	86	6
黑龙江　Heilongjiang	0	80	280	440	0	0	0	0
上　海　Shanghai	2	1128	1653	5337	1250	1156	458	24
江　苏　Jiangsu	1	592	919	2663	547	547	240	5
浙　江　Zhejiang	2	397	1470	2369	499	495	220	1
安　徽　Anhui	0	0	0	0	0	0	0	0
福　建　Fujian	1	300	350	1054	229	227	124	1
江　西　Jiangxi	1	251	458	1168	340	335	124	0
山　东　Shandong	1	552	1312	2575	383	371	144	3
河　南　Henan	1	358	756	1723	302	302	159	2
湖　北　Hubei	2	1568	2952	8072	1126	1081	530	42
湖　南　Hunan	1	467	1201	2443	520	506	272	3
广　东　Guangdong	1	317	914	1781	490	486	209	4
广　西　Guangxi	0	0	285	720	233	228	107	4
海　南　Hainan	0	0	0	0	0	0	0	0
重　庆　Chongqing	1	949	1938	5692	1117	959	400	39
四　川　Sichuan	0	0	0	0	0	0	0	0
贵　州　Guizhou	0	0	598	758	0	0	0	0
云　南　Yunnan	1	346	972	1965	330	317	154	1
西　藏　Tibet	0	0	0	0	0	0	0	0
陕　西　Shaanxi	1	802	1465	4641	892	854	372	48
甘　肃　Gansu	1	372	610	2260	389	367	198	9
青　海　Qinghai	0	0	0	0	0	0	0	0
宁　夏　Ningxia	0	0	0	0	0	0	0	0
新　疆　Xinjiang	0	0	0	0	0	0	0	0

校基本情况

Institutions of Political Science & Law

单位:人

工数 & Workers 教职工 in College or Uni. Proper 教师 Teachers 副教授 Asso. Professors	讲师 Lecturers	助教 Assistants	教员 Instructors	教辅人员 Supporting Staff	行政人员 Adm. Personnel	工勤人员 Workers	科研机构人员 Personnel in Affiliated Research Org.	校办工厂、农场职工 Employees in School-run Factories, Farms	附设机构人员 Personnel in Other Subsidiary Units
1499	2479	1191	263	1490	4641	2482	198	63	456
438	486	95	52	468	1218	664	59	1	165
0	0	0	0	0	0	0	0	0	0
73	143	81	54	70	328	540	10	39	0
0	0	0	0	0	0	0	0	0	0
0	0	0	0	0	0	0	0	0	0
135	181	84	5	115	394	127	0	0	19
22	41	13	4	58	88	23	8	0	0
0	0	0	0	0	0	0	0	0	0
102	254	51	27	137	372	189	22	15	57
30	93	78	34	40	214	53	0	0	0
36	98	84	1	42	165	68	4	0	0
0	0	0	0	0	0	0	0	0	0
21	45	56	1	24	78	1	2	0	0
23	43	47	11	25	139	47	0	0	5
42	47	51	1	20	160	47	0	0	12
29	65	51	12	21	101	21	0	0	0
126	224	131	7	79	350	122	6	0	39
57	105	106	1	35	176	23	0	0	14
53	91	50	11	96	124	57	4	0	0
31	55	13	4	33	61	27	5	0	0
0	0	0	0	0	0	0	0	0	0
118	176	46	21	110	247	202	43	0	115
0	0	0	0	0	0	0	0	0	0
0	0	0	0	0	0	0	0	0	0
24	77	40	12	16	121	26	4	0	9
0	0	0	0	0	0	0	0	0	0
95	168	61	0	60	236	186	28	0	10
44	87	53	5	41	69	59	3	8	11
0	0	0	0	0	0	0	0	0	0
0	0	0	0	0	0	0	0	0	0
0	0	0	0	0	0	0	0	0	0

高等体育院

Basic Statistics of

地区 Region	学校数(所) Institutions	本专科学生数 Undergraduate Students 毕业生数 Graduates	招生数 Students Admitted	在校学生数 Enrolments	教职 Teachers, Staff 合计 Total	校本部 Teachers, Staff & Workers 计 Subtotal	专任 Full-time 计 Subtotal	教授 Professors
总计 Total	14	4957	9336	24809	7008	6492	3225	237
北京 Beijing	1	512	810	2634	919	919	367	36
天津 Tianjin	1	249	525	1539	422	422	197	9
河北 Hebei	1	233	385	988	217	215	102	7
山西 Shanxi	0	0	0	0	0	0	0	0
内蒙古 Inner Mongolia	0	0	0	0	0	0	0	0
辽宁 Liaoning	1	431	796	2101	672	596	297	17
吉林 Jilin	1	183	505	1168	187	179	103	11
黑龙江 Heilongjiang	1	305	550	1587	365	365	165	17
上海 Shanghai	1	469	865	2350	780	636	343	33
江苏 Jiangsu	1	174	388	1074	290	279	119	8
浙江 Zhejiang	0	0	0	0	0.	0	0	0
安徽 Anhui	0	0	0	0	0	0	0	0
福建 Fujian	0	0	0	0	0	0	0	0
江西 Jiangxi	0	0	0	0	0	0	0	0
山东 Shandong	1	171	408	1100	352	323	130	13
河南 Henan	0	0	0	0	0	0	0	0
湖北 Hubei	1	502	880	2387	836	711	407	24
湖南 Hunan	0	0	0	0	0	0	0	0
广东 Guangdong	1	587	886	2377	491	448	221	19
广西 Guangxi	1	293	356	656	127	124	68	3
海南 Hainan	0	0	0	0	0	0	0	0
重庆 Chongqing	0	0	0	0	0	0	0	0
四川 Sichuan	1	426	1022	2449	667	667	381	19
贵州 Guizhou	0	0	0	0	0	0	0	0
云南 Yunnan	0	0	0	0	0	0	0	0
西藏 Tibet	0	0	0	0	0	0	0	0
陕西 Shaanxi	1	422	960	2399	683	608	325	21
甘肃 Gansu	0	0	0	0	0	0	0	0
青海 Qinghai	0	0	0	0	0	0	0	0
宁夏 Ningxia	0	0	0	0	0	0	0	0
新疆 Xinjiang	0	0	0	0	0	0	0	0

校基本情况

Institutions of Physical Culture

单位：人

工 数 & Workers									
教 职 工 in College or Uni. Proper							科研机构人员 Personnel in Affiliated Research Org.	校办工厂、农场职工 Employees in School－run Factories, Farms	附设机构人员 Personnel in Other Subsidiary Units
教 师 Teachers				教辅人员 Supporting Staff	行政人员 Adm. Personnel	工勤人员 Workers			
副教授 Asso. Professors	讲 师 Lecturers	助 教 Assistants	教 员 Instrructors						
912	1279	684	113	549	1495	1223	71	38	407
132	136	61	2	116	263	173	0	0	0
62	83	36	7	17	122	86	0	0	0
31	32	23	9	13	64	36	0	0	2
0	0	0	0	0	0	0	0	0	0
0	0	0	0	0	0	0	0	0	0
79	136	57	8	13	153	133	0	0	76
35	18	27	12	10	32	34	0	0	8
66	52	30	0	34	106	60	0	0	0
88	144	52	26	64	124	105	24	14	106
37	42	22	10	34	102	24	11	0	0
0	0	0	0	0	0	0	0	0	0
0	0	0	0	0	0	0	0	0	0
0	0	0	0	0	0	0	0	0	0
0	0	0	0	0	0	0	0	0	0
50	34	33	0	42	93	58	7	22	0
0	0	0	0	0	0	0	0	0	0
95	176	110	2	20	89	195	18	0	107
0	0	0	0	0	0	0	0	0	0
70	79	49	4	43	129	55	10	2	31
15	37	12	1	4	29	23	1	0	2
0	0	0	0	0	0	0	0	0	0
0	0	0	0	0	0	0	0	0	0
75	170	104	13	82	94	110	0	0	0
0	0	0	0	0	0	0	0	0	0
0	0	0	0	0	0	0	0	0	0
0	0	0	0	0	0	0	0	0	0
77	140	68	19	57	95	131	0	0	75
0	0	0	0	0	0	0	0	0	0
0	0	0	0	0	0	0	0	0	0
0	0	0	0	0	0	0	0	0	0
0	0	0	0	0	0	0	0	0	0

高 等 艺 术 院

Basic Statistics of

地　区 Region	学校数(所) Institutions	本专科学生数 Undergraduate Students			教职 Teachers, Staff			
		毕业生数 Graduates	招生数 Students Admitted	在校学生数 Enrolments	合计 Total	校本部 Teachers, Staff & Workers		
						计 Subtotal	专任 Full-time	
							计 Subtotal	教授 Professors
总　计 Total	29	4563	9190	24368	11770	10965	5744	590
北　京 Beijing	7	695	1119	3381	2618	2373	1082	166
天　津 Tianjin	2	273	455	1511	696	650	369	55
河　北 Hebei	0	0	0	0	0	0	0	0
山　西 Shanxi	0	0	0	0	0	0	0	0
内蒙古 Inner Mongolia	0	88	121	460	398	390	247	2
辽　宁 Liaoning	2	397	740	1855	883	871	476	56
吉　林 Jilin	1	249	455	1209	395	391	257	29
黑龙江 Heilongjiang	0	0	0	0	0	0	0	0
上　海 Shanghai	2	180	361	1062	778	601	280	34
江　苏 Jiangsu	1	124	659	1172	447	390	225	24
浙　江 Zhejiang	1	103	238	664	408	370	195	32
安　徽 Anhui	0	0	0	0	0	0	0	0
福　建 Fujian	0	0	0	0	0	0	0	0
江　西 Jiangxi	0	0	0	0	0	0	0	0
山　东 Shandong	2	406	852	2135	739	731	365	34
河　南 Henan	0	0	0	0	0	0	0	0
湖　北 Hubei	2	254	594	1960	728	727	373	28
湖　南 Hunan	0	0	0	0	0	0	0	0
广　东 Guangdong	2	359	856	1950	745	713	368	32
广　西 Guangxi	1	204	285	1003	399	390	216	12
海　南 Hainan	0	0	0	0	0	0	0	0
重　庆 Chongqing	1	339	561	1352	417	385	198	22
四　川 Sichuan	1	171	528	1134	402	348	210	10
贵　州 Guizhou	0	0	0	0	0	0	0	0
云　南 Yunnan	1	275	519	1268	494	465	227	10
西　藏 Tibet	0	0	0	0	0	0	0	0
陕　西 Shaanxi	2	298	744	1863	832	779	421	39
甘　肃 Gansu	0	0	0	0	0	0	0	0
青　海 Qinghai	0	0	0	0	0	0	0	0
宁　夏 Ningxia	0	0	0	0	0	0	0	0
新　疆 Xinjiang	1	148	103	389	391	391	235	5

校基本情况

Institutions of Art

单位:人

工数 & Workers 教职工 in College or Uni. Proper 教师 Teachers 副教授 Asso. Professors	讲师 Lecturers	助教 Assistants	教员 Instructors	教辅人员 Supporting Staff	行政人员 Adm. Personnel	工勤人员 Workers	科研机构人员 Personnel in Affiliated Research Org.	校办工厂、农场职工 Employees in School-run Factories, Farms	附设机构人员 Personnel in Other Subsidiary Units
1682	1984	1150	338	1004	2659	1558	208	233	364
333	326	189	68	373	587	331	58	126	61
86	143	76	9	45	148	88	12	11	23
0	0	0	0	0	0	0	0	0	0
0	0	0	0	0	0	0	0	0	0
30	105	84	26	49	76	18	8	0	0
134	159	80	47	73	199	123	6	0	6
82	86	45	15	30	56	48	0	0	4
0	0	0	0	0	0	0	0	0	0
95	83	49	19	49	180	92	30	17	130
98	71	30	2	25	95	45	26	12	19
75	55	32	1	42	79	54	0	2	36
0	0	0	0	0	0	0	0	0	0
0	0	0	0	0	0	0	0	0	0
0	0	0	0	0	0	0	0	0	0
106	159	53	13	45	203	118	8	0	0
0	0	0	0	0	0	0	0	0	0
127	122	76	20	47	213	94	1	0	0
0	0	0	0	0	0	0	0	0	0
102	140	87	7	59	177	109	29	0	3
72	68	44	20	38	115	21	5	0	4
0	0	0	0	0	0	0	0	0	0
74	65	30	7	22	73	92	0	15	17
53	74	59	14	13	67	58	16	5	33
0	0	0	0	0	0	0	0	0	0
65	87	52	13	26	111	101	8	12	9
0	0	0	0	0	0	0	0	0	0
96	152	111	23	45	189	124	1	33	19
0	0	0	0	0	0	0	0	0	0
0	0	0	0	0	0	0	0	0	0
0	0	0	0	0	0	0	0	0	0
54	89	53	34	23	91	42	0	0	0

高 等 民 族 院

Basic Statistics of

地　区 Region	学校数(所) Institutions	本专科学生数 Undergraduate Students			教职 Teachers, Staff			
					合　计 Total	校本部 Teachers, Staff & Workers		
						计 Subtotal	专任 Full-time	
		毕业生数 Graduates	招生数 Students Admitted	在校学生数 Enrolments			计 Subtotal	教授 Professors
总　计　Total	12	8597	14891	42751	10621	9485	4780	292
北　京　Beijing	1	999	969	3799	1763	1485	722	72
天　津　Tianjin	0	0	0	0	0	0	0	0
河　北　Hebei	0	0	0	0	0	0	0	0
山　西　Shanxi	0	0	0	0	0	0	0	0
内蒙古　Inner Mongolia	0	0	0	0	0	0	0	0
辽　宁　Liaoning	1	0	890	1533	289	289	129	7
吉　林　Jilin	0	0	0	0	0	0	0	0
黑龙江　Heilongjiang	0	0	0	0	0	0	0	0
上　海　Shanghai	0	0	0	0	0	0	0	0
江　苏　Jiangsu	0	0	0	0	0	0	0	0
浙　江　Zhejiang	0	0	0	0	0	0	0	0
安　徽　Anhui	0	0	0	0	0	0	0	0
福　建　Fujian	0	0	0	0	0	0	0	0
江　西　Jiangxi	0	0	0	0	0	0	0	0
山　东　Shandong	0	0	0	0	0	0	0	0
河　南　Henan	0	0	0	0	0	0	0	0
湖　北　Hubei	2	2188	3506	11179	2192	1843	1044	70
湖　南　Hunan	0	0	0	0	0	0	0	0
广　东　Guangdong	0	0	0	0	0	0	0	0
广　西　Guangxi	1	1038	1866	5423	1003	951	462	30
海　南　Hainan	0	0	0	0	0	0	0	0
重　庆　Chongqing	0	0	0	0	0	0	0	0
四　川　Sichuan	1	1074	1211	4445	993	935	408	27
贵　州　Guizhou	1	618	1486	3489	880	825	449	23
云　南　Yunnan	1	685	1352	3764	911	817	428	25
西　藏　Tibet	1	408	708	1588	561	529	241	5
陕　西　Shaanxi	0	0	0	0	0	0	0	0
甘　肃　Gansu	1	702	1405	3573	979	867	449	19
青　海　Qinghai	1	482	611	1690	554	482	200	8
宁　夏　Ningxia	1	403	887	2268	496	462	248	6
新　疆　Xinjiang	0	0	0	0	0	0	0	0

校基本情况

Institutions of Nationalities

工　　数

& Workers

单位:人

教职工 in College or Uni. Proper							科研机构人员 Personnel in Affiliated Research Org.	校办工厂、农场职工 Employees in School-run Factories, Farms	附设机构人员 Personnel in Other Subsidiary Units
教师 Teachers				教辅人员 Supporting Staff	行政人员 Adm. Personnel	工勤人员 Workers			
副教授 Asso. Professors	讲师 Lecturers	助教 Assistants	教员 Instructors						
1333	2045	833	277	1092	2060	1553	222	139	775
234	342	52	22	92	320	351	33	68	177
0	0	0	0	0	0	0	0	0	0
0	0	0	0	0	0	0	0	0	0
0	0	0	0	0	0	0	0	0	0
0	0	0	0	0	0	0	0	0	0
48	48	21	5	43	95	22	0	0	0
0	0	0	0	0	0	0	0	0	0
0	0	0	0	0	0	0	0	0	0
0	0	0	0	0	0	0	0	0	0
0	0	0	0	0	0	0	0	0	0
0	0	0	0	0	0	0	0	0	0
0	0	0	0	0	0	0	0	0	0
0	0	0	0	0	0	0	0	0	0
0	0	0	0	0	0	0	0	0	0
0	0	0	0	0	0	0	0	0	0
0	0	0	0	0	0	0	0	0	0
288	405	177	104	326	204	269	40	19	290
0	0	0	0	0	0	0	0	0	0
0	0	0	0	0	0	0	0	0	0
145	158	86	43	112	230	147	0	0	52
0	0	0	0	0	0	0	0	0	0
0	0	0	0	0	0	0	0	0	0
142	188	44	7	124	234	169	40	18	0
112	209	93	12	64	236	76	9	0	46
149	175	69	10	104	167	118	49	0	45
48	123	59	6	47	128	113	0	32	0
0	0	0	0	0	0	0	0	0	0
95	212	89	34	56	224	138	20	0	92
36	77	62	17	51	143	88	29	0	43
36	108	81	17	73	79	62	2	2	30
0	0	0	0	0	0	0	0	0	0

普通高等学校女学

Number of Female Students, Teachers, Staff &

地区 Region	本专科学生数 Undergraduate Students			教职 Teachers, Staff			
					校本部 Teachers, Staff & Workers		
						专任 Full-time	
	毕业生数 Graduates	招生数 Students Admitted	在校学生数 Enrolments	合计 Total	计 Subtotal	计 Subtotal	教授 Professors
总计 Total	323238	625400	1620554	438130	358489	158974	5933
北京 Beijing	19833	33177	97974	53700	41662	15578	1289
天津 Tianjin	8248	13772	38627	11055	9067	3998	293
河北 Hebei	18641	34091	81116	17902	14489	7250	166
山西 Shanxi	8686	16983	43096	10260	8983	4244	112
内蒙古 Inner Mongolia	5395	8658	24321	7216	6332	3290	89
辽宁 Liaoning	20975	39869	103461	25712	22521	11203	289
吉林 Jilin	12124	21813	57441	15724	13304	6459	241
黑龙江 Heilongjiang	12754	28288	69111	17978	13837	6476	298
上海 Shanghai	17715	29929	82776	24965	18594	6981	299
江苏 Jiangsu	21676	48092	121130	27766	22661	9974	363
浙江 Zhejiang	11077	23170	57601	12090	10046	4313	99
安徽 Anhui	6161	16808	42246	9450	7846	3756	105
福建 Fujian	7064	14019	36760	8252	6971	3189	68
江西 Jiangxi	7349	12881	35147	9752	7385	3235	113
山东 Shandong	19680	34996	88131	19338	16355	7804	324
河南 Henan	13778	27914	65595	15881	13355	6680	179
湖北 Hubei	16164	35693	91103	28324	22288	9345	344
湖南 Hunan	13174	28062	69612	17025	14212	5968	129
广东 Guangdong	19054	34691	88847	19589	15788	6666	147
广西 Guangxi	6255	12537	34673	8078	6876	2993	67
海南 Hainan	1305	1757	5354	1497	1146	511	13
重庆 Chongqing	7141	13901	36829	9226	7608	3413	113
四川 Sichuan	12927	26428	69122	17323	14578	6105	212
贵州 Guizhou	3586	9226	21198	5818	5381	2377	61
云南 Yunnan	6470	12085	31306	8095	7228	3375	115
西藏 Tibet	431	678	1631	621	550	277	1
陕西 Shaanxi	13036	24852	64934	19296	15305	6839	278
甘肃 Gansu	4423	8113	22405	6159	5127	2281	43
青海 Qinghai	1106	1568	4601	1407	1341	698	4
宁夏 Ningxia	1184	2073	6120	1729	1564	788	28
新疆 Xinjiang	5826	9276	28286	6902	6089	2908	51

生和女教职工数

Workers in Regular Higher Educational Institutions

单位:人

工 数 & Workers — 教 职 工 in College or Uni. Proper — 教 师 Teachers: 副教授 Asso. Professors	讲 师 Lecturers	助 教 Assistants	教 员 Instructors	教辅人员 Supporting Staff	行政人员 Adm. Personnel	工勤人员 Workers	科研机构人员 Personnel in Affiliated Research Org.	校办工厂、农场职工 Employees in School-run Factories, Farms	附设机构人员 Personnel in Other Subsidiary Units
37896	65359	39855	9931	69874	73423	56218	17592	19608	42441
4686	6382	2598	623	11642	8163	6279	6719	1570	3749
1213	1512	765	215	1815	1938	1316	522	485	981
1636	2867	1910	671	2492	2483	2264	260	961	2192
851	1882	1140	259	1548	1699	1492	114	286	877
738	1476	844	143	1250	1136	656	46	456	382
2824	4941	2642	507	3762	4709	2847	739	797	1655
1500	2567	1824	327	2470	2518	1857	396	645	1379
1987	2359	1533	299	2568	2562	2231	411	1112	2618
1671	3285	1464	262	3827	4147	3639	1387	1993	2991
2176	3752	2910	773	4371	4722	3594	872	1741	2492
891	1822	1151	350	1904	2006	1823	355	487	1202
851	1445	1020	335	1504	1400	1186	372	216	1016
601	1178	1100	242	1150	1568	1064	199	287	795
774	1134	1047	167	1402	1484	1264	76	1269	1022
2069	3048	1886	477	2879	3276	2396	482	742	1759
1443	2798	1788	472	2236	2556	1883	151	1056	1319
2292	3315	2438	956	4378	5038	3527	952	1126	3958
1350	2449	1497	543	2450	2963	2831	567	631	1615
1608	3057	1630	224	3486	3632	2004	649	466	2686
590	1262	887	187	1259	1512	1112	95	434	673
106	239	133	20	214	224	197	23	189	139
807	1485	869	139	1336	1807	1052	288	264	1066
1399	2547	1493	454	2624	3396	2453	760	455	1530
433	995	715	173	950	1322	732	99	126	212
859	1376	808	217	1223	1513	1117	141	86	640
17	117	126	16	80	113	80	6	19	46
1352	3005	1817	387	2605	2899	2962	652	899	2440
407	1046	613	172	902	900	1044	201	384	447
59	309	272	54	240	224	179	15	0	51
160	351	176	73	267	271	238	19	60	86
546	1358	759	194	1040	1242	899	24	366	423

地区 Region	学校数(所) Schools	毕业生数 Graduates	招生数 Entrants			在校学生数 Enrolment		
			计 Total	招高中毕业生数 Graduates From Senior Sec. School	招初中毕业生数 Graduates From Junior Sec. School		合计 Total	
								计 Subtotal
总计 Total	3962	1401451	1633761	114271	1519490	5154984	528636	498781
北京 Beijing	112	27266	34294	1201	33093	123379	12658	11908
天津 Tianjin	82	20220	22642	304	22338	88413	10394	10052
河北 Hebei	172	68016	85156	9547	75609	255162	28466	26929
山西 Shanxi	127	38235	62146	5680	56466	170816	18452	17776
内蒙古 Inner Mongolia	105	21113	41182	6917	34265	101396	14835	14408
辽宁 Liaoning	151	40100	42839	341	42498	156847	22602	21410
吉林 Jilin	119	39285	33470	2372	31098	142055	16399	15472
黑龙江 Heilongjiang	112	39353	46585	1906	44679	128485	17440	16079
上海 Shanghai	87	25905	35302	36	35266	130609	12889	11465
江苏 Jiangsu	206	123461	124574	3829	120745	475856	27516	25991
浙江 Zhejiang	149	50772	51565	1011	50554	165227	14851	14137
安徽 Anhui	159	48023	84723	11408	73315	205217	18438	17600
福建 Fujian	118	32075	43034	287	42747	128881	12825	12273
江西 Jiangxi	101	45460	62482	5651	56831	161755	13598	12699
山东 Shandong	251	106740	122331	11036	111295	344062	39274	37198
河南 Henan	180	98258	113799	9201	104598	347095	31107	28820
湖北 Hubei	220	122331	89643	8453	81190	354369	31136	29206
湖南 Hunan	157	65341	81239	983	80256	272556	23658	22009
广东 Guangdong	248	81678	86906	1509	85397	279608	25134	24451
广西 Guangxi	126	37553	48471	1514	46957	161281	17522	15621
海南 Hainan	34	8291	10254	599	9655	28399	3256	3129
重庆 Chongqing	78	27076	27291	862	26429	91954	10114	8954
四川 Sichuan	209	73860	79840	4417	75423	256921	27441	25791
贵州 Guizhou	109	33272	44124	2357	41767	118175	12470	12180
云南 Yunnan	135	34961	36370	3164	33206	119219	15261	14924
西藏 Tibet	15	1427	1664	52	1612	5672	1264	1248
陕西 Shaanxi	114	36811	50744	9318	41426	145737	16627	14902
甘肃 Gansu	113	20739	25067	3124	21943	73442	12964	12591
青海 Qinghai	35	4252	4050	1088	2962	12600	3072	3046
宁夏 Ningxia	25	4459	6003	966	5037	16370	3043	2935
新疆 Xinjiang	113	25118	35971	5138	30833	93426	13930	13577

校基本情况

Specialized Secondary Schools

单位:人

教职工数 Teachers, Staff & Workers										兼任教师数(不在教工数中) Part-time Teachers
校本部教职工 Employees in the School Proper								校办厂、场职工 Employees in School-run Factories & Farms	附设机构人员 Employees in Subsidiary Units	
专任教师 Full-time Teachers					教辅人员 Supporting Staff	行政人员 Adm. Personnel	工勤人员 Workers			
计 Subtotal	高级讲师 Senior Lecturers	讲师 Lecturers	助理讲师 Assistant Lecturers	教员 Instructors						
273645	48736	119881	94479	10549	47066	96118	81952	17814	12041	11321
5780	1099	2627	1894	160	1360	2593	2175	480	270	430
5399	1139	2455	1612	193	828	2135	1690	191	151	227
14578	2370	6260	5181	767	2493	4918	4940	952	585	328
9568	1523	4062	3462	521	1575	3570	3063	384	292	67
7672	1123	3747	2533	269	1575	2839	2322	254	173	128
11286	2927	5168	2896	295	2250	4185	3689	779	413	266
8409	1739	3496	2974	200	1403	3296	2364	771	156	60
7787	2451	3446	1774	116	1601	3305	3386	825	536	419
5274	848	2800	1434	192	1194	2325	2672	1002	422	437
14783	2420	6011	5475	877	2388	4730	4090	1291	234	2021
7765	1136	3766	2474	389	1455	2637	2280	452	262	985
9898	2008	4193	3328	369	1598	3335	2769	467	371	220
7162	992	2982	2938	250	1038	2275	1798	336	216	421
7278	1274	3225	2561	218	1270	2242	1909	629	270	339
21311	4286	8404	7809	812	3356	7441	5090	1312	764	464
16781	3200	6816	6119	646	2487	5145	4407	1292	995	398
16614	3378	7479	5099	658	2972	5495	4125	968	962	541
11934	2612	5185	3667	470	2230	4224	3621	1067	582	972
14353	1734	5993	6003	623	2292	4444	3362	255	428	671
8941	1436	4421	2857	227	1467	2503	2710	414	1487	228
1736	218	635	782	101	223	595	575	49	78	107
4791	926	1990	1717	158	1015	1657	1491	658	502	166
13469	2563	5937	4578	391	2715	5353	4254	1083	567	560
6976	758	3082	2904	232	867	2876	1461	105	185	229
8278	967	4203	2867	241	1134	2684	2828	135	202	168
740	18	279	426	17	50	225	233	16	0	1
7814	1517	3471	2483	343	1581	3045	2462	1127	598	322
6699	835	3067	2632	165	1083	2267	2542	216	157	47
1777	130	667	900	80	219	525	525	0	26	0
1563	281	771	407	104	251	570	551	78	30	34
7229	828	3243	2693	465	1096	2684	2568	226	127	65

中等技术学

Basic Statistics of

地区 Region	学校数(所) Schools	毕业生数 Graduates	招生数 Entrants			在校学生数 Enrolment	合计 Total	
			计 Total	招高中毕业生数 Graduates From Senior Sec. School	招初中毕业生数 Graduates From Junior Sec. School			计 Subtotal
总计 Total	3147	1092478	1342516	88854	1253662	4249768	421445	394665
北京 Beijing	94	23640	33744	1201	32543	119267	10610	9912
天津 Tianjin	72	17318	20005	304	19701	79418	8994	8727
河北 Hebei	139	47200	65722	4454	61268	200176	22021	20575
山西 Shanxi	104	28250	43640	3770	39870	131683	14923	14340
内蒙古 Inner Mongolia	84	16311	35304	6770	28534	84579	11863	11481
辽宁 Liaoning	139	32942	39316	341	38975	137975	20618	19496
吉林 Jilin	96	30070	28151	1852	26299	116749	13179	12395
黑龙江 Heilongjiang	83	29862	40237	1906	38331	103235	13686	12423
上海 Shanghai	85	25382	34845	36	34809	128341	12694	11279
江苏 Jiangsu	170	109306	112190	1895	110295	426380	22091	20991
浙江 Zhejiang	120	39473	46186	1011	45175	145272	12085	11545
安徽 Anhui	118	37528	71707	5941	65766	167948	14282	13519
福建 Fujian	92	21450	39461	265	39196	109615	9728	9258
江西 Jiangxi	77	33209	48579	2677	45902	126496	10518	9650
山东 Shandong	191	88762	106443	9333	97110	296292	30974	29262
河南 Henan	137	63355	76097	9201	66896	244072	23526	21388
湖北 Hubei	191	102330	75241	7285	67956	297931	25539	24021
湖南 Hunan	127	54811	70043	983	69060	233114	19526	18012
广东 Guangdong	202	62192	73398	1509	71889	228606	19095	18496
广西 Guangxi	97	28720	37416	1380	36036	129581	13284	11478
海南 Hainan	26	4785	6892	349	6543	18812	2191	2100
重庆 Chongqing	46	21495	22028	862	21166	75788	7432	6350
四川 Sichuan	138	56913	62264	4061	58203	205185	20764	19187
贵州 Guizhou	83	24684	34167	2322	31845	89178	9600	9323
云南 Yunnan	107	24852	26816	3164	23652	89294	11612	11292
西藏 Tibet	10	640	923	52	871	3178	803	789
陕西 Shaanxi	92	27212	37835	7225	30610	113030	13652	12003
甘肃 Gansu	91	16369	20240	3079	17161	57525	10481	10155
青海 Qinghai	24	2526	3000	732	2268	8216	2223	2197
宁夏 Ningxia	21	2761	4306	845	3461	11903	2475	2388
新疆 Xinjiang	91	18130	26320	4049	22271	70929	10976	10633

校基本情况

Secondary Technical Schools

单位：人

教职工数 Teachers, Staff & Workers										兼任教师数（不在教工数中） Part-time Teachers
校本部教职工 Employees in the School Proper								校办厂、场职工 Employees in School-run Factories & Farms	附设机构人员 Employees in Subsidiary Units	
专任教师 Full-time Teachers					教辅人员 Supporting Staff	行政人员 Adm. Personnel	工勤人员 Workers			
计 Subtotal	高级讲师 Senior Lecturers	讲师 Lecturers	助理讲师 Assistant Lecturers	教员 Instructors						
211778	39269	94869	70148	7492	38629	78872	65386	15773	11007	11046
4850	884	2243	1597	126	1105	2177	1780	453	245	430
4678	1020	2154	1362	142	715	1845	1489	159	108	227
10940	1996	4865	3544	535	1925	3842	3868	867	579	308
7648	1249	3318	2690	391	1353	2910	2429	320	263	57
6076	910	2996	1942	228	1333	2285	1787	209	173	126
10183	2668	4659	2610	246	2116	3806	3391	729	393	266
6611	1509	2879	2080	143	1229	2624	1931	656	128	60
5762	1873	2471	1339	79	1387	2500	2774	748	515	397
5184	835	2756	1404	189	1187	2269	2639	993	422	437
11788	1935	4883	4271	699	1951	3911	3341	913	187	2014
6241	931	3029	1965	316	1208	2200	1896	359	181	950
7514	1596	3210	2436	272	1161	2693	2151	428	335	218
5330	765	2284	2084	197	875	1700	1353	303	167	421
5316	956	2383	1858	119	1022	1854	1458	617	251	278
16768	3593	6664	5938	573	2472	6083	3939	1041	671	464
12212	2288	4994	4436	494	2044	3814	3318	1204	934	381
13039	2791	6153	3704	391	2535	5054	3393	728	790	541
9788	2090	4272	3028	398	1856	3414	2954	967	547	942
10428	1355	4491	4186	396	1757	3714	2597	216	383	643
6299	1074	3219	1888	118	1146	2034	1999	400	1406	228
1098	130	410	507	51	142	496	364	13	78	107
3382	696	1524	1072	90	713	1224	1031	603	479	166
9758	1956	4558	3026	218	2070	4324	3035	1017	560	548
5145	588	2379	2086	92	744	2258	1176	100	177	224
6118	728	3144	2064	182	906	2149	2119	135	185	168
441	10	174	254	3	36	167	145	14	0	1
6039	1204	2716	1880	239	1387	2567	2010	1113	536	306
5233	651	2462	2011	109	942	1822	2158	190	136	47
1226	102	509	572	43	169	431	371	0	26	0
1265	233	633	324	75	209	480	434	59	28	34
5418	653	2437	1990	338	934	2225	2056	219	124	57

中等工业学

Basic Statistics of

地 区 Region	学校数(所) Schools	毕业生数 Graduates	招生数 Entrants			在校学生数 Enrolment		
			计 Total	招高中毕业生数 Graduates From Senior Sec. School	招初中毕业生数 Graduates From Junior Sec. School		合 计 Total	计 Subtotal
总 计 Total	1022	462262	555803	25717	530086	1886145	167458	154386
北 京 Beijing	30	14711	22126	1006	21120	78067	5059	4543
天 津 Tianjin	23	8535	9845	182	9663	39032	4162	3944
河 北 Hebei	41	14702	22041	1315	20726	69091	8394	7554
山 西 Shanxi	25	9833	13376	1074	12302	42389	4597	4416
内蒙古 Inner Mongolia	26	6147	12114	1342	10772	32242	4344	4222
辽 宁 Liaoning	49	17935	17335	307	17028	72552	10152	9262
吉 林 Jilin	26	11005	7686	327	7359	36652	3661	3451
黑龙江 Heilongjiang	24	8416	10522	150	10372	29098	4265	3901
上 海 Shanghai	38	14866	20474	0	20474	80046	7862	6667
江 苏 Jiangsu	77	78715	81601	1132	80469	316447	11810	11038
浙 江 Zhejiang	33	14327	15048	269	14779	51141	3703	3527
安 徽 Anhui	49	18008	33248	1615	31633	80532	6446	6133
福 建 Fujian	31	7630	15185	0	15185	44237	3821	3522
江 西 Jiangxi	24	13672	19573	603	18970	54756	3762	3389
山 东 Shandong	68	36017	44636	2649	41987	125373	13012	12062
河 南 Henan	40	23628	28581	2689	25892	99521	8603	8099
湖 北 Hubei	72	39879	29382	2702	26680	121999	10918	10230
湖 南 Hunan	48	20194	27537	226	27311	97707	7897	7131
广 东 Guangdong	64	25039	30983	16	30967	104333	7268	7035
广 西 Guangxi	34	10845	14280	0	14280	52587	4460	4243
海 南 Hainan	6	746	1215	0	1215	3118	307	299
重 庆 Chongqing	14	8890	7859	125	7734	28997	2724	2124
四 川 Sichuan	44	22878	21352	637	20715	76776	8979	7870
贵 州 Guizhou	22	6731	11008	964	10044	28064	2736	2678
云 南 Yunnan	24	5663	5808	501	5307	22223	3214	3101
西 藏 Tibet	0	0	0	0	0	0	0	0
陕 西 Shaanxi	29	10193	14999	2907	12092	45919	5804	4872
甘 肃 Gansu	27	6178	7868	1391	6477	23240	4469	4323
青 海 Qinghai	8	581	787	55	732	2285	749	746
宁 夏 Ningxia	5	610	802	45	757	2564	748	690
新 疆 Xinjiang	21	5688	8532	1488	7044	25157	3532	3314

校基本情况

Secondary Industrial Schools

单位: 人

教职工数 Teachers, Staff & Workers										兼任教师数(不在教工数中) Part-time Teachers
校本部教职工 Employees in the School Proper								校办厂、场职工 Employees in School-run Factories & Farms	附设机构人员 Employees in Subsidiary Units	
专任教师 Full-time Teachers					教辅人员 Supporting Staff	行政人员 Adm. Personnel	工勤人员 Workers			
计 Subtotal	高级讲师 Senior Lecturers	讲师 Lecturers	助理讲师 Assistant Lecturers	教员 Instructors						
82194	15506	37188	26597	2903	15712	30387	26093	9339	3733	5017
2252	415	1030	732	75	515	1018	758	337	179	126
1960	493	941	477	49	390	848	746	137	81	39
4024	811	1837	1229	147	690	1326	1514	552	288	53
2288	450	1132	671	35	463	863	802	127	54	15
2083	346	1055	642	40	514	878	747	65	57	47
4753	1217	2298	1179	59	1044	1667	1798	570	320	103
1823	575	819	414	15	367	662	599	159	51	8
1899	668	766	431	34	495	674	833	299	65	230
3029	456	1560	888	125	691	1428	1519	912	283	247
6513	970	2652	2401	490	1001	1801	1723	662	110	1646
1895	267	966	573	89	363	700	569	142	34	217
3366	657	1446	1094	169	524	1225	1018	252	61	180
1909	316	858	665	70	335	671	607	243	56	56
1805	339	832	591	43	410	777	397	167	206	161
7041	1395	2706	2699	241	1047	2392	1582	633	317	280
4687	772	1886	1809	220	678	1410	1324	396	108	136
5373	1074	2634	1478	187	1124	2264	1469	417	271	117
3892	792	1688	1253	159	752	1267	1220	562	204	379
4046	496	1718	1639	193	728	1360	901	140	93	217
2339	395	1193	682	69	462	745	697	192	25	109
151	12	57	77	5	11	92	45	8	0	42
1078	208	532	305	33	288	423	335	505	95	89
3858	749	1737	1266	106	862	1797	1353	810	299	167
1495	191	734	549	21	250	621	312	33	25	89
1666	194	865	553	54	288	620	527	75	38	31
0	0	0	0	0	0	0	0	0	0	0
2433	595	1069	723	46	578	1083	778	643	289	186
2063	304	991	720	48	408	827	1025	101	45	11
410	32	149	206	23	80	143	113	0	3	0
361	70	188	91	12	59	131	139	44	14	0
1702	247	849	560	46	295	674	643	156	62	36

中等农业学

Basic Statistics of

地区 Region		学校数(所) Schools	毕业生数 Graduates	招生数 Entrants 计 Total	招高中毕业生数 Graduates From Senior Sec. School	招初中毕业生数 Graduates From Junior Sec. School	在校学生数 Enrolment	合计 Total	计 Subtotal
总计	Total	335	133848	157890	6608	151282	496859	49727	46443
北京	Beijing	1	875	1204	0	1204	3456	336	301
天津	Tianjin	3	687	633	0	633	3781	292	292
河北	Hebei	21	7981	10856	447	10409	36830	3010	2955
山西	Shanxi	14	3600	4739	322	4417	16304	1988	1895
内蒙古	Inner Mongolia	12	2768	5556	335	5221	12590	1888	1690
辽宁	Liaoning	11	2822	3877	0	3877	13693	2128	1966
吉林	Jilin	9	5615	3642	12	3630	18270	1857	1805
黑龙江	Heilongjiang	10	6148	8160	280	7880	19436	2492	1998
上海	Shanghai	3	1675	2027	0	2027	7348	467	441
江苏	Jiangsu	9	5790	6253	546	5707	19887	1839	1682
浙江	Zhejiang	11	5153	5079	114	4965	16646	1110	1072
安徽	Anhui	13	3992	7926	450	7476	18551	1369	1324
福建	Fujian	12	3867	8098	0	8098	20346	1357	1352
江西	Jiangxi	12	4460	5771	58	5713	15735	1661	1445
山东	Shandong	17	8545	13269	76	13193	33868	3548	3215
河南	Henan	6	4427	6096	1215	4881	17551	1238	1212
湖北	Hubei	12	11658	4213	494	3719	22746	2065	1873
湖南	Hunan	22	11101	11602	0	11602	41650	3738	3516
广东	Guangdong	13	5534	6078	0	6078	17839	1484	1452
广西	Guangxi	9	3773	4447	0	4447	17389	1187	1117
海南	Hainan	6	1710	2071	15	2056	5825	666	656
重庆	Chongqing	7	4207	3396	120	3276	13524	1021	992
四川	Sichuan	16	7579	6750	52	6698	26726	2109	2037
贵州	Guizhou	15	4232	5318	30	5288	15183	1760	1704
云南	Yunnan	19	4288	5424	95	5329	17381	2034	1992
西藏	Tibet	1	108	237	0	237	746	114	104
陕西	Shaanxi	12	3686	4969	757	4212	16217	2073	1646
甘肃	Gansu	13	2295	3106	257	2849	9390	1616	1526
青海	Qinghai	2	485	664	162	502	1651	312	291
宁夏	Ningxia	3	612	1012	197	815	2910	509	480
新疆	Xinjiang	21	4175	5417	574	4843	13390	2459	2412

校基本情况

Secondary Agricultural Schools

单位：人

教职工数 Teachers, Staff & Workers										兼任教师数（不在教工数中） Part-time Teachers
校本部教职工 Employees in the School Proper								校办厂、场职工 Employees in School-run Factories & Farms	附设机构人员 Employees in Subsidiary Units	
专任教师 Full-time Teachers					教辅人员 Supporting Staff	行政人员 Adm. Personnel	工勤人员 Workers			
计 Subtotal	高级讲师 Senior Lecturers	讲师 Lecturers	助理讲师 Assistant Lecturers	教员 Instructors						
24558	4045	10435	9200	878	5051	7764	9070	2665	619	791
128	43	44	33	8	65	43	65	35	0	11
133	28	66	32	7	31	73	55	0	0	26
1622	240	662	656	64	322	431	580	39	16	0
958	142	393	383	40	207	406	324	84	9	17
919	134	426	309	50	217	212	342	121	77	32
998	282	435	257	24	213	381	374	129	33	17
878	209	359	304	6	190	296	441	52	0	5
850	253	346	240	11	210	368	570	381	113	8
210	28	105	70	7	44	64	123	26	0	20
882	149	338	364	31	223	265	312	147	10	0
608	76	255	243	34	141	161	162	24	14	60
700	101	317	265	17	133	217	274	37	8	5
789	63	307	392	27	140	231	192	5	0	110
748	121	324	284	19	209	186	302	210	6	14
1872	438	743	634	57	339	517	487	237	96	23
692	141	272	250	29	142	136	242	22	4	109
985	175	434	367	9	248	273	367	146	46	42
1875	348	817	640	70	406	612	623	190	32	160
791	67	287	398	39	137	235	289	28	4	54
578	72	324	173	9	116	178	245	58	12	0
359	41	122	169	27	47	119	131	3	7	9
574	124	257	186	7	122	156	140	29	0	0
1050	209	502	329	10	266	378	343	63	9	20
914	80	348	477	9	140	353	297	45	11	2
1138	118	518	467	35	119	319	416	15	27	1
66	0	22	44	0	5	11	22	10	0	0
797	110	363	259	65	172	284	393	412	15	10
767	74	337	338	18	177	223	359	60	30	36
154	10	71	64	9	36	60	41	0	21	0
256	47	121	68	20	49	84	91	15	14	0
1267	122	520	505	120	185	492	468	42	5	0

中等林业学

Basic Statistics of

地区 Region	学校数(所) Schools	毕业生数 Graduates	招生数 Entrants 计 Total	招高中毕业生数 Graduates From Senior Sec. School	招初中毕业生数 Graduates From Junior Sec. School	在校学生数 Enrolments	合计 Total	计 Subtotal
总计 Total	52	17804	25648	1752	23896	78012	8682	8209
北京 Beijing	1	173	183	0	183	622	95	95
天津 Tianjin	1	295	481	0	481	1885	170	170
河北 Hebei	1	251	410	0	410	1310	186	179
山西 Shanxi	1	427	555	0	555	1950	197	168
内蒙古 Inner Mongolia	2	273	445	0	445	1529	285	283
辽宁 Liaoning	1	334	548	0	548	1447	243	239
吉林 Jilin	3	951	805	68	737	3788	604	597
黑龙江 Heilongjiang	6	2277	4161	0	4161	9807	1363	1336
上海 Shanghai	1	132	309	0	309	788	101	101
江苏 Jiangsu	1	361	474	0	474	1519	251	233
浙江 Zhejiang	2	1152	1566	148	1418	3975	282	278
安徽 Anhui	2	496	1107	50	1057	2571	225	223
福建 Fujian	2	482	1148	0	1148	4044	305	272
江西 Jiangxi	2	1111	1114	132	982	3711	355	329
山东 Shandong	1	423	625	0	625	1757	341	307
河南 Henan	3	827	1437	26	1411	4683	431	419
湖北 Hubei	4	2742	2445	767	1678	7505	646	563
湖南 Hunan	1	621	977	158	819	2691	211	211
广东 Guangdong	2	411	621	0	621	1741	217	198
广西 Guangxi	3	955	1348	0	1348	5310	446	340
海南 Hainan	0	0	0	0	0	0	0	0
重庆 Chongqing	0	0	0	0	0	0	0	0
四川 Sichuan	1	598	1131	30	1101	3733	343	287
贵州 Guizhou	2	416	656	0	656	2138	288	288
云南 Yunnan	2	517	504	86	418	2270	261	261
西藏 Tibet	0	0	0	0	0	0	0	0
陕西 Shaanxi	3	1042	1173	127	1046	3729	264	262
甘肃 Gansu	2	332	855	0	855	2165	274	272
青海 Qinghai	0	0	0	0	0	0	0	0
宁夏 Ningxia	1	80	160	0	160	490	82	82
新疆 Xinjiang	1	125	410	160	250	854	216	216

校基本情况

Secondary Forestry Schools

单位:人

教职工数 Teachers, Staff & Workers										兼任教师数(不在教工数中) Part-time Teachers
校本部教职工 Employees in the School Proper								校办厂、场职工 Employees in School-run Factories & Farms	附设机构人员 Employees in Subsidiary Units	
专任教师 Full-time Teachers					教辅人员 Supporting Staff	行政人员 Adm. Personnel	工勤人员 Workers			
计 Subtotal	高级讲师 Senior Lecturers	讲师 Lecturers	助理讲师 Assistant Lecturers	教员 Instructors						
4180	916	1882	1304	78	848	1487	1694	330	143	85
36	4	23	8	1	12	24	23	0	0	0
85	15	47	23	0	6	32	47	0	0	0
100	12	45	42	1	20	34	25	7	0	7
82	16	30	36	0	17	37	32	29	0	0
152	20	63	69	0	25	79	27	2	0	0
117	26	50	40	1	43	30	49	0	4	0
296	103	139	51	3	69	110	122	2	5	0
574	195	250	125	4	91	266	405	23	4	0
35	5	15	15	0	17	20	29	0	0	0
103	35	40	22	6	22	68	40	0	18	0
178	25	95	50	8	27	25	48	0	4	24
124	23	60	41	0	22	35	42	0	2	0
161	34	86	37	4	21	52	38	31	2	28
199	38	73	86	2	43	26	61	23	3	0
110	35	57	18	0	38	76	83	34	0	1
260	67	95	79	19	21	38	100	5	7	0
350	59	157	128	6	78	68	67	60	23	21
108	37	55	16	0	31	30	42	0	0	0
95	19	57	19	0	23	46	34	0	19	4
206	31	109	64	2	37	62	35	54	52	0
0	0	0	0	0	0	0	0	0	0	0
0	0	0	0	0	0	0	0	0	0	0
125	32	61	32	0	30	79	53	56	0	0
163	7	69	83	4	22	67	36	0	0	0
131	21	59	51	0	26	57	47	0	0	0
0	0	0	0	0	0	0	0	0	0	0
125	15	43	67	0	38	32	67	2	0	0
139	22	51	59	7	39	31	63	2	0	0
0	0	0	0	0	0	0	0	0	0	0
38	8	23	4	3	8	12	24	0	0	0
88	12	30	39	7	22	51	55	0	0	0

中等医药学

Basic Statistics of

地区 Region	学校数(所) Schools	毕业生数 Graduates	招生数 Entrants 计 Total	招高中毕业生数 Graduates From Senior Sec. School	招初中毕业生数 Graduates From Junior Sec. School	在校学生数 Enrolments	合计 Total	计 Subtotal
总计 Total	525	137255	175854	4853	171001	534161	67752	60799
北京 Beijing	36	2985	1858	0	1858	9203	1764	1735
天津 Tianjin	8	1851	1164	0	1164	5577	633	631
河北 Hebei	20	6858	11884	40	11844	33120	2717	2631
山西 Shanxi	15	4456	6705	0	6705	18724	2444	2209
内蒙古 Inner Mongolia	16	1609	4079	406	3673	8293	1950	1893
辽宁 Liaoning	21	3113	3189	34	3155	11129	2678	2666
吉林 Jilin	10	1752	3920	45	3875	12422	1549	1215
黑龙江 Heilongjiang	16	4703	6087	0	6087	16579	2204	1965
上海 Shanghai	20	2046	1958	0	1958	7520	1538	1530
江苏 Jiangsu	19	6118	6307	0	6307	21267	2371	2342
浙江 Zhejiang	17	4178	5192	0	5192	16484	2088	2003
安徽 Anhui	21	4203	8004	390	7614	19479	2485	2168
福建 Fujian	15	3192	4010	0	4010	11775	1531	1429
江西 Jiangxi	13	5596	8554	35	8519	22066	1713	1692
山东 Shandong	29	11311	11962	492	11470	38343	4472	4240
河南 Henan	22	9812	11521	789	10732	37470	5688	4102
湖北 Hubei	26	13165	12211	937	11274	47877	3936	3676
湖南 Hunan	14	7211	8703	0	8703	27076	2854	2489
广东 Guangdong	37	10361	11228	0	11228	36117	3485	3283
广西 Guangxi	18	3342	6422	0	6422	16271	3613	2213
海南 Hainan	4	931	1529	100	1429	3944	413	384
重庆 Chongqing	10	3110	4358	0	4358	13063	1795	1364
四川 Sichuan	28	8148	14073	268	13805	38623	3737	3417
贵州 Guizhou	14	3237	5397	70	5327	12947	1559	1425
云南 Yunnan	17	4455	3443	246	3197	13104	1828	1736
西藏 Tibet	2	110	218	0	218	637	185	185
陕西 Shaanxi	14	4505	5561	311	5250	16762	2441	2169
甘肃 Gansu	14	1688	1960	220	1740	6274	1540	1510
青海 Qinghai	7	603	364	0	364	1228	474	472
宁夏 Ningxia	3	438	573	0	573	1760	397	397
新疆 Xinjiang	19	2168	3420	470	2950	9027	1670	1628

校基本情况

Secondary Health Schools

单位:人

教职工数 Teachers, Staff & Workers										兼任教师数(不在教工数中) Part-time Teachers
校本部教职工 Employees in the School Proper								校办厂、场职工 Employees in School-run Factories & Farms	附设机构人员 Employees in Subsidiary Units	
专任教师 Full-time Teachers					教辅人员 Supporting Staff	行政人员 Adm. Personnel	工勤人员 Workers			
计 Subtotal	高级讲师 Senior Lecturers	讲师 Lecturers	助理讲师 Assistant Lecturers	教员 Instructors						
31793	7136	14681	9283	693	7626	11432	9948	1846	5107	1690
835	138	393	301	3	228	357	315	26	3	151
367	67	183	115	2	81	103	80	0	2	0
1276	243	557	430	46	322	542	491	66	20	211
1203	258	511	376	58	261	397	348	42	193	0
982	148	501	308	25	307	345	259	21	36	47
1290	354	592	318	26	439	552	385	12	0	91
638	140	279	214	5	150	248	179	294	40	37
932	309	414	198	11	259	411	363	3	236	0
721	135	459	122	5	181	276	352	8	0	38
1118	261	487	349	21	285	456	483	21	8	109
1034	239	536	235	24	255	365	349	2	83	0
1241	361	545	323	12	227	390	310	86	231	3
759	153	308	272	26	219	230	221	0	102	89
986	256	454	275	1	188	247	271	0	21	75
2318	618	985	690	25	426	952	544	72	160	59
2036	530	855	601	50	572	798	696	780	806	54
1939	467	907	520	45	500	641	596	0	260	123
1308	441	551	283	33	326	501	354	114	251	148
1891	335	851	661	44	375	553	464	5	197	158
1216	240	643	321	12	227	338	432	88	1312	14
193	41	83	63	6	59	61	71	2	27	16
725	190	334	185	16	188	252	199	47	384	0
1798	401	937	428	32	433	683	503	80	240	113
771	124	380	256	11	151	341	162	20	114	100
971	162	517	268	24	152	271	342	0	92	0
100	4	40	56	0	7	42	36	0	0	0
1079	243	444	350	42	352	386	352	56	216	23
844	107	369	344	24	152	224	290	0	30	0
264	20	100	133	11	19	68	121	0	2	0
185	43	98	43	1	65	72	75	0	0	10
773	108	368	245	52	220	330	305	1	41	21

中等财经学

Basic Statistics of Secondary

地 区 Region	学校数(所) Schools	毕业生数 Graduates	招生数 Entrants			在校学生数 Enrolments		
			计 Total	招高中毕业生数 Graduates From Senior Sec. School	招初中毕业生数 Graduates From Junior Sec. School		合计 Total	计 Subtotal
总 计 Total	573	200701	251834	18864	232970	756852	66465	64715
北 京 Beijing	8	2863	5484	0	5484	16785	1330	1272
天 津 Tianjin	8	2134	2453	69	2384	9667	1038	1015
河 北 Hebei	26	11216	12954	1592	11362	37291	4426	4002
山 西 Shanxi	22	6425	10071	942	9129	30454	2563	2533
内蒙古 Inner Mongolia	15	2943	8318	2450	5868	19148	1917	1914
辽 宁 Liaoning	18	4684	6752	0	6752	21233	1864	1835
吉 林 Jilin	13	4445	4449	324	4125	18934	1603	1587
黑龙江 Heilongjiang	16	5732	7749	150	7599	20146	1791	1766
上 海 Shanghai	10	5038	8281	0	8281	26223	1212	1167
江 苏 Jiangsu	32	13275	12658	57	12601	51321	3571	3528
浙 江 Zhejiang	26	7970	11046	96	10950	31832	2638	2418
安 徽 Anhui	20	7069	14758	1349	13409	32629	2336	2303
福 建 Fujian	18	4453	8234	0	8234	21835	1562	1554
江 西 Jiangxi	14	4908	7902	313	7589	18049	1732	1500
山 东 Shandong	37	20335	22138	2764	19374	58871	4978	4883
河 南 Henan	33	15396	15679	1900	13779	51448	4420	4411
湖 北 Hubei	34	16394	11463	401	11062	46334	4486	4425
湖 南 Hunan	25	9664	12783	235	12548	37552	3461	3312
广 东 Guangdong	37	12284	15537	0	15537	42377	2989	2956
广 西 Guangxi	20	5638	6729	50	6679	25284	2077	2069
海 南 Hainan	6	910	1543	124	1419	4135	371	361
重 庆 Chongqing	7	2521	3086	0	3086	11070	808	804
四 川 Sichuan	29	11684	11166	777	10389	38481	3479	3466
贵 州 Guizhou	19	4765	6753	1128	5625	17592	1851	1822
云 南 Yunnan	23	5955	7014	517	6497	21829	2415	2355
西 藏 Tibet	3	221	312	0	312	1112	225	221
陕 西 Shaanxi	16	4298	6626	1870	4756	19308	1705	1693
甘 肃 Gansu	15	2083	2614	390	2224	6550	1186	1138
青 海 Qinghai	3	540	831	435	396	1930	355	355
宁 夏 Ningxia	4	495	898	235	663	2109	387	387
新 疆 Xinjiang	16	4363	5553	696	4857	15323	1689	1663

校基本情况

Finance & Economics Schools

单位:人

教职工数 Teachers, Staff & Workers										兼任教师数(不在教工数中) Part-time Teachers
校本部教职工 Employees in the School Proper								校办厂、场职工 Employees in School-run Factories & Farms	附设机构人员 Employees in Subsidiary Units	
专任教师 Full-time Teachers					教辅人员 Supporting Staff	行政人员 Adm. Personnel	工勤人员 Workers			
计 Subtotal	高级讲师 Senior Lecturers	讲师 Lecturers	助理讲师 Assistant Lecturers	教员 Instructors						
34874	6177	16212	11403	1082	5103	14497	10241	1082	668	1370
587	75	281	216	15	112	313	260	7	51	17
527	127	249	139	12	59	218	211	8	15	0
2077	407	968	629	73	318	865	742	197	227	15
1321	208	596	470	47	219	542	451	25	5	25
1059	155	559	316	29	178	365	312	0	3	0
991	267	475	236	13	111	438	295	16	13	0
803	174	382	234	13	151	388	245	12	4	0
831	274	386	168	3	129	430	376	14	11	139
529	98	290	123	18	140	221	277	45	0	14
1894	304	822	666	102	258	832	544	39	4	131
1279	177	661	387	54	234	437	468	186	34	115
1342	289	526	463	64	131	496	334	22	11	10
947	93	411	418	25	89	310	208	4	4	17
810	117	368	303	22	120	336	234	217	15	23
2663	534	1122	908	99	410	1179	631	43	52	101
2650	506	1150	922	72	399	828	534	0	9	62
2378	565	1142	582	89	332	1133	582	14	47	129
1824	350	874	521	79	292	736	460	101	48	140
1654	200	743	670	41	217	674	411	22	11	121
1154	207	551	389	7	166	401	348	8	0	27
199	18	76	103	2	19	89	54	0	10	40
439	68	183	177	11	36	160	169	4	0	33
1767	323	804	585	55	285	848	566	1	12	60
1016	111	464	417	24	113	485	208	2	27	0
1231	137	665	395	34	190	504	430	45	15	64
108	1	52	52	3	15	42	56	4	0	0
888	168	474	229	17	160	429	216	0	12	82
633	64	343	225	1	75	241	189	26	22	0
209	24	98	87	0	17	67	62	0	0	0
210	40	105	47	18	18	116	43	0	0	5
854	96	392	326	40	110	374	325	20	6	0

中等政法学

Basic Statistics of Secondary

地　区 Region	学校数(所) Schools	毕业生数 Graduates	招生数 Entrants			在校学生数 Enrolments		
			计 Total	招高中毕业生数 Graduates From Senior Sec. School	招初中毕业生数 Graduates From Junior Sec. School		合　计 Total	计 Subtotal
总　计　Total	142	41098	49979	24812	25167	115064	14869	14757
北　京　Beijing	4	852	801	151	650	4001	301	301
天　津　Tianjin	3	924	922	38	884	2755	456	442
河　北　Hebei	8	2517	2924	986	1938	7683	1108	1101
山　西　Shanxi	5	1566	4522	1200	3322	9287	810	805
内蒙古　Inner Mongolia	6	953	2043	1467	576	3301	611	611
辽　宁　Liaoning	6	853	0	0	0	172	423	423
吉　林　Jilin	4	822	1026	1026	0	2023	486	486
黑龙江　Heilongjiang	5	1181	1726	1326	400	2897	685	685
上　海　Shanghai	3	489	19	0	19	226	164	164
江　苏　Jiangsu	4	1424	611	160	451	2282	454	449
浙　江　Zhejiang	7	1603	733	384	349	3118	547	539
安　徽　Anhui	4	1725	2448	1677	771	4883	479	469
福　建　Fujian	4	959	813	265	548	2355	363	360
江　西　Jiangxi	5	1204	2348	1424	924	3543	356	356
山　东　Shandong	8	3083	2952	2081	871	6091	999	989
河　南　Henan	7	2960	3059	2009	1050	6240	715	715
湖　北　Hubei	9	3753	5968	1435	4533	12952	694	663
湖　南　Hunan	3	1281	2034	258	1776	7839	243	243
广　东　Guangdong	11	3407	2990	1320	1670	7493	848	848
广　西　Guangxi	4	1858	1330	1330	0	3245	574	569
海　南　Hainan	2	359	364	110	254	1123	167	167
重　庆　Chongqing	1	409	409	409	0	859	126	126
四　川　Sichuan	4	1738	2658	2051	607	5075	581	581
贵　州　Guizhou	4	702	511	100	411	1310	513	513
云　南　Yunnan	5	1089	1322	1142	180	3257	384	384
西　藏　Tibet	1	81	52	52	0	317	80	80
陕　西　Shaanxi	4	1433	2158	1062	1096	4048	371	367
甘　肃　Gansu	2	482	713	460	253	1342	215	215
青　海　Qinghai	2	278	280	80	200	758	216	216
宁　夏　Ningxia	2	287	510	191	319	1278	165	165
新　疆　Xinjiang	5	826	1733	618	1115	3311	735	725

校基本情况

Politics & Law Schools

单位:人

教职工数 Teachers, Staff & Workers										兼任教师数(不在教工数中) Part-time Teachers
校本部教职工 Employees in the School Proper								校办厂、场职工 Employees in School-run Factories & Farms	附设机构人员 Employees in Subsidiary Units	
专任教师 Full-time Teachers					教辅人员 Supporting Staff	行政人员 Adm. Personnel	工勤人员 Workers			
计 Subtotal	高级讲师 Senior Lecturers	讲师 Lecturers	助理讲师 Assistant Lecturers	教员 Instructors						
6752	1018	2871	2495	368	1258	4738	2009	32	80	113
122	25	52	45	0	27	105	47	0	0	0
196	42	86	63	5	37	170	39	14	0	0
485	76	212	157	40	115	296	205	0	7	0
296	57	107	98	34	73	272	164	3	2	0
307	46	157	77	27	47	223	34	0	0	0
186	38	80	51	17	34	182	21	0	0	0
225	63	91	57	14	26	197	38	0	0	0
268	63	120	82	3	100	191	126	0	0	20
50	10	19	21	0	23	55	36	0	0	0
188	17	59	111	1	30	144	87	0	5	0
220	29	88	84	19	21	229	69	1	7	0
205	32	86	84	3	50	143	71	10	0	0
188	18	74	84	12	33	108	31	0	3	0
174	14	88	72	0	14	117	51	0	0	5
432	82	161	155	34	59	376	122	4	6	0
366	62	154	145	5	99	180	70	0	0	0
371	60	164	133	14	43	205	44	0	31	48
118	7	33	49	29	10	51	64	0	0	1
396	41	174	172	9	71	259	122	0	0	5
263	37	161	60	5	66	156	84	0	5	16
102	11	31	55	5	3	37	25	0	0	0
63	7	34	3	19	27	32	4	0	0	4
278	69	110	91	8	76	180	47	0	0	0
222	9	95	106	12	38	165	88	0	0	13
206	17	109	72	8	16	116	46	0	0	0
44	0	14	30	0	3	26	7	0	0	1
161	26	71	61	3	22	142	42	0	4	0
96	5	47	44	0	10	88	21	0	0	0
114	8	50	56	0	15	71	16	0	0	0
96	13	43	40	0	5	36	28	0	0	0
314	34	101	137	42	65	186	160	0	10	0

中 等 体 育 学
Basic Statistics of Secondary

地 区 Region	学校数(所) Schools	毕业生数 Graduates	招生数 Entrants 计 Total	招高中毕业生数 Graduates From Senior Sec. School	招初中毕业生数 Graduates From Junior Sec. School	在校学生数 Enrolments	合计 Total	计 Subtotal
总 计 **Total**	181	22063	28145	111	28034	81936	15059	14551
北 京 Beijing	7	263	625	44	581	1601	616	616
天 津 Tianjin	5	269	369	0	369	1091	289	289
河 北 Hebei	10	1137	1322	0	1322	4085	839	835
山 西 Shanxi	7	760	1020	0	1020	3704	943	933
内蒙古 Inner Mongolia	1	717	925	0	925	2701	88	88
辽 宁 Liaoning	14	1408	1643	0	1643	4671	1124	1109
吉 林 Jilin	6	642	850	0	850	2280	523	511
黑龙江 Heilongjiang	3	813	822	0	822	2470	421	335
上 海 Shanghai	3	68	280	36	244	640	500	391
江 苏 Jiangsu	12	1070	1015	0	1015	3205	701	679
浙 江 Zhejiang	5	302	426	0	426	1185	416	416
安 徽 Anhui	3	544	2043	0	2043	4056	335	313
福 建 Fujian	3	336	381	0	381	1268	108	108
江 西 Jiangxi	3	688	941	0	941	2369	264	264
山 东 Shandong	16	1882	2208	0	2208	7431	1493	1489
河 南 Henan	8	1707	2898	0	2898	7371	693	692
湖 北 Hubei	10	3093	2411	12	2399	9071	910	792
湖 南 Hunan	5	463	863	0	863	2415	395	391
广 东 Guangdong	17	1526	1746	0	1746	4942	1105	1065
广 西 Guangxi	1	244	273	0	273	777	176	176
海 南 Hainan	1	69	61	0	61	181	149	115
重 庆 Chongqing	1	153	154	0	154	623	97	93
四 川 Sichuan	3	291	441	19	422	1116	129	129
贵 州 Guizhou	2	690	1002	0	1002	2255	335	335
云 南 Yunnan	7	826	981	0	981	2819	655	642
西 藏 Tibet	1	24	38	0	38	85	57	57
陕 西 Shaanxi	9	1114	1155	0	1155	3634	537	537
甘 肃 Gansu	10	446	510	0	510	1542	584	574
青 海 Qinghai	1	39	40	0	40	120	47	47
宁 夏 Ningxia	1	59	51	0	51	171	56	56
新 疆 Xinjiang	6	420	651	0	651	2057	474	474

校基本情况
Physical Culture Schools

单位:人

教职工数 Teachers, Staff & Workers										兼任教师数(不在教工数中) Part-time Teachers
校本部教职工 Employees in the School Proper								校办厂、场职工 Employees in School-run Factories & Farms	附设机构人员 Employees in Subsidiary Units	
专任教师 Full-time Teachers					教辅人员 Supporting Staff	行政人员 Adm. Personnel	工勤人员 Workers			
计 Subtotal	高级讲师 Senior Lecturers	讲师 Lecturers	助理讲师 Assistant Lecturers	教员 Instructors						
8074	1357	3864	2575	278	891	3044	2542	31	477	153
234	39	126	69	0	13	169	200	0	0	8
163	26	71	62	4	12	68	46	0	0	0
459	83	214	151	11	42	161	173	4	0	0
561	37	232	246	46	67	176	129	10	0	0
57	12	25	20	0	3	16	12	0	0	0
604	138	276	163	27	58	236	211	2	13	0
287	69	149	67	2	12	127	85	0	12	0
155	55	79	21	0	58	66	56	0	86	0
183	39	97	42	5	10	84	114	0	109	3
419	81	190	132	16	63	151	46	0	22	17
182	31	94	56	1	103	71	60	0	0	0
192	37	89	62	4	7	59	55	0	22	20
86	15	47	24	0	0	21	1	0	0	7
138	22	79	34	3	16	70	40	0	0	0
901	211	350	284	56	50	301	237	3	1	0
402	56	179	154	13	36	139	115	1	0	0
482	100	230	136	16	65	115	130	6	112	0
236	39	126	64	7	10	75	70	0	4	45
549	75	249	209	16	90	228	198	0	40	10
76	21	35	20	0	26	36	38	0	0	0
24	1	4	19	0	0	71	20	0	34	0
48	6	32	10	0	1	34	10	4	0	0
71	9	34	28	0	0	52	6	0	0	25
218	32	130	50	6	7	81	29	0	0	13
328	32	196	84	16	67	102	145	0	13	5
33	1	15	17	0	0	14	10	0	0	0
306	21	166	109	10	18	109	104	0	0	0
341	35	177	128	1	20	90	123	1	9	0
27	3	22	2	0	0	14	6	0	0	0
36	3	21	9	3	0	12	8	0	0	0
276	28	130	103	15	37	96	65	0	0	0

中等艺术学

Basic Statistics of

地区 Region	学校数(所) Schools	毕业生数 Graduates	招生数 Entrants			在校学生数 Enrolments		
			计 Total	招高中毕业生数 Graduates From Senior Sec. School	招初中毕业生数 Graduates From Junior Sec. School		合计 Total	计 Subtotal
总计 Total	168	24822	37182	1207	35975	118270	17103	16786
北京 Beijing	6	654	1045	0	1045	3810	1034	974
天津 Tianjin	4	403	489	15	474	1631	395	395
河北 Hebei	6	723	1447	74	1373	3956	736	736
山西 Shanxi	11	944	1808	18	1790	7153	1131	1131
内蒙古 Inner Mongolia	4	607	1177	308	869	3719	650	650
辽宁 Liaoning	12	1124	2632	0	2632	7526	1477	1472
吉林 Jilin	2	859	1793	0	1793	5332	257	257
黑龙江 Heilongjiang	2	453	830	0	830	2201	365	337
上海 Shanghai	6	362	720	0	720	2612	696	664
江苏 Jiangsu	12	1956	2658	0	2658	8533	868	825
浙江 Zhejiang	6	698	1176	0	1176	3178	455	451
安徽 Anhui	4	1031	1253	160	1093	3179	492	471
福建 Fujian	6	431	1041	0	1041	2857	649	629
江西 Jiangxi	3	1013	1223	0	1223	3492	461	461
山东 Shandong	10	2403	2778	19	2759	9413	1305	1251
河南 Henan	15	3201	4531	33	4498	14149	1467	1467
湖北 Hubei	15	2194	1741	164	1577	7235	1005	1005
湖南 Hunan	5	1057	1747	106	1641	4914	412	404
广东 Guangdong	13	1346	1652	173	1479	5765	992	952
广西 Guangxi	3	698	975	0	975	3255	300	300
海南 Hainan	1	60	109	0	109	486	118	118
重庆 Chongqing	3	136	345	0	345	915	193	191
四川 Sichuan	4	527	1219	77	1142	4119	476	476
贵州 Guizhou	2	308	368	0	368	1444	26	26
云南 Yunnan	2	334	392	0	392	1071	211	211
西藏 Tibet	1	16	23	0	23	103	75	75
陕西 Shaanxi	4	775	1003	0	1003	3062	344	344
甘肃 Gansu	2	63	249	0	249	767	145	145
青海 Qinghai	1	0	34	0	34	244	70	70
宁夏 Ningxia	1	81	120	17	103	339	97	97
新疆 Xinjiang	2	365	604	43	561	1810	201	201

校基本情况

Secondary Art Schools

单位:人

教职工数 Teachers, Staff & Workers										兼任教师数(不在教工数中) Part-time Teachers
校本部教职工 Employees in the School Proper								校办厂、场职工 Employees in School-run Factories & Farms	附设机构人员 Employees in Subsidiary Units	
专任教师 Full-time Teachers					教辅人员 Supporting Staff	行政人员 Adm. Personnel	工勤人员 Workers			
计 Subtotal	高级讲师 Senior Lecturers	讲师 Lecturers	助理讲师 Assistant Lecturers	教员 Instructors						
11007	1948	4433	3919	707	1205	2698	1876	197	120	852
597	140	287	146	24	131	134	112	48	12	117
263	60	142	60	1	20	50	62	0	0	20
510	81	232	125	72	40	107	79	0	0	4
793	69	280	359	85	46	161	131	0	0	0
455	31	174	193	57	16	134	45	0	0	0
987	290	372	260	65	133	185	167	0	5	46
180	26	100	54	0	36	12	29	0	0	0
200	42	90	55	13	37	67	33	28	0	0
357	63	174	96	24	57	108	142	2	30	104
554	92	246	184	32	55	129	87	40	3	111
302	47	122	104	29	25	82	42	0	4	19
290	75	121	91	3	61	94	26	21	0	0
473	72	183	185	33	34	71	51	20	0	84
356	26	130	171	29	19	39	47	0	0	0
818	156	318	327	17	85	211	137	15	39	0
964	137	342	400	85	77	234	192	0	0	20
626	173	247	190	16	115	196	68	0	0	11
254	50	55	134	15	15	92	43	0	8	64
596	70	236	254	36	48	199	109	21	19	55
214	59	93	52	10	14	39	33	0	0	50
70	6	37	21	6	3	27	18	0	0	0
119	37	26	52	4	4	43	25	2	0	40
261	70	103	86	2	62	92	61	0	0	89
26	4	14	7	1	0	0	0	0	0	7
127	17	65	42	3	26	32	26	0	0	11
57	4	19	34	0	3	13	2	0	0	0
205	26	86	82	11	27	81	31	0	0	0
96	7	45	44	0	12	23	14	0	0	0
48	5	19	24	0	2	8	12	0	0	0
65	7	28	12	18	2	13	17	0	0	0
144	6	47	75	16	0	22	35	0	0	0

其他中等技术

Basic Statistics of Other

地区 Region		学校数(所) Schools	毕业生数 Graduates	招生数 Entrants			在校学生数 Enrolments	
				计 Total	招高中毕业生数 Graduates From Senior Sec. School	招初中毕业生数 Graduates From Junior Sec. School	合计 Total	计 Subtotal
总计	**Total**	149	52625	60181	4930	55251	182469	14330	14019
北京	Beijing	1	264	418	0	418	1722	75	75
天津	Tianjin	17	2220	3649	0	3649	13999	1559	1549
河北	Hebei	6	1815	1884	0	1884	6810	605	582
山西	Shanxi	4	239	844	214	630	1718	250	250
内蒙古	Inner Mongolia	2	294	647	462	185	1056	130	130
辽宁	Liaoning	7	669	3340	0	3340	5552	529	524
吉林	Jilin	23	3979	3980	50	3930	17048	2639	2486
黑龙江	Heilongjiang	1	139	180	0	180	601	100	100
上海	Shanghai	1	706	777	0	777	2938	154	154
江苏	Jiangsu	4	597	613	0	613	1919	226	215
浙江	Zhejiang	13	4090	5920	0	5920	17713	846	841
安徽	Anhui	2	460	920	250	670	2068	115	115
福建	Fujian	1	100	551	0	551	898	32	32
江西	Jiangxi	1	557	1153	112	1041	2775	214	214
山东	Shandong	5	4763	5875	1252	4623	15145	826	826
河南	Henan	3	1397	2295	540	1755	5639	271	271
湖北	Hubei	9	9452	5407	373	5034	22212	879	794
湖南	Hunan	4	3219	3797	0	3797	11270	315	315
广东	Guangdong	8	2284	2563	0	2563	7999	707	707
广西	Guangxi	5	1367	1612	0	1612	5463	451	451
海南	Hainan	0	0	0	0	0	0	0	0
重庆	Chongqing	3	2069	2421	208	2213	6737	668	656
四川	Sichuan	9	3470	3474	150	3324	10536	931	924
贵州	Guizhou	3	3603	3154	30	3124	8245	532	532
云南	Yunnan	8	1725	1928	577	1351	5340	610	610
西藏	Tibet	1	80	43	0	43	178	67	67
陕西	Shaanxi	1	166	191	191	0	351	113	113
甘肃	Gansu	6	2802	2365	361	2004	6255	452	452
青海	Qinghai	0	0	0	0	0	0	0	0
宁夏	Ningxia	1	99	180	160	20	282	34	34
新疆	Xinjiang	0	0	0	0	0	0	0	0

学校基本情况

Secondary Technical Schools

单位:人

教职工数 Teachers, Staff & Workers										兼任教师数(不在教工数中) Part-time Teachers
校本部教职工 Employees in the School Proper								校办厂、场职工 Employees in School-run Factories & Farms	附设机构人员 Employees in Subsidiary Units	
专任教师 Full-time Teachers					教辅人员 Supporting Staff	行政人员 Adm. Personnel	工勤人员 Workers			
计 Subtotal	高级讲师 Senior Lecturers	讲师 Lecturers	助理讲师 Assistant Lecturers	教员 Instructors						
8346	1166	3303	3372	505	935	2825	1913	251	60	975
59	5	7	47	0	2	14	0	0	0	0
984	162	369	391	62	79	283	203	0	10	142
387	43	138	125	81	56	80	59	2	21	18
146	12	37	51	46	0	56	48	0	0	0
62	18	36	8	0	26	33	9	0	0	0
257	56	81	106	14	41	135	91	0	5	9
1481	150	561	685	85	228	584	193	137	16	10
53	14	20	19	0	8	27	12	0	0	0
70	1	37	27	5	24	13	47	0	0	11
117	26	49	42	0	14	65	19	4	7	0
543	40	212	233	58	39	130	129	4	1	515
54	21	20	13	0	6	34	21	0	0	0
18	1	10	7	0	4	6	4	0	0	30
100	23	35	42	0	3	56	55	0	0	0
613	124	222	223	44	18	79	116	0	0	0
155	17	61	76	1	20	51	45	0	0	0
535	118	238	170	9	30	159	70	85	0	50
173	26	73	68	6	14	50	78	0	0	5
410	52	176	164	18	68	160	69	0	0	19
253	12	110	127	4	32	79	87	0	0	12
0	0	0	0	0	0	0	0	0	0	0
336	56	126	154	0	47	124	149	12	0	0
550	94	270	181	5	56	215	103	7	0	74
320	30	145	141	4	23	145	44	0	0	0
320	30	150	132	8	22	128	140	0	0	56
33	0	12	21	0	3	19	12	0	0	0
45	0	0	0	45	20	21	27	0	0	5
254	33	102	109	10	49	75	74	0	0	0
0	0	0	0	0	0	0	0	0	0	0
18	2	6	10	0	3	4	9	0	0	19
0	0	0	0	0	0	0	0	0	0	0

中等师范学

Basic Statistics of

地　　区 Region	学校数(所) Schools	毕业生数 Graduates	招　生　数 Entrants			在校学生数 Enrolments		
			计 Total	招高中毕业生数 Graduates From Senior Sec. School	招初中毕业生数 Graduates From Junior Sec. School		合　计 Total	计 Subtotal
总　计 Total	815	308973	291245	25417	265828	905216	107191	104116
北　京 Beijing	18	3626	550	0	550	4112	2048	1996
天　津 Tianjin	10	2902	2637	0	2637	8995	1400	1325
河　北 Hebei	33	20816	19434	5093	14341	54986	6445	6354
山　西 Shanxi	23	9985	18506	1910	16596	39133	3529	3436
内蒙古 Inner Mongolia	21	4802	5878	147	5731	16817	2972	2927
辽　宁 Liaoning	12	7158	3523	0	3523	18872	1984	1914
吉　林 Jilin	23	9215	5319	520	4799	25306	3220	3077
黑龙江 Heilongjiang	29	9491	6348	0	6348	25250	3754	3656
上　海 Shanghai	2	523	457	0	457	2268	195	186
江　苏 Jiangsu	36	14155	12384	1934	10450	49476	5425	5000
浙　江 Zhejiang	29	11299	5379	0	5379	19955	2766	2592
安　徽 Anhui	41	10495	13016	5467	7549	37269	4156	4081
福　建 Fujian	26	10625	3573	22	3551	19266	3097	3015
江　西 Jiangxi	24	12251	13903	2974	10929	35259	3080	3049
山　东 Shandong	60	17978	15888	1703	14185	47770	8300	7936
河　南 Henan	43	34903	37702	0	37702	103023	7581	7432
湖　北 Hubei	29	20001	14402	1168	13234	56438	5597	5185
湖　南 Hunan	30	10530	11196	0	11196	39442	4132	3997
广　东 Guangdong	46	19486	13508	0	13508	51002	6039	5955
广　西 Guangxi	29	8833	11055	134	10921	31700	4238	4143
海　南 Hainan	8	3506	3362	250	3112	9587	1065	1029
重　庆 Chongqing	32	5581	5263	0	5263	16166	2682	2604
四　川 Sichuan	71	16947	17576	356	17220	51736	6677	6604
贵　州 Guizhou	26	8588	9957	35	9922	28997	2870	2857
云　南 Yunnan	28	10109	9554	0	9554	29925	3649	3632
西　藏 Tibet	5	787	741	0	741	2494	461	459
陕　西 Shaanxi	22	9599	12909	2093	10816	32707	2975	2899
甘　肃 Gansu	22	4370	4827	45	4782	15917	2483	2436
青　海 Qinghai	11	1726	1050	356	694	4384	849	849
宁　夏 Ningxia	4	1698	1697	121	1576	4467	568	547
新　疆 Xinjiang	22	6988	9651	1089	8562	22497	2954	2944

校基本情况

Teacher Training Schools

单位:人

教职工数 Teachers, Staff & Workers										兼任教师数(不在教工数中) Part-time Teachers
校本部教职工 Employees in the School Proper								校办厂、场职工 Employees in School-run Factories & Farms	附设机构人员 Employees in Subsidiary Units	
专任教师 Full-time Teachers					教辅人员 Supporting Staff	行政人员 Adm. Personnel	工勤人员 Workers			
计 Subtotal	高级讲师 Senior Lecturers	讲师 Lecturers	助理讲师 Assistant Lecturers	教员 Instructors						
61867	9467	25012	24331	3057	8437	17246	16566	2041	1034	275
930	215	384	297	34	255	416	395	27	25	0
721	119	301	250	51	113	290	201	32	43	0
3638	374	1395	1637	232	568	1076	1072	85	6	20
1920	274	744	772	130	222	660	634	64	29	10
1596	213	751	591	41	242	554	535	45	0	2
1103	259	509	286	49	134	379	298	50	20	0
1798	230	617	894	57	174	672	433	115	28	0
2025	578	975	435	37	214	805	612	77	21	22
90	13	44	30	3	7	56	33	9	0	0
2995	485	1128	1204	178	437	819	749	378	47	7
1524	205	737	509	73	247	437	384	93	81	35
2384	412	983	892	97	437	642	618	39	36	2
1832	227	698	854	53	163	575	445	33	49	0
1962	318	842	703	99	248	388	451	12	19	61
4543	693	1740	1871	239	884	1358	1151	271	93	0
4569	912	1822	1683	152	443	1331	1089	88	61	17
3575	587	1326	1395	267	437	441	732	240	172	0
2146	522	913	639	72	374	810	667	100	35	30
3925	379	1502	1817	227	535	730	765	39	45	28
2642	362	1202	969	109	321	469	711	14	81	0
638	88	225	275	50	81	99	211	36	0	0
1409	230	466	645	68	302	433	460	55	23	0
3711	607	1379	1552	173	645	1029	1219	66	7	12
1831	170	703	818	140	123	618	285	5	8	5
2160	239	1059	803	59	228	535	709	0	17	0
299	8	105	172	14	14	58	88	2	0	0
1775	313	755	603	104	194	478	452	14	62	16
1466	184	605	621	56	141	445	384	26	21	0
551	28	158	328	37	50	94	154	0	0	0
298	48	138	83	29	42	90	117	19	2	0
1811	175	806	703	127	162	459	512	7	3	8

中等师范学校中幼

Basic Statistics of Pre-primary

地区 Region	学校数(所) Schools	毕业生数 Graduates	招生数 Entrants 计 Total	招生数 Entrants 招高中毕业生数 Graduates From Senior Sec. School	招生数 Entrants 招初中毕业生数 Graduates From Junior Sec. School	在校学生数 Enrolments	合计 Total	计 Subtotal
总计 Total	61	18604	18900	268	18632	59823	7858	7312
北京 Beijing	1	214	94	0	94	493	135	135
天津 Tianjin	2	587	719	0	719	2100	398	355
河北 Hebei	4	805	1068	0	1068	3092	235	235
山西 Shanxi	4	930	2657	0	2657	6524	466	430
内蒙古 Inner Mongolia	2	487	630	0	630	1727	217	217
辽宁 Liaoning	2	540	280	0	280	1317	294	290
吉林 Jilin	5	1839	1352	0	1352	5446	843	807
黑龙江 Heilongjiang	3	872	780	0	780	2226	331	331
上海 Shanghai	0	163	102	0	102	960	80	75
江苏 Jiangsu	4	1026	562	0	562	2702	402	366
浙江 Zhejiang	3	862	617	0	617	2023	353	273
安徽 Anhui	3	663	958	258	700	2906	310	276
福建 Fujian	2	854	542	0	542	2002	305	267
江西 Jiangxi	1	209	240	0	240	810	89	89
山东 Shandong	4	1021	965	0	965	2925	663	570
河南 Henan	1	389	398	0	398	1260	161	161
湖北 Hubei	4	2185	1079	10	1069	4662	646	581
湖南 Hunan	2	749	831	0	831	2564	343	325
广东 Guangdong	4	1781	1522	0	1522	4902	513	508
广西 Guangxi	1	287	496	0	496	1142	165	144
海南 Hainan	0	0	0	0	0	0	0	0
重庆 Chongqing	2	670	964	0	964	2571	297	266
四川 Sichuan	1	214	524	0	524	957	100	100
贵州 Guizhou	1	188	202	0	202	628	71	70
云南 Yunnan	1	184	230	0	230	696	98	98
西藏 Tibet	0	0	0	0	0	0	0	0
陕西 Shaanxi	1	276	285	0	285	914	120	120
甘肃 Gansu	1	185	123	0	123	732	86	86
青海 Qinghai	1	59	0	0	0	124	19	19
宁夏 Ningxia	0	0	0	0	0	0	0	0
新疆 Xinjiang	1	365	680	0	680	1418	118	118

儿师范学校基本情况

Teacher Training Schools

单位:人

教职工数 Teachers, Staff & Workers										兼任教师数(不在教工数中) Part-time Teachers
校本部教职工 Employees in the School Proper								校办厂、场职工 Employees in School-run Factories & Farms	附设机构人员 Employees in Subsidiary Units	
专任教师 Full-time Teachers					教辅人员 Supporting Staff	行政人员 Adm. Personnel	工勤人员 Workers			
计 Subtotal	高级讲师 Senior Lecturers	讲师 Lecturers	助理讲师 Assistant Lecturers	教员 Instructors						
4296	767	1720	1597	212	555	1467	994	127	419	1
55	22	20	13	0	25	25	30	0	0	0
197	47	107	37	6	24	60	74	0	43	0
150	10	63	67	10	20	48	17	0	0	0
256	37	72	114	33	10	94	70	10	26	0
138	21	67	50	0	17	29	33	0	0	0
168	41	61	44	22	16	69	37	4	0	0
462	51	159	231	21	47	201	97	10	26	0
199	64	87	42	6	15	91	26	0	0	0
27	4	12	11	0	7	22	19	5	0	0
201	37	89	66	9	27	85	53	8	28	0
160	36	73	48	3	29	53	31	22	58	0
172	34	60	67	11	27	46	31	15	19	0
154	13	75	63	3	9	80	24	3	35	0
61	7	21	28	5	0	28	0	0	0	0
291	44	114	114	19	61	115	103	28	65	0
96	23	45	22	6	0	42	23	0	0	0
404	89	132	176	7	43	65	69	0	65	0
198	46	69	62	21	20	47	60	8	10	0
318	37	135	140	6	42	83	65	5	0	0
77	21	40	16	0	16	26	25	0	21	0
0	0	0	0	0	0	0	0	0	0	0
139	40	41	54	4	64	30	33	9	22	0
59	12	27	20	0	4	28	9	0	0	0
47	10	22	11	4	3	16	4	0	1	1
49	4	26	17	2	7	27	15	0	0	0
0	0	0	0	0	0	0	0	0	0	0
62	2	28	25	7	8	30	20	0	0	0
51	8	25	18	0	10	13	12	0	0	0
17	1	12	4	0	0	2	0	0	0	0
0	0	0	0	0	0	0	0	0	0	0
88	6	38	37	7	4	12	14	0	0	0

中等专业学校女学

Number of Female Students, Teachers, Staff

地区 Region	毕业生数 Graduates	招生数 Entrants			在校学生数 Enrolments		
		计 Total	招高中毕业生数 Graduates From Senior Sec. School	招初中毕业生数 Graduates From Junior Sec. School		合计 Total	计 Subtotal
总计 Total	731473	917006	48914	868092	2874488	227468	214546
北京 Beijing	15079	17670	440	17230	64501	6807	6481
天津 Tianjin	11243	12193	154	12039	47481	5072	4914
河北 Hebei	38365	49402	5208	44194	146674	13007	12517
山西 Shanxi	20540	36871	2565	34306	101453	8282	8018
内蒙古 Inner Mongolia	10378	21801	2786	19015	54165	6989	6845
辽宁 Liaoning	23890	25527	162	25365	97844	10248	9878
吉林 Jilin	22405	19701	1068	18633	84217	7874	7395
黑龙江 Heilongjiang	23009	26195	784	25411	76449	7946	7373
上海 Shanghai	13939	17304	12	17292	65086	5919	5420
江苏 Jiangsu	65080	66727	1549	65178	261052	11124	10453
浙江 Zhejiang	29931	32901	506	32395	103412	6700	6384
安徽 Anhui	20673	47868	5289	42579	111859	6786	6405
福建 Fujian	18394	27215	58	27157	78065	5284	5046
江西 Jiangxi	22448	35651	1869	33782	91569	5407	5032
山东 Shandong	57869	73944	4430	69514	205792	16226	15377
河南 Henan	52625	66183	3946	62237	202785	12809	11599
湖北 Hubei	61165	46272	3517	42755	185445	12691	11870
湖南 Hunan	32817	48044	389	47655	154804	9772	9018
广东 Guangdong	45274	49437	395	49042	158858	11511	11193
广西 Guangxi	19857	28622	475	28147	91348	7965	6836
海南 Hainan	4058	6163	229	5934	16507	1355	1275
重庆 Chongqing	11504	14798	311	14487	47230	4115	3549
四川 Sichuan	34157	43332	1589	41743	134774	10772	10146
贵州 Guizhou	13632	19524	812	18712	50260	5431	5286
云南 Yunnan	17708	18505	1212	17293	60308	6779	6617
西藏 Tibet	625	800	12	788	2842	523	518
陕西 Shaanxi	17859	28055	4461	23594	78364	6392	5713
甘肃 Gansu	9134	11566	1150	10416	33970	4626	4515
青海 Qinghai	2064	2209	610	1599	6603	1262	1248
宁夏 Ningxia	2607	3812	599	3213	10084	1392	1353
新疆 Xinjiang	13144	18714	2327	16387	50687	6402	6272

生和女教职工数

& Workers in Specialized Secondary Schools

单位: 人

教职工数 Teachers, Staff & Workers										兼任教师数不在教(工数中) Part-time Teachers
校本部教职工 Employees in the School Proper								校办厂、场职工 Employees in School-run Factories & Farms	附设机构人员 Employees in Subsidiary Units	
专任教师 Full-time Teachers					教辅人员 Supporting Staff	行政人员 Adm. Personnel	工勤人员 Workers			
计 Subtotal	高级讲师 Senior Lecturers	讲师 Lecturers	助理讲师 Assistant Lecturers	教员 Instructors						
121792	17008	53940	45634	5210	26888	36719	29147	6363	6559	3950
3465	516	1641	1217	91	854	1309	853	213	113	208
2981	462	1419	972	128	467	912	554	73	85	101
7521	963	3205	2921	432	1477	1711	1808	246	244	130
4725	571	1982	1933	239	1001	1315	977	104	160	20
3892	458	1907	1392	135	964	1198	791	83	61	60
5784	1256	2841	1519	168	1224	1764	1106	143	227	117
4617	746	1926	1835	110	807	1315	656	411	68	41
4066	1158	1880	966	62	915	1245	1147	281	292	155
2482	263	1323	790	106	613	1070	1255	328	171	151
6170	766	2475	2514	415	1176	1655	1452	546	125	682
3543	412	1640	1277	214	882	1019	940	164	152	373
3520	667	1499	1230	124	878	1177	830	147	234	51
2959	250	1232	1360	117	630	782	675	99	139	146
2715	359	1182	1076	98	753	859	705	251	124	101
9614	1581	3706	3876	451	1866	2331	1566	430	419	182
7088	1092	2895	2790	311	1293	1809	1409	617	593	110
6249	1005	2796	2193	255	1734	2263	1624	350	471	226
4806	850	2150	1595	211	1320	1485	1407	438	316	301
6507	581	2710	2892	324	1358	1812	1516	89	229	204
3644	424	1839	1292	89	845	1055	1292	138	991	60
623	46	208	324	45	146	213	293	41	39	46
1863	281	777	738	67	577	633	476	251	315	54
5306	746	2469	1910	181	1374	2156	1310	335	291	185
2993	236	1385	1259	113	522	1249	522	43	102	77
3711	302	1935	1349	125	668	1053	1185	34	128	56
303	2	121	173	7	42	89	84	5	0	0
3045	403	1360	1133	149	870	994	804	359	320	89
2438	173	1113	1067	85	627	678	772	49	62	3
782	42	300	400	40	120	194	152	0	14	0
774	119	388	216	51	173	208	198	33	6	8
3606	278	1636	1425	267	712	1166	788	62	68	13

普通中学校数、

Number of General Secondary Schools

地区 Region		学校数(所) Schools				计 Total	小计 Subtotal
		计 Total	初级中学 Junior Sec. Schools	高级中学 Senior Sec. Schools	完全中学 Complete Sec. Schools		
总计	**Total**	77213	63086	4270	9857	1239727	1044904
北京	Beijing	754	479	33	242	15558	11835
天津	Tianjin	712	504	57	151	12072	9701
河北	Hebei	4949	4272	358	319	76749	65887
山西	Shanxi	3284	2867	167	250	36069	30874
内蒙古	Inner Mongolia	1710	1366	111	233	24584	20307
辽宁	Liaoning	2429	1964	313	152	39881	32369
吉林	Jilin	1722	1431	153	138	26143	21630
黑龙江	Heilongjiang	2699	2232	231	236	44764	38672
上海	Shanghai	869	536	88	245	16617	11659
江苏	Jiangsu	3727	2860	188	679	65453	51471
浙江	Zhejiang	2995	2373	343	279	46469	36598
安徽	Anhui	3792	3139	60	593	56011	48053
福建	Fujian	1893	1453	16	424	43498	37448
江西	Jiangxi	2739	2274	43	422	42430	36602
山东	Shandong	4586	3892	488	206	99205	83802
河南	Henan	6120	5432	493	195	90835	80419
湖北	Hubei	3301	2713	322	266	53910	43810
湖南	Hunan	4502	3815	251	436	65228	55415
广东	Guangdong	3914	3000	86	828	79980	68242
广西	Guangxi	3012	2592	90	330	48904	43474
海南	Hainan	501	404	2	95	7370	6422
重庆	Chongqing	1552	1281	4	267	25354	21643
四川	Sichuan	4375	3587	59	729	66096	56474
贵州	Guizhou	1896	1592	32	272	26272	23222
云南	Yunnan	2225	1818	10	397	32392	28544
西藏	Tibet	97	81	8	8	1034	829
陕西	Shaanxi	2586	2021	173	392	37316	30625
甘肃	Gansu	1667	1257	25	385	23430	19446
青海	Qinghai	448	277	10	161	4581	3492
宁夏	Ningxia	432	337	10	85	6020	4895
新疆	Xinjiang	1725	1237	46	442	25502	21044

班数(总计)

and Classes (Regional Aggregates)

班数(个) Classes							
初中 Junior Sec. Schools				高中 Senior Sec. Schools			
一年级 Grade 1	二年级 Grade 2	三年级 Grade 3	四年级 Grade 4	小计 Subtotal	一年级 Grade 1	二年级 Grade 2	三年级 Grade 3
385319	343781	304003	11801	194823	71772	63728	59323
4272	3872	3652	39	3723	1312	1242	1169
3419	3501	2773	8	2371	866	778	727
23952	21683	19336	916	10862	3940	3598	3324
10811	10139	9686	238	5195	1989	1675	1531
6976	6614	6090	627	4277	1579	1351	1347
12182	10671	9373	143	7512	2691	2532	2289
7935	7159	6430	106	4513	1599	1514	1400
14118	12910	9492	2152	6092	2147	2043	1902
4175	3869	3608	7	4958	1724	1707	1527
19345	17044	15065	17	13982	4853	4716	4413
13550	11807	11229	12	9871	3669	3369	2833
17109	16008	14911	25	7958	2936	2598	2424
12855	12473	12120	0	6050	2418	1946	1686
13510	12219	10869	4	5828	2248	1805	1775
28820	25798	22814	6370	15403	5729	4971	4703
30208	26603	23324	284	10416	3965	3250	3201
16593	14386	12459	372	10100	3856	3234	3010
20479	18479	16456	1	9813	3720	3222	2871
24557	22753	20912	20	11738	4310	3888	3540
16767	14229	12459	19	5430	2170	1729	1531
2461	2144	1817	0	948	370	301	277
8892	7257	5486	8	3711	1340	1270	1101
22744	18681	15017	32	9622	3470	3196	2956
9092	7600	6529	1	3050	1170	932	948
10462	9321	8493	268	3848	1362	1245	1241
311	271	247	0	205	89	64	52
11685	10244	8690	6	6691	2535	2100	2056
7224	6335	5780	107	3984	1394	1268	1322
1275	1173	1042	2	1089	370	335	384
1755	1596	1533	11	1125	386	378	361
7785	6942	6311	6	4458	1565	1471	1422

普通中学校数、

Number of General Secondary

地区 Region	学校数(所) Schools 计 Total	初级中学 Junior Sec. Schools	高级中学 Senior Sec. Schools	完全中学 Complete Sec. Schools	计 Total	小计 Subtotal
总计 Total	14223	8702	1496	4025	262734	185213
北京 Beijing	363	177	24	162	8355	5724
天津 Tianjin	359	239	13	107	5905	4473
河北 Hebei	726	486	61	179	13020	9311
山西 Shanxi	470	278	57	135	7831	5614
内蒙古 Inner Mongolia	368	219	49	100	6895	4979
辽宁 Liaoning	790	510	172	108	15637	11399
吉林 Jilin	472	307	80	85	9244	6477
黑龙江 Heilongjiang	800	559	116	125	14044	10601
上海 Shanghai	502	302	56	144	10333	7097
江苏 Jiangsu	587	376	25	186	11197	7976
浙江 Zhejiang	502	276	108	118	9881	6278
安徽 Anhui	488	278	20	190	8094	5651
福建 Fujian	242	131	9	102	5644	3948
江西 Jiangxi	316	167	18	131	5800	3876
山东 Shandong	847	564	169	114	19593	13157
河南 Henan	869	596	128	145	13548	9694
湖北 Hubei	1129	756	163	210	19851	13575
湖南 Hunan	658	406	42	210	10349	7129
广东 Guangdong	662	329	35	298	14994	10975
广西 Guangxi	275	175	19	81	5530	4141
海南 Hainan	41	25	1	15	799	595
重庆 Chongqing	490	357	2	131	8610	6875
四川 Sichuan	538	283	22	233	9237	6063
贵州 Guizhou	253	168	14	71	3798	2780
云南 Yunnan	219	110	7	102	3350	2251
西藏 Tibet	19	11	6	2	317	200
陕西 Shaanxi	574	314	44	216	9423	6746
甘肃 Gansu	228	102	8	118	4253	2866
青海 Qinghai	67	21	5	41	892	639
宁夏 Ningxia	57	36	6	15	1042	728
新疆 Xinjiang	312	144	17	151	5268	3395

班数(城市)

Schools and Classes (Urban)

班数(个) Classes								
初中 Junior Sec. Schools				高中 Senior Sec. Schools				
一年级 Grade 1	二年级 Grade 2	三年级 Grade 3	四年级 Grade 4	小计 Subtotal	一年级 Grade 1	二年级 Grade 2	三年级 Grade 3
66576	60488	55084	3065	77521	28675	25574	23272
2003	1870	1838	13	2631	917	879	835
1417	1526	1522	8	1432	524	475	433
3321	2988	2842	160	3709	1361	1254	1094
1954	1825	1779	56	2217	872	716	629
1659	1579	1449	292	1916	751	602	563
3939	3961	3374	125	4238	1578	1436	1224
2349	2123	1950	55	2767	991	949	827
3981	3473	2687	460	3443	1204	1179	1060
2479	2341	2277	0	3236	1155	1127	954
3032	2600	2333	11	3221	1141	1080	1000
2329	2015	1922	12	3603	1368	1229	1006
2033	1874	1728	16	2443	900	810	733
1329	1310	1309	0	1696	672	554	470
1394	1291	1187	4	1924	729	608	587
4458	3907	3573	1219	6436	2422	2061	1953
3524	3133	2919	118	3854	1480	1211	1163
4853	4411	3949	362	6276	2429	2016	1831
2633	2355	2140	1	3220	1177	1067	976
3917	3638	3400	20	4019	1461	1325	1233
1545	1352	1230	14	1389	589	422	378
219	199	177	0	204	80	65	59
2743	2317	1809	6	1735	623	606	506
2377	1941	1718	27	3174	1113	1064	997
1043	929	808	0	1018	376	321	321
798	717	699	37	1099	382	360	357
72	69	59	0	117	50	39	28
2454	2258	2032	2	2677	990	855	832
1007	928	890	41	1387	476	459	452
236	214	189	0	253	86	82	85
260	232	236	0	314	107	106	101
1218	1112	1059	6	1873	671	617	585

普通中学校数、

Number of General Secondary Schools

地区 Region	学校数(所) Schools					
	计 Total	初级中学 Junior Sec. Schools	高级中学 Senior Sec. Schools	完全中学 Complete Sec. Schools	计 Total	小计 Subtotal
总　计 Total	19905	13963	1918	4024	368246	277666
北　京 Beijing	199	127	8	64	4182	3235
天　津 Tianjin	156	88	25	43	2778	2062
河　北 Hebei	1392	1037	246	109	25270	19000
山　西 Shanxi	456	313	61	82	7597	5273
内蒙古 Inner Mongolia	401	246	53	102	7681	5634
辽　宁 Liaoning	374	243	104	27	7041	4391
吉　林 Jilin	629	507	72	50	9831	8124
黑龙江 Heilongjiang	684	510	94	80	12666	10447
上　海 Shanghai	322	200	32	90	5768	4144
江　苏 Jiangsu	1478	1004	105	369	28897	20603
浙　江 Zhejiang	1852	1461	231	160	29989	23792
安　徽 Anhui	400	214	18	168	8006	4971
福　建 Fujian	867	600	7	260	23986	20203
江　西 Jiangxi	933	667	18	248	17620	14141
山　东 Shandong	414	249	111	54	10568	5930
河　南 Henan	1315	1042	241	32	22161	16942
湖　北 Hubei	281	171	92	18	5430	3136
湖　南 Hunan	1351	1060	115	176	22334	17623
广　东 Guangdong	1069	788	29	252	23730	19043
广　西 Guangxi	579	379	46	154	10513	7437
海　南 Hainan	71	31	0	40	1850	1305
重　庆 Chongqing	553	425	2	126	9612	7797
四　川 Sichuan	1699	1202	36	461	28362	22219
贵　州 Guizhou	323	194	17	112	5432	3813
云　南 Yunnan	559	326	3	230	9998	7628
西　藏 Tibet	77	69	2	6	711	623
陕　西 Shaanxi	752	528	106	118	13442	10087
甘　肃 Gansu	230	92	16	122	4549	2793
青　海 Qinghai	139	45	4	90	1796	1145
宁　夏 Ningxia	82	38	4	40	1770	1121
新　疆 Xinjiang	268	107	20	141	4676	3004

班数(县镇)

and Classes (County Seats & Towns)

班数(个) Classes							
初中 Junior Sec. Schools				高中 Senior Sec. Schools			
一年级 Grade 1	二年级 Grade 2	三年级 Grade 3	四年级 Grade 4	小计 Subtotal	一年级 Grade 1	二年级 Grade 2	三年级 Grade 3
102800	91452	81576	1838	90580	33282	29515	27783
1197	1052	960	26	947	346	317	284
788	695	579	0	716	262	232	222
6971	6194	5494	341	6270	2247	2049	1974
1790	1728	1690	65	2324	868	750	706
1892	1862	1734	146	2047	718	655	674
1644	1430	1307	10	2650	896	889	865
2935	2699	2449	41	1707	594	549	564
3743	3474	2635	595	2219	787	725	707
1536	1391	1210	7	1624	536	551	537
7944	6793	5866	0	8294	2865	2793	2636
8808	7670	7314	0	6197	2276	2117	1804
1785	1643	1539	4	3035	1126	988	921
6986	6754	6463	0	3783	1512	1218	1053
5239	4708	4194	0	3479	1359	1069	1051
2102	1797	1640	391	4638	1760	1484	1394
6347	5545	4914	136	5219	1947	1628	1644
1198	1025	909	4	2294	852	729	713
6464	5860	5299	0	4711	1830	1531	1350
6865	6339	5839	0	4687	1720	1560	1407
2764	2459	2210	4	3076	1188	1013	875
476	439	390	0	545	216	173	156
3217	2591	1989	0	1815	653	610	552
8914	7350	5950	5	6143	2241	2033	1869
1442	1258	1113	0	1619	637	494	488
2742	2492	2337	57	2370	849	761	760
237	200	186	0	88	39	25	24
3840	3354	2890	3	3355	1290	1047	1018
1031	911	849	2	1756	631	546	579
415	383	347	0	651	222	203	226
395	368	357	1	649	221	220	208
1093	988	923	0	1672	594	556	522

普通中学校数、

Number of General Secondary

地　区 Region	学校数(所) Schools					
	计 Total	初级中学 Junior Sec. Schools	高级中学 Senior Sec. Schools	完全中学 Complete Sec. Schools	计 Total	小计 Subtotal
总　计 **Total**	43085	40421	856	1808	608747	582025
北　京 Beijing	192	175	1	16	3021	2876
天　津 Tianjin	197	177	19	1	3389	3166
河　北 Hebei	2831	2749	51	31	38459	37576
山　西 Shanxi	2358	2276	49	33	20641	19987
内蒙古 Inner Mongolia	941	901	9	31	10008	9694
辽　宁 Liaoning	1265	1211	37	17	17203	16579
吉　林 Jilin	621	617	1	3	7068	7029
黑龙江 Heilongjiang	1215	1163	21	31	18054	17624
上　海 Shanghai	45	34	0	11	516	418
江　苏 Jiangsu	1662	1480	58	124	25359	22892
浙　江 Zhejiang	641	636	4	1	6599	6528
安　徽 Anhui	2904	2647	22	235	39911	37431
福　建 Fujian	784	722	0	62	13868	13297
江　西 Jiangxi	1490	1440	7	43	19010	18585
山　东 Shandong	3325	3079	208	38	69044	64715
河　南 Henan	3936	3794	124	18	55126	53783
湖　北 Hubei	1891	1786	67	38	28629	27099
湖　南 Hunan	2493	2349	94	50	32545	30663
广　东 Guangdong	2183	1883	22	278	41256	38224
广　西 Guangxi	2158	2038	25	95	32861	31896
海　南 Hainan	389	348	1	40	4721	4522
重　庆 Chongqing	509	499	0	10	7132	6971
四　川 Sichuan	2138	2102	1	35	28497	28192
贵　州 Guizhou	1320	1230	1	89	17042	16629
云　南 Yunnan	1447	1382	0	65	19044	18665
西　藏 Tibet	1	1	0	0	6	6
陕　西 Shaanxi	1260	1179	23	58	14451	13792
甘　肃 Gansu	1209	1063	1	145	14628	13787
青　海 Qinghai	242	211	1	30	1893	1708
宁　夏 Ningxia	293	263	0	30	3208	3046
新　疆 Xinjiang	1145	986	9	150	15558	14645

班数(农村)

Schools and Classes (Rural)

班数(个) Classes							
初中 Junior Sec. Schools				高中 Senior Sec. Schools			
一年级 Grade 1	二年级 Grade 2	三年级 Grade 3	四年级 Grade 4	小计 Subtotal	一年级 Grade 1	二年级 Grade 2	三年级 Grade 3
215943	191841	167343	6898	26722	9815	8639	8268
1072	950	854	0	145	49	46	50
1214	1280	672	0	223	80	71	72
13660	12501	11000	415	883	332	295	256
7067	6586	6217	117	654	249	209	196
3425	3173	2907	189	314	110	94	110
6599	5280	4692	8	624	217	207	200
2651	2337	2031	10	39	14	16	9
6394	5963	4170	1097	430	156	139	135
160	137	121	0	98	33	29	36
8369	7651	6866	6	2467	847	843	777
2413	2122	1993	0	71	25	23	23
13291	12491	11644	5	2480	910	800	770
4540	4409	4348	0	571	234	174	163
6877	6220	5488	0	425	160	128	137
22260	20094	17601	4760	4329	1547	1426	1356
20337	17925	15491	30	1343	538	411	394
10542	8950	7601	6	1530	575	489	466
11382	10264	9017	0	1882	713	624	545
13775	12776	11673	0	3032	1129	1003	900
12458	10418	9019	1	965	393	294	278
1766	1506	1250	0	199	74	63	62
2932	2349	1688	2	161	64	54	43
11453	9390	7349	0	305	116	99	90
6607	5413	4608	1	413	157	117	139
6922	6112	5457	174	379	131	124	124
2	2	2	0	0	0	0	0
5391	4632	3768	1	659	255	198	206
5186	4496	4041	64	841	287	263	291
624	576	506	2	185	62	50	73
1100	996	940	10	162	58	52	52
5474	4842	4329	0	913	300	298	315

普通中学毕业生数、招生数、毕业班学生数(总计)

Number of Graduates, Entrants & Graduates for Next Year in General Secondary Schools (Regional Aggregates)

单位:人

地区 Region	毕业生数 Graduates		招生数 Entrants		毕业班学生数 Graduates for Next Year	
	初中 Junior Sec. Schools	高中 Senior Sec. Schools	初中 Junior Sec. Schools	高中 Senior Sec. Schools	初中 Junior Sec. Schools	高中 Senior Sec. Schools
总计 Total	15898024	2629091	21496821	3963239	16213682	3055893
北京 Beijing	153172	40660	172706	56998	142440	48766
天津 Tianjin	134120	27851	147610	42209	123456	34268
河北 Hebei	1087879	158174	1398981	232230	1129853	186668
山西 Shanxi	471653	68621	566980	108843	486847	79319
内蒙古 Inner Mongolia	278031	58982	358115	84933	277672	67537
辽宁 Liaoning	511067	106998	611679	143871	433365	119896
吉林 Jilin	325646	63451	406895	87356	322239	71161
黑龙江 Heilongjiang	492606	82932	742265	110095	489634	92317
上海 Shanghai	181205	53743	194585	80679	163495	72478
江苏 Jiangsu	779242	195838	1022124	255847	763663	231074
浙江 Zhejiang	586390	112696	673365	183876	534931	140751
安徽 Anhui	873489	111465	1057898	170838	903416	132716
福建 Fujian	578425	64024	673874	125433	642689	82281
江西 Jiangxi	613866	86523	777091	129423	653446	92511
山东 Shandong	1412180	236588	1874521	347516	1370432	277463
河南 Henan	1384707	155035	1956971	244256	1449822	175780
湖北 Hubei	695967	146673	996724	233902	714653	166704
湖南 Hunan	849006	133018	1160327	207529	866238	147133
广东 Guangdong	1091006	165284	1374296	241505	1159659	185556
广西 Guangxi	642821	74042	919914	125697	667249	83203
海南 Hainan	99537	13219	136223	21080	102854	14089
重庆 Chongqing	249665	36823	472596	70488	251613	52670
四川 Sichuan	689732	114797	1233499	193508	682964	145128
贵州 Guizhou	312633	41231	494406	62904	328721	46303
云南 Yunnan	376522	51543	555057	74290	426600	58009
西藏 Tibet	9700	2392	13784	4383	10012	2243
陕西 Shaanxi	423535	89293	647268	141084	467623	99825
甘肃 Gansu	251425	53867	379672	75439	277992	61200
青海 Qinghai	42788	13924	61345	17556	42724	15176
宁夏 Ningxia	69926	17001	86335	19670	72009	17903
新疆 Xinjiang	230083	52403	329715	69801	255371	55765

普通中学毕业生数、招生数、毕业班学生数(城市)

Number of Graduates, Entrants & Graduates for Next Year in General Secondary Schools (Urban)

单位:人

地区 Region	毕业生数 Graduates		招生数 Entrants		毕业班学生数 Graduates for Next Year	
	初中 Junior Sec. Schools	高中 Senior Sec. Schools	初中 Junior Sec. Schools	高中 Senior Sec. Schools	初中 Junior Sec. Schools	高中 Senior Sec. Schools
总计 Total	2743332	989019	3453372	1519240	2680094	1181850
北京 Beijing	79221	27579	78997	38913	72515	34174
天津 Tianjin	75537	16851	60784	24847	67652	20658
河北 Hebei	146849	47909	177211	75131	138309	60041
山西 Shanxi	86391	28459	104754	47544	89656	33212
内蒙古 Inner Mongolia	66508	25261	87138	38710	69179	29684
辽宁 Liaoning	192644	53325	206421	81850	168888	62800
吉林 Jilin	110535	36793	124211	54467	105398	43621
黑龙江 Heilongjiang	143314	44544	208655	61428	131154	52014
上海 Shanghai	116779	31921	114836	53798	104648	44908
江苏 Jiangsu	115853	40742	146873	56101	107252	49075
浙江 Zhejiang	99721	39179	118898	67581	95432	49364
安徽 Anhui	89852	30143	110023	50011	89904	38020
福建 Fujian	61078	18507	65513	32518	63439	22354
江西 Jiangxi	60337	29027	74754	39682	63630	30346
山东 Shandong	198816	93760	257752	143694	191643	113523
河南 Henan	147867	53316	196382	84822	145189	62013
湖北 Hubei	199696	88120	268872	142539	199763	99238
湖南 Hunan	103859	41556	140432	63422	105634	49132
广东 Guangdong	161306	56803	206137	77596	169581	62900
广西 Guangxi	52966	16323	76657	25678	56764	18767
海南 Hainan	8314	2714	11381	4029	8937	3021
重庆 Chongqing	77605	15263	131638	30051	77966	22671
四川 Sichuan	83790	39187	121882	61647	77157	51081
贵州 Guizhou	36093	13618	53464	20268	38066	15818
云南 Yunnan	32117	14428	40891	20514	33088	17209
西藏 Tibet	2824	1469	3333	2743	2664	1379
陕西 Shaanxi	93564	33074	131108	52083	100238	39069
甘肃 Gansu	40213	18448	53515	25288	42801	21341
青海 Qinghai	7641	3505	12272	4310	7985	3814
宁夏 Ningxia	10024	4092	12551	5458	10675	5060
新疆 Xinjiang	42018	23103	56037	32517	44887	25543

普通中学毕业生数、招生数、毕业班学生数(县镇)

Number of Graduates, Entrants & Graduates for Next Year in General Secondary Schools (County Seats & Towns)

单位:人

地区 Region	毕业生数 Graduates		招生数 Entrants		毕业班学生数 Graduates for Next Year	
	初中 Junior Sec. Schools	高中 Senior Sec. Schools	初中 Junior Sec. Schools	高中 Senior Sec. Schools	初中 Junior Sec. Schools	高中 Senior Sec. Schools
总　计 Total	4241585	1282215	5689309	1892528	4337128	1469010
北　京 Beijing	40078	11214	50580	15967	38199	12669
天　津 Tianjin	25473	8525	34931	13117	26131	10231
河　北 Hebei	312092	98325	393426	136448	311990	111427
山　西 Shanxi	91027	32188	105277	48349	93952	37273
内蒙古 Inner Mongolia	83491	29401	102142	41165	83895	33075
辽　宁 Liaoning	72329	44163	86958	50524	61479	47138
吉　林 Jilin	118939	26147	150705	32435	119056	27143
黑龙江 Heilongjiang	134144	32894	198606	40860	134350	34630
上　海 Shanghai	59103	21037	73087	25473	54161	26149
江　苏 Jiangsu	296727	117795	413872	153226	286985	140870
浙　江 Zhejiang	387208	72555	440732	114948	351222	90248
安　徽 Anhui	84726	45223	106101	67653	89557	52528
福　建 Fujian	315560	39884	375130	79931	349752	51451
江　西 Jiangxi	234188	51961	306911	81218	255446	55876
山　东 Shandong	103120	77973	146635	111318	107311	88640
河　南 Henan	291209	85386	411606	127457	307757	94758
湖　北 Hubei	50679	36234	77213	52220	54866	41561
湖　南 Hunan	277854	65838	380021	102171	288515	70751
广　东 Guangdong	319445	69077	385846	102975	336961	78785
广　西 Guangxi	113700	46050	157627	76930	120590	52195
海　南 Hainan	23243	8394	28095	13267	24279	9048
重　庆 Chongqing	102411	20472	185467	37058	98812	28229
四　川 Sichuan	284529	72642	484892	125777	282051	90747
贵　州 Guizhou	55537	22982	76450	34735	56796	24950
云　南 Yunnan	106204	32335	147019	46929	118840	35904
西　藏 Tibet	6816	923	10391	1640	7304	864
陕　西 Shaanxi	142793	48556	214481	76200	160856	52591
甘　肃 Gansu	38409	25473	57303	34645	45011	28888
青　海 Qinghai	14773	8308	19037	10736	13486	9329
宁　夏 Ningxia	18589	11131	20695	11617	18478	11018
新　疆 Xinjiang	37189	19129	48073	25539	39040	20044

普通中学毕业生数、招生数、毕业班学生数(农村)

Number of Graduates, Entrants & Graduates for Next Year in General Secondary Schools (Rural)

单位:人

地区 Region	毕业生数 Graduates		招生数 Entrants		毕业班学生数 Graduates for Next Year	
	初中 Junior Sec. Schools	高中 Senior Sec. Schools	初中 Junior Sec. Schools	高中 Senior Sec. Schools	初中 Junior Sec. Schools	高中 Senior Sec. Schools
总计 Total	8913107	357857	12354140	551471	9196460	405033
北京 Beijing	33873	1867	43129	2118	31726	1923
天津 Tianjin	33110	2475	51895	4245	29673	3379
河北 Hebei	628938	11940	828344	20651	679554	15200
山西 Shanxi	294235	7974	356949	12950	303239	8834
内蒙古 Inner Mongolia	128032	4320	168835	5058	124598	4778
辽宁 Liaoning	246094	9510	318300	11497	202998	9958
吉林 Jilin	96172	511	131979	454	97785	397
黑龙江 Heilongjiang	215148	5494	335004	7807	224130	5673
上海 Shanghai	5323	785	6662	1408	4686	1421
江苏 Jiangsu	366662	37301	461379	46520	369426	41129
浙江 Zhejiang	99461	962	113735	1347	88277	1139
安徽 Anhui	698911	36099	841774	53174	723955	42168
福建 Fujian	201787	5633	233231	12984	229498	8476
江西 Jiangxi	319341	5535	395426	8523	334370	6289
山东 Shandong	1110244	64855	1470134	92504	1071478	75300
河南 Henan	945631	16333	1348983	31977	996876	19009
湖北 Hubei	445592	22319	650639	39143	460024	25905
湖南 Hunan	467293	25624	639874	41936	472089	27250
广东 Guangdong	610255	39404	782313	60934	653117	43871
广西 Guangxi	476155	11669	685630	23089	489895	12241
海南 Hainan	67980	2111	96747	3784	69638	2020
重庆 Chongqing	69649	1088	155491	3379	74835	1770
四川 Sichuan	321413	2968	626725	6084	323756	3300
贵州 Guizhou	221003	4631	364492	7901	233859	5535
云南 Yunnan	238201	4780	367147	6847	274672	4896
西藏 Tibet	60	0	60	0	44	0
陕西 Shaanxi	187178	7663	301679	12801	206529	8165
甘肃 Gansu	172803	9946	268854	15506	190180	10971
青海 Qinghai	20374	2111	30036	2510	21253	2033
宁夏 Ningxia	41313	1778	53089	2595	42856	1825
新疆 Xinjiang	150876	10171	225605	11745	171444	10178

普通中学在校

Enrolment of General Secondary

地 区 Region	合 计 Total	初中 Junior Secondary Schools 计 Subtotal	一 年 级 Grade 1	二 年 级 Grade 2	三 年 级 Grade 3
总 计 Total	67712749	57215671	21556031	18710291	16317095
北 京 Beijing	634895	473422	173897	155359	142755
天 津 Tianjin	542705	428334	148473	156063	123554
河 北 Hebei	4474303	3844420	1399226	1249138	1150398
山 西 Shanxi	1868638	1590282	567786	521987	490452
内蒙古 Inner Mongolia	1221959	995456	358996	322871	287118
辽 宁 Liaoning	1961673	1562444	611985	507609	435993
吉 林 Jilin	1336757	1094484	407194	357019	325100
黑龙江 Heilongjiang	2356487	2046920	742495	672315	504877
上 海 Shanghai	774646	539780	196354	179529	163617
江 苏 Jiangsu	3408878	2666953	1022835	879703	763707
浙 江 Zhejiang	2281459	1786620	674115	577087	534922
安 徽 Anhui	3398493	2944687	1058428	981734	903352
福 建 Fujian	2281355	1973559	675103	655767	642689
江 西 Jiangxi	2468362	2146164	779651	712909	653449
山 东 Shandong	6204328	5264908	1875054	1626943	1409114
河 南 Henan	5688611	5077959	1966200	1644357	1451596
湖 北 Hubei	3180863	2587432	998427	855829	717020
湖 南 Hunan	3560453	3028566	1161506	1000781	866249
广 东 Guangdong	4439061	3797987	1374380	1263408	1159465
广 西 Guangxi	2670224	2360700	921965	770596	667373
海 南 Hainan	412376	359666	137454	119358	102854
重 庆 Chongqing	1282599	1095743	477279	366354	251807
四 川 Sichuan	3364576	2856294	1236911	935097	683261
贵 州 Guizhou	1386285	1228515	498952	400842	328638
云 南 Yunnan	1674413	1480201	559099	480580	427764
西 藏 Tibet	44207	34756	13615	11129	10012
陕 西 Shaanxi	2044138	1693914	655827	570229	467694
甘 肃 Gansu	1185891	984753	382312	317746	280721
青 海 Qinghai	207214	160155	62276	53278	44540
宁 夏 Ningxia	294520	237254	87727	77472	71652
新 疆 Xinjiang	1062380	873343	330509	287202	255352

学生数(总计)

Schools (Regional Aggregates)

单位:人

四年级 Grade 4	高中 Senior Secondary Schools 计 Subtotal	一年级 Grade 1	二年级 Grade 2	三年级 Grade 3	合计中住宿生 of the total Boarding Students
632254	10497078	3972694	3468491	3055893	19738875
1411	161473	57918	54789	48766	54455
244	114371	42343	37760	34268	34101
45658	629883	232412	210803	186668	758315
10057	278356	108906	90131	79319	602173
26471	226503	85076	73890	67537	310986
6857	399229	143925	135408	119896	241700
5171	242273	87394	83718	71161	132851
127233	309567	110103	107147	92317	276241
280	234866	81219	81169	72478	48899
708	741925	256536	254315	231074	777739
496	494839	184394	169694	140751	751871
1173	453806	172711	148379	132716	703559
0	307796	125873	99642	82281	592418
155	322198	130410	99277	92511	947316
353797	939420	347539	314418	277463	1539319
15806	610652	244882	189990	175780	2440594
16156	593431	234280	192447	166704	1608330
30	531887	207761	176993	147133	1237060
734	641074	241529	213989	185556	1081286
766	309524	125294	101027	83203	1772001
0	52710	21801	16820	14089	97748
303	186856	70512	63674	52670	529644
1025	508282	193614	169540	145128	1028750
83	157770	62990	48477	46303	273091
12758	194212	74839	61364	58009	919042
0	9451	4360	2848	2243	19286
164	350224	141466	108933	99825	526180
3974	201138	75471	64467	61200	199393
61	47059	17585	14298	15176	34685
403	57266	19696	19667	17903	56556
280	189037	69855	63417	55765	143286

普通中学在校

Enrolment of General Secondary

地区 Region		合计 Total	初中 Junior Secondary Schools			
			计 Subtotal	一年级 Grade 1	二年级 Grade 2	三年级 Grade 3
总计	**Total**	13455752	9394809	3461014	3071777	2709810
北京	Beijing	338222	226226	79304	73527	72929
天津	Tianjin	264429	195959	60941	67024	67750
河北	Hebei	685497	480686	177344	154816	140749
山西	Shanxi	411303	291452	104827	94313	89876
内蒙古	Inner Mongolia	354146	252461	87485	81134	71459
辽宁	Liaoning	804054	585268	206495	201211	171401
吉林	Jilin	498075	346866	124178	114046	105596
黑龙江	Heilongjiang	725375	551297	208702	181188	135252
上海	Shanghai	482419	330365	116029	109688	104648
江苏	Jiangsu	537529	378036	147140	123262	107252
浙江	Zhejiang	495423	317431	119057	102471	95407
安徽	Anhui	432647	300265	109983	99743	89859
福建	Fujian	275686	193546	65574	64533	63439
江西	Jiangxi	312831	209964	75343	70833	63633
山东	Shandong	1136458	751370	257770	226362	202897
河南	Henan	726327	511014	196617	163277	145675
湖北	Hubei	1081067	722700	268291	236147	202516
湖南	Hunan	536962	367003	140569	120759	105645
广东	Guangdong	775876	565431	205788	189839	169070
广西	Guangxi	275891	207432	80400	67318	59172
海南	Hainan	40959	30474	11390	10147	8937
重庆	Chongqing	397888	317068	131745	106937	78130
四川	Sichuan	464742	295662	121933	95472	77434
贵州	Guizhou	190619	137696	53787	45843	38066
云南	Yunnan	168255	111677	40965	35416	33548
西藏	Tibet	14963	8992	3349	2979	2664
陕西	Shaanxi	482826	349204	131376	117498	100235
甘肃	Gansu	215395	145061	53738	46493	43043
青海	Qinghai	42116	30125	12272	9868	7985
宁夏	Ningxia	50070	34068	12551	10842	10675
新疆	Xinjiang	237702	150010	56071	48791	44868

学生数(城市)

Schools (Urban)

单位:人

	高 中 Senior Secondary Schools				
四年级 Grade 4	计 Subtotal	一年级 Grade 1	二年级 Grade 2	三年级 Grade 3	合计中住宿生 Of the total Boarding Students
152208	4060943	1522348	1355906	1182689	1898152
466	111996	39607	38215	34174	20460
244	68470	24914	22898	20658	5843
7777	204811	75181	69589	60041	116868
2436	119851	47547	39092	33212	71682
12383	101685	38712	33289	29684	39381
6161	218786	81887	74099	62800	46664
3046	151209	54490	53098	43621	42127
26155	174078	61429	60635	52014	50267
0	152054	54004	53142	44908	16480
382	159493	56336	54082	49075	37323
496	177992	67812	60816	49364	119487
680	132382	50093	44269	38020	41118
0	82140	32602	27184	22354	34305
155	102867	39750	32771	30346	39174
64341	385088	143712	127853	113523	198144
5445	215313	84931	68369	62013	139623
15746	358367	142565	116564	99238	298535
30	169959	63524	57303	49132	100450
734	210445	77612	69933	62900	72901
542	68459	26238	22615	19606	64830
0	10485	4031	3433	3021	6224
256	80820	30057	28092	22671	117308
823	169080	61691	56308	51081	73095
0	52923	20275	16830	15818	19108
1748	56578	20797	18572	17209	40047
0	5971	2767	1825	1379	2582
95	133622	52263	42290	39069	46346
1787	70334	25205	23788	21341	10632
0	11991	4310	3867	3814	537
0	16002	5458	5484	5060	1253
280	87692	32548	29601	25543	25358

普通中学在校

Enrolment of General Secondary

地 区 Region	合 计 Total	初中 Junior Secondary Schools			
		计 Subtotal	一年级 Grade 1	二年级 Grade 2	三年级 Grade 3
总 计 Total	20140440	15123148	5703313	4965180	4357056
北 京 Beijing	177514	134201	51057	44099	38100
天 津 Tianjin	127016	92295	34943	31221	26131
河 北 Hebei	1460803	1089096	393476	358374	320378
山 西 Shanxi	427461	301101	105596	97911	94915
内蒙古 Inner Mongolia	402354	292074	102152	96972	86848
辽 宁 Liaoning	366672	218511	87017	69645	61506
吉 林 Jilin	493299	403550	150770	129587	121472
黑龙江 Heilongjiang	664669	549213	198680	177996	137914
上 海 Shanghai	271042	192286	73539	64184	54283
江 苏 Jiangsu	1488972	1041930	414119	340826	286985
浙 江 Zhejiang	1483554	1170403	441204	377961	351238
安 徽 Anhui	471288	292748	106362	96701	89570
福 建 Fujian	1282452	1087498	376061	361685	349752
江 西 Jiangxi	1043765	846180	307846	282634	255700
山 东 Shandong	703431	402702	146653	124513	109152
河 南 Henan	1406129	1083863	413542	350946	310963
湖 北 Hubei	338983	196694	77285	64393	54910
湖 南 Hunan	1258093	999160	380018	330641	288501
广 东 Guangdong	1344021	1070067	386308	349295	334464
广 西 Guangxi	600706	410617	154712	137562	118155
海 南 Hainan	112953	79363	28125	26959	24279
重 庆 Chongqing	528054	429817	187327	143678	98812
四 川 Sichuan	1474634	1149421	486397	381003	281819
贵 州 Guizhou	285407	199356	76934	65626	56796
云 南 Yunnan	519974	399554	148410	129604	119048
西 藏 Tibet	29090	25610	10206	8100	7304
陕 西 Shaanxi	760373	573593	218022	194626	160888
甘 肃 Gansu	246159	152672	58021	49518	45091
青 海 Qinghai	79417	50736	19380	16752	14604
宁 夏 Ningxia	93543	58955	21024	19453	18438
新 疆 Xinjiang	198612	129882	48127	42715	39040

学生数(县镇)

Schools (County Seats & Towns)

单位:人

	高 中 Senior Secondary Schools				
四年级 Grade 4	计 Subtotal	一年级 Grade 1	二年级 Grade 2	三年级 Grade 3	合计中住宿生 Of the total Boarding Students
97599	5017292	1899040	1650105	1468147	6533533
945	43313	16122	14522	12669	24287
0	34721	13170	11320	10231	20083
16868	371707	136580	123700	111427	438287
2679	126360	48409	40678	37273	127462
6102	110280	41300	35905	33075	115327
343	148161	50541	50482	47138	95221
1721	89749	32450	30156	27143	71031
34623	115456	40867	39959	34630	91234
280	78756	25769	26838	26149	30520
0	447042	153576	152596	140870	381146
0	313151	115234	107669	90248	518690
115	178540	67701	58311	52528	111109
0	194954	80274	63229	51451	327907
0	197585	81684	60025	55876	406581
22384	300729	111320	100769	88640	241390
8412	322266	127934	99574	94758	634792
106	142289	54863	45865	41561	165110
0	258933	102294	85888	70751	464879
0	273954	102908	92321	78725	369079
188	190089	76102	62671	51316	364234
0	33590	13761	10781	9048	27837
0	98237	37076	32932	28229	282837
202	325213	125838	108628	90747	561701
0	86051	34812	26289	24950	59332
2492	120420	47131	37385	35904	261113
0	3480	1593	1023	864	16704
57	186780	76369	57820	52591	200846
42	93487	35427	29096	28964	53280
0	28681	10743	8609	9329	20082
40	34588	11634	11936	11018	22095
0	68730	25558	23128	20044	29337

普通中学在校

Enrolment of General Secondary

地　区 Region	合　计 Total	初中 Junior Secondary Schools 计 Subtotal	一年级 Grade 1	二年级 Grade 2	三年级 Grade 3
总　计　Total	34116557	32697714	12391704	10673334	9250229
北　京　Beijing	119159	112995	43536	37733	31726
天　津　Tianjin	151260	140080	52589	57818	29673
河　北　Hebei	2328003	2274638	828406	735948	689271
山　西　Shanxi	1029874	997729	357363	329763	305661
内蒙古　Inner Mongolia	465459	450921	169359	144765	128811
辽　宁　Liaoning	790947	758665	318473	236753	203086
吉　林　Jilin	345383	344068	132246	113386	98032
黑龙江　Heilongjiang	966443	946410	335113	313131	231711
上　海　Shanghai	21185	17129	6786	5657	4686
江　苏　Jiangsu	1382377	1246987	461576	415615	369470
浙　江　Zhejiang	302482	298786	113854	96655	88277
安　徽　Anhui	2494558	2351674	842083	785290	723923
福　建　Fujian	723217	692515	233468	229549	229498
江　西　Jiangxi	1111766	1090020	396462	359442	334116
山　东　Shandong	4364439	4110836	1470631	1276068	1097065
河　南　Henan	3556155	3483082	1356041	1130134	994958
湖　北　Hubei	1760813	1668038	652851	555289	459594
湖　南　Hunan	1765398	1662403	640919	549381	472103
广　东　Guangdong	2319164	2162489	782284	724274	655931
广　西　Guangxi	1793627	1742651	686853	565716	490046
海　南　Hainan	258464	249829	97939	82252	69638
重　庆　Chongqing	356657	348858	158207	115739	74865
四　川　Sichuan	1425200	1411211	628581	458622	324008
贵　州　Guizhou	910259	891463	368231	289373	233776
云　南　Yunnan	986184	968970	369724	315560	275168
西　藏　Tibet	154	154	60	50	44
陕　西　Shaanxi	800939	771117	306429	258105	206571
甘　肃　Gansu	724337	687020	270553	221735	192587
青　海　Qinghai	85681	79294	30624	26658	21951
宁　夏　Ningxia	150907	144231	54152	47177	42539
新　疆　Xinjiang	626066	593451	226311	195696	171444

学生数(农村)

Schools (Rural)

单位:人

四年级 Grade 4	高中 Senior Secondary Schools 计 Subtotal	一年级 Grade 1	二年级 Grade 2	三年级 Grade 3	合计中住宿生 Of the total Boarding Students
382447	1418843	551306	462480	405057	11307190
0	6164	2189	2052	1923	9708
0	11180	4259	3542	3379	8175
21013	53365	20651	17514	15200	203160
4942	32145	12950	10361	8834	403029
7986	14538	5064	4696	4778	156278
353	32282	11497	10827	9958	99815
404	1315	454	464	397	19693
66455	20033	7807	6553	5673	134740
0	4056	1446	1189	1421	1899
326	135390	46624	47637	41129	359270
0	3696	1348	1209	1139	113694
378	142884	54917	45799	42168	551332
0	30702	12997	9229	8476	230206
0	21746	8976	6481	6289	501561
267072	253603	92507	85796	75300	1099785
1949	73073	32017	22047	19009	1666179
304	92775	36852	30018	25905	1144685
0	102995	41943	33802	27250	671731
0	156675	61009	51735	43931	639306
36	50976	22954	15741	12281	1342937
0	8635	4009	2606	2020	63687
47	7799	3379	2650	1770	129499
0	13989	6085	4604	3300	393954
83	18796	7903	5358	5535	194651
8518	17214	6911	5407	4896	617882
0	0	0	0	0	0
12	29822	12834	8823	8165	278988
2145	37317	14839	11583	10895	135481
61	6387	2532	1822	2033	14066
363	6676	2604	2247	1825	33208
0	32615	11749	10688	10178	88591

普通中学学生

Number of Female Students in

地 区 Region		合 计 Total	初中 Junior Secondary Schools			
			计 Subtotal	一 年 级 Grade 1	二 年 级 Grade 2	三 年 级 Grade 3
总 计	**Total**	31092443	26765358	10111133	8747206	7605134
北 京	Beijing	312848	230937	84907	75622	69701
天 津	Tianjin	266908	210135	73255	75964	60806
河 北	Hebei	2151475	1865439	679333	608424	555890
山 西	Shanxi	891187	767496	273412	251291	237731
内蒙古	Inner Mongolia	583079	475382	169840	154700	137666
辽 宁	Liaoning	948906	760051	297132	247329	212216
吉 林	Jilin	640820	526429	194585	173296	155993
黑龙江	Heilongjiang	1141365	992786	362048	326921	243460
上 海	Shanghai	382698	262423	95595	86915	79793
江 苏	Jiangsu	1505945	1225535	472019	404880	348303
浙 江	Zhejiang	1054332	842436	319418	271512	251260
安 徽	Anhui	1519485	1361758	494459	456023	410794
福 建	Fujian	1038158	925378	317106	306328	301944
江 西	Jiangxi	1083831	974807	358832	322665	293240
山 东	Shandong	2863466	2481484	890514	763082	659951
河 南	Henan	2625208	2381477	926217	770417	677191
湖 北	Hubei	1394118	1172179	454361	386454	323252
湖 南	Hunan	1612181	1415536	547262	466786	401469
广 东	Guangdong	1979223	1735795	630862	577084	527490
广 西	Guangxi	1197114	1077593	417955	350671	308600
海 南	Hainan	180901	162762	62132	54630	46000
重 庆	Chongqing	592570	512853	224416	169509	118770
四 川	Sichuan	1545434	1337204	577506	439456	319720
贵 州	Guizhou	574178	517000	212399	168509	136062
云 南	Yunnan	765588	680425	255721	222412	196315
西 藏	Tibet	19997	16280	6406	5252	4622
陕 西	Shaanxi	945524	799755	310339	268069	221260
甘 肃	Gansu	514724	437763	171254	140749	123887
青 海	Qinghai	96002	73832	28411	24442	20954
宁 夏	Ningxia	134970	109400	40484	35266	33424
新 疆	Xinjiang	530208	433028	162953	142548	127370

总数中女学生数

General Secondary Schools

单位:人

四年级 Grade 4	高中 Senior Secondary Schools 计 Subtotal	一年级 Grade 1	二年级 Grade 2	三年级 Grade 3	合计中住宿生 Of the total Boarding Students
301885	4327085	1653556	1426252	1247277	8617622
707	81911	29391	27573	24947	23705
110	56773	21376	18637	16760	17040
21792	286036	107082	94393	84561	337551
5062	123691	48513	39660	35518	286961
13176	107697	40609	35095	31993	144279
3374	188855	69200	63670	55985	116706
2555	114391	41739	39432	33220	61080
60357	148579	52997	51540	44042	123063
120	120275	42011	41145	37119	7264
333	280410	99539	95906	84965	312207
246	211896	79430	72497	59969	336076
482	157727	61667	51345	44715	273477
0	112780	48392	35901	28487	263593
70	109024	44286	33605	31133	397317
167937	381982	142205	128584	111193	712071
7652	243731	97505	76273	69953	1106534
8112	221939	90284	71067	60588	675224
19	196645	79507	64650	52488	527432
359	243428	93579	80539	69310	441999
367	119521	49629	38571	31321	774031
0	18139	7583	5719	4837	38446
158	79717	29983	27131	22603	233110
522	208230	80109	68867	59254	439174
30	57178	22677	17880	16621	105229
5977	85163	33015	26979	25169	421541
0	3717	1703	1163	851	7759
87	145769	58530	45131	42108	250131
1873	76961	28331	24877	23753	75663
25	22170	8115	6769	7286	13873
226	25570	8927	8857	7786	24801
157	97180	35642	32796	28742	70285

普通中学教

Number of Teachers, Staff & Workers in General

地区 Region	教职工 Teachers, Staff &				
	合计 Total	专任教师 Full-time Teachers			行政人员 Adm. Personnel
		计 Total	初中 Junior Sec. Schools	高中 Senior Sec. Schools	
总计 Total	4753600	3840556	3148117	692439	473446
北京 Beijing	72312	48165	36142	12023	15422
天津 Tianjin	53126	38414	30129	8285	10247
河北 Hebei	286488	239832	199293	40539	23959
山西 Shanxi	153144	122659	102689	19970	14224
内蒙古 Inner Mongolia	104656	78208	62921	15287	13123
辽宁 Liaoning	175820	139497	114086	25411	26808
吉林 Jilin	118687	90943	73417	17526	19805
黑龙江 Heilongjiang	183112	143036	119454	23582	22525
上海 Shanghai	77522	50844	37051	13793	18121
江苏 Jiangsu	264160	203756	153615	50141	27083
浙江 Zhejiang	157835	131360	101168	30192	13995
安徽 Anhui	183396	152890	126699	26191	14838
福建 Fujian	143086	117312	98017	19295	15068
江西 Jiangxi	155552	135034	112773	22261	8313
山东 Shandong	414538	333884	275678	58206	37558
河南 Henan	343265	290943	250044	40899	26451
湖北 Hubei	231764	191343	152091	39252	15365
湖南 Hunan	248658	212435	176341	36094	14174
广东 Guangdong	265253	218899	179712	39187	26264
广西 Guangxi	160076	121738	104998	16740	18610
海南 Hainan	29546	22442	19083	3359	2156
重庆 Chongqing	97605	76158	63679	12479	11283
四川 Sichuan	256567	207305	172376	34929	26025
贵州 Guizhou	90523	76654	65962	10692	7687
云南 Yunnan	122821	98927	85416	13511	8744
西藏 Tibet	4861	4045	3259	786	270
陕西 Shaanxi	142131	115007	91427	23580	17693
甘肃 Gansu	83172	70711	56478	14233	6003
青海 Qinghai	19090	16260	11859	4401	1387
宁夏 Ningxia	23510	19660	15738	3922	1531
新疆 Xinjiang	91324	72195	56522	15673	8714

职 工 数（总 计）

Secondary Schools (Regional Aggregates)

单位:人

数 Workers			代课教师 Substitute Teachers	临 时 工 Temporary Workers	兼任教师 Part－time Teachers
工勤人员 Workers	校办工厂、农场职工 Employees in School－run Factories & Farms				
	计 Total	其中:由厂、场收入支付工资的职工 Employees maintained by income of School－run businesses			
402649	36949	17110	112872	102061	21819
6996	1729	608	1807	3386	491
3516	949	223	649	504	577
20901	1796	1032	9236	9204	597
15169	1092	673	6028	5426	674
12410	915	300	3263	1281	470
9179	336	116	1519	2614	1017
6970	969	646	809	815	101
15804	1747	1200	3244	2184	445
6538	2019	0	1676	1035	1680
27619	5702	3578	6017	10362	491
9745	2735	1990	6092	8722	2947
14845	823	259	2472	4649	1204
10111	595	354	6475	2015	949
11572	633	261	1970	2350	424
40393	2703	786	1686	2509	276
24368	1503	770	2237	2041	1499
22138	2918	1292	3732	4095	445
20064	1985	955	2593	1564	440
19612	478	225	12416	10301	323
19185	543	151	16961	4549	1284
4871	77	53	261	456	117
9280	884	97	2536	2089	318
21716	1521	381	4124	3406	2492
5849	333	204	3896	2628	496
14856	294	132	3501	7885	407
535	11	0	73	188	262
8884	547	195	3389	2085	765
6039	419	237	2131	1428	122
1361	82	61	96	313	52
2155	164	92	287	725	19
9968	447	239	1696	1252	435

普通中学教

Number of Teachers, Staff & Workers in General

地区 Region		教职工 Teachers, Staff &				
		合计 Total	专任教师 Full-time Teachers			行政人员 Adm. Personnel
			计 Total	初中 Junior Sec. Schools	高中 Senior Sec. Schools	
总计	Total	1203374	898508	629000	269508	179347
北京	Beijing	41208	25881	17606	8275	9644
天津	Tianjin	28434	19059	14358	4701	6453
河北	Hebei	61889	46523	33430	13093	8447
山西	Shanxi	39728	29311	21204	8107	5556
内蒙古	Inner Mongolia	32466	23463	16751	6712	5906
辽宁	Liaoning	68824	53901	40738	13163	11427
吉林	Jilin	47028	34666	24586	10080	8802
黑龙江	Heilongjiang	67154	50437	37264	13173	10451
上海	Shanghai	47960	31612	22958	8654	11431
江苏	Jiangsu	53559	37311	26078	11233	8077
浙江	Zhejiang	38672	29094	18157	10937	4577
安徽	Anhui	34562	27338	19348	7990	4233
福建	Fujian	23089	17796	12087	5709	3362
江西	Jiangxi	26654	22132	14737	7395	2261
山东	Shandong	96858	72279	48176	24103	13512
河南	Henan	65474	49145	34642	14503	10159
湖北	Hubei	94414	73882	49711	24171	9776
湖南	Hunan	47595	36523	24796	11727	4809
广东	Guangdong	60676	45886	32339	13547	9063
广西	Guangxi	20465	15516	11867	3649	2946
海南	Hainan	3465	2673	1976	697	281
重庆	Chongqing	34747	26341	20669	5672	4640
四川	Sichuan	43966	32680	21057	11623	6117
贵州	Guizhou	16817	13260	9744	3516	2187
云南	Yunnan	15782	11580	7698	3882	1971
西藏	Tibet	1613	1309	850	459	112
陕西	Shaanxi	38969	29765	20596	9169	6357
甘肃	Gansu	18362	14237	9485	4752	2401
青海	Qinghai	4332	3335	2278	1057	623
宁夏	Ningxia	4409	3535	2463	1072	373
新疆	Xinjiang	24203	18038	11351	6687	3393

职工数（城市）

Secondary Schools (Urban)

单位:人

数 Workers			代课教师 Substitute Teachers	临时工 Temporary Workers	兼任教师 Part-time Teachers
工勤人员 Workers	校办工厂、农场职工 Employees in School-run Factories & Farms				
	计 Total	其中:由厂、场收入支付工资的职工 Employees maintained by income of School-run businesses			
102788	22731	12534	13731	19478	12736
4238	1445	565	716	1792	409
2161	761	175	484	134	551
5881	1038	712	802	1407	517
4205	656	409	762	991	495
2621	476	165	352	471	401
3326	170	58	412	1386	806
2798	762	569	72	296	90
5084	1182	854	316	783	387
3637	1280	0	1352	534	1354
4345	3826	3241	613	872	421
3202	1799	1487	583	1505	1835
2634	357	83	414	452	361
1525	406	314	87	139	158
2063	198	36	65	120	275
9407	1660	590	636	447	147
5384	786	475	11	713	933
9049	1707	886	1055	1604	372
4978	1285	785	215	234	402
5446	281	122	2054	2118	172
1889	114	66	493	464	864
477	34	30	24	54	53
3242	524	36	452	625	121
4385	784	218	441	575	419
1170	200	131	194	273	174
2112	119	67	114	428	127
181	11	0	45	21	45
2517	330	139	676	546	575
1502	222	157	29	161	47
324	50	46	13	23	51
396	105	54	44	48	7
2609	163	64	205	262	167

普通中学教

Number of Teachers, Staff & Workers in General

地区 Region	教职工 Teachers, Staff &				
	合计 Total	专任教师 Full-time Teachers			行政人员 Adm. Personnel
		计 Total	初中 Junior Sec. Schools	高中 Senior Sec. Schools	
总计 Total	1485485	1179747	856280	323467	146675
北京 Beijing	18664	12969	9737	3232	3769
天津 Tianjin	13036	9390	6736	2654	2598
河北 Hebei	103428	84372	60535	23837	8699
山西 Shanxi	36335	27945	18705	9240	3414
内蒙古 Inner Mongolia	33924	25258	17927	7331	3844
辽宁 Liaoning	36160	27325	17540	9785	5748
吉林 Jilin	45440	35106	27794	7312	7107
黑龙江 Heilongjiang	54855	42428	33703	8725	6897
上海 Shanghai	27248	17654	12803	4851	6180
江苏 Jiangsu	119393	93065	63227	29838	11709
浙江 Zhejiang	99418	84683	65672	19011	7941
安徽 Anhui	32371	24953	15038	9915	3182
福建 Fujian	77349	63682	51814	11868	7536
江西 Jiangxi	65655	56220	43091	13129	3365
山东 Shandong	51963	37671	21010	16661	6236
河南 Henan	92281	75443	54941	20502	7057
湖北 Hubei	25935	20879	11554	9325	1416
湖南 Hunan	87846	74234	56661	17573	4921
广东 Guangdong	80909	67322	51922	15400	6569
广西 Guangxi	43460	31452	21657	9795	4924
海南 Hainan	8342	5901	4019	1882	607
重庆 Chongqing	39516	30171	23917	6254	4515
四川 Sichuan	118194	93370	71130	22240	12421
贵州 Guizhou	22463	17857	12201	5656	2181
云南 Yunnan	42107	32484	24146	8338	3401
西藏 Tibet	3217	2709	2382	327	155
陕西 Shaanxi	52340	42441	30403	12038	5967
甘肃 Gansu	19208	15342	9044	6298	1454
青海 Qinghai	8008	6647	4058	2589	520
宁夏 Ningxia	7838	6180	3943	2237	658
新疆 Xinjiang	18582	14594	8970	5624	1684

职 工 数（县 镇）

Secondary Schools（County Seats & Towns）

单位：人

数 Workers			代课教师 Substitute Teachers	临时工 Temporary Workers	兼任教师 Part－time Teachers
工勤人员 Workers	校办工厂、农场职工 Employees in School－run Factories & Farms				
	计 Total	其中：由厂、场收入支付工资的职工 Employees maintained by income of School－run businesses			
148650	10413	3212	26294	36966	5866
1720	206	29	488	1087	53
892	156	39	63	280	17
9681	676	309	2008	4971	34
4610	366	235	1047	1859	132
4531	291	90	425	233	41
3013	74	15	130	575	165
3066	161	73	334	432	11
5176	354	170	665	444	33
2686	728	0	226	469	266
13076	1543	261	2230	5338	47
5895	899	494	3850	6111	1088
3950	286	90	237	867	541
5973	158	31	4731	1242	538
5744	326	184	598	1022	78
7499	557	57	363	454	75
9247	534	231	703	618	504
3234	406	138	215	427	3
8141	550	154	652	575	19
6846	172	95	2313	3181	81
6806	278	31	992	617	212
1817	17	0	54	118	30
4484	346	61	762	584	161
11776	627	146	1165	1232	1030
2347	78	34	197	489	141
6078	144	62	450	2093	45
353	0	0	28	166	217
3766	166	45	1091	583	140
2259	153	68	146	317	57
809	32	15	44	141	1
949	51	36	9	255	2
2226	78	19	78	186	104

普通中学教

Number of Teachers, Staff & Workers in General

地区 Region	合计 Total	专任教师 Full-time Teachers 计 Total	初中 Junior Sec. Schools	高中 Senior Sec. Schools	行政人员 Adm. Personnel
					教职工 Teachers, Staff &
总计 Total	2064741	1762301	1662837	99464	147424
北京 Beijing	12440	9315	8799	516	2009
天津 Tianjin	11656	9965	9035	930	1196
河北 Hebei	121171	108937	105328	3609	6813
山西 Shanxi	77081	65403	62780	2623	5254
内蒙古 Inner Mongolia	38266	29487	28243	1244	3373
辽宁 Liaoning	70836	58271	55808	2463	9633
吉林 Jilin	26219	21171	21037	134	3896
黑龙江 Heilongjiang	61103	50171	48487	1684	5177
上海 Shanghai	2314	1578	1290	288	510
江苏 Jiangsu	91208	73380	64310	9070	7297
浙江 Zhejiang	19745	17583	17339	244	1477
安徽 Anhui	116463	100599	92313	8286	7423
福建 Fujian	42648	35834	34116	1718	4170
江西 Jiangxi	63243	56682	54945	1737	2687
山东 Shandong	265717	223934	206492	17442	17810
河南 Henan	185510	166355	160461	5894	9235
湖北 Hubei	111415	96582	90826	5756	4173
湖南 Hunan	113217	101678	94884	6794	4444
广东 Guangdong	123668	105691	95451	10240	10632
广西 Guangxi	96151	74770	71474	3296	10740
海南 Hainan	17739	13868	13088	780	1268
重庆 Chongqing	23342	19646	19093	553	2128
四川 Sichuan	94407	81255	80189	1066	7487
贵州 Guizhou	51243	45537	44017	1520	3319
云南 Yunnan	64932	54863	53572	1291	3372
西藏 Tibet	31	27	27	0	3
陕西 Shaanxi	50822	42801	40428	2373	5369
甘肃 Gansu	45602	41132	37949	3183	2148
青海 Qinghai	6750	6278	5523	755	244
宁夏 Ningxia	11263	9945	9332	613	500
新疆 Xinjiang	48539	39563	36201	3362	3637

职 工 数（农 村）

Secondary Schools（Rural）

单位：人

数 Workers			代课教师 Substitute Teachers	临时工 Temporary Workers	兼任教师 Part-time Teachers
工勤人员 Workers	校办工厂、农场职工 Employees in School-run Factories & Farms				
	计 Total	其中：由厂、场收入支付工资的职工 Employees maintained by income of School-run businesses			
151211	3805	1364	72847	45617	3217
1038	78	14	603	507	29
463	32	9	102	90	9
5339	82	11	6426	2826	46
6354	70	29	4219	2576	47
5258	148	45	2486	577	28
2840	92	43	977	653	46
1106	46	4	403	87	0
5544	211	176	2263	957	25
215	11	0	98	32	60
10198	333	76	3174	4152	23
648	37	9	1659	1106	24
8261	180	86	1821	3330	302
2613	31	9	1657	634	253
3765	109	41	1307	1208	71
23487	486	139	687	1608	54
9737	183	64	1523	710	62
9855	805	268	2462	2064	70
6945	150	16	1726	755	19
7320	25	8	8049	5002	70
10490	151	54	15476	3468	208
2577	26	23	183	284	34
1554	14	0	1322	880	36
5555	110	17	2518	1599	1043
2332	55	39	3505	1866	181
6666	31	3	2937	5364	235
1	0	0	0	1	0
2601	51	11	1622	956	50
2278	44	12	1956	950	18
228	0	0	39	149	0
810	8	2	234	422	10
5133	206	156	1413	804	164

普通中学教职工总

Number of General Secondary School Teachers,

地区 Region	教职工 Teachers, Staff &				
	合计 Total	专任教师 Full-time Teachers			行政人员 Adm. Personnel
		计 Total	初中 Junior Sec. Schools	高中 Senior Sec. Schools	
总计 Total	63852	41171	40928	243	1542
北京 Beijing	0	0	0	0	0
天津 Tianjin	61	0	0	0	7
河北 Hebei	3551	2431	2394	37	63
山西 Shanxi	7205	5276	5264	12	93
内蒙古 Inner Mongolia	2617	1182	1169	13	54
辽宁 Liaoning	5846	4153	4071	82	513
吉林 Jilin	1159	673	669	4	56
黑龙江 Heilongjiang	7334	6187	6180	7	221
上海 Shanghai	0	0	0	0	0
江苏 Jiangsu	4243	191	191	0	38
浙江 Zhejiang	526	33	33	0	9
安徽 Anhui	816	156	154	2	3
福建 Fujian	0	0	0	0	0
江西 Jiangxi	1528	684	682	2	6
山东 Shandong	11210	8354	8353	1	201
河南 Henan	6190	5680	5657	23	116
湖北 Hubei	2745	1251	1247	4	28
湖南 Hunan	3141	1471	1468	3	5
广东 Guangdong	1172	586	575	11	22
广西 Guangxi	1083	662	662	0	20
海南 Hainan	136	82	82	0	4
重庆 Chongqing	138	84	84	0	0
四川 Sichuan	787	484	467	17	15
贵州 Guizhou	243	205	204	1	2
云南 Yunnan	12	0	0	0	0
西藏 Tibet	0	0	0	0	0
陕西 Shaanxi	876	702	702	0	58
甘肃 Gansu	1084	595	585	10	1
青海 Qinghai	51	6	6	0	0
宁夏 Ningxia	23	0	0	0	0
新疆 Xinjiang	75	43	29	14	7

数中民办教职工数

Staff & Workers Maintained by the Communities

单位:人

数 Workers			代课教师 Substitute Teachers	临时工 Temporary Workers	兼任教师 Part-time Teachers
工勤人员 Workers	校办工厂、农场职工 Employees in School-run Factories & Farms				
	计 Total	其中:由厂、场收入支付工资的职工 Employees maintained by income of School-run businesses			
15073	6066	5543	23748	19170	281
0	0	0	0	0	0
19	35	28	13	36	0
988	69	56	6263	2737	1
1799	37	31	388	578	9
1290	91	65	1796	289	0
1152	28	28	797	707	15
37	393	393	86	166	4
329	597	511	1120	640	0
0	0	0	0	0	0
1049	2965	2850	2553	4118	17
12	472	462	634	1483	2
648	9	2	210	544	25
0	0	0	152	150	4
778	60	53	214	222	61
2607	48	22	371	763	0
378	16	1	866	565	10
1289	177	138	1543	1343	46
914	751	685	441	340	0
508	56	41	2114	2307	9
369	32	7	1167	869	2
46	4	4	7	24	0
54	0	0	113	9	0
255	33	33	381	224	0
36	0	0	108	35	0
6	6	6	0	0	0
0	0	0	0	5	0
101	15	13	1500	617	69
363	125	68	907	387	3
3	42	42	0	3	0
22	1	0	0	0	0
21	4	4	4	9	4

普通中学教职工总

Number of Female Teachers, Staff &

地区 Region		教职工 Teachers, Staff &				
		合计 Total	专任教师 Full-time Teachers			行政人员 Adm. Personnel
			计 Total	初中 Junior Sec. Schools	高中 Senior Sec. Schools	
总计	**Total**	1827092	1550341	1308691	241650	121910
北京	Beijing	44078	31962	24678	7284	8039
天津	Tianjin	29913	23497	18874	4623	4621
河北	Hebei	142072	130133	110266	19867	5202
山西	Shanxi	67864	59707	51782	7925	3278
内蒙古	Inner Mongolia	48424	40077	33232	6845	4104
辽宁	Liaoning	91675	79378	65380	13998	9148
吉林	Jilin	61324	52163	42870	9293	6501
黑龙江	Heilongjiang	94042	79114	66927	12187	8227
上海	Shanghai	42097	29006	22294	6712	9101
江苏	Jiangsu	87037	70104	55195	14909	5626
浙江	Zhejiang	65728	56979	45729	11250	3501
安徽	Anhui	44949	37682	32488	5194	2581
福建	Fujian	47801	40617	34985	5632	2879
江西	Jiangxi	40597	35562	30332	5230	1191
山东	Shandong	148420	130663	110502	20161	7188
河南	Henan	126427	113773	101299	12474	5623
湖北	Hubei	70932	58347	48489	9858	3889
湖南	Hunan	84626	74858	65243	9615	2236
广东	Guangdong	100917	84796	72027	12769	5845
广西	Guangxi	56942	44722	39792	4930	2958
海南	Hainan	9544	6482	5677	805	446
重庆	Chongqing	32381	26630	23291	3339	2656
四川	Sichuan	80088	67744	58674	9070	5203
贵州	Guizhou	26825	22737	19772	2965	1624
云南	Yunnan	46933	36521	32592	3929	2293
西藏	Tibet	1717	1417	1154	263	81
陕西	Shaanxi	50428	44684	37119	7565	3202
甘肃	Gansu	22261	19406	16229	3177	1002
青海	Qinghai	7695	6750	5101	1649	375
宁夏	Ningxia	8658	7403	6156	1247	324
新疆	Xinjiang	44697	37427	30542	6885	2966

数中女教职工数

Workers in General Secondary Schools

单位：人

数 Workers			代课教师 Substitute Teachers	临时工 Temporary Workers	兼任教师 Part-time Teachers
工勤人员 Workers	校办工厂、农场职工 Employees in School-run Factories & Farms				
	计 Total	其中：由厂、场收入支付工资的职工 Employees maintained by income of School-run businesses			
140803	14038	7673	51920	43095	6605
3281	796	288	1185	1242	327
1424	371	90	393	91	350
6036	701	445	5752	2312	79
4477	402	266	3256	1706	235
3933	310	126	1527	426	156
3052	97	45	841	1115	543
2210	450	290	370	352	37
5913	788	435	1478	786	250
3287	703	0	885	467	785
9020	2287	1863	2465	4079	156
4100	1148	937	3031	4519	985
4427	259	123	787	1937	222
4101	204	154	2461	964	122
3614	230	105	662	772	95
9612	957	344	425	464	55
6543	488	288	974	550	343
7691	1005	547	1267	1929	157
6729	803	475	1014	665	77
10086	190	73	5984	5370	52
9027	235	55	7976	2736	419
2569	47	36	83	232	27
2863	232	19	976	735	66
6653	488	185	1530	1188	261
2353	111	87	1258	1371	85
8004	115	66	1763	4961	123
212	7	0	23	65	102
2389	153	77	1789	631	283
1722	131	61	712	415	17
554	16	4	43	129	17
826	105	63	135	430	6
4095	209	126	875	456	173

职业中学校数、班数、

Number of Schools, Classes, Graduates & Students

地区 Region	学校数(所) Schools 计 Total	初中 Junior Sec. Schools	高中 Senior Sec. Schools	初高中合设 Junior & Senior Sec. Schools
总计 Total	9636	1319	7828	489
北京 Beijing	168	0	168	0
天津 Tianjin	127	0	118	9
河北 Hebei	494	69	409	16
山西 Shanxi	359	94	219	46
内蒙古 Inner Mongolia	443	275	135	33
辽宁 Liaoning	450	46	400	4
吉林 Jilin	284	42	234	8
黑龙江 Heilongjiang	269	54	197	18
上海 Shanghai	71	2	69	0
江苏 Jiangsu	415	1	412	2
浙江 Zhejiang	534	1	519	14
安徽 Anhui	742	357	336	49
福建 Fujian	266	5	248	13
江西 Jiangxi	314	35	258	21
山东 Shandong	505	8	473	24
河南 Henan	696	12	674	10
湖北 Hubei	354	72	273	9
湖南 Hunan	611	41	550	20
广东 Guangdong	435	8	401	26
广西 Guangxi	271	34	182	55
海南 Hainan	43	0	38	5
重庆 Chongqing	190	4	181	5
四川 Sichuan	383	15	354	14
贵州 Guizhou	270	95	153	22
云南 Yunnan	209	20	176	13
西藏 Tibet	3	0	1	2
陕西 Shaanxi	371	10	344	17
甘肃 Gansu	177	7	155	15
青海 Qinghai	31	3	23	5
宁夏 Ningxia	35	2	30	3
新疆 Xinjiang	116	7	98	11

毕业生数和招生数(总计)

Admitted in Vocational Schools (Regional Aggregates)

班数(个) Classes		毕业生数(人) Graduates		招生数(人) Students Admitted	
初中 Junior	高中 Senior	初中 Junior	高中 Senior	初中 Junior	高中 Senior
16500	104427	241425	1436865	337591	1603783
1	3089	94	34380	0	31004
14	2001	912	19097	296	23790
881	7912	15680	117964	17344	152189
784	2168	11189	33621	15950	41091
3032	2109	31536	21259	53600	32658
85	4927	1653	58407	1311	55030
805	2406	10721	48217	23292	39510
615	2199	11497	29331	8209	27287
16	2548	41	30356	127	28601
13	5645	156	73967	196	58731
21	6902	454	74516	238	110378
4314	4060	83304	65711	106307	61003
81	4635	1650	51215	1286	71717
529	2566	8965	38671	8598	54627
145	9198	3469	143197	1999	143377
157	9784	2673	176829	2105	167436
742	2958	13091	48315	17441	38083
214	5424	3716	65678	4559	83365
155	4604	2830	63143	2965	79538
932	2205	11153	28398	15526	27836
8	271	52	2873	183	3924
51	2293	387	27158	1031	29196
224	4507	2205	50165	3229	64416
781	953	9481	15841	16362	17040
1063	2184	3301	31738	21787	36985
4	15	208	262	100	467
177	3799	2065	51329	3624	83076
47	1366	1251	15779	766	20414
57	267	1118	3173	841	4276
28	440	1078	2944	744	6085
524	992	5495	13331	7575	10653

职业中学校数、班数、

Number of Schools, Classes, Graduates & Students

地区 Region	学校数(所) Schools 计 Total	初中 Junior Sec. Schools	高中 Senior Sec. Schools	初高中合设 Junior & Senior Sec. Schools
总计 Total	3763	30	3615	118
北京 Beijing	109	0	109	0
天津 Tianjin	94	0	87	7
河北 Hebei	182	1	175	6
山西 Shanxi	112	4	97	11
内蒙古 Inner Mongolia	63	0	58	5
辽宁 Liaoning	306	1	301	4
吉林 Jilin	130	3	123	4
黑龙江 Heilongjiang	98	1	94	3
上海 Shanghai	45	2	43	0
江苏 Jiangsu	107	1	105	1
浙江 Zhejiang	250	1	244	5
安徽 Anhui	152	2	147	3
福建 Fujian	100	0	96	4
江西 Jiangxi	108	0	102	6
山东 Shandong	224	0	218	6
河南 Henan	295	2	293	0
湖北 Hubei	204	6	195	3
湖南 Hunan	313	1	306	6
广东 Guangdong	128	1	118	9
广西 Guangxi	120	0	106	14
海南 Hainan	5	0	4	1
重庆 Chongqing	93	2	88	3
四川 Sichuan	118	0	117	1
贵州 Guizhou	69	1	64	4
云南 Yunnan	55	0	52	3
西藏 Tibet	1	0	0	1
陕西 Shaanxi	173	0	171	2
甘肃 Gansu	35	0	35	0
青海 Qinghai	10	0	9	1
宁夏 Ningxia	16	0	16	0
新疆 Xinjiang	48	1	42	5

毕业生数和招生数(城市)

Admitted in Vocational Schools (Urban)

班数(个) Classes		毕业生数(人) Graduates		招生数(人) Students Admitted	
初中 Junior	高中 Senior	初中 Junior	高中 Senior	初中 Junior	高中 Senior
555	52807	7730	696479	8723	749175
1	2254	94	23739	0	21870
10	1628	605	14349	0	20163
43	3156	659	43863	855	57863
100	1115	1448	16141	2415	20731
14	955	113	10747	193	14716
19	3753	84	43046	232	43506
37	1208	317	19582	329	15406
9	1442	147	16900	82	17229
16	1788	41	19560	127	20649
12	1423	138	17383	196	10149
5	3454	184	35754	52	55346
39	1931	431	32425	676	24794
0	2016	0	20469	0	30781
0	1070	0	13354	0	21313
14	5046	104	77350	171	77495
21	4768	197	78179	156	70073
52	2265	1807	37492	1106	26735
20	2825	85	35370	180	41739
6	1787	28	27044	39	27985
29	1282	0	16594	135	15758
6	88	52	766	65	1269
23	1347	173	15113	422	14891
2	1890	40	22269	43	26175
17	396	114	8383	334	7789
23	753	161	11130	372	12674
0	6	0	176	0	87
9	1656	91	22901	180	34468
5	512	426	5996	80	6597
2	116	28	879	38	1375
0	286	0	1780	0	4176
21	591	163	7745	245	5373

职业中学校数、班数、

Number of Schools, Classes, Graduates & Students

地区 Region		学校数(所) Schools			
		计 Total	初中 Junior Sec. Schools	高中 Senior Sec. Schools	初高中合设 Junior & Senior Sec. Schools
总计	**Total**	3206	173	2821	212
北京	Beijing	35	0	35	0
天津	Tianjin	24	0	23	1
河北	Hebei	225	17	201	7
山西	Shanxi	87	4	59	24
内蒙古	Inner Mongolia	94	20	54	20
辽宁	Liaoning	56	2	54	0
吉林	Jilin	105	17	87	1
黑龙江	Heilongjiang	112	21	83	8
上海	Shanghai	25	0	25	0
江苏	Jiangsu	215	0	214	1
浙江	Zhejiang	275	0	266	9
安徽	Anhui	99	9	76	14
福建	Fujian	132	2	122	8
江西	Jiangxi	129	8	113	8
山东	Shandong	89	5	79	5
河南	Henan	220	1	212	7
湖北	Hubei	47	6	39	2
湖南	Hunan	196	17	171	8
广东	Guangdong	129	7	116	6
广西	Guangxi	85	0	55	30
海南	Hainan	15	0	13	2
重庆	Chongqing	79	2	75	2
四川	Sichuan	226	8	208	10
贵州	Guizhou	105	16	76	13
云南	Yunnan	110	3	98	9
西藏	Tibet	2	0	1	1
陕西	Shaanxi	158	3	147	8
甘肃	Gansu	63	1	61	1
青海	Qinghai	17	2	13	2
宁夏	Ningxia	15	1	11	3
新疆	Xinjiang	37	1	34	2

毕业生数和招生数(县镇)

Admitted in Vocational Schools (County Seats & Towns)

班数(个) Classes		毕业生数(人) Graduates		招生数(人) Students Admitted	
初中 Junior	高中 Senior	初中 Junior	高中 Senior	初中 Junior	高中 Senior
3084	37096	41852	530359	60164	612065
0	614	0	7772	0	7275
0	251	0	3184	0	2195
235	4147	3961	65347	4785	83481
181	626	2594	9643	3647	12669
467	851	4784	8075	8450	14038
2	740	100	10326	0	7111
368	923	4238	20509	9721	17848
188	633	3944	9807	1636	8656
0	745	0	10330	0	7494
1	3270	18	41835	0	35998
16	3364	270	38089	186	53817
180	1087	3848	18974	4280	17746
66	2184	1335	25772	1049	34026
165	1141	2984	20010	2415	26132
62	1463	1643	23301	320	23233
7	3204	86	66864	10	61906
52	453	903	6645	1439	7253
41	1947	877	24011	1091	30931
130	1238	2448	16073	2531	22690
211	642	939	8940	4254	8135
2	83	0	978	118	1160
25	844	214	10998	584	12671
134	2331	959	24985	1884	33966
194	488	2231	6886	4596	7997
154	1145	351	16709	3618	19560
4	9	208	86	100	380
80	1756	846	23154	1832	39745
14	466	17	5420	17	7158
30	134	521	1841	610	2403
17	127	858	941	254	1617
58	190	675	2854	737	2774

职业中学校数、班数、

Number of Schools, Classes, Graduates & Students

地区 Region	学校数(所) Schools 计 Total	初中 Junior Sec. Schools	高中 Senior Sec. Schools	初高中合设 Junior & Senior Sec. Schools
总计 Total	2667	1116	1392	159
北京 Beijing	24	0	24	0
天津 Tianjin	9	0	8	1
河北 Hebei	87	51	33	3
山西 Shanxi	160	86	63	11
内蒙古 Inner Mongolia	286	255	23	8
辽宁 Liaoning	88	43	45	0
吉林 Jilin	49	22	24	3
黑龙江 Heilongjiang	59	32	20	7
上海 Shanghai	1	0	1	0
江苏 Jiangsu	93	0	93	0
浙江 Zhejiang	9	0	9	0
安徽 Anhui	491	346	113	32
福建 Fujian	34	3	30	1
江西 Jiangxi	77	27	43	7
山东 Shandong	192	3	176	13
河南 Henan	181	9	169	3
湖北 Hubei	103	60	39	4
湖南 Hunan	102	23	73	6
广东 Guangdong	178	0	167	11
广西 Guangxi	66	34	21	11
海南 Hainan	23	0	21	2
重庆 Chongqing	18	0	18	0
四川 Sichuan	39	7	29	3
贵州 Guizhou	96	78	13	5
云南 Yunnan	44	17	26	1
西藏 Tibet	0	0	0	0
陕西 Shaanxi	40	7	26	7
甘肃 Gansu	79	6	59	14
青海 Qinghai	4	1	1	2
宁夏 Ningxia	4	1	3	0
新疆 Xinjiang	31	5	22	4

毕业生数和招生数(农村)

Admitted in Vocational Schools (Rural)

班数(个) Classes		毕业生数(人) Graduates		招生数(人) Students Admitted	
初中 Junior	高中 Senior	初中 Junior	高中 Senior	初中 Junior	高中 Senior
12861	14524	191843	210027	268704	242543
0	221	0	2869	0	1859
4	122	307	1564	296	1432
603	609	11060	8754	11704	10845
503	427	7147	7837	9888	7691
2551	303	26639	2437	44957	3904
64	434	1469	5035	1079	4413
400	275	6166	8126	13242	6256
418	124	7406	2624	6491	1402
0	15	0	466	0	458
0	952	0	14749	0	12584
0	84	0	673	0	1215
4095	1042	79025	14312	101351	18463
15	435	315	4974	237	6910
364	355	5981	5307	6183	7182
69	2689	1722	42546	1508	42649
129	1812	2390	31786	1939	35457
638	240	10381	4178	14896	4095
153	652	2754	6297	3288	10695
19	1579	354	20026	395	28863
692	281	10214	2864	11137	3943
0	100	0	1129	0	1495
3	102	0	1047	25	1634
88	286	1206	2911	1302	4275
570	69	7136	572	11432	1254
886	286	2789	3899	17797	4751
0	0	0	0	0	0
88	387	1128	5274	1612	8863
28	388	808	4363	669	6659
25	17	569	453	193	498
11	27	220	223	490	292
445	211	4657	2732	6593	2506

职业中学在校学生

Enrolment and Number of Graduates for Next Year

地 区 Region	合 计 Total	在校学 Enrolment 初 中 Junior Sec. Schools 计 Subtotal	一年级 Grade 1	二年级 Grade 2	三年级 Grade 3
总 计 Total	5339170	900751	339306	300519	260926
北 京 Beijing	106964	23	0	0	23
天 津 Tianjin	78110	707	707	0	0
河 北 Hebei	465441	49950	17347	16845	15758
山 西 Shanxi	140187	38737	15965	11458	11314
内蒙古 Inner Mongolia	225891	141657	53614	44831	43212
辽 宁 Liaoning	194860	2913	1311	992	610
吉 林 Jilin	142846	44117	23292	11427	9398
黑龙江 Heilongjiang	116937	36332	8209	17675	10448
上 海 Shanghai	102088	327	127	96	104
江 苏 Jiangsu	196677	573	196	190	187
浙 江 Zhejiang	284123	660	238	222	200
安 徽 Anhui	467026	291150	106313	99869	84968
福 建 Fujian	180585	4408	1286	1647	1475
江 西 Jiangxi	152038	27808	8908	9741	9159
山 东 Shandong	426107	6599	1999	1806	2794
河 南 Henan	537477	8821	2131	1951	4739
湖 北 Hubei	162219	43814	17449	14281	12084
湖 南 Hunan	227864	9416	4591	2237	2588
广 东 Guangdong	206510	8791	2965	3048	2778
广 西 Guangxi	126117	46963	15526	15573	15864
海 南 Hainan	9411	295	183	42	70
重 庆 Chongqing	82377	2321	1031	834	456
四 川 Sichuan	174942	9786	3240	2295	4251
贵 州 Guizhou	79529	39626	16461	12747	10418
云 南 Yunnan	138907	51481	22565	20129	8787
西 藏 Tibet	740	106	100	6	0
陕 西 Shaanxi	186945	8508	3624	2820	2064
甘 肃 Gansu	49866	1755	766	522	467
青 海 Qinghai	10049	1774	843	415	516
宁 夏 Ningxia	16466	1497	744	274	479
新 疆 Xinjiang	49871	19836	7575	6546	5715

数、毕业班学生数(总计)

in Vocational Schools (Regional Aggregates)

单位:人

生 数

计 Subtotal	高中 Senior Sec. Schools 二年制 2-year 一年级 Grade 1	二年级 Grade 2	三年制 3-year 一年级 Grade 1	二年级 Grade 2	三年级 Grade 3	四年制 4-year	毕业班学生数 Graduates for Next Year 初中 Junior Sec. Schools	高中 Senior Sec. Schools
4438419	306708	288179	1274898	1293088	1192346	83200	263967	1506104
106941	1861	3375	25265	30927	29354	16159	23	36748
77403	41	64	15486	18362	17331	26119	889	21592
415491	27740	24582	123134	130262	109276	497	15758	136771
101450	13863	12323	27296	25641	22086	241	11314	34650
84234	5902	3459	26758	27260	20845	10	33718	24314
191947	1876	3096	53098	68753	64864	260	610	68026
98729	21318	17207	17889	20949	20523	843	16623	37907
80605	6243	9470	21044	24039	19587	222	10448	29279
101761	2315	3505	24277	30455	33643	7566	57	39350
196104	9443	9092	48891	60963	65147	2568	187	74881
283463	8680	18233	100805	84069	69568	2108	200	88064
175876	9696	7778	51309	49696	57373	24	84968	65151
176177	14428	7307	56824	47938	48369	1311	1475	55911
124230	19091	16758	35848	29424	23054	55	8276	40210
419508	18656	17451	124342	133113	124093	1853	2794	143879
528656	18143	23441	149000	171131	160097	6844	4739	186705
118405	3887	3508	31896	33371	36072	9671	11265	41425
218448	14108	10050	68984	66394	57745	1167	2588	68146
197719	11475	12498	68116	56077	49349	204	2778	61900
79154	3227	2326	24486	24752	24363	0	15864	26635
9116	1564	808	2481	2314	1949	0	70	2749
80056	10827	11774	18423	20721	18311	0	456	30085
165156	16814	14949	47599	44321	41317	156	4251	56266
39903	5514	4758	11526	9078	9027	0	10418	13785
87426	15894	16763	21104	18017	15648	0	14694	32411
634	106	0	361	0	167	0	80	183
178437	35677	26328	46283	37826	28443	3880	1497	56097
48111	3221	2827	16966	12667	11466	964	717	14348
8275	2106	1591	1746	1462	1370	0	821	3811
14969	332	304	5753	5185	3395	0	674	3586
30035	2660	2554	7908	7921	8514	478	5715	11239

职业中学在校学生

Enrolment and Number of Graduates for Next Year

在校学 Enrolment

地区 Region	合计 Total	初中 Junior Sec. Schools 计 Subtotal	一年级 Grade 1	二年级 Grade 2	三年级 Grade 3
总计 Total	2259771	21636	9166	6658	5812
北京 Beijing	76340	23	0	0	23
天津 Tianjin	65344	411	411	0	0
河北 Hebei	162375	2181	855	1046	280
山西 Shanxi	61448	5362	2415	1260	1687
内蒙古 Inner Mongolia	39228	482	193	154	135
辽宁 Liaoning	153628	644	232	155	257
吉林 Jilin	46911	648	329	200	119
黑龙江 Heilongjiang	53028	273	82	142	49
上海 Shanghai	71094	327	127	96	104
江苏 Jiangsu	48636	556	196	190	170
浙江 Zhejiang	147149	142	52	35	55
安徽 Anhui	84733	1751	676	645	430
福建 Fujian	78293	0	0	0	0
江西 Jiangxi	46906	0	0	0	0
山东 Shandong	234448	391	171	98	122
河南 Henan	240626	479	156	143	180
湖北 Hubei	92615	2985	1106	1034	845
湖南 Hunan	116873	436	212	84	140
广东 Guangdong	76584	78	39	25	14
广西 Guangxi	50792	252	135	54	63
海南 Hainan	3282	177	65	42	70
重庆 Chongqing	48380	937	422	354	161
四川 Sichuan	74679	73	43	30	0
贵州 Guizhou	20412	651	334	87	230
云南 Yunnan	33844	948	372	315	261
西藏 Tibet	200	0	0	0	0
陕西 Shaanxi	82648	489	180	207	102
甘肃 Gansu	17378	210	80	70	60
青海 Qinghai	3612	47	38	0	9
宁夏 Ningxia	10090	0	0	0	0
新疆 Xinjiang	18195	683	245	192	246

数、毕业班学生数(城市)

in Vocational Schools (Urban)

单位:人

生数								
	高中 Senior Sec. Schools						毕业班学生数 Graduates for Next Year	
计 Subtotal	二年制 2-year		三年制 3-year			四年制 4-year	初中 Junior Sec. Schools	高中 Senior Sec. Schools
	一年级 Grade 1	二年级 Grade 2	一年级 Grade 1	二年级 Grade 2	三年级 Grade 3			
2238135	86458	89853	643270	696070	651182	71302	6468	759943
76317	261	850	18090	21435	20237	15444	23	25007
64933	6	9	11979	14383	13198	25358	593	17255
160194	11291	8553	45586	51634	42668	462	280	53555
56086	4903	4075	15829	17064	14102	113	1687	18290
38746	3125	1137	11591	12433	10460	0	171	11597
152984	450	1046	42991	55820	52590	87	257	53658
46263	4872	5121	10461	13053	12613	143	193	17791
52755	2581	4529	14648	17291	13563	143	49	18235
70767	795	1213	17997	21925	22152	6685	57	25354
48080	521	381	9617	17822	19627	112	170	20008
147007	2242	6001	52864	45627	38580	1693	55	44843
82982	1609	1777	23187	25624	30761	24	430	32538
78293	4197	2100	26212	23386	21478	920	0	23651
46906	7326	5660	14107	10383	9375	55	0	15051
234057	5152	5617	72031	78531	70980	1746	122	77850
240147	3904	5112	65211	80596	79673	5651	180	86759
89630	1606	1694	22888	25591	28731	9120	845	32072
116437	6856	5058	34730	35683	33237	873	140	38524
76506	1270	1564	26721	24618	22280	53	14	23897
50540	756	520	15059	17006	17199	0	63	17719
3105	190	0	1079	1058	778	0	70	778
47443	3546	4585	11345	14365	13602	0	161	18187
74606	3760	4962	22412	21897	21469	106	0	26431
19761	1779	1651	6010	5202	5119	0	230	6770
32896	3346	4807	9336	8347	7060	0	261	11867
200	36	0	51	0	113	0	0	113
82159	8787	9254	25235	20517	16839	1527	102	26671
17168	98	687	6357	5041	4476	509	60	5189
3565	515	770	860	926	494	0	9	1264
10090	80	29	4096	3787	2098	0	0	2127
17512	598	1091	4690	5025	5630	478	246	6892

职业中学在校学生

Enrolment and Number of Graduates for Next Year

地区 Region	合计 Total	在校学 Enrolment 初中 Junior Sec. Schools 计 Subtotal	一年级 Grade 1	二年级 Grade 2	三年级 Grade 3
总计 Total	1738468	156817	60193	49773	46851
北京 Beijing	23815	0	0	0	0
天津 Tianjin	8258	0	0	0	0
河北 Hebei	238210	13250	4786	4014	4450
山西 Shanxi	37212	9526	3647	3473	2406
内蒙古 Inner Mongolia	57697	22937	8454	7246	7237
辽宁 Liaoning	25778	61	0	35	26
吉林 Jilin	58334	17812	9721	4264	3827
黑龙江 Heilongjiang	33421	10113	1636	4604	3873
上海 Shanghai	29763	0	0	0	0
江苏 Jiangsu	114320	17	0	0	17
浙江 Zhejiang	134047	518	186	187	145
安徽 Anhui	59712	11366	4281	3724	3361
福建 Fujian	85424	3697	1049	1413	1235
江西 Jiangxi	69504	8718	2418	3342	2958
山东 Shandong	70145	1724	320	240	1164
河南 Henan	184520	962	10	13	939
湖北 Hubei	22164	3241	1439	1101	701
湖南 Hunan	78952	1700	1091	348	261
广东 Guangdong	61915	7678	2531	2697	2450
广西 Guangxi	29018	9840	4254	3244	2342
海南 Hainan	3048	118	118	0	0
重庆 Chongqing	31040	1311	584	452	275
四川 Sichuan	86372	5847	1884	1202	2761
贵州 Guizhou	27927	10351	4613	3243	2495
云南 Yunnan	51697	7762	3621	2345	1796
西藏 Tibet	540	106	100	6	0
陕西 Shaanxi	81961	3957	1832	1246	879
甘肃 Gansu	16056	155	17	121	17
青海 Qinghai	4975	848	610	47	191
宁夏 Ningxia	5061	907	254	274	379
新疆 Xinjiang	7582	2295	737	892	666

数、毕业班学生数(县镇)

in Vocational Schools (County Seats & Towns)

单位:人

生数							毕业班学生数 Graduates for Next Year	
	高中 Senior Sec. Schools							
计 Subtotal	二年制 2-year		三年制 3-year			四年制 4-year	初中 Junior Sec. Schools	高中 Senior Sec. Schools
	一年级 Grade 1	二年级 Grade 2	一年级 Grade 1	二年级 Grade 2	三年级 Grade 3			
1581651	156821	139425	452784	432188	390792	9641	49707	534292
23815	1125	1614	5791	7622	6948	715	0	8661
8258	35	55	2075	2582	2750	761	0	2954
224960	15480	13574	67672	70156	58043	35	4450	72196
27686	3956	3342	8725	6112	5551	0	2406	8893
34760	2632	1836	11408	11241	7643	0	5769	9479
25717	698	1244	6422	8579	8774	0	26	10018
40522	11475	8534	6143	6690	6980	700	7456	15634
23308	3159	4383	5497	5496	4694	79	3873	9156
29763	1359	2031	6063	8380	11333	597	0	13577
114303	5989	6160	29654	34955	35139	2406	17	41910
133529	6050	11830	47114	37713	30407	415	145	42238
48346	2404	1540	15342	13327	15733	0	3361	17273
81727	8213	3936	25720	20360	23107	391	1235	27205
60786	9852	9419	16492	14584	10439	0	2958	20120
68421	5831	4297	17402	20187	20704	0	1164	25255
183558	10087	13527	52412	55732	51479	321	939	65327
18923	1001	775	6124	5345	5127	551	701	6058
77252	4845	4043	25966	23579	18525	294	261	22690
54237	3435	3465	19374	14963	13000	0	2450	16465
19178	1450	1128	6562	5112	4926	0	2531	6000
2930	223	178	937	847	745	0	0	923
29729	6083	6270	6642	6097	4637	0	275	10907
80525	12341	9303	21625	19686	17520	50	2761	26823
17576	3518	2856	4479	3351	3372	0	2495	6228
43935	9325	8857	10240	8036	7477	0	2140	16334
434	70	0	310	0	54	0	80	70
78004	21490	11919	17627	15024	10053	1891	656	22419
15901	1731	1106	5362	3889	3378	435	17	4480
4127	1305	821	872	523	606	0	496	2082
4154	252	275	1365	1186	1076	0	379	1238
5287	1407	1107	1367	834	572	0	666	1679

职业中学在校学生

Enrolment and Number of Graduates for Next Year

地区 Region	合计 Total	初中 Junior Sec. Schools 计 Subtotal	一年级 Grade 1	二年级 Grade 2	三年级 Grade 3
		在校学 Enrolment			
总计 Total	1340931	722298	269947	244088	208263
北京 Beijing	6809	0	0	0	0
天津 Tianjin	4508	296	296	0	0
河北 Hebei	64856	34519	11706	11785	11028
山西 Shanxi	41527	23849	9903	6725	7221
内蒙古 Inner Mongolia	128966	118238	44967	37431	35840
辽宁 Liaoning	15454	2208	1079	802	327
吉林 Jilin	37601	25657	13242	6963	5452
黑龙江 Heilongjiang	30488	25946	6491	12929	6526
上海 Shanghai	1231	0	0	0	0
江苏 Jiangsu	33721	0	0	0	0
浙江 Zhejiang	2927	0	0	0	0
安徽 Anhui	322581	278033	101356	95500	81177
福建 Fujian	16868	711	237	234	240
江西 Jiangxi	35628	19090	6490	6399	6201
山东 Shandong	121514	4484	1508	1468	1508
河南 Henan	112331	7380	1965	1795	3620
湖北 Hubei	47440	37588	14904	12146	10538
湖南 Hunan	32039	7280	3288	1805	2187
广东 Guangdong	68011	1035	395	326	314
广西 Guangxi	46307	36871	11137	12275	13459
海南 Hainan	3081	0	0	0	0
重庆 Chongqing	2957	73	25	28	20
四川 Sichuan	13891	3866	1313	1063	1490
贵州 Guizhou	31190	28624	11514	9417	7693
云南 Yunnan	53366	42771	18572	17469	6730
西藏 Tibet	0	0	0	0	0
陕西 Shaanxi	22336	4062	1612	1367	1083
甘肃 Gansu	16432	1390	669	331	390
青海 Qinghai	1462	879	195	368	316
宁夏 Ningxia	1315	590	490	0	100
新疆 Xinjiang	24094	16858	6593	5462	4803

数、毕业班学生数(农村)

in Vocational Schools (Rural)

单位:人

生数 计 Subtotal	高中 Senior Sec. Schools 二年制 2-year 一年级 Grade 1	二年制 2-year 二年级 Grade 2	三年制 3-year 一年级 Grade 1	三年制 3-year 二年级 Grade 2	三年制 3-year 三年级 Grade 3	四年制 4-year	毕业班学生数 Graduates for Next Year 初中 Junior Sec. Schools	毕业班学生数 Graduates for Next Year 高中 Senior Sec. Schools
618633	63429	58901	178844	164830	150372	2257	207792	211869
6809	475	911	1384	1870	2169	0	0	3080
4212	0	0	1432	1397	1383	0	296	1383
30337	969	2455	9876	8472	8565	0	11028	11020
17678	5004	4906	2742	2465	2433	128	7221	7467
10728	145	486	3759	3586	2742	10	27778	3238
13246	728	806	3685	4354	3500	173	327	4350
11944	4971	3552	1285	1206	930	0	8974	4482
4542	503	558	899	1252	1330	0	6526	1888
1231	161	261	217	150	158	284	0	419
33721	2933	2551	9620	8186	10381	50	0	12963
2927	388	402	827	729	581	0	0	983
44548	5683	4461	12780	10745	10879	0	81177	15340
16157	2018	1271	4892	4192	3784	0	240	5055
16538	1913	1679	5249	4457	3240	0	5318	5039
117030	7673	7537	34909	34395	32409	107	1508	40774
104951	4152	4802	31377	34803	28945	872	3620	34619
9852	1280	1039	2884	2435	2214	0	9719	3295
24759	2407	949	8288	7132	5983	0	2187	6932
66976	6770	7469	22021	16496	14069	151	314	21538
9436	1021	678	2865	2634	2238	0	13270	2916
3081	1151	630	465	409	426	0	0	1048
2884	1198	919	436	259	72	0	20	991
10025	713	684	3562	2738	2328	0	1490	3012
2566	217	251	1037	525	536	0	7693	787
10595	3223	3099	1528	1634	1111	0	12293	4210
0	0	0	0	0	0	0	0	0
18274	5400	5155	3421	2285	1551	462	739	7007
15042	1392	1034	5247	3737	3612	20	640	4679
583	286	0	14	13	270	0	316	465
725	0	0	292	212	221	0	295	221
7236	655	356	1851	2062	2312	0	4803	2668

职业中学学生

Number of Female Students

地区 Region		合计 Total	在校学 Enrolment 初中 Junior Sec. Schools 计 Subtotal	一年级 Grade 1	二年级 Grade 2	三年级 Grade 3
总 计	**Total**	2547269	407583	153465	137055	117063
北 京	Beijing	57240	0	0	0	0
天 津	Tianjin	43409	331	331	0	0
河 北	Hebei	245618	23908	8322	8010	7576
山 西	Shanxi	68406	17363	6320	5467	5576
内蒙古	Inner Mongolia	104835	66155	24930	20719	20506
辽 宁	Liaoning	101430	1491	662	490	339
吉 林	Jilin	68424	19403	9793	5535	4075
黑龙江	Heilongjiang	57655	16131	3628	7882	4621
上 海	Shanghai	55651	97	40	30	27
江 苏	Jiangsu	85112	263	88	82	93
浙 江	Zhejiang	138560	94	39	47	8
安 徽	Anhui	211645	130748	48645	44591	37512
福 建	Fujian	89879	2168	610	828	730
江 西	Jiangxi	58192	11887	3958	4206	3723
山 东	Shandong	189141	2682	797	705	1180
河 南	Henan	253050	4038	962	1152	1924
湖 北	Hubei	75348	19459	7961	6324	5174
湖 南	Hunan	106574	4213	2015	1061	1137
广 东	Guangdong	99999	4202	1384	1510	1308
广 西	Guangxi	55322	20505	6747	7029	6729
海 南	Hainan	4359	159	94	25	40
重 庆	Chongqing	40737	910	400	322	188
四 川	Sichuan	81816	4408	1417	973	2018
贵 州	Guizhou	33655	16379	6831	5344	4204
云 南	Yunnan	65086	24540	10826	9480	4234
西 藏	Tibet	371	50	48	2	0
陕 西	Shaanxi	92433	4049	1779	1346	924
甘 肃	Gansu	24463	821	386	226	209
青 海	Qinghai	5293	1027	575	219	233
宁 夏	Ningxia	8833	652	318	153	181
新 疆	Xinjiang	24733	9450	3559	3297	2594

总数中女学生数

in Vocational Schools

单位:人

生数							毕业班学生数 Graduates for Next Year	
	高中 Senior Sec. Schools							
计 Subtotal	二年制 2-year		三年制 3-year			四年制 4-year	初中 Junior Sec. Schools	高中 Senior Sec. Schools
	一年级 Grade 1	二年级 Grade 2	一年级 Grade 1	二年级 Grade 2	三年级 Grade 3			
2139686	126700	119838	604126	638818	605126	45078	117556	737871
57240	775	1810	13477	16765	15590	8823	0	19667
43078	23	31	8465	10410	10087	14062	431	12427
221710	12890	11189	65231	70442	61661	297	7576	74417
51043	6771	5690	13488	13186	11871	37	5576	17598
38680	2030	1578	12153	12827	10088	4	15743	11666
99939	885	1510	26665	36117	34555	207	339	36120
49021	9499	7759	9530	11370	10422	441	6701	17981
41524	2850	4680	11136	12588	10170	100	4621	14950
55554	1073	1969	12994	16536	18896	4086	18	22085
84849	3097	3219	20133	27187	29868	1345	93	33472
138466	3271	7380	46817	42990	36600	1408	8	44063
80897	3683	2721	23197	23246	28042	8	37512	30763
87711	6126	3404	26909	24743	25934	595	730	29226
46305	5991	5235	13138	12579	9310	52	3254	14460
186459	7578	7062	53282	59673	57658	1206	1180	65799
249012	7590	9995	70161	79860	78063	3343	1924	89534
55889	1499	1149	14428	15641	17655	5517	4750	20101
102361	6083	4534	31735	31120	28360	529	1137	33000
95797	4990	5600	31914	28243	24953	97	1308	30540
34817	1059	944	10112	10996	11706	0	6746	12584
4200	563	311	1137	1136	1053	0	40	1361
39827	4882	5510	8985	10499	9951	0	188	15617
77408	6313	5419	22489	21864	21175	148	2018	26594
17276	1812	1742	5369	4127	4226	0	4204	5968
40546	5278	5821	11133	9778	8536	0	7028	14357
321	64	0	149	0	108	0	43	119
88384	16348	10550	23753	20741	14960	2032	697	26700
23642	1259	1070	8301	6429	6067	516	369	7156
4266	1188	894	758	685	741	0	443	1989
8181	149	104	2840	2950	2138	0	297	2060
15283	1081	958	4247	4090	4682	225	2582	5497

职业中学教

Number of Teachers, Staff & Workers in

地区 Region	教职工 Teachers, Staff &				
	合计 Total	专任教师 Full-time Teachers			行政人员 Adm. Personnel
		计 Total	初中 Junior Sec. Schools	高中 Senior Sec. Schools	
总计 Total	472254	335501	39420	296081	68158
北京 Beijing	13195	7691	0	7691	3740
天津 Tianjin	7636	4859	32	4827	1875
河北 Hebei	34631	25002	2748	22254	3968
山西 Shanxi	14041	10180	2516	7664	1688
内蒙古 Inner Mongolia	20412	15536	8682	6854	2155
辽宁 Liaoning	19443	13691	134	13557	4075
吉林 Jilin	13143	8919	1856	7063	2895
黑龙江 Heilongjiang	13289	9032	859	8173	2333
上海 Shanghai	7137	4107	52	4055	1944
江苏 Jiangsu	31035	22381	59	22322	3900
浙江 Zhejiang	19825	14802	53	14749	2618
安徽 Anhui	24968	19882	10512	9370	2654
福建 Fujian	14510	10770	276	10494	2152
江西 Jiangxi	11695	7784	876	6908	1012
山东 Shandong	41289	27838	892	26946	6497
河南 Henan	36357	26677	426	26251	4278
湖北 Hubei	17046	12518	2684	9834	2123
湖南 Hunan	24775	17632	695	16937	2914
广东 Guangdong	19297	15086	421	14665	2426
广西 Guangxi	10697	7307	966	6341	1513
海南 Hainan	1488	1086	17	1069	152
重庆 Chongqing	9784	6494	214	6280	1657
四川 Sichuan	21318	14794	555	14239	3210
贵州 Guizhou	7225	5500	2169	3331	922
云南 Yunnan	9835	6900	654	6246	1038
西藏 Tibet	70	46	4	42	14
陕西 Shaanxi	14030	9001	382	8619	2785
甘肃 Gansu	6371	4615	90	4525	690
青海 Qinghai	1067	807	76	731	115
宁夏 Ningxia	1263	966	80	886	123
新疆 Xinjiang	5382	3598	440	3158	692

职 工 数（总 计）

Vocational Schools (Regional Aggregates)

单位：人

数 Workers			代课教师 Substitute Teachers	临时工 Temporary Workers	兼任教师 Part-time Teachers
工勤人员 Workers	校办工厂、农场职工 Employers in School-run Factories & Farms				
	计 Total	其中：由厂、场收入支付工资的职工 Employers maintained by income of school-run businesses			
56163	12432	6447	13065	15459	26159
1535	229	80	347	884	497
745	157	43	343	120	567
4253	1408	976	537	2040	1263
1764	409	224	813	725	515
2444	277	32	876	315	324
1616	61	31	273	667	624
1084	245	191	86	183	284
1540	384	168	106	158	190
824	262	0	118	144	269
3733	1021	668	1208	1698	1155
1940	465	350	1682	1963	4284
2160	272	164	776	769	1397
1454	134	56	1083	243	1251
1160	1739	1519	235	249	1037
5635	1319	289	134	433	1084
4360	1042	404	67	844	1554
1995	410	201	486	374	910
3592	637	222	194	227	1283
1708	77	7	781	841	316
1667	210	126	325	361	1642
243	7	0	25	46	27
1285	348	131	260	266	382
2971	343	57	409	436	1132
718	85	18	328	280	333
1810	87	9	154	542	1438
10	0	0	3	15	9
1810	434	205	1130	357	1969
874	192	146	157	113	110
127	18	7	10	27	1
138	36	28	15	62	45
968	124	95	104	77	267

职业中学教

Number of Teachers, Staff & Workers in

地区 Region	教职工 Teachers, Staff & 合计 Total	专任教师 Full-time Teachers 计 Total	初中 Junior Sec. Schools	高中 Senior Sec. Schools	行政人员 Adm. Personnel
总计 Total	205524	137522	1513	136009	37867
北京 Beijing	9590	5363	0	5363	2966
天津 Tianjin	5853	3633	32	3601	1486
河北 Hebei	12420	8341	67	8274	1818
山西 Shanxi	5739	3793	317	3476	924
内蒙古 Inner Mongolia	4643	3325	62	3263	836
辽宁 Liaoning	13647	9650	20	9630	2876
吉林 Jilin	6935	4377	66	4311	1742
黑龙江 Heilongjiang	7490	4980	25	4955	1405
上海 Shanghai	4952	2850	45	2805	1404
江苏 Jiangsu	9465	6439	46	6393	1460
浙江 Zhejiang	8992	6425	10	6415	1340
安徽 Anhui	6344	4129	112	4017	1328
福建 Fujian	6265	4521	4	4517	1053
江西 Jiangxi	3489	2565	0	2565	480
山东 Shandong	19350	12191	46	12145	3481
河南 Henan	14816	10402	55	10347	2419
湖北 Hubei	10599	7395	196	7199	1694
湖南 Hunan	12145	8188	57	8131	1794
广东 Guangdong	7392	5557	19	5538	1126
广西 Guangxi	4392	2968	26	2942	768
海南 Hainan	447	376	17	359	46
重庆 Chongqing	5048	3197	48	3149	988
四川 Sichuan	7599	5083	4	5079	1346
贵州 Guizhou	1727	1249	47	1202	267
云南 Yunnan	3096	2243	95	2148	356
西藏 Tibet	37	26	1	25	4
陕西 Shaanxi	6316	3754	29	3725	1547
甘肃 Gansu	2518	1764	20	1744	330
青海 Qinghai	369	279	13	266	53
宁夏 Ningxia	540	380	0	380	67
新疆 Xinjiang	3309	2079	34	2045	463

职工数（城市）

Vocational Schools（Urban）

单位:人

数 Workers			代课教师 Substitute Teachers	临时工 Temporary Workers	兼任教师 Part-time Teachers
工勤人员 Workers	校办工厂、农场职工 Employers in School-run Factories & Farms				
	计 Total	其中:由厂、场收入支付工资的职工 Employers maintained by income of school-run businesses			
22993	7142	3678	5171	5629	16838
1096	165	75	232	447	323
587	147	43	323	44	555
1533	728	595	190	372	574
769	253	171	372	267	225
368	114	1	88	50	226
1069	52	28	208	497	591
585	231	191	20	107	22
821	284	147	38	85	95
528	170	0	78	74	178
776	790	641	81	176	318
959	268	217	627	889	3411
775	112	92	450	197	965
610	81	49	241	83	805
315	129	102	115	67	717
2512	1166	265	107	153	896
1481	514	121	0	567	855
1175	335	177	343	240	854
1739	424	216	124	77	1005
658	51	5	252	276	209
575	81	31	121	223	860
25	0	0	4	13	8
583	280	108	79	37	193
939	231	33	180	196	805
182	29	8	64	65	226
481	16	8	25	110	146
7	0	0	2	12	0
737	278	155	640	181	1539
313	111	103	74	33	25
37	0	0	2	4	1
65	28	27	14	48	38
693	74	69	77	39	173

职业中学教

Number of Teachers, Staff & Workers in

地区 Region	教职工 Teachers, Staff &				
	合计 Total	专任教师 Full-time Teachers			行政人员 Adm. Personnel
		计 Total	初中 Junior Sec. Schools	高中 Senior Sec. Schools	
总计 Total	171676	123305	8169	115136	21307
北京 Beijing	2292	1553	0	1553	444
天津 Tianjin	1158	746	0	746	291
河北 Hebei	17570	13003	789	12214	1771
山西 Shanxi	4197	3165	657	2508	425
内蒙古 Inner Mongolia	5636	4025	1391	2634	598
辽宁 Liaoning	4157	2803	8	2795	899
吉林 Jilin	4658	3299	889	2410	917
黑龙江 Heilongjiang	4726	3217	390	2827	807
上海 Shanghai	2022	1168	7	1161	498
江苏 Jiangsu	17227	12636	13	12623	2002
浙江 Zhejiang	10621	8203	43	8160	1259
安徽 Anhui	4395	3282	563	2719	498
福建 Fujian	7014	5229	226	5003	958
江西 Jiangxi	5426	3697	288	3409	361
山东 Shandong	7895	5411	228	5183	1166
河南 Henan	14423	10531	47	10484	1339
湖北 Hubei	2691	1944	226	1718	242
湖南 Hunan	9100	6742	102	6640	814
广东 Guangdong	6059	4682	350	4332	711
广西 Guangxi	4587	3039	415	2624	547
海南 Hainan	543	349	0	349	64
重庆 Chongqing	4067	2841	137	2704	564
四川 Sichuan	12118	8579	349	8230	1626
贵州 Guizhou	3328	2379	552	1827	477
云南 Yunnan	5130	3462	161	3301	563
西藏 Tibet	33	20	3	17	10
陕西 Shaanxi	6091	4050	178	3872	997
甘肃 Gansu	2149	1524	10	1514	201
青海 Qinghai	670	501	43	458	61
宁夏 Ningxia	602	478	60	418	52
新疆 Xinjiang	1091	747	44	703	145

职 工 数（县 镇）

Vocational Schools（County Seats & Towns）

单位:人

数 Workers			代课教师 Substitute Teachers	临时工 Temporary Workers	兼任教师 Part-time Teachers
工勤人员 Workers	校办工厂、农场职工 Employers in School-run Factories & Farms				
	计 Total	其中:由厂、场收入支付工资的职工 Employers maintained by income of school-run businesses			
23363	3701	1740	5190	6942	6283
250	45	0	105	337	134
112	9	0	14	56	9
2196	600	379	244	1410	639
508	99	39	224	253	164
897	116	17	87	54	75
450	5	2	15	73	20
428	14	0	47	44	234
602	100	21	34	50	56
271	85	0	29	51	91
2382	207	20	991	1167	753
971	188	124	998	1040	837
538	77	28	78	211	265
775	52	7	795	153	345
654	714	564	69	137	219
1227	91	20	17	101	151
2094	459	259	55	124	398
461	44	17	63	52	38
1379	165	6	45	122	242
654	12	1	226	300	68
882	119	95	77	79	125
126	4	0	12	11	18
599	63	23	168	201	172
1813	100	24	199	225	287
431	41	7	114	123	97
1045	60	1	66	311	329
3	0	0	1	3	9
899	145	46	357	148	395
383	41	23	44	42	78
90	18	7	8	23	0
64	8	1	1	14	0
179	20	9	7	27	35

职业中学教

Number of Teachers, Staff & Workers in

地区 Region	教职工 Teachers, Staff & 合计 Total	专任教师 Full-time Teachers 计 Total	初中 Junior Sec. Schools	高中 Senior Sec. Schools	行政人员 Adm. Personnel
总计 Total	95054	74674	29738	44936	8984
北京 Beijing	1313	775	0	775	330
天津 Tianjin	625	480	0	480	98
河北 Hebei	4641	3658	1892	1766	379
山西 Shanxi	4105	3222	1542	1680	339
内蒙古 Inner Mongolia	10133	8186	7229	957	721
辽宁 Liaoning	1639	1238	106	1132	300
吉林 Jilin	1550	1243	901	342	236
黑龙江 Heilongjiang	1073	835	444	391	121
上海 Shanghai	163	89	0	89	42
江苏 Jiangsu	4343	3306	0	3306	438
浙江 Zhejiang	212	174	0	174	19
安徽 Anhui	14229	12471	9837	2634	828
福建 Fujian	1231	1020	46	974	141
江西 Jiangxi	2780	1522	588	934	171
山东 Shandong	14044	10236	618	9618	1850
河南 Henan	7118	5744	324	5420	520
湖北 Hubei	3756	3179	2262	917	187
湖南 Hunan	3530	2702	536	2166	306
广东 Guangdong	5846	4847	52	4795	589
广西 Guangxi	1718	1300	525	775	198
海南 Hainan	498	361	0	361	42
重庆 Chongqing	669	456	29	427	105
四川 Sichuan	1601	1132	202	930	238
贵州 Guizhou	2170	1872	1570	302	178
云南 Yunnan	1609	1195	398	797	119
西藏 Tibet	0	0	0	0	0
陕西 Shaanxi	1623	1197	175	1022	241
甘肃 Gansu	1704	1327	60	1267	159
青海 Qinghai	28	27	20	7	1
宁夏 Ningxia	121	108	20	88	4
新疆 Xinjiang	982	772	362	410	84

职工数（农村）

Vocational Schools (Rural)

单位:人

数 Workers			代课教师 Substitute Teachers	临时工 Temporary Workers	兼任教师 Part-time Teachers
工勤人员 Workers	校办工厂、农场职工 Employers in School-run Factories & Farms				
	计 Total	其中:由厂、场收入支付工资的职工 Employers maintained by income of school-run businesses			
9807	1589	1029	2704	2888	3038
189	19	5	10	100	40
46	1	0	6	20	3
524	80	2	103	258	50
487	57	14	217	205	126
1179	47	14	701	211	23
97	4	1	50	97	13
71	0	0	19	32	28
117	0	0	34	23	39
25	7	0	11	19	0
575	24	7	136	355	84
10	9	9	57	34	36
847	83	44	248	361	167
69	1	0	47	7	101
191	896	853	51	45	101
1896	62	4	10	179	37
785	69	24	12	153	301
359	31	7	80	82	18
474	48	0	25	28	36
396	14	1	303	265	39
210	10	0	127	59	657
92	3	0	9	22	1
103	5	0	13	28	17
219	12	0	30	15	40
105	15	3	150	92	10
284	11	0	63	121	963
0	0	0	0	0	0
174	11	4	133	28	35
178	40	20	39	38	7
0	0	0	0	0	0
9	0	0	0	0	7
96	30	17	20	11	59

职业中学教职工总

Number of Female Teachers, Staff

地区 Region	教职工 Teachers, Staff &				
	合计 Total	专任教师 Full-time Teachers			行政人员 Adm. Personnel
		计 Total	初中 Junior Sec. Schools	高中 Senior Sec. Schools	
总计 Total	187984	141465	12640	128825	21144
北京 Beijing	8118	5150	0	5150	2110
天津 Tianjin	4210	2977	3	2974	864
河北 Hebei	16898	13803	1352	12451	1052
山西 Shanxi	6057	4990	1153	3837	400
内蒙古 Inner Mongolia	7942	6632	3335	3297	532
辽宁 Liaoning	10995	8537	41	8496	1837
吉林 Jilin	6545	4975	889	4086	1116
黑龙江 Heilongjiang	6604	5009	269	4740	872
上海 Shanghai	3673	2243	33	2210	963
江苏 Jiangsu	11549	8521	31	8490	1091
浙江 Zhejiang	8116	6239	22	6217	806
安徽 Anhui	5798	4556	2023	2533	527
福建 Fujian	5562	4207	76	4131	652
江西 Jiangxi	3286	2043	133	1910	185
山东 Shandong	15497	11748	326	11422	1615
河南 Henan	13402	10470	157	10313	1036
湖北 Hubei	5772	4176	676	3500	726
湖南 Hunan	8789	6566	209	6357	703
广东 Guangdong	7265	5755	122	5633	632
广西 Guangxi	4041	2673	363	2310	420
海南 Hainan	446	312	6	306	29
重庆 Chongqing	3621	2470	52	2418	547
四川 Sichuan	7339	5446	182	5264	835
贵州 Guizhou	2231	1689	505	1184	223
云南 Yunnan	4068	2728	225	2503	312
西藏 Tibet	21	13	2	11	6
陕西 Shaanxi	4955	3551	166	3385	651
甘肃 Gansu	1941	1437	38	1399	116
青海 Qinghai	432	345	24	321	25
宁夏 Ningxia	489	398	38	360	30
新疆 Xinjiang	2322	1806	189	1617	231

数中女教职工数

& Workers in Vocational Schools

单位:人

数 Workers			代课教师 Substitute Teachers	临时工 Temporary Workers	兼任教师 Part-time Teachers
工勤人员 Workers	校办工厂、农场职工 Employers in School-run Factories & Farms				
	计 Total	其中:由厂、场收入支付工资的职工 Employers maintained by income of school-run businesses			
20529	4846	2881	4328	5351	7655
762	96	46	184	330	256
307	62	13	164	32	238
1486	557	430	254	558	404
546	121	93	317	177	152
718	60	4	359	126	108
603	18	12	146	342	345
342	112	88	9	39	127
543	180	89	29	44	74
388	79	0	47	65	111
1497	440	291	333	589	266
868	203	164	603	834	1461
622	93	75	186	240	254
674	29	0	292	100	315
338	720	679	43	98	198
1589	545	107	10	100	253
1395	501	238	16	105	357
719	151	101	134	120	270
1316	204	90	56	74	366
861	17	2	255	357	31
852	96	60	127	171	373
103	2	0	3	36	0
453	151	74	82	77	145
971	87	20	132	120	306
308	11	2	106	103	98
1001	27	3	61	311	355
2	0	0	1	6	3
593	160	96	290	111	647
297	91	86	42	42	28
57	5	1	0	10	0
46	15	15	0	17	18
272	13	2	47	17	96

小学校数、班数、招生

Number of Schools, Classes, Graduates & Students

地 区 Region	学校数(所) Schools	教学点数(个) Teaching Sites	班		
			计 Total	一 年 级 Grade 1	二 年 级 Grade 2
总 计 Total	582291	186065	3967402	675692	671761
北 京 Beijing	2352	0	26611	3559	3590
天 津 Tianjin	2642	0	21803	3535	3660
河 北 Hebei	39770	7943	260705	38325	39336
山 西 Shanxi	38804	4720	133139	19322	18636
内蒙古 Inner Mongolia	10849	7114	81024	14341	14154
辽 宁 Liaoning	13748	1249	112642	17384	17343
吉 林 Jilin	9595	2321	84673	12849	13231
黑龙江 Heilongjiang	14754	4123	109973	19733	19415
上 海 Shanghai	1222	2	21511	3028	3106
江 苏 Jiangsu	21253	2681	184216	29189	30771
浙 江 Zhejiang	13848	1398	95985	17667	14965
安 徽 Anhui	25476	6400	171904	34155	32932
福 建 Fujian	14355	8332	123556	20932	21257
江 西 Jiangxi	22617	6823	128765	25737	24202
山 东 Shandong	29453	9514	230404	39761	44697
河 南 Henan	41404	8596	296561	57462	58820
湖 北 Hubei	25107	5927	179191	29978	29743
湖 南 Hunan	37143	4811	204321	30287	32666
广 东 Guangdong	24556	10801	248544	43360	42335
广 西 Guangxi	16155	31911	200174	31277	30441
海 南 Hainan	4199	1286	32482	6550	6079
重 庆 Chongqing	15223	1121	77042	13279	13017
四 川 Sichuan	45133	6254	235339	40245	39487
贵 州 Guizhou	18508	10298	142845	25707	24635
云 南 Yunnan	22705	25459	166517	27457	26845
西 藏 Tibet	820	3033	13469	3333	3079
陕 西 Shaanxi	34336	2712	162942	24223	23174
甘 肃 Gansu	22560	5841	102726	20702	18719
青 海 Qinghai	3448	829	17784	3722	3156
宁 夏 Ningxia	3460	780	21456	4790	4179
新 疆 Xinjiang	6796	3786	79098	13803	14091

数、毕业生数(总计)

Admitted in Primary Schools (Regional Aggregates)

班数(个) Classes					毕业生数(人) Graduates	招生数(人) Students Admitted
三年级 Grade 3	四年级 Grade 4	五年级 Grade 5	六年级 Grade 6	复式班 Multiple-grade Classes		
690769	676582	644894	396976	210728	23137366	20295337
4161	4880	5048	5266	107	175656	94358
3919	3898	3890	2587	314	156584	104452
42913	43783	42631	35717	18000	1445217	1161498
19698	19584	20007	3250	32642	627540	623393
14849	14135	13965	1743	7837	435682	349917
18856	19182	19830	19496	551	644042	503795
14330	14438	14566	14345	914	446250	331776
20440	20680	20687	5599	3419	785711	464113
3232	3812	4070	4263	0	194399	106123
33143	32462	30258	24343	4050	1051895	1017876
15691	15939	16287	9847	5589	678254	654599
33036	31571	30312	2870	7028	1200173	1139910
22683	21759	20669	10178	6078	695885	528644
24415	23448	22406	849	7708	838959	732469
47876	46825	45043	5277	925	1914045	1160371
59674	57558	53990	4738	4319	2050056	1936465
30412	30776	28142	23618	6522	1112412	997103
35888	36230	30315	26887	12048	1223723	790897
41640	40200	38949	38398	3662	1433779	1498378
30704	30777	30603	27251	19121	1018442	806377
5552	5093	4652	4309	247	152363	161165
13013	12488	11999	12071	1175	517933	452845
39901	39095	36856	34949	4806	1327862	1240217
23666	22022	20273	18695	7847	656238	815402
25809	24401	22399	20484	19122	656091	705991
2901	1907	1223	967	59	30725	58939
23683	23538	22026	20839	25459	717291	715705
17940	16674	15446	5412	7833	424250	538695
2939	2691	2529	1010	1737	68728	95983
3857	3520	3342	908	860	99380	116583
13948	13216	12481	10810	749	357801	391298

小学校数、班数、招生

Number of Schools, Classes, Graduates & Students

地区 Region		学校数(所) Schools	教学点数(个) Teaching Sites	班		
				计 Total	一年级 Grade 1	二年级 Grade 2
总计	**Total**	32602	5939	406866	66840	66048
北京	Beijing	651	0	10456	1524	1485
天津	Tianjin	477	0	6970	969	1025
河北	Hebei	1746	292	20784	3216	3189
山西	Shanxi	810	109	11380	1981	1969
内蒙古	Inner Mongolia	587	52	8938	1644	1577
辽宁	Liaoning	1306	4	21881	3397	3189
吉林	Jilin	753	18	12799	1971	1918
黑龙江	Heilongjiang	1122	128	16880	2986	2885
上海	Shanghai	538	0	11742	1549	1593
江苏	Jiangsu	1615	219	20512	3097	3132
浙江	Zhejiang	1037	46	13544	2519	2184
安徽	Anhui	1030	113	13025	2163	2187
福建	Fujian	615	115	8948	1420	1488
江西	Jiangxi	513	61	6615	1254	1259
山东	Shandong	2045	538	24414	4119	4217
河南	Henan	1827	267	22598	3811	3909
湖北	Hubei	3520	526	36082	6117	6074
湖南	Hunan	1729	252	17299	2585	2732
广东	Guangdong	2068	959	31305	5631	5363
广西	Guangxi	841	129	11123	1750	1784
海南	Hainan	127	1	1700	289	299
重庆	Chongqing	2560	122	17430	2964	2841
四川	Sichuan	746	156	10937	1823	1745
贵州	Guizhou	662	103	7116	1207	1189
云南	Yunnan	333	83	4507	748	729
西藏	Tibet	25	8	438	68	71
陕西	Shaanxi	2192	149	19917	3151	3148
甘肃	Gansu	501	1281	6392	1075	1065
青海	Qinghai	103	28	1469	243	234
宁夏	Ningxia	99	0	1650	264	264
新疆	Xinjiang	424	180	8015	1305	1304

数、毕业生数(城市)

Admitted in Primary Schools (Urban)

班数 (个) Classes 三年级 Grade 3	四年级 Grade 4	五年级 Grade 5	六年级 Grade 6	复式班 Multiple-grade Classes	毕业生数(人) Graduates	招生数(人) Students Admitted
69496	72628	73280	57353	1221	3292056	2798203
1554	1842	1975	2074	2	76634	45488
1065	1268	1363	1280	0	62725	37794
3524	3703	3794	3308	50	157356	133825
2091	2094	2039	1166	40	93985	93749
1737	1735	1732	513	0	77614	72172
3599	3875	4231	3588	2	204328	148538
2138	2202	2308	2262	0	117109	87222
3182	3325	3430	1072	0	200269	131932
1691	2120	2297	2492	0	114180	50822
3365	3626	3704	3495	93	148463	125422
2244	2361	2364	1803	69	103992	105157
2233	2345	2293	1751	53	104817	103899
1585	1622	1622	1203	8	64948	58259
1289	1340	1344	93	36	65222	57887
4584	4826	4987	1641	40	239118	167117
4150	4287	4237	2201	3	180743	174601
6212	6423	6293	4889	74	272910	250293
2948	3128	3043	2821	42	132173	105374
5326	5176	5013	4783	13	205487	256787
1815	1886	1912	1950	26	80315	65493
306	289	273	244	0	11980	14035
2861	2855	2782	3096	31	136934	102024
1794	1857	1894	1816	8	95040	84176
1194	1189	1183	1131	23	46890	49624
747	780	795	706	2	34795	32117
74	75	74	76	0	3320	3339
3203	3303	3268	3250	594	133687	113377
1116	1172	1127	833	4	46705	47504
249	256	251	236	0	11678	12970
272	278	284	288	0	12070	11654
1348	1390	1368	1292	8	56569	55552

小学校数、班数、招生

Number of Schools, Classes, Graduates & Students

地区 Region		学校数(所) Schools	教学点数(个) Teaching Sites	班 计 Total	一年级 Grade 1	二年级 Grade 2
总计	Total	81162	14752	661794	110958	110475
北京	Beijing	580	0	6825	885	900
天津	Tianjin	506	0	5470	942	925
河北	Hebei	4131	470	33591	4981	5075
山西	Shanxi	2380	309	12875	2321	2214
内蒙古	Inner Mongolia	610	112	7985	1457	1481
辽宁	Liaoning	714	22	9967	1497	1459
吉林	Jilin	1413	431	16070	2440	2466
黑龙江	Heilongjiang	1049	178	13293	2311	2346
上海	Shanghai	307	0	6867	1060	1048
江苏	Jiangsu	7547	900	67320	10309	10759
浙江	Zhejiang	8620	839	61862	11544	9785
安徽	Anhui	1595	334	13156	2635	2506
福建	Fujian	3721	1449	40312	6861	7421
江西	Jiangxi	7322	2249	46362	9359	8827
山东	Shandong	1182	348	12147	2168	2296
河南	Henan	5295	1030	44375	8181	8501
湖北	Hubei	1099	260	9831	1641	1602
湖南	Hunan	9902	966	59274	8557	9384
广东	Guangdong	1945	458	28387	4783	4741
广西	Guangxi	1426	1547	18161	2845	2864
海南	Hainan	136	12	2267	391	374
重庆	Chongqing	4349	324	23507	4026	3957
四川	Sichuan	3737	245	33770	5358	5297
贵州	Guizhou	1432	390	13042	2250	2211
云南	Yunnan	1650	833	15635	2597	2555
西藏	Tibet	94	82	1171	209	195
陕西	Shaanxi	6707	479	40503	6203	6150
甘肃	Gansu	797	351	6573	1224	1174
青海	Qinghai	352	13	2713	504	487
宁夏	Ningxia	120	10	1738	321	312
新疆	Xinjiang	444	111	6745	1098	1163

数、毕业生数(县镇)

Admitted in Primary Schools (County Seats & Towns)

数 (个) Classes						
三年级 Grade 3	四年级 Grade 4	五年级 Grade 5	六年级 Grade 6	复式班 Multiple-grade Classes	毕业生数(人) Graduates	招生数(人) Students Admitted
116734	116972	113861	72979	19815	4616602	3966688
1070	1279	1318	1359	14	46415	23683
959	957	953	707	27	32289	28396
5650	5846	5974	4752	1313	217187	179629
2301	2242	2289	164	1344	88628	87605
1584	1601	1602	208	52	68267	53739
1624	1679	1787	1911	10	76955	63178
2663	2720	2764	2705	312	98188	73241
2515	2618	2654	814	35	129555	80108
1046	1157	1235	1321	0	60126	42373
11831	11896	11207	9423	1895	413713	373897
10260	10387	10548	6302	3036	443820	431824
2556	2475	2411	273	300	108501	106430
8234	7984	7725	1762	325	296209	217234
8986	8688	8316	256	1930	299752	283434
2509	2507	2509	154	4	129024	85246
8924	8744	8387	1332	306	357040	312771
1623	1661	1590	1436	278	74469	71497
10439	10722	9247	8417	2508	376712	234883
4743	4655	4654	4739	72	220208	225634
2934	3023	3104	2533	858	123009	94084
385	379	380	358	0	20641	18898
3988	3859	3735	3733	209	166248	152518
5499	5544	5726	6199	147	279509	231057
2189	2153	2052	1973	214	75131	80638
2546	2503	2494	2337	603	86194	87535
199	197	188	183	0	6118	7072
6303	6373	5968	5711	3795	207595	200613
1181	1148	1124	583	139	43220	47787
481	479	460	236	66	16149	17135
318	323	319	145	0	14370	14310
1194	1173	1141	953	23	41360	40239

小学校数、班数、招生

Number of Schools, Classes, Graduates & Students

地区 Region		学校数(所) Schools	教学点数(个) Teaching Sites	班		
				计 Total	一年级 Grade 1	二年级 Grade 2
总计	Total	468527	165374	2898742	497894	495238
北京	Beijing	1121	0	9330	1150	1205
天津	Tianjin	1659	0	9363	1624	1710
河北	Hebei	33893	7181	206330	30128	31072
山西	Shanxi	35614	4302	108884	15020	14453
内蒙古	Inner Mongolia	9652	6950	64101	11240	11096
辽宁	Liaoning	11728	1223	80794	12490	12695
吉林	Jilin	7429	1872	55804	8438	8847
黑龙江	Heilongjiang	12583	3817	79800	14436	14184
上海	Shanghai	377	2	2902	419	465
江苏	Jiangsu	12091	1562	96384	15783	16880
浙江	Zhejiang	4191	513	20579	3604	2996
安徽	Anhui	22851	5953	145723	29357	28239
福建	Fujian	10019	6768	74296	12651	12348
江西	Jiangxi	14782	4513	75788	15124	14116
山东	Shandong	26226	8628	193843	33474	38184
河南	Henan	34282	7299	229588	45470	46410
湖北	Hubei	20488	5141	133278	22220	22067
湖南	Hunan	25512	3593	127748	19145	20550
广东	Guangdong	20543	9384	188852	32946	32231
广西	Guangxi	13888	30235	170890	26682	25793
海南	Hainan	3936	1273	28515	5870	5406
重庆	Chongqing	8314	675	36105	6289	6219
四川	Sichuan	40650	5853	190632	33064	32445
贵州	Guizhou	16414	9805	122687	22250	21235
云南	Yunnan	20722	24543	146375	24112	23561
西藏	Tibet	701	2943	11860	3056	2813
陕西	Shaanxi	25437	2084	102522	14869	13876
甘肃	Gansu	21262	4209	89761	18403	16480
青海	Qinghai	2993	788	13602	2975	2435
宁夏	Ningxia	3241	770	18068	4205	3603
新疆	Xinjiang	5928	3495	64338	11400	11624

数、毕业生数(农村)

Admitted in Primary Schools (Rural)

数 (个) Classes					毕业生数(人) Graduates	招生数(人) Students Admitted
三年级 Grade 3	四年级 Grade 4	五年级 Grade 5	六年级 Grade 6	复式班 Multiple grade Classes		
504539	486982	457753	266644	189692	15228708	13530446
1537	1759	1755	1833	91	52607	25187
1895	1673	1574	600	287	61570	38262
33739	34234	32863	27657	16637	1070674	848044
15306	15248	15679	1920	31258	444927	442039
11528	10799	10631	1022	7785	289801	224006
13633	13628	13812	13997	539	362759	292079
9529	9516	9494	9378	602	230953	171313
14743	14737	14603	3713	3384	455887	252073
495	535	538	450	0	20093	12928
17947	16940	15347	11425	2062	489719	518557
3187	3191	3375	1742	2484	130442	117618
28247	26751	25608	846	6675	986855	929581
12864	12153	11322	7213	5745	334728	253151
14140	13420	12746	500	5742	473985	391148
40783	39492	37547	3482	881	1545903	908008
46600	44527	41366	1205	4010	1512273	1449093
22577	22692	20259	17293	6170	765033	675313
22501	22380	18025	15649	9498	714838	450640
31571	30369	29282	28876	3577	1008084	1015957
25955	25868	25587	22768	18237	815118	646800
4861	4425	3999	3707	247	119742	128232
6164	5774	5482	5242	935	214751	198303
32608	31694	29236	26934	4651	953313	924984
20283	18680	17038	15591	7610	534217	685140
22516	21118	19110	17441	18517	535102	586339
2628	1635	961	708	59	21287	48528
14177	13862	12790	11878	21070	376009	401715
15643	14354	13195	3996	7690	334325	443404
2209	1956	1818	538	1671	40901	65878
3267	2919	2739	475	860	72940	90619
11406	10653	9972	8565	718	259872	295507

六年制小学校数、班

Number of Schools, Classes, Students Admitted

地　　区 Region	学校数(所) Schools	教学点数(个) Teaching Sites	班		
			计 Total	一　年　级 Grade 1	二　年　级 Grade 2
总　计　Total	370317	124784	2689058	436328	431150
北　京　Beijing	2342	0	26376	3509	3546
天　津　Tianjin	2464	0	15493	2248	2358
河　北　Hebei	33861	6298	234342	34777	35024
山　西　Shanxi	4291	791	23240	3226	3219
内蒙古　Inner Mongolia	1273	877	11990	1563	1686
辽　宁　Liaoning	13495	1249	109351	16766	16788
吉　林　Jilin	9164	1862	81827	11721	12665
黑龙江　Heilongjiang	3192	436	20838	2240	2502
上　海　Shanghai	1014	2	21440	3015	3093
江　苏　Jiangsu	19502	2423	172857	27892	29353
浙　江　Zhejiang	9127	601	62270	12691	8995
安　徽　Anhui	1918	403	19372	3420	3004
福　建　Fujian	7870	4990	71159	11753	11715
江　西　Jiangxi	2095	357	11437	3097	1985
山　东　Shandong	3247	1673	31837	4662	5321
河　南　Henan	2364	889	29601	4576	4806
湖　北　Hubei	24223	5760	170738	28451	28199
湖　南　Hunan	35767	4612	197738	28854	31310
广　东　Guangdong	24556	10801	248544	43360	42335
广　西　Guangxi	14477	25866	179839	27813	27313
海　南　Hainan	3997	1242	32425	6541	6068
重　庆　Chongqing	15207	1111	76885	13210	12956
四　川　Sichuan	45014	6128	234241	39980	39225
贵　州　Guizhou	18508	10298	142845	25707	24635
云　南　Yunnan	22285	24971	162510	26521	25948
西　藏　Tibet	752	2020	10871	2442	2315
陕　西　Shaanxi	34333	2712	162932	24221	23172
甘　肃　Gansu	5922	2281	39165	6932	6521
青　海　Qinghai	1319	387	8202	1704	1413
宁　夏　Ningxia	688	44	5973	1081	1046
新　疆　Xinjiang	6050	3700	72720	12355	12634

数、招生数、毕业生数

& Graduates in 6-year Primary Schools

班数 (个) Classes 三年级 Grade 3	四年级 Grade 4	五年级 Grade 5	六年级 Grade 6	复式班 Multiple-grade Classes	毕业生数(人) Graduates	招生数(人) Students Admitted
441897	435922	412939	396976	133846	14325089	13184354
4117	4830	5001	5266	107	173891	92832
2522	2695	2769	2587	314	102002	60663
38090	38774	37167	35717	14793	1245605	1055715
3347	3329	3284	3250	3585	111386	120315
1813	1812	1804	1743	1569	63349	50911
18209	18481	19060	19496	551	604378	477552
13790	14093	14299	14345	914	428874	294672
2764	2916	4115	5599	702	248074	56306
3218	3797	4054	4263	0	193904	105727
30590	29558	27082	24343	4039	903130	958224
8951	9070	9278	9847	3438	378224	476817
3081	3153	3034	2870	810	124962	148496
12287	11582	10817	10178	2827	336665	274057
1898	1319	1278	849	1011	32783	72314
5587	5557	5381	5277	52	198090	133797
5180	5214	5023	4738	64	181261	169702
28758	29110	26080	23618	6522	960033	930126
34453	35092	29323	26887	11819	1166727	757147
41640	40200	38949	38398	3662	1433779	1498088
27414	27371	27237	27251	15440	884414	731650
5538	5078	4644	4309	247	139899	161099
13002	12480	11991	12071	1175	517511	450314
39663	38925	36693	34949	4806	1316573	1229671
23666	22022	20273	18695	7847	656238	815402
24981	23735	21779	20484	19062	636588	681046
2239	1661	1191	967	56	28561	46271
23681	23536	22024	20839	25459	717206	715618
6512	6254	5738	5412	1796	154108	197210
1320	1228	1096	1010	431	29087	41888
1020	977	939	908	2	30881	32829
12566	12073	11536	10810	746	326906	347895

小学在校学生数和

Enrolment and Number of Graduates for

地 区 Region	在校学生数 Enrolment 合 计 Total	一 年 级 Grade 1	二 年 级 Grade 2	三 年 级 Grade 3
总 计 Total	135479642	20900537	22801386	25338360
北 京 Beijing	836655	95378	101731	126419
天 津 Tianjin	773064	105073	116863	136114
河 北 Hebei	8643540	1166643	1297816	1518427
山 西 Shanxi	3452505	631193	655330	708831
内蒙古 Inner Mongolia	2136772	351661	384638	452410
辽 宁 Liaoning	3666131	507669	513163	611794
吉 林 Jilin	2603849	335021	372338	458170
黑龙江 Heilongjiang	3101578	467917	517419	613349
上 海 Shanghai	881499	106720	116352	129776
江 苏 Jiangsu	7411888	1056115	1223243	1383185
浙 江 Zhejiang	3633125	657848	575564	630158
安 徽 Anhui	6419167	1144745	1246741	1338164
福 建 Fujian	3868492	544348	667860	788269
江 西 Jiangxi	4399376	764448	864092	937660
山 东 Shandong	8707249	1164856	1492153	1849962
河 南 Henan	11869651	2008989	2312072	2532076
湖 北 Hubei	6984361	1010201	1108496	1225313
湖 南 Hunan	7213955	797242	1024309	1305564
广 东 Guangdong	9209566	1498450	1524438	1577667
广 西 Guangxi	5694639	829365	879521	951977
海 南 Hainan	1051079	178127	183760	183678
重 庆 Chongqing	2802741	460114	452604	473076
四 川 Sichuan	8270859	1286569	1323186	1427185
贵 州 Guizhou	5009598	820753	861966	896980
云 南 Yunnan	4808006	761103	820168	869111
西 藏 Tibet	310437	59643	58004	56918
陕 西 Shaanxi	4921827	759865	818231	864597
甘 肃 Gansu	3131747	651757	611554	615495
青 海 Qinghai	500723	106304	100783	95200
宁 夏 Ningxia	658157	146715	127863	126473
新 疆 Xinjiang	2507406	425705	449128	454362

毕业班学生数(总计)

Next Year in Primary Schools (Regional Aggregates)

单位:人

生数 四年级 Grade 4	五年级 Grade 5	六年级 Grade 6	毕业班学生数 Graduates for Next Year
25737577	25097535	15604247	24550473
159082	170733	183312	185137
149570	154290	111154	150914
1617724	1645751	1397179	1594261
688734	646943	121474	642853
445110	436534	66419	435704
646027	697534	689944	725401
475277	485052	477991	488685
655313	663712	183868	713183
162517	175873	190261	190928
1385145	1316743	1047457	1169633
658130	677415	434010	718775
1308728	1240045	140744	1226928
771792	741885	354338	717657
924106	879262	29808	859614
1957184	1997853	245241	2002415
2494801	2308659	213054	2292836
1303402	1269526	1067423	1200903
1433940	1393974	1258926	1308526
1555339	1538919	1514753	1514903
1011723	1048770	973283	1055442
178874	171185	155455	155761
464941	452662	499344	499704
1427680	1405098	1401141	1408013
884288	815315	730296	730296
845862	798884	712878	733700
51999	46391	37482	37540
872733	836156	770245	770321
572484	492905	187552	465746
86743	79173	32520	76080
116081	106968	34057	104850
432248	403325	342638	373764

小学在校学生数和

Enrolment and Number of Graduates for

地区 Region	在校学生 Enrolment 合计 Total	一年级 Grade 1	二年级 Grade 2	三年级 Grade 3
总计 Total	18377600	2809608	2842118	3174356
北京 Beijing	356990	45521	46669	51042
天津 Tianjin	305425	37917	42477	46291
河北 Hebei	916928	134174	130813	156790
山西 Shanxi	548580	93959	91383	103614
内蒙古 Inner Mongolia	415399	72198	67270	83533
辽宁 Liaoning	1055297	148591	141787	172959
吉林 Jilin	633879	87376	86690	106288
黑龙江 Heilongjiang	797228	132035	129057	151808
上海 Shanghai	476557	50862	56839	66766
江苏 Jiangsu	895910	125900	131196	146893
浙江 Zhejiang	616145	105284	93143	102078
安徽 Anhui	659359	103996	108354	115692
福建 Fujian	394652	58685	62270	71924
江西 Jiangxi	327732	57979	61620	65767
山东 Shandong	1127701	167184	181158	215788
河南 Henan	1131735	175606	188867	212335
湖北 Hubei	1639349	252641	259653	282099
湖南 Hunan	800315	105545	115803	136820
广东 Guangdong	1461313	256852	249040	253346
广西 Guangxi	444739	65704	69036	71748
海南 Hainan	92748	14844	16372	17231
重庆 Chongqing	626096	102730	98173	100274
四川 Sichuan	522353	84463	80565	85011
贵州 Guizhou	314232	49888	50670	53001
云南 Yunnan	205537	32259	31631	33757
西藏 Tibet	21167	3388	3352	3602
陕西 Shaanxi	791624	115165	121142	129996
甘肃 Gansu	293082	48370	46073	51831
青海 Qinghai	77998	12976	12414	13617
宁夏 Ningxia	77563	11658	11985	12923
新疆 Xinjiang	349967	55858	56616	59532

毕业班学生数(城市)

Next Year in Primary Schools (Urban)

单位:人

生数			毕业班学生数 Graduates for Next Year
四年级 Grade 4	五年级 Grade 5	六年级 Grade 6	
3395633	3471658	2684227	3469520
64751	71660	77347	78165
57225	62450	59065	62687
168604	176160	150387	176482
104126	99191	56307	97263
84079	83259	25060	82602
191855	213825	186280	221241
112309	121082	120134	126068
162325	167355	54648	180950
90338	99067	112685	112685
163434	170285	158202	163946
112046	114352	89242	116877
121943	119172	90202	112755
74526	73980	53267	70198
69425	69402	3539	69055
233837	246633	83101	250991
223110	218780	113037	211761
303627	307797	233532	287472
151079	151615	139453	145248
244286	237229	220560	220710
76275	79629	82347	82592
16230	14973	13098	13404
101235	101201	122483	122843
89370	91985	90959	96261
55030	54465	51178	51178
36972	37810	33108	36508
3681	3579	3565	3565
140993	143846	140482	140558
53874	53748	39186	52548
13712	13287	11992	12903
13512	13860	13625	13625
61824	59981	56156	56379

小学在校学生数和

Enrolment and Number of Graduates for

地　区 Region	在校学生 Enrolment 合　计 Total	一年级 Grade 1	二年级 Grade 2	三年级 Grade 3
总　计 Total	26360773	4030543	4322982	4853832
北　京 Beijing	221605	24074	25610	33421
天　津 Tianjin	186897	28498	29280	32241
河　北 Hebei	1277440	180333	190943	222807
山　西 Shanxi	467104	88395	89898	97533
内蒙古 Inner Mongolia	328490	53740	56035	68802
辽　宁 Liaoning	443935	63348	60809	72485
吉　林 Jilin	564885	74512	81202	98141
黑龙江 Heilongjiang	514367	80771	85706	99777
上　海 Shanghai	302737	42793	44276	45788
江　苏 Jiangsu	2758433	381870	436743	499904
浙　江 Zhejiang	2370024	434060	379102	413380
安　徽 Anhui	598175	107631	115719	123647
福　建 Fujian	1523154	222781	272471	326533
江　西 Jiangxi	1666211	294885	326789	354195
山　东 Shandong	598033	85291	105087	127551
河　南 Henan	1946096	316695	371002	411061
湖　北 Hubei	463346	71698	73543	78579
湖　南 Hunan	2191379	236129	303014	391319
广　东 Guangdong	1383913	225560	227075	233387
广　西 Guangxi	650563	97056	100805	109817
海　南 Hainan	119270	18654	18969	20740
重　庆 Chongqing	952992	153896	153385	161872
四　川 Sichuan	1558028	233779	235520	255476
贵　州 Guizhou	512553	80765	83788	87897
云　南 Yunnan	606934	92570	96355	107071
西　藏 Tibet	42579	6612	6234	6880
陕　西 Shaanxi	1383478	208616	224957	239141
甘　肃 Gansu	283573	51481	51081	52793
青　海 Qinghai	96516	17559	17175	18081
宁　夏 Ningxia	82187	14604	14432	15492
新　疆 Xinjiang	265876	41887	45977	48021

毕业班学生数(县镇)

Next Year in Primary Schools (County Seats & Towns)

单位:人

生数 四年级 Grade 4	五年级 Grade 5	六年级 Grade 6	毕业班学生数 Graduates for Next Year
4991326	4939136	3222954	4906094
42872	46473	49155	50162
34109	34728	28041	36894
238057	243897	201403	239008
94542	89113	7623	88940
69810	70708	9395	70917
75881	81954	89458	89766
102944	104974	103112	106789
107386	108526	32201	113928
52511	56574	60795	61177
520376	501757	417783	456870
428948	440536	273998	470631
121290	114494	15394	112705
319259	309963	72147	306793
348458	332091	9793	324211
134651	136547	8906	136042
407446	386845	53047	383275
83006	82569	73951	79075
435175	425835	399907	402882
230096	232353	235442	235442
117020	121914	103951	117176
20537	20460	19910	19910
162535	155095	166209	166209
259692	272785	300776	302035
91442	87222	81439	81439
106924	106842	97172	100044
8145	7684	7024	7024
244708	240215	225841	225841
52436	49746	26036	46527
18276	17147	8278	16581
15683	15307	6669	14912
47111	44782	38098	42889

小学在校学生数和

Enrolment and Number of Graduates for

地区 Region	在校学生数 Enrolment 合计 Total	一年级 Grade 1	二年级 Grade 2	三年级 Grade 3
总计 Total	90741269	14060386	15636286	17310172
北京 Beijing	258060	25783	29452	41956
天津 Tianjin	280742	38658	45106	57582
河北 Hebei	6449172	852136	976060	1138830
山西 Shanxi	2436821	448839	474049	507684
内蒙古 Inner Mongolia	1392883	225723	261333	300075
辽宁 Liaoning	2166899	295730	310567	366350
吉林 Jilin	1405085	173133	204446	253741
黑龙江 Heilongjiang	1789983	255111	302656	361764
上海 Shanghai	102205	13065	15237	17222
江苏 Jiangsu	3757545	548345	655304	736388
浙江 Zhejiang	646956	118504	103319	114700
安徽 Anhui	5161633	933118	1022668	1098825
福建 Fujian	1950686	262882	333119	389812
江西 Jiangxi	2405433	411584	475683	517698
山东 Shandong	6981515	912381	1205908	1506623
河南 Henan	8791820	1516688	1752203	1908680
湖北 Hubei	4881666	685862	775300	864635
湖南 Hunan	4222261	455568	605492	777425
广东 Guangdong	6364340	1016038	1048323	1090934
广西 Guangxi	4599337	666605	709680	770412
海南 Hainan	839061	144629	148419	145707
重庆 Chongqing	1223653	203488	201046	210930
四川 Sichuan	6190478	968327	1007101	1086698
贵州 Guizhou	4182813	690100	727508	756082
云南 Yunnan	3995535	636274	692182	728283
西藏 Tibet	246691	49643	48418	46436
陕西 Shaanxi	2746725	436084	472132	495460
甘肃 Gansu	2555092	551906	514400	510871
青海 Qinghai	326209	75769	71194	63502
宁夏 Ningxia	498407	120453	101446	98058
新疆 Xinjiang	1891563	327960	346535	346809

毕业班学生数(农村)

Next Year in Primary Schools (Rural)

单位:人

生数			毕业班学生数
四年级 Grade 4	五年级 Grade 5	六年级 Grade 6	Graduates for Next Year
17350618	16686741	9697066	16174859
51459	52600	56810	56810
58236	57112	24048	51333
1211063	1225694	1045389	1178771
490066	458639	57544	456650
291221	282567	31964	282185
378291	401755	414206	414394
260024	258996	254745	255828
385602	387831	97019	418305
19668	20232	16781	17066
701335	644701	471472	548817
117136	122527	70770	131267
1065495	1006379	35148	1001468
378007	357942	228924	340666
506223	477769	16476	466348
1588696	1614673	153234	1615382
1864245	1703034	46970	1697800
916769	879160	759940	834356
847686	816524	719566	760396
1080957	1069337	1058751	1058751
818428	847227	786985	855674
142107	135752	122447	122447
201171	196366	210652	210652
1078618	1040328	1009406	1009717
737816	673628	597679	597679
701966	654232	582598	597148
40173	35128	26893	26951
487032	452095	403922	403922
466174	389411	122330	366671
54755	48739	12250	46596
86886	77801	13763	76313
323313	298562	248384	274496

六年制小学在校学生

Enrolment and Number of Graduates for

地区 Region	在校学 Enrolment			
	合计 Total	一年级 Grade 1	二年级 Grade 2	三年级 Grade 3
总计 Total	92283826	13629075	14517623	16002087
北京 Beijing	828721	93834	100260	124959
天津 Tianjin	578965	72133	81029	93037
河北 Hebei	7829439	1060475	1153236	1342175
山西 Shanxi	758884	122470	123123	134290
内蒙古 Inner Mongolia	377786	50739	56163	68554
辽宁 Liaoning	3520173	481417	489868	583134
吉林 Jilin	2506840	302266	353670	438795
黑龙江 Heilongjiang	619040	56787	67784	83737
上海 Shanghai	878761	106253	115864	129244
江苏 Jiangsu	6961022	1011757	1170239	1278975
浙江 Zhejiang	2400246	481723	351215	361134
安徽 Anhui	904924	153186	144150	153498
福建 Fujian	2158705	279450	344607	407300
江西 Jiangxi	394126	108046	77080	77820
山东 Shandong	1224057	133847	172141	206048
河南 Henan	1271703	171003	195596	228120
湖北 Hubei	6440150	921737	1012308	1115849
湖南 Hunan	6989811	763622	984183	1256533
广东 Guangdong	9208323	1497939	1524234	1577473
广西 Guangxi	5372982	782725	826716	889826
海南 Hainan	1049017	177863	183363	183132
重庆 Chongqing	2796691	457580	450275	472586
四川 Sichuan	8226328	1275957	1312960	1417294
贵州 Guizhou	5009598	820753	861966	896980
云南 Yunnan	4686346	735883	793900	842172
西藏 Tibet	272257	47125	45414	47134
陕西 Shaanxi	4921433	759778	818152	864522
甘肃 Gansu	1354892	244748	231317	242588
青海 Qinghai	240199	47782	44101	41379
宁夏 Ningxia	215785	34577	35680	37962
新疆 Xinjiang	2286622	375620	397029	405837

数和毕业班学生数

Next Year in 6-year Primary Schools

单位:人

生数 四年级 Grade 4	五年级 Grade 5	六年级 Grade 6	毕业班学生数 Graduates for Next Year
16379485	16151309	15604247	15604247
157448	168908	183312	183312
107082	114530	111154	111154
1427705	1448669	1397179	1397179
131963	125564	121474	121474
68662	67249	66419	66419
613733	662077	689944	689944
459760	474358	477991	477991
92467	134397	183868	183868
161933	175206	190261	190261
1258027	1194567	1047457	1047457
379514	392650	434010	434010
159485	153861	140744	140744
394444	378566	354338	354338
51916	49456	29808	29808
226101	240679	245241	245241
235053	228877	213054	213054
1186787	1136046	1067423	1067423
1382173	1344374	1258926	1258926
1555155	1538769	1514753	1514753
933821	966611	973283	973283
178325	170879	155455	155455
464604	452302	499344	499344
1420750	1398226	1401141	1401141
884288	815315	730296	730296
823451	778062	712878	712878
48769	46333	37482	37482
872656	836080	770245	770245
233976	214711	187552	187552
38804	35613	32520	32520
37334	36175	34057	34057
393299	372199	342638	342638

小学在校学生数和毕业

Number of Female Students

地区 Region	在校学生 Enrolment			
	合计 Total	一年级 Grade 1	二年级 Grade 2	三年级 Grade 3
总计 Total	64548651	9937953	10867208	12072020
北京 Beijing	402995	46088	48575	60318
天津 Tianjin	375615	50314	56939	65863
河北 Hebei	4225172	571299	639107	739128
山西 Shanxi	1669385	306640	316027	343938
内蒙古 Inner Mongolia	1022610	167125	184631	217100
辽宁 Liaoning	1759754	241639	245449	291968
吉林 Jilin	1263749	161219	179830	221375
黑龙江 Heilongjiang	1505585	227376	251457	297100
上海 Shanghai	424324	51378	56089	62122
江苏 Jiangsu	3504763	497114	574208	652648
浙江 Zhejiang	1717235	309245	271185	295928
安徽 Anhui	3053000	538210	588855	639419
福建 Fujian	1842890	251082	313391	379197
江西 Jiangxi	2090088	361255	409786	445870
山东 Shandong	4186074	560937	716009	888439
河南 Henan	5727144	976900	1117844	1220762
湖北 Hubei	3326181	474576	534612	584282
湖南 Hunan	3454264	377706	490614	625190
广东 Guangdong	4360306	709428	723707	745445
广西 Guangxi	2626723	385361	408292	438089
海南 Hainan	482283	81918	84035	84773
重庆 Chongqing	1328436	216983	214602	224229
四川 Sichuan	3923442	607516	623855	676677
贵州 Guizhou	2313150	387829	404507	417865
云南 Yunnan	2242933	358901	384113	405972
西藏 Tibet	138895	27805	26565	25346
陕西 Shaanxi	2344879	360779	387466	413916
甘肃 Gansu	1479779	308203	292113	285917
青海 Qinghai	232650	50620	46971	43997
宁夏 Ningxia	310162	69815	61047	59503
新疆 Xinjiang	1214185	202692	215327	219644

班学生总数中女生数

in Primary Schools

单位:人

生数			
四年级 Grade 4	五年级 Grade 5	六年级 Grade 6	毕业班学生数 Graduates for Next Year
12283684	11976936	7410850	11598326
76440	82396	89178	90073
72307	75348	54844	54844
787258	805567	682813	776125
332526	312632	57622	309994
214837	207608	31309	207640
309781	336747	334170	351396
230758	237765	232802	237418
318496	321576	89580	346500
77732	85113	91890	92225
658119	626025	496649	553547
310341	321574	208962	341562
629126	589821	67569	585969
374267	358334	166619	345076
441501	417837	13839	402314
938344	963051	119294	965796
1199906	1108562	103170	1095979
620343	606172	506196	531625
688495	668694	603565	626626
738124	728233	715369	715433
466442	481923	446616	495516
81709	78810	71038	71146
221534	214308	236780	237020
678620	670551	666223	669106
407630	372253	323066	323066
394056	370795	329096	339269
22774	20263	16142	16137
416051	399666	367001	367029
271135	232621	89790	207373
39905	36170	14987	34551
54332	49262	16203	24306
210795	197259	168468	183665

小学教职

Number of Teachers, Staff & Workers

地区 Region	合计 Total	专任教师 Full-time Teachers	行政人员 Adm. Personnel	工勤人员 Workers
	教职 Teachers, Staff			
总计 Total	6471159	5860455	430146	169427
北京 Beijing	74114	61121	9237	3459
天津 Tianjin	59002	48293	7857	2621
河北 Hebei	339219	315423	18158	5412
山西 Shanxi	193963	177563	11736	4542
内蒙古 Inner Mongolia	154492	135975	11297	6748
辽宁 Liaoning	222460	191011	28124	3155
吉林 Jilin	176366	152052	18214	5569
黑龙江 Heilongjiang	236864	206807	19960	9753
上海 Shanghai	64869	47479	12077	4471
江苏 Jiangsu	316583	284115	21715	8572
浙江 Zhejiang	175299	159962	10558	4131
安徽 Anhui	293206	276616	13244	3021
福建 Fujian	197912	183601	11437	2790
江西 Jiangxi	237666	224835	8508	4168
山东 Shandong	451063	418828	21417	10082
河南 Henan	476183	446613	22193	7195
湖北 Hubei	307676	278689	16143	11613
湖南 Hunan	325706	307404	8963	8906
广东 Guangdong	414314	357429	48422	8236
广西 Guangxi	230925	198950	24525	7176
海南 Hainan	56417	50130	3542	2742
重庆 Chongqing	135463	120229	9866	5167
四川 Sichuan	374910	336356	24055	13786
贵州 Guizhou	183879	170680	11021	2170
云南 Yunnan	216538	201125	10013	5353
西藏 Tibet	14418	13726	298	393
陕西 Shaanxi	196011	178655	13937	3307
甘肃 Gansu	135004	128839	3807	2268
青海 Qinghai	29130	27452	917	666
宁夏 Ningxia	36018	34096	1172	748
新疆 Xinjiang	145489	126401	7733	11207

工 数（总 计）

in Primary Schools (Regional Aggregates)

单位:人

工数 & Workers: 校办工厂、农场职工 Employers in School－run Factories & Farms: 计 Total	其中:由厂、场收入支付工资的职工 Employers maintained by income of school－run businesses	代课教师 Substitute Teachers	临时工 Temporary Workers	兼任教师 Part－time Teachers
11131	2681	706535	92125	12535
297	102	1316	3218	63
231	41	1579	503	308
226	29	85173	2473	88
122	31	19716	2343	128
472	101	13856	1280	391
170	45	6177	2449	204
531	285	2292	1253	46
344	48	8158	2458	73
842	0	386	626	258
2181	514	30408	10696	74
648	124	4906	5390	607
325	93	8139	1519	117
84	2	8714	781	556
155	90	14010	1751	294
736	145	6335	912	171
182	18	40637	8020	602
1231	375	48852	3525	560
433	155	15718	2415	71
227	23	46716	6604	79
274	49	111146	1563	1567
3	0	2954	368	64
201	13	8088	3993	303
713	154	28984	10391	2783
8	2	41655	3684	571
47	14	47968	6650	96
1	0	2492	206	991
112	18	64965	3103	214
90	38	18330	1561	188
95	73	1141	456	4
2	1	2412	749	14
148	98	13312	1185	1050

小学教职

Number of Teachers, Staff & Workers

地区 Region	教职 Teachers, Staff			
	合计 Total	专任教师 Full-time Teachers	行政人员 Adm. Personnel	工勤人员 Workers
总计 Total	1070312	918705	99123	47499
北京 Beijing	33433	26728	4726	1748
天津 Tianjin	26361	20381	4072	1744
河北 Hebei	52471	45821	4374	2124
山西 Shanxi	34556	29640	2892	1975
内蒙古 Inner Mongolia	26820	22763	2754	1092
辽宁 Liaoning	60455	49711	9157	1528
吉林 Jilin	41819	34214	5222	2060
黑龙江 Heilongjiang	53772	44087	6464	3056
上海 Shanghai	32156	23527	6439	2016
江苏 Jiangsu	50978	44892	3742	1478
浙江 Zhejiang	31132	27818	1679	1410
安徽 Anhui	34212	31383	1741	976
福建 Fujian	21778	19862	1281	607
江西 Jiangxi	18312	16960	926	418
山东 Shandong	73543	64037	5638	3307
河南 Henan	59048	52084	4577	2276
湖北 Hubei	87671	76637	6337	3888
湖南 Hunan	43748	39235	2402	1984
广东 Guangdong	73021	60919	8165	3827
广西 Guangxi	23982	21206	1891	847
海南 Hainan	4484	3745	266	473
重庆 Chongqing	38836	33609	3105	2000
四川 Sichuan	32122	27651	2674	1616
贵州 Guizhou	16664	14925	1202	530
云南 Yunnan	11722	10248	732	727
西藏 Tibet	1557	1432	54	71
陕西 Shaanxi	39747	34151	3861	1676
甘肃 Gansu	15828	14220	922	630
青海 Qinghai	3931	3601	219	107
宁夏 Ningxia	4105	3742	186	176
新疆 Xinjiang	22048	19476	1423	1132

工 数（城 市）

in Primary Schools (Urban)

单位:人

工 数 & Workers		代课教师 Substitute Teachers	临时工 Temporary Workers	兼任教师 Part-time Teachers
校办工厂、农场职工 Employers in School-run Factories & Farms				
计 Total	其中:由厂、场收入支付工资的职工 Employers maintained by income of school-run businesses			
4985	1425	28450	12631	4480
231	90	130	2000	40
164	40	56	190	287
152	27	1453	293	65
49	19	1102	421	99
211	47	356	240	239
59	16	114	789	100
323	170	25	75	3
165	23	276	278	60
174	0	285	363	233
866	476	896	513	29
225	45	276	769	381
112	2	486	173	4
28	0	105	63	31
8	1	250	42	204
561	112	186	124	103
111	18	356	418	216
809	213	4751	1054	299
127	27	550	151	45
110	6	6469	2029	52
38	14	2525	342	1175
0	0	65	47	6
122	8	1334	729	100
181	3	335	177	201
7	2	775	322	40
15	6	77	51	42
0	0	32	0	42
59	16	4624	604	148
56	38	96	116	43
4	0	36	32	3
1	1	60	45	0
17	5	369	181	190

小学教职

Number of Teachers, Staff & Workers

地区 Region	教职 Teachers, Staff			
	合计 Total	专任教师 Full-time Teachers	行政人员 Adm. Personnel	工勤人员 Workers
总计 **Total**	1332805	1194309	91031	43590
北京 Beijing	18422	15213	2317	860
天津 Tianjin	15454	12757	2085	570
河北 Hebei	58738	53636	3396	1645
山西 Shanxi	26915	24181	1746	943
内蒙古 Inner Mongolia	24579	20749	2327	1370
辽宁 Liaoning	27661	24122	2831	642
吉林 Jilin	42117	34376	6031	1609
黑龙江 Heilongjiang	41036	34500	3943	2445
上海 Shanghai	24960	17561	4805	1973
江苏 Jiangsu	122520	108797	8794	3960
浙江 Zhejiang	109883	100739	6568	2239
安徽 Anhui	28949	26924	1448	446
福建 Fujian	73823	66926	5618	1252
江西 Jiangxi	87500	82968	3093	1358
山东 Shandong	34481	31402	1633	1392
河南 Henan	80563	74711	3619	2181
湖北 Hubei	22747	20593	1045	965
湖南 Hunan	99907	94623	2224	2823
广东 Guangdong	63248	55999	5633	1537
广西 Guangxi	37227	32315	2777	2093
海南 Hainan	6917	5929	283	705
重庆 Chongqing	43130	38413	2947	1719
四川 Sichuan	83072	71543	7166	4008
贵州 Guizhou	26306	24261	1490	554
云南 Yunnan	31497	28494	1890	1102
西藏 Tibet	2985	2655	126	203
陕西 Shaanxi	54738	50263	3568	877
甘肃 Gansu	14232	13142	486	598
青海 Qinghai	6416	6024	207	179
宁夏 Ningxia	5363	5026	123	213
新疆 Xinjiang	17419	15467	812	1129

工 数（县 镇）

in Primary Schools (County Seats & Towns)

单位:人

工 数 & Workers 校办工厂、农场职工 Employers in School-run Factories & Farms 计 Total	其中:由厂、场收入支付工资的职工 Employers maintained by income of school-run businesses	代课教师 Substitute Teachers	临时工 Temporary Workers	兼任教师 Part-time Teachers
3875	715	81370	16603	2177
32	0	385	470	18
42	1	672	172	14
61	2	8067	445	14
45	10	1407	190	6
133	24	374	117	13
66	11	345	122	13
101	11	416	558	11
148	23	489	117	0
621	0	41	210	20
969	28	11424	3617	8
337	75	2946	3446	200
131	70	271	176	20
27	2	2963	154	395
81	65	4526	459	15
54	9	15	54	4
52	0	7820	1480	271
144	68	2053	128	4
237	126	3802	438	15
79	14	2672	695	1
42	23	5006	67	14
0	0	27	49	11
51	5	1834	641	126
355	133	2019	891	690
1	0	1909	247	23
11	2	1895	885	6
1	0	91	38	205
30	1	16732	488	8
6	0	761	92	6
6	6	137	50	0
1	0	18	45	0
11	6	253	62	46

小学教职

Number of Teachers, Staff & Workers

地区 Region	教职 Teachers, Staff			
	合计 Total	专任教师 Full-time Teachers	行政人员 Adm. Personnel	工勤人员 Workers
总计 Total	4068042	3747441	239992	78338
北京 Beijing	22259	19180	2194	851
天津 Tianjin	17187	15155	1700	307
河北 Hebei	228010	215966	10388	1643
山西 Shanxi	132492	123742	7098	1624
内蒙古 Inner Mongolia	103093	92463	6216	4286
辽宁 Liaoning	134344	117178	16136	985
吉林 Jilin	92430	83462	6961	1900
黑龙江 Heilongjiang	142056	128220	9553	4252
上海 Shanghai	7753	6391	833	482
江苏 Jiangsu	143085	130426	9179	3134
浙江 Zhejiang	34284	31405	2311	482
安徽 Anhui	230045	218309	10055	1599
福建 Fujian	102311	96813	4538	931
江西 Jiangxi	131854	124907	4489	2392
山东 Shandong	343039	323389	14146	5383
河南 Henan	336572	319818	13997	2738
湖北 Hubei	197258	181459	8761	6760
湖南 Hunan	182051	173546	4337	4099
广东 Guangdong	278045	240511	34624	2872
广西 Guangxi	169716	145429	19857	4236
海南 Hainan	45016	40456	2993	1564
重庆 Chongqing	53497	48207	3814	1448
四川 Sichuan	259716	237162	14215	8162
贵州 Guizhou	140909	131494	8329	1086
云南 Yunnan	173319	162383	7391	3524
西藏 Tibet	9876	9639	118	119
陕西 Shaanxi	101526	94241	6508	754
甘肃 Gansu	104944	101477	2399	1040
青海 Qinghai	18783	17827	491	380
宁夏 Ningxia	26550	25328	863	359
新疆 Xinjiang	106022	91458	5498	8946

工数（农村）

in Primary Schools (Rural)

单位:人

工数 & Workers				
校办工厂、农场职工 Employers in School-run Factories & Farms		代课教师 Substitute Teachers	临时工 Temporary Workers	兼任教师 Part-time Teachers
计 Total	其中:由厂、场收入支付工资的职工 Employers maintained by income of school-run businesses			
2271	541	596715	62891	5878
34	12	801	748	5
25	0	851	141	7
13	0	75653	1735	9
28	2	17207	1732	23
128	30	13126	923	139
45	18	5718	1538	91
107	104	1851	620	32
31	2	7393	2063	13
47	0	60	53	5
346	10	18088	6566	37
86	4	1684	1175	26
82	21	7382	1170	93
29	0	5646	564	130
66	24	9234	1250	75
121	24	6134	734	64
19	0	32461	6122	115
278	94	42048	2343	257
69	2	11366	1826	11
38	3	37575	3880	26
194	12	103615	1154	378
3	0	2862	272	47
28	0	4920	2623	77
177	18	26630	9323	1892
0	0	38971	3115	508
21	6	45996	5714	48
0	0	2369	168	744
23	1	43609	2011	58
28	0	17473	1353	139
85	67	968	374	1
0	0	2334	659	14
120	87	12690	942	814

小学教职工总数

Number of Primary School Teachers, Staff

地区 Region	教职 Teachers, Staff 合计 Total	专任教师 Full-time Teachers	行政人员 Adm. Personnel	工勤人员 Workers
总计 Total	519420	496643	8035	13753
北京 Beijing	0	0	0	0
天津 Tianjin	3	0	0	0
河北 Hebei	30035	29293	218	521
山西 Shanxi	37407	36626	239	522
内蒙古 Inner Mongolia	15023	14060	163	750
辽宁 Liaoning	19787	18715	763	301
吉林 Jilin	6149	5862	98	23
黑龙江 Heilongjiang	29187	28273	706	154
上海 Shanghai	0	0	0	0
江苏 Jiangsu	2003	1055	39	656
浙江 Zhejiang	193	162	9	8
安徽 Anhui	35213	34572	227	347
福建 Fujian	73	61	7	5
江西 Jiangxi	31848	30571	113	1149
山东 Shandong	82230	79981	485	1730
河南 Henan	61372	59709	1119	540
湖北 Hubei	68792	63080	2661	2884
湖南 Hunan	12420	11543	35	816
广东 Guangdong	11698	10995	239	447
广西 Guangxi	7791	7479	170	130
海南 Hainan	3683	3659	3	21
重庆 Chongqing	4898	4762	4	131
四川 Sichuan	15900	13625	146	2097
贵州 Guizhou	8862	8690	77	95
云南 Yunnan	513	497	1	15
西藏 Tibet	3373	3373	0	0
陕西 Shaanxi	18267	17737	470	58
甘肃 Gansu	10767	10533	6	188
青海 Qinghai	1423	1393	3	27
宁夏 Ningxia	70	26	1	43
新疆 Xinjiang	440	311	33	95

中民办教职工数

& Workers Maintained by the Communities

单位:人

工数 & Workers		代课教师 Substitute Teachers	临时工 Temporary Workers	兼任教师 Part－time Teachers
校办工厂、农场职工 Employers in School－run Factories & Farms				
计 Total	其中:由厂、场收入支付工资的职工 Employers maintained by income of school－run businesses			
989	705	293433	32570	979
0	0	0	0	0
3	3	950	38	37
3	2	70197	1188	1
20	12	1994	311	19
50	25	9833	479	18
8	5	5446	1366	29
166	166	537	1021	0
54	0	3186	1630	0
0	0	0	0	0
253	203	14710	6407	1
14	8	961	1659	2
67	56	2749	681	85
0	0	904	148	0
15	15	4430	439	42
34	25	5618	598	2
4	0	22650	5514	45
167	104	42605	1970	313
26	0	4967	1034	0
17	11	13143	2157	8
12	7	13032	259	0
0	0	72	14	0
1	0	497	823	1
32	26	7885	1968	195
0	0	8274	460	13
0	0	15	0	0
0	0	676	1	16
2	0	47293	1440	8
40	36	9951	822	115
0	0	716	131	0
0	0	115	3	0
1	1	27	9	29

小学教职工总数

Number of Female Teachers, Staff &

教职

Teachers, Staff

地区 Region	合计 Total	专任教师 Full-time Teachers	行政人员 Adm. Personnel	工勤人员 Workers
总计 Total	3087871	2909652	102162	72650
北京 Beijing	53893	46546	5223	1993
天津 Tianjin	39761	34232	3951	1502
河北 Hebei	201165	195063	4031	1983
山西 Shanxi	119267	114243	2947	2028
内蒙古 Inner Mongolia	78320	72573	3277	2326
辽宁 Liaoning	136140	123503	11313	1273
吉林 Jilin	101608	92530	6763	2074
黑龙江 Heilongjiang	137359	124352	8584	4253
上海 Shanghai	44516	34945	6964	2384
江苏 Jiangsu	140622	132826	3827	3533
浙江 Zhejiang	98450	93980	2069	2212
安徽 Anhui	101940	99205	1486	1134
福建 Fujian	98429	95816	1228	1363
江西 Jiangxi	91494	88235	1353	1810
山东 Shandong	186277	178745	4276	2957
河南 Henan	217673	210678	4418	2492
湖北 Hubei	127137	119415	3218	4184
湖南 Hunan	152670	147492	1820	3267
广东 Guangdong	217163	205673	6781	4619
广西 Guangxi	96036	89669	2603	3697
海南 Hainan	21380	19160	322	1896
重庆 Chongqing	59406	55386	2033	1934
四川 Sichuan	158923	149341	4363	5003
贵州 Guizhou	65238	62664	1576	996
云南 Yunnan	84869	79992	1638	3224
西藏 Tibet	5699	5488	75	136
陕西 Shaanxi	88165	84290	2641	1202
甘肃 Gansu	45403	43840	556	986
青海 Qinghai	12769	12300	191	261
宁夏 Ningxia	16171	15624	164	382
新疆 Xinjiang	89928	81846	2471	5546

中女教职工数

Workers in Primary Schools

单位:人

工 数 & Workers		代课教师 Substitute Teachers	临时工 Temporary Workers	兼任教师 Part-time Teachers
校办工厂、农场职工 Employers in School-run Factories & Farms				
计 Total	其中:由厂、场收入支付工资的职工 Employers maintained by income of school-run businesses			
3407	1035	403713	49294	4972
131	45	1092	1407	45
76	20	1316	183	235
88	9	66714	1066	44
49	15	15383	1353	58
144	47	7981	598	298
51	14	4877	1512	128
241	115	1220	628	25
170	22	4935	1159	49
223	0	320	400	203
436	168	18570	6331	16
189	31	3623	3910	339
115	40	4078	923	7
22	1	6042	536	74
96	48	6774	622	111
299	66	3501	373	88
85	14	25785	4517	291
320	178	20266	1768	243
91	32	8526	1300	15
90	11	30694	3788	23
67	19	60828	965	757
2	0	1087	190	5
53	2	3779	1840	120
216	63	12096	4447	518
2	0	13916	1546	127
15	6	20673	3868	58
0	0	651	59	399
32	10	41963	1922	127
21	9	7540	847	48
17	0	406	150	1
1	1	1097	591	9
65	49	7980	495	511

小学学龄儿童

Net Enrolment Rate of School－age

地　区 Region	校内外学龄儿童总数 Total Number of School－age Children	小　学　在　校 Breakdown of 合　计 Total	不足七周岁 Under 7 years	七周岁 7 years
总　计　Total	129913742	128727848	1319731	19328122
北　京　Beijing	791848	791425	86656	97376
天　津　Tianjin	727512	727074	23947	99891
河　北　Hebei	8470570	8461826	25186	1140297
山　西　Shanxi	3373547	3362950	0	610111
内蒙古　Inner Mongolia	2036215	2024897	9688	309108
辽　宁　Liaoning	3504103	3481240	0	474994
吉　林　Jilin	2565301	2561208	0	320726
黑龙江　Heilongjiang	2966436	2919843	0	428094
上　海　Shanghai	835637	835540	97077	112044
江　苏　Jiangsu	7112867	7100943	372411	1000988
浙　江　Zhejiang	3462035	3460247	0	523234
安　徽　Anhui	6239073	6211273	78198	1104906
福　建　Fujian	3634625	3628297	25895	523970
江　西　Jiangxi	4055238	4039591	14820	690267
山　东　Shandong	8459662	8426601	134177	1122467
河　南　Henan	11425743	11407029	25520	1926391
湖　北　Hubei	6691603	6658754	334990	1002665
湖　南　Hunan	7016787	6931867	0	805579
广　东　Guangdong	9003106	8976317	0	1421714
广　西　Guangxi	5465154	5385380	0	773007
海　南　Hainan	947951	944289	0	152095
重　庆　Chongqing	2731368	2723873	0	414096
四　川　Sichuan	8088405	7722536	0	1155340
贵　州　Guizhou	4385022	4306563	0	660495
云　南　Yunnan	4490157	4445187	7607	648029
西　藏　Tibet	325561	271776	48	45693
陕　西　Shaanxi	4766455	4737114	83339	704968
甘　肃　Gansu	2914073	2874003	0	505374
青　海　Qinghai	481168	450039	0	81530
宁　夏　Ningxia	600623	582642	172	105972
新　疆　Xinjiang	2345897	2277524	0	366701

入学率情况

Children in Primary Schools

单位：人

学龄儿童年龄分组 Students by age						学龄儿童入学率(%) Net Enrolment Rate of School-age Children
八周岁 8 years	九周岁 9 years	十周岁 10 years	十一周岁 11 years	十二周岁 12 years	十三周岁及以上 13 years and over	
21727647	24740786	24744616	23592342	13272878	1726	99.09
115778	149967	164990	176658	0	0	99.95
110120	138855	148310	142862	62475	614	99.94
1283828	1493807	1592285	1611732	1314691	0	99.90
641644	700670	672881	605735	131909	0	99.69
366713	438263	430927	387370	81726	1102	99.44
495356	608882	635167	681891	584950	0	99.35
367676	456109	468276	474695	473726	0	99.84
495810	602023	627324	595947	170645	0	98.43
122172	156809	172963	174475	0	0	99.99
1177078	1354298	1337469	1281987	576712	0	99.83
547811	638328	647007	662756	441111	0	99.95
1199366	1330029	1264663	1181084	53027	0	99.55
659609	787851	742870	640206	247896	0	99.83
797190	885032	857277	762390	32605	10	99.61
1483637	1854349	1901836	1760914	169221	0	99.61
2267760	2453936	2400644	2165635	167143	0	99.84
1093795	1241221	1232526	1121037	632520	0	99.51
1050924	1322784	1387337	1313490	1051753	0	98.79
1464514	1532410	1525199	1509983	1522497	0	99.70
828868	908378	963541	989554	922032	0	98.54
160543	162438	161461	158362	149390	0	99.61
417907	469448	440996	438468	542958	0	99.73
1234856	1411752	1376354	1333414	1210820	0	95.48
687175	767222	755239	732534	703898	0	98.21
705530	803130	790548	761192	729151	0	99.00
48530	47613	48556	44070	37266	0	83.48
777036	840257	849537	816918	665059	0	99.38
531704	553174	539400	503725	240626	0	98.62
84336	90484	86191	75696	31802	0	93.53
110766	119793	114048	105817	26074	0	97.01
399615	421474	408794	381745	299195	0	97.09

小学女学龄儿童

Net Enrolment Rate of Female School－age

地　区 Region	校内外学龄儿童总数 Total Number of School－age Children	小　学　在　校 Breakdown of		
		合　计 Total	不足七周岁 Under 7 years	七周岁 7 years
总　计 Total	62131991	61538530	631125	9211228
北　京 Beijing	383214	382984	42361	46727
天　津 Tianjin	353649	353414	12295	48264
河　北 Hebei	4145116	4140935	12185	558175
山　西 Shanxi	1634898	1629746	0	296589
内蒙古 Inner Mongolia	978024	972721	4820	147665
辽　宁 Liaoning	1681286	1670850	0	227154
吉　林 Jilin	1245641	1243807	0	153054
黑龙江 Heilongjiang	1443680	1421102	0	207480
上　海 Shanghai	404459	404411	47181	54206
江　苏 Jiangsu	3373083	3366540	176261	471990
浙　江 Zhejiang	1642319	1641570	0	246588
安　徽 Anhui	2964198	2951824	37165	518714
福　建 Fujian	1728865	1725866	12107	240587
江　西 Jiangxi	1934238	1927210	7065	326234
山　东 Shandong	4069614	4055853	65100	541984
河　南 Henan	5523651	5515649	11993	934807
湖　北 Hubei	3191736	3177438	159131	471775
湖　南 Hunan	3361909	3323037	0	383116
广　东 Guangdong	4270726	4256766	0	674631
广　西 Guangxi	2532661	2497834	0	358530
海　南 Hainan	439212	437505	0	70504
重　庆 Chongqing	1297290	1294495	0	195781
四　川 Sichuan	3852044	3672772	0	548975
贵　州 Guizhou	2063338	2018603	0	309294
云　南 Yunnan	2123723	2098434	3882	305145
西　藏 Tibet	159128	123960	29	21013
陕　西 Shaanxi	2274060	2261164	39461	338383
甘　肃 Gansu	1398941	1372454	0	246553
青　海 Qinghai	229812	212313	0	38920
宁　夏 Ningxia	289591	277267	89	50630
新　疆 Xinjiang	1141885	1110006	0	177760

入学率情况

Children in Primary Schools

单位: 人

学龄儿童年龄分组 Students by age						学龄儿童入学率(%) Net Enrolment Rate of School-age Children
八周岁 8 years	九周岁 9 years	十周岁 10 years	十一周岁 11 years	十二周岁 12 years	十三周岁及以上 13 years and over	
10382658	11836244	11842831	11300850	6332895	699	99.04
55957	72410	79625	85904	0	0	99.94
53519	66806	72400	69574	30326	230	99.93
630509	732807	775521	790774	640964	0	99.90
312542	339513	326680	293073	61349	0	99.68
175359	211114	207673	186953	38672	465	99.46
237014	291456	305157	329633	280436	0	99.38
179068	220163	229139	231172	231211	0	99.85
241756	294805	305471	288801	82789	0	98.44
59239	75526	83617	84642	0	0	99.99
557695	643175	636056	605840	275523	0	99.81
258711	300987	307170	315010	213104	0	99.95
568647	634433	602096	565736	25033	0	99.58
308595	376844	359595	310091	118047	0	99.83
380357	421555	412070	364751	15174	4	99.64
711203	891107	913419	852778	80262	0	99.66
1097443	1186523	1157832	1046784	80267	0	99.86
522979	592080	590213	535925	305335	0	99.55
503680	633171	665349	630531	507190	0	98.84
695132	725209	724123	716145	721526	0	99.67
383552	423121	446519	457410	428702	0	98.62
74212	75243	74944	72833	69769	0	99.61
199141	222590	210128	208552	258303	0	99.78
587793	670967	652320	635950	576767	0	95.35
320644	360871	353959	344213	329622	0	97.83
332639	380012	373616	358847	344293	0	98.81
22066	21717	22403	20115	16617	0	77.90
372815	399760	404262	390325	316158	0	99.43
253767	264792	255373	237340	114629	0	98.11
39599	43110	40831	35323	14530	0	92.39
53248	57106	54535	49382	12277	0	95.74
193777	207271	200735	186443	144020	0	97.21

特殊教育学校基本情况(包括盲

Basic Statistics of Special Education Schools (Including

地　区 Region	学校数(所) Schools	班　数(个) Classes		毕业生数 Graduates		
		小　学 Primary Schools	初　中 Junior Sec. Schools	计 Total	小　学 Primary Schools	初　中 Junior Sec. Schools
总　计 Total	1520	19959	2028	38143	31434	6709
北　京 Beijing	29	386	62	1538	873	665
天　津 Tianjin	24	147	17	416	341	75
河　北 Hebei	96	673	41	1005	870	135
山　西 Shanxi	45	297	48	575	506	69
内蒙古 Inner Mongolia	27	180	9	186	156	30
辽　宁 Liaoning	80	684	74	785	525	260
吉　林 Jilin	51	532	44	856	773	83
黑龙江 Heilongjiang	70	2084	89	990	822	168
上　海 Shanghai	35	354	114	762	383	379
江　苏 Jiangsu	125	1764	116	3526	2940	586
浙　江 Zhejiang	62	1312	203	3315	2556	759
安　徽 Anhui	69	421	33	1859	1584	275
福　建 Fujian	74	1395	148	5891	5151	740
江　西 Jiangxi	31	138	11	877	758	119
山　东 Shandong	142	1057	201	1868	1453	415
河　南 Henan	118	674	74	1448	1257	191
湖　北 Hubei	70	431	37	793	549	244
湖　南 Hunan	58	1839	435	2366	1823	543
广　东 Guangdong	63	417	58	2225	1991	234
广　西 Guangxi	44	913	21	1342	1254	88
海　南 Hainan	1	20	6	142	120	22
重　庆 Chongqing	42	241	9	840	670	170
四　川 Sichuan	63	635	42	943	871	72
贵　州 Guizhou	24	2565	75	684	644	40
云　南 Yunnan	19	176	24	1024	879	145
西　藏 Tibet	1	2	0	0	0	0
陕　西 Shaanxi	29	214	4	1030	999	31
甘　肃 Gansu	10	279	14	684	541	143
青　海 Qinghai	6	42	3	36	31	5
宁　夏 Ningxia	5	30	5	53	53	0
新　疆 Xinjiang	7	57	11	84	61	23

聋哑学校及弱智儿童辅读学校)

Schools for the Blind, the Deaf－mute & the Retarded)

单位:人

招生数 Students Admitted			在校学生数 Enrolment			教职工数 Teachers, Staff & Workers	
计 Total	小学 Primary Schools	初中 Junior Sec. Schools	计 Total	小学 Primary Schools	初中 Junior Sec. Schools	计 Total	其中:专任教师 Of which: Full－time Teachers
50074	40484	9590	371625	336651	34974	45119	31377
956	478	478	8246	6392	1854	1009	729
362	284	78	2722	2484	238	688	484
1606	1428	178	9939	9353	586	2158	1377
1334	1217	117	4906	4611	295	1143	845
402	369	33	3236	2813	423	692	548
913	774	139	7267	6343	924	2517	1855
709	650	59	7111	6662	449	2015	1441
1091	920	171	8860	8211	649	3269	2473
902	547	355	7529	6131	1398	1604	973
4539	3853	686	39321	36886	2435	3736	2725
2437	1531	906	21840	18159	3681	1382	1120
2286	1925	361	19525	18133	1392	1247	894
6089	4077	2012	43201	37621	5580	1322	1086
965	848	117	5389	4966	423	394	323
2661	2093	568	16362	14420	1942	4994	3252
2264	2029	235	12302	11631	671	2839	2207
1212	1038	174	7706	6737	969	1563	1150
4198	3435	763	22804	20195	2609	3052	860
2782	2258	524	29806	26740	3066	1261	990
2521	2342	179	20545	19638	907	1957	1438
411	355	56	2120	1881	239	83	58
1926	1325	601	9007	7640	1367	585	469
1163	1049	114	10771	10270	501	1437	1148
2188	2118	70	15688	15355	333	2079	1422
1623	1253	370	16304	14916	1388	559	426
30	30	0	68	68	0	7	7
1041	986	55	10634	10488	146	596	433
1049	923	126	4653	4300	353	388	297
165	158	7	2666	2626	40	128	97
74	48	26	416	375	41	115	79
175	143	32	681	606	75	300	171

特殊教育学校中盲

Basic Statistics of Schools for

地 区 Region	学校数(所) Schools	班数(个) Classes		毕业生数 Graduates		
		小学 Primary Schools	初中 Junior Sec. Schools	计 Total	小学 Primary Schools	初中 Junior Sec. Schools
总 计 Total	1102	7827	971	10502	7619	2883
北 京 Beijing	7	65	46	282	94	188
天 津 Tianjin	9	51	17	152	82	70
河 北 Hebei	80	444	36	416	362	54
山 西 Shanxi	26	198	46	361	316	45
内蒙古 Inner Mongolia	18	121	9	95	73	22
辽 宁 Liaoning	52	368	62	551	340	211
吉 林 Jilin	24	239	42	319	254	65
黑龙江 Heilongjiang	65	614	66	508	371	137
上 海 Shanghai	16	83	48	341	179	162
江 苏 Jiangsu	73	574	102	863	502	361
浙 江 Zhejiang	45	330	35	507	332	175
安 徽 Anhui	57	289	25	427	324	103
福 建 Fujian	36	331	32	533	429	104
江 西 Jiangxi	26	95	10	248	207	41
山 东 Shandong	119	812	120	1133	802	331
河 南 Henan	99	582	70	802	647	155
湖 北 Hubei	68	361	26	454	331	123
湖 南 Hunan	55	368	39	769	616	153
广 东 Guangdong	23	164	38	297	223	74
广 西 Guangxi	27	231	1	234	222	12
海 南 Hainan	1	17	6	24	23	1
重 庆 Chongqing	41	136	8	155	124	31
四 川 Sichuan	57	276	21	179	122	57
贵 州 Guizhou	17	470	10	71	64	7
云 南 Yunnan	12	109	21	304	219	85
西 藏 Tibet	1	2	0	0	0	0
陕 西 Shaanxi	24	156	4	101	97	4
甘 肃 Gansu	8	235	12	221	136	85
青 海 Qinghai	5	29	3	22	18	4
宁 夏 Ningxia	4	25	5	51	51	0
新 疆 Xinjiang	7	52	11	82	59	23

注:本表不包括普校附设的盲聋哑班的学生数

Nomber of students in the blind and deaf-mute classes attached to regular schools are not included.

聋哑学校基本情况

the Blind & the Deaf－mute

单位:人

招生数 Students Admitted			在校学生数 Enrolment			教职工数 Teachers Staff & Workers	
计 Total	小学 Primary Schools	初中 Junior Sec. Schools	计 Total	小学 Primary Schools	初中 Junior Sec. Schools	计 Total	其中:专任教师 Of which: Full－time Teachers
17464	14405	3059	101108	89505	11603	31490	22097
207	74	133	1412	820	592	440	287
138	63	75	713	475	238	353	244
978	872	106	4624	4281	343	1664	1183
632	554	78	2891	2692	199	889	624
261	243	18	1571	1453	118	556	425
609	498	111	4837	4069	768	1891	1357
377	322	55	3621	3221	400	1479	985
580	455	125	4548	4028	520	2550	1793
377	167	210	1526	958	568	867	471
1337	1084	253	7395	6317	1078	2632	1718
557	431	126	4054	3605	449	1065	834
819	706	113	5059	4701	358	1090	755
792	578	214	5642	4916	726	863	664
299	245	54	1483	1291	192	317	261
1715	1370	345	10132	8640	1492	4313	2755
1492	1279	213	7639	7047	592	2558	1965
770	687	83	3977	3744	233	1467	1062
1227	1022	205	5850	5058	792	1134	817
595	524	71	5251	4507	744	625	497
624	574	50	4385	4262	123	778	510
163	132	31	530	447	83	78	53
283	252	31	1658	1581	77	503	395
500	427	73	2861	2665	196	1006	756
500	492	8	2513	2455	58	504	345
593	422	171	2285	1901	384	487	360
30	30	0	30	30	0	7	7
284	279	5	1641	1613	28	536	406
463	426	37	1490	1374	116	343	259
36	29	7	549	529	20	103	81
67	41	26	368	327	41	100	65
159	127	32	573	498	75	292	163

幼儿园基本

Basic Statistics of Kindergartens

地区 Region	园数(所) Kindergartens 计 Total	班数(个) Classes 计 Total	其中:小学附设学前班 of which: Pre-school Classes Attached to Primary Schools	入园人数(人) Children Admitted 计 Total	其中:小学附设学前班 of which: Pre-school Classes Attached to Primary Schools
总计 Total	181136	781450	403426	16175393	10551583
北京 Beijing	2180	8708	1028	89463	28247
天津 Tianjin	882	6635	3538	135359	97050
河北 Hebei	5691	42278	34900	1025896	872852
山西 Shanxi	10550	37135	18996	661257	335522
内蒙古 Inner Mongolia	1771	14653	9867	272521	212099
辽宁 Liaoning	9935	29813	13317	481840	284501
吉林 Jilin	4440	17930	10572	310209	222897
黑龙江 Heilongjiang	4830	21732	14267	408498	283537
上海 Shanghai	956	8364	1464	97669	17141
江苏 Jiangsu	14573	52821	14087	821377	280726
浙江 Zhejiang	14864	38637	6357	562744	137789
安徽 Anhui	3314	29778	19005	835182	625214
福建 Fujian	12522	28910	8304	463737	164235
江西 Jiangxi	7602	20183	11547	514200	331353
山东 Shandong	33849	68245	21092	1101846	536117
河南 Henan	2943	49667	38998	1451980	1269747
湖北 Hubei	3729	28039	17578	642096	480439
湖南 Hunan	4448	29577	24735	583649	482082
广东 Guangdong	11836	63566	24677	1345465	819718
广西 Guangxi	3639	26405	18997	647923	538235
海南 Hainan	652	4343	2313	89116	61981
重庆 Chongqing	6007	19052	8542	414336	244652
四川 Sichuan	12016	53887	22884	1234075	658404
贵州 Guizhou	1340	13008	9763	409758	341478
云南 Yunnan	1568	17936	11964	456163	366779
西藏 Tibet	36	164	78	3713	1839
陕西 Shaanxi	1662	26003	21228	545368	452272
甘肃 Gansu	2040	12778	7248	320918	227963
青海 Qinghai	189	2330	1691	59509	45677
宁夏 Ningxia	261	2584	1734	64469	54242
新疆 Xinjiang	811	6289	2655	125057	76795

情况（总计）

(Regional Aggregates)

在园幼儿数（人） Children Enrolled		教职工数（人） Teachers, Staff & Workers			
			其中: of which		
计 Total	其中:小学附设学前班 Of which: Pre-school Classes Attached to Primary Schools	计 Total	园长 Kindergarten Heads	教师 Teachers	保健员 Health Nurses
23262588	11911894	1158302	85479	872422	63211
237055	31261	29367	2058	13216	1117
211977	97050	18607	1360	11223	474
1175759	938427	51208	1587	44529	2317
1036280	473614	50534	3916	41384	1839
346840	222059	18977	1333	14482	1051
838133	367622	54582	5732	37881	3169
446623	258230	26080	3278	18623	2138
510631	294964	34884	3152	25962	2086
245245	37513	25831	1527	15743	1085
1552234	399013	92111	6567	74784	4772
1083790	204975	61549	5495	47902	4050
1116123	714733	29683	2763	24297	1080
819102	214355	47945	3184	40033	2049
626009	348424	29179	2280	24124	1680
1666397	620283	110127	9571	90164	3156
1785233	1406701	33037	2004	21171	897
856859	519461	44030	3275	32828	2775
643161	494833	39678	1737	32988	3713
2130453	907101	123815	10528	79748	8296
783482	562724	31782	2080	24416	2267
124656	69173	7077	655	4929	1104
625666	294592	26231	1699	21088	1243
1923949	796934	69773	3657	58165	3837
468373	345079	17220	1022	14160	1377
577493	366779	25256	1427	18618	1637
5274	2383	397	26	237	83
656051	488523	21349	1216	15474	1397
407489	238723	14666	1085	10669	687
66795	46282	2784	186	1999	256
83374	56388	3550	183	2413	262
212082	93695	16993	896	9172	1317

成人高等学校基本情况(总计)(不包

Basic Statistics of Adult Higher Educational

(Evening Schools & Divisions of Correspondence run by Regular

地 区 Region	学校数(所) Schools 计 Total	其中:中央部委所属学校数 Inst. Under Central Ministries & Agencies	本专科学生数 Undergraduate Students 毕业生数 Graduates	招生数 Students Admitted	在校学生数 Enrolments	合 计 Total	校 Teachers, 计 Subtotal	专 任 Full-time 小 计 Subtotal	教 授 Prof.
总 计 Total	871	119	411687	538654	1274789	200054	192068	97644	1726
北 京 Beijing	69	33	23585	26868	71033	16952	16050	7281	385
天 津 Tianjin	39	5	12264	14344	34918	6947	6847	3439	49
河 北 Hebei	28	7	13329	20879	45188	7034	6800	3202	80
山 西 Shanxi	24	1	9431	12526	28021	5484	5318	2684	23
内蒙古 Inner Mongolia	16	0	6702	8617	18379	3468	3444	1713	16
辽 宁 Liaoning	49	6	21161	21175	56465	10732	10447	5098	90
吉 林 Jilin	29	4	16245	14964	38099	6212	5874	2810	77
黑龙江 Heilongjiang	50	8	19297	23119	55606	12407	11968	6263	124
上 海 Shanghai	39	5	5665	10378	26056	7694	7142	3299	48
江 苏 Jiangsu	41	5	18999	30373	69776	11820	11533	6510	65
浙 江 Zhejiang	24	4	12770	20851	57020	6255	6142	3269	40
安 徽 Anhui	24	3	12843	15673	37150	4848	4784	2427	8
福 建 Fujian	18	1	9972	13330	31869	2654	2545	1287	12
江 西 Jiangxi	20	1	10295	14359	32720	3944	3421	1841	32
山 东 Shandong	40	4	31765	44893	104739	14335	13831	7131	106
河 南 Henan	40	3	21661	22817	54108	8933	8756	4731	44
湖 北 Hubei	41	10	20254	26134	58123	10387	10014	5308	72
湖 南 Hunan	33	4	25086	30701	75544	7335	6635	3388	60
广 东 Guangdong	54	3	22845	41887	94129	12345	12157	6274	121
广 西 Guangxi	14	0	9836	11141	33574	3811	3598	1864	22
海 南 Hainan	4	0	448	574	1581	257	245	137	2
重 庆 Chongqing	22	1	7846	10945	24620	3654	3385	1768	22
四 川 Sichuan	48	4	30267	35261	83290	11752	10980	5401	86
贵 州 Guizhou	14	0	9351	13682	27851	2397	2346	1246	18
云 南 Yunnan	11	1	5103	5705	13369	2033	2009	1051	2
西 藏 Tibet	0	0	0	0	0	0	0	0	0
陕 西 Shaanxi	31	4	14838	17603	37814	6413	6189	3054	51
甘 肃 Gansu	18	1	5262	6736	14376	2353	2287	1272	16
青 海 Qinghai	2	0	733	1726	3525	597	594	400	6
宁 夏 Ningxia	5	0	1632	2430	6441	685	631	392	26
新 疆 Xinjiang	24	1	12202	18963	39405	6316	6096	3104	23

括普通高等学校函授部、夜大学)

Institutions (Regional Aggregates)

Institutions of Higher Education are not Included in Aggregates)

单位:人

教职工数 Teachers, Staff & Workers										兼任教师 Part-time Teachers
本部教职工 Staff & Workers in the School Proper							科研机构人员 Personnel in Affiliated Research Org.	校办厂、场职工 Employers in School-run Factories, Farms	附设机构人员 Personnel in Other Subsidiary Units	
教师 Teachers				教辅人员 Supporting Staff	行政人员 Adm. Personnel	工勤人员 Workers				
副教授 Asso. Prof.	讲师 Lecturers	助教 Assistants	教员 Instructors							
23244	45870	22223	4581	23870	44321	26233	1079	3690	32173	5291
1745	2932	1411	808	2312	4423	2034	110	433	359	3873
1007	1699	614	70	911	1549	948	14	46	40	1499
783	1369	814	156	963	1296	1339	48	47	139	507
599	1275	677	110	632	1204	798	12	118	36	203
361	925	365	46	525	729	477	3	21	0	288
1568	2431	886	123	1405	2362	1582	76	144	65	1046
777	1284	626	46	764	1525	775	38	4	296	423
1993	2874	1051	221	1335	2374	1996	95	139	205	1379
741	1940	459	111	990	1544	1309	94	275	183	614
1137	2992	1817	499	1306	2280	1437	29	187	71	1954
654	1632	796	147	670	1376	827	3	93	17	1450
625	1199	473	122	597	1171	589	4	58	2	1201
302	616	307	50	261	760	237	9	54	46	1102
467	857	387	98	428	683	469	30	461	32	763
1450	3013	2230	332	1771	3197	1732	54	317	133	1325
1071	2069	1249	298	983	2032	1010	36	100	41	1011
1294	2413	1267	262	1358	2222	1126	92	230	51	1132
826	1735	647	120	667	1671	909	13	320	367	1530
1354	2965	1644	190	1481	2980	1422	103	30	55	3354
394	980	406	62	379	836	519	76	46	91	747
12	46	69	8	22	50	36	0	12	0	97
432	962	307	45	349	784	484	20	91	158	2001
1474	2562	1103	176	1360	2834	1385	34	176	562	4267
288	623	278	39	228	629	243	11	22	18	641
169	560	267	53	264	375	319	1	7	16	300
0	0	0	0	0	0	0	0	0	0	0
744	1487	650	122	864	1426	845	27	165	32	1767
230	660	309	57	223	467	325	14	23	29	158
74	221	99	0	65	83	46	0	3	0	205
80	173	104	9	45	118	76	1	27	26	168
593	1376	911	201	712	1341	939	32	41	147	286

成人高等学校本、专科学生数(总计)

Number of Students in Adult Higher Educational
(Evening Schools & Divisions of Correspondence run by

地区 Region	毕业生数 Graduates			招生数 Students Admitted		
	计 Total	本科 Normal Courses	专科 Short-cycle Courses	计 Total	本科 Normal Courses	专科 Short-cycle Courses
总计 Total	411687	19365	392322	538654	33028	505626
北京 Beijing	23585	1609	21976	26868	3234	23634
天津 Tianjin	12264	227	12037	14344	27	14317
河北 Hebei	13329	69	13260	20879	479	20400
山西 Shanxi	9431	606	8825	12526	1354	11172
内蒙古 Inner Mongolia	6702	417	6285	8617	361	8256
辽宁 Liaoning	21161	386	20775	21175	713	20462
吉林 Jilin	16245	639	15606	14964	703	14261
黑龙江 Heilongjiang	19297	223	19074	23119	948	22171
上海 Shanghai	5665	498	5167	10378	476	9902
江苏 Jiangsu	18999	1741	17258	30373	2028	28345
浙江 Zhejiang	12770	911	11859	20851	698	20153
安徽 Anhui	12843	1019	11824	15673	1591	14082
福建 Fujian	9972	514	9458	13330	1568	11762
江西 Jiangxi	10295	510	9785	14359	923	13436
山东 Shandong	31765	1264	30501	44893	3157	41736
河南 Henan	21661	904	20757	22817	1686	21131
湖北 Hubei	20254	468	19786	26134	1580	24554
湖南 Hunan	25086	2015	23071	30701	2207	28494
广东 Guangdong	22845	2236	20609	41887	3591	38296
广西 Guangxi	9836	224	9612	11141	508	10633
海南 Hainan	448	0	448	574	0	574
重庆 Chongqing	7846	95	7751	10945	374	10571
四川 Sichuan	30267	954	29313	35261	2584	32677
贵州 Guizhou	9351	727	8624	13682	727	12955
云南 Yunnan	5103	87	5016	5705	0	5705
西藏 Tibet						
陕西 Shaanxi	14838	559	14279	17603	895	16708
甘肃 Gansu	5262	231	5031	6736	377	6359
青海 Qinghai	733	0	733	1726	0	1726
宁夏 Ningxia	1632	0	1632	2430	0	2430
新疆 Xinjiang	12202	232	11970	18963	239	18724

(不包括普通高等学校函授部、夜大学)

Institutions by Type of Courses (Regional Aggregates)
Institutions of Higher Education are not Included in Aggregates)

单位:人

在校学生数 Enrolment			毕业班学生数 Graduates for Next Year		
计 Total	本科 Normal Courses	专科 Short－cycle Courses	计 Total	本科 Normal Courses	专科 Short－cycle Courses
1274789	75739	1199050	440954	23261	417693
71033	7289	63744	25464	2175	23289
34918	321	34597	13573	206	13367
45188	803	44385	14542	176	14366
28021	2528	25493	9871	631	9240
18379	942	17437	6771	342	6429
56465	1801	54664	20996	660	20336
38099	1804	36295	13511	709	12802
55606	1954	53652	20687	596	20091
26056	1672	24384	7389	541	6848
69776	4720	65056	21610	1741	19869
57020	6150	50870	16038	1687	14351
37150	3065	34085	12834	845	11989
31869	3133	28736	10528	810	9718
32720	1924	30796	11270	702	10568
104739	7168	97571	37723	2237	35486
54108	3269	50839	21246	929	20317
58123	2984	55139	18841	768	18073
75544	5532	70012	28211	1967	26244
94129	7325	86804	28129	2160	25969
33574	1184	32390	10240	287	9953
1581	0	1581	766	0	766
24620	907	23713	8496	295	8201
83290	4492	78798	32595	1113	31482
27851	1633	26218	10312	707	9605
13369	187	13182	4931	93	4838
37814	1801	36013	14040	516	13524
14376	658	13718	5975	281	5694
3525	0	3525	1207	0	1207
6441	0	6441	2175	0	2175
39405	493	38912	10983	87	10896

广 播 电 视 大

Basic Statistics of

地 区 Region	学校数(所) Schools 计 Total	其中:中央部委所属学校数 Inst. under Central Ministries & Agencies	本专科学生数 Undergraduate Students 毕业生数 Graduates	招生数 Students Admitted	在校学生数 Enrolments	合 计 Total	校 Teachers, 计 Subtotal	专 任 Full-time 小计 Subtotal	教授 Prof.
总 计 **Total**	45	1	170210	196230	489155	53177	51684	25687	178
北 京 Beijing	2	1	1586	1705	5262	1121	965	392	2
天 津 Tianjin	1	0	4889	4313	11695	1021	1011	357	3
河 北 Hebei	1	0	4571	8500	18572	1679	1665	726	6
山 西 Shanxi	1	0	2512	2480	6807	820	817	334	4
内蒙古 Inner Mongolia	1	0	2088	3503	7637	1019	1006	404	3
辽 宁 Liaoning	3	0	8539	7975	23453	2487	2468	1197	16
吉 林 Jilin	2	0	9111	7695	18079	1496	1496	708	11
黑龙江 Heilongjiang	2	0	7673	7983	18861	3697	3583	1726	22
上 海 Shanghai	1	0	1081	1265	3801	352	284	84	5
江 苏 Jiangsu	2	0	9645	13830	33827	5730	5670	3143	7
浙 江 Zhejiang	2	0	8708	10837	28918	2525	2511	1370	6
安 徽 Anhui	1	0	4542	4368	11827	1093	1093	490	0
福 建 Fujian	2	0	6118	6170	16758	900	853	359	0
江 西 Jiangxi	1	0	3956	5910	14886	705	699	361	2
山 东 Shandong	2	0	13722	13635	34778	6734	6592	3582	13
河 南 Henan	1	0	9506	6467	15986	1966	1885	895	3
湖 北 Hubei	2	0	9012	11758	25483	4227	4104	2323	8
湖 南 Hunan	1	0	10298	12674	33762	1117	1117	454	2
广 东 Guangdong	3	0	7180	11224	29857	3373	3354	1769	12
广 西 Guangxi	1	0	3709	3313	11722	891	887	408	3
海 南 Hainan	1	0	419	514	1325	124	124	69	2
重 庆 Chongqing	1	0	3865	6550	14231	646	632	262	5
四 川 Sichuan	2	0	12924	11700	32055	2916	2396	1060	7
贵 州 Guizhou	1	0	4095	6201	12321	687	676	330	5
云 南 Yunnan	1	0	4258	3800	10120	800	777	370	0
西 藏 Tibet	0	0	0	0	0	0	0	0	0
陕 西 Shaanxi	2	0	6468	8889	17594	1882	1868	985	22
甘 肃 Gansu	1	0	2228	2940	6140	187	183	67	2
青 海 Qinghai	1	0	310	1018	1957	414	414	264	5
宁 夏 Ningxia	1	0	874	1333	3367	164	164	70	2
新 疆 Xinjiang	2	0	6323	7680	18074	2404	2390	1128	0

学基本情况

Radio/TV Universities

单位:人

教职工数 Teachers, Staff & Workers											兼任教师 Part-time Teachers
本部教职工 Staff & Workers in the School Proper								科研机构人员 Personnel in Affiliated Research Org.	校办厂、场职工 Employers in School-run Factories, Farms	附设机构人员 Personnel in Other Subsidiary Units	
教师 Teachers				教辅人员 Supporting Staff	行政人员 Adm. Personnel	工勤人员 Workers					
副教授 Asso. Prof.	讲师 Lecturers	助教 Assistants	教员 Instructors								
4555	11819	7575	1560	7313	13158	5526	157	393	9431	9450	
115	199	69	7	84	398	91	16	3	137	809	
94	203	45	12	208	329	117	3	7	0	792	
141	364	171	44	318	387	234	6	8	0	290	
67	167	79	17	109	272	102	0	3	0	6	
66	209	116	10	176	294	132	0	13	0	254	
329	511	297	44	388	614	269	4	3	12	320	
145	348	190	14	302	415	71	0	0	0	250	
368	785	451	100	545	865	447	9	11	94	594	
18	53	8	0	112	74	14	10	38	20	49	
374	1344	1089	329	636	1178	713	4	46	10	1174	
198	689	403	74	314	532	295	0	14	0	1307	
104	236	99	51	157	370	76	0	0	0	698	
57	170	110	22	114	320	60	0	6	41	532	
89	168	87	15	118	156	64	2	0	4	576	
520	1447	1397	205	880	1419	711	24	49	69	740	
154	351	292	95	249	592	149	25	15	41	636	
459	1027	656	173	572	797	412	8	94	21	527	
91	247	85	29	128	411	124	0	0	0	871	
239	809	626	83	371	860	354	12	2	5	1985	
71	253	69	12	89	287	103	4	0	0	458	
9	26	27	5	10	36	9	0	0	0	74	
48	151	55	3	109	190	71	0	0	14	1285	
218	542	274	19	323	822	191	18	52	450	2875	
65	156	90	14	94	216	36	0	3	8	439	
57	211	87	15	122	184	101	0	7	16	79	
0	0	0	0	0	0	0	0	0	0	0	
202	455	254	52	310	471	102	4	10	0	1476	
20	33	6	6	57	54	5	4	0	0	0	
53	144	62	0	50	58	42	0	0	0	193	
11	45	12	0	20	67	7	0	0	0	57	
173	476	369	110	348	490	424	4	9	1	104	

广播电视大学

Number of Students in Radio/TV

地区 Region	毕业生数 Graduates			招生数 Students Admitted		
	计 Total	本科 Normal Courses	专科 Short－cycle Courses	计 Total	本科 Normal Courses	专科 Short－cycle Courses
总 计 Total	170210	1104	169106	196230	1128	195102
北 京 Beijing	1586	248	1338	1705	0	1705
天 津 Tianjin	4889	176	4713	4313	0	4313
河 北 Hebei	4571		4571	8500		8500
山 西 Shanxi	2512		2512	2480		2480
内蒙古 Inner Mongolia	2088		2088	3503		3503
辽 宁 Liaoning	8539		8539	7975		7975
吉 林 Jilin	9111		9111	7695		7695
黑龙江 Heilongjiang	7673		7673	7983		7983
上 海 Shanghai	1081	176	905	1265	0	1265
江 苏 Jiangsu	9645	220	9425	13830	220	13610
浙 江 Zhejiang	8708	0	8708	10837	0	10837
安 徽 Anhui	4542		4542	4368		4368
福 建 Fujian	6118		6118	6170		6170
江 西 Jiangxi	3956		3956	5910		5910
山 东 Shandong	13722		13722	13635		13635
河 南 Henan	9506		9506	6467		6467
湖 北 Hubei	9012	0	9012	11758	134	11624
湖 南 Hunan	10298		10298	12674		12674
广 东 Guangdong	7180	120	7060	11224	680	10544
广 西 Guangxi	3709	77	3632	3313	94	3219
海 南 Hainan	419		419	514		514
重 庆 Chongqing	3865		3865	6550		6550
四 川 Sichuan	12924		12924	11700		11700
贵 州 Guizhou	4095		4095	6201		6201
云 南 Yunnan	4258	87	4171	3800	0	3800
西 藏 Tibet						
陕 西 Shaanxi	6468		6468	8889		8889
甘 肃 Gansu	2228		2228	2940		2940
青 海 Qinghai	310		310	1018		1018
宁 夏 Ningxia	874		874	1333		1333
新 疆 Xinjiang	6323		6323	7680		7680

本、专科学生数

Universities by Type of Courses

单位:人

在校学生数 Enrolment			毕业班学生数 Graduates for Next Year		
计 Total	本科 Normal Courses	专科 Short－cycle Courses	计 Total	本科 Normal Courses	专科 Short－cycle Courses
489155	3295	485860	175680	1228	174452
5262	360	4902	1673	184	1489
11695	233	11462	4994	163	4831
18572		18572	5681		5681
6807		6807	2895		2895
7637		7637	2806		2806
23453		23453	8141		8141
18079		18079	6054		6054
18861		18861	7305		7305
3801	478	3323	1182	244	938
33827	621	33206	10820	201	10619
28918	119	28799	9756	40	9716
11827		11827	4989		4989
16758		16758	6065		6065
14886		14886	4687		4687
34778		34778	14688		14688
15986		15986	6566		6566
25483	222	25261	8448	76	8372
33762		33762	12008		12008
29857	781	29076	9746	127	9619
11722	294	11428	3805	100	3705
1325		1325	570		570
14231		14231	4468		4468
32055		32055	14350		14350
12321		12321	4416		4416
10120	187	9933	4153	93	4060
17594		17594	6169		6169
6140		6140	2482		2482
1957		1957	659		659
3367		3367	1154		1154
18074		18074	4950		4950

职工高等学

Basic Statistics of

地区 Region	学校数(所) Schools 计 Total	其中:中央部委所属学校数 Inst. Under Central Ministries & Agencies	本专科学生数 Undergraduate Students 毕业生数 Graduates	招生数 Students Admitted	在校学生数 Enrolments	合计 Total	校 Teachers, 计 Subtotal	专任 Full-time 小计 Subtotal	教授 Prof.
总 计 Total	507	73	101741	143953	348215	81469	77262	41096	676
北 京 Beijing	36	9	10395	9491	30529	9793	9308	4510	188
天 津 Tianjin	30	2	5365	7162	17818	4529	4457	2557	32
河 北 Hebei	13	4	4361	6246	13538	3214	3001	1420	44
山 西 Shanxi	11	0	2606	2758	7625	2566	2480	1329	12
内蒙古 Inner Mongolia	5	0	953	1292	2669	515	505	261	1
辽 宁 Liaoning	39	6	7345	9564	22594	6351	6132	3008	46
吉 林 Jilin	17	2	3980	4062	12219	2408	2248	1166	17
黑龙江 Heilongjiang	35	7	7723	8905	22699	5992	5802	3065	58
上 海 Shanghai	34	5	3952	7911	19621	6474	6015	2865	30
江 苏 Jiangsu	24	3	3964	7426	17352	2860	2735	1731	15
浙 江 Zhejiang	15	3	1047	4729	8356	2020	1939	1045	14
安 徽 Anhui	13	3	2464	3786	8572	1896	1856	1024	2
福 建 Fujian	8	0	534	1436	3462	435	435	269	1
江 西 Jiangxi	12	1	2920	4171	8906	1400	1364	858	2
山 东 Shandong	22	3	7958	12294	28936	3917	3670	1803	10
河 南 Henan	19	1	4110	5262	15223	3009	2935	1688	17
湖 北 Hubei	23	8	4443	5757	13523	3319	3137	1702	26
湖 南 Hunan	22	2	7432	9322	20243	4442	3754	2126	32
广 东 Guangdong	25	2	4504	9968	22090	3376	3265	1763	63
广 西 Guangxi	3	0	497	833	2173	422	378	229	0
海 南 Hainan	2	0	29	60	256	133	121	68	0
重 庆 Chongqing	16	1	2382	2297	5973	2095	1845	1008	12
四 川 Sichuan	25	4	3476	5283	12623	3821	3700	2024	24
贵 州 Guizhou	6	0	1696	2608	4862	541	522	320	0
云 南 Yunnan	6	1	450	1319	2372	808	807	441	0
西 藏 Tibet	0	0	0	0	0	0	0	0	0
陕 西 Shaanxi	18	4	2382	3219	7651	2095	1927	997	2
甘 肃 Gansu	12	1	1368	1415	3667	1155	1117	699	1
青 海 Qinghai	1	0	423	708	1568	183	180	136	1
宁 夏 Ningxia	4	0	758	1097	3074	521	467	322	24
新 疆 Xinjiang	11	1	2224	3572	8021	1179	1160	662	2

校基本情况

Workers' Colleges

单位: 人

教职工数 Teachers, Staff & Workers										兼任教师 Part-time Teachers
本部教职工 Staff & Workers in the School Proper							科研机构人员 Personnel in Affiliated Research Org.	校办厂、场职工 Employers in School-run Factories, Farms	附设机构人员 Personnel in Other Subsidiary Units	
教师 Teachers				教辅人员 Supporting Staff	行政人员 Adm. Personnel	工勤人员 Workers				
副教授 Asso. Prof.	讲师 Lecturers	助教 Assistants	教员 Instructors							
9906	20236	8481	1797	9125	16017	11024	452	2201	1554	11367
843	1769	984	726	1459	2373	966	60	351	74	2442
740	1266	478	41	470	869	561	7	35	30	650
338	635	344	59	372	501	708	42	32	139	201
276	630	360	51	293	476	382	6	48	32	177
74	158	26	2	68	117	59	2	8	0	7
851	1561	484	66	770	1343	1011	67	99	53	618
306	527	289	27	222	540	320	0	3	157	164
967	1521	452	67	486	1069	1182	30	58	102	665
652	1685	395	103	772	1263	1115	71	226	162	514
331	911	400	74	303	451	250	10	72	43	732
257	526	210	38	204	434	256	0	66	15	127
289	518	200	15	194	403	235	0	40	0	463
43	155	53	17	25	109	32	0	0	0	195
211	428	176	41	116	268	122	12	24	0	138
461	839	440	53	486	814	567	24	180	43	335
371	767	439	94	344	520	383	11	63	0	277
414	818	409	35	395	673	367	22	133	27	244
459	1114	448	73	373	774	481	2	320	366	504
444	828	382	46	543	685	274	51	22	38	821
62	113	48	6	33	77	39	0	37	7	133
3	20	42	3	12	14	27	0	12	0	23
260	550	167	19	151	401	285	15	91	144	570
471	1018	471	40	443	712	521	2	69	50	408
77	180	58	5	47	78	77	0	16	3	124
81	230	120	10	95	121	150	1	0	0	204
0	0	0	0	0	0	0	0	0	0	0
281	519	167	28	211	435	284	3	139	26	223
108	418	149	23	82	181	155	10	23	5	140
21	77	37	0	15	25	4	0	3	0	12
69	128	92	9	25	51	69	1	27	26	111
146	327	161	26	116	240	142	3	4	12	145

职工高等学校

Number of Students in Workers'

地　区 Region	毕业生数 Graduates			招生数 Students Admitted		
	计 Total	本　科 Normal Courses	专　科 Short－cycle Courses	计 Total	本　科 Normal Courses	专　科 Short－cycle Courses
总　计　Total	101741	1012	100729	143953	2302	141651
北　京　Beijing	10395	122	10273	9491	812	8679
天　津　Tianjin	5365		5365	7162		7162
河　北　Hebei	4361	69	4292	6246	479	5767
山　西　Shanxi	2606	60	2546	2758	70	2688
内蒙古　Inner Mongolia	953		953	1292		1292
辽　宁　Liaoning	7345	101	7244	9564	32	9532
吉　林　Jilin	3980	52	3928	4062	0	4062
黑龙江　Heilongjiang	7723	63	7660	8905	80	8825
上　海　Shanghai	3952	322	3630	7911	476	7435
江　苏　Jiangsu	3964		3964	7426		7426
浙　江　Zhejiang	1047		1047	4729		4729
安　徽　Anhui	2464		2464	3786		3786
福　建　Fujian	534		534	1436		1436
江　西　Jiangxi	2920		2920	4171		4171
山　东　Shandong	7958		7958	12294		12294
河　南　Henan	4110		4110	5262		5262
湖　北　Hubei	4443	50	4393	5757	249	5508
湖　南　Hunan	7432		7432	9322		9322
广　东　Guangdong	4504		4504	9968		9968
广　西　Guangxi	497		497	833		833
海　南　Hainan	29		29	60		60
重　庆　Chongqing	2382		2382	2297		2297
四　川　Sichuan	3476	41	3435	5283	85	5198
贵　州　Guizhou	1696		1696	2608		2608
云　南　Yunnan	450		450	1319		1319
西　藏　Tibet						
陕　西　Shaanxi	2382		2382	3219		3219
甘　肃　Gansu	1368		1368	1415		1415
青　海　Qinghai	423		423	708		708
宁　夏　Ningxia	758		758	1097		1097
新　疆　Xinjiang	2224	132	2092	3572	19	3553

本、专科学生数

Colleges by Type of Courses

单位:人

在校学生数 Enrolment			毕业班学生数 Graduates for Next Year		
计 Total	本科 Normal Courses	专科 Short-cycle Courses	计 Total	本科 Normal Courses	专科 Short-cycle Courses
348215	4609	343606	112923	1197	111726
30529	1192	29337	10561	304	10257
17818		17818	6473		6473
13538	803	12735	4141	176	3965
7625	130	7495	2696	60	2636
2669		2669	757		757
22594	137	22457	7866	75	7791
12219	111	12108	4152	54	4098
22699	131	22568	8480	51	8429
19621	1194	18427	5454	297	5157
17352		17352	4563		4563
8356		8356	1486		1486
8572		8572	2526		2526
3462		3462	956		956
8906		8906	3033		3033
28936		28936	8983		8983
15223		15223	5194		5194
13523	600	12923	3986	78	3908
20243		20243	8311		8311
22090		22090	5884		5884
2173		2173	611		611
256		256	196		196
5973		5973	2397		2397
12623	140	12483	4116	55	4061
4862		4862	1682		1682
2372		2372	487		487
7651		7651	2618		2618
3667		3667	1495		1495
1568		1568	548		548
3074		3074	1021		1021
8021	171	7850	2250	47	2203

农民高等学

Basic Statistics

地区 Region	学校数(所) Schools		本专科学生数 Undergraduate Students			校 Teachers,			
	计 Total	其中:中央部委所属学校数 Inst. Under Central Ministries & Agencies	毕业生数 Graduates	招生数 Students Admitted	在校学生数 Enrolments	合计 Total	计 Subtotal	专任 Full-time	
								小计 Subtotal	教授 Prof.
总计 Total	3	0	481	428	953	206	205	127	0
吉林 Jilin	3	0	481	428	953	206	205	127	0

注:农民高等学校都是专科学生数。

Note: All students in Peasants' colleges are enrolled in short-cycle courses.

独立函授学

Basic Statistics of

地区 Region	学校数(所) Schools		本专科学生数 Undergraduate Students			校 Teachers,			
	计 Total	其中:中央部委所属学校数 Inst. Under Central Ministries & Agencies	毕业生数 Graduates	招生数 Students Admitted	在校学生数 Enrolment	合计 Total	计 Subtotal	专任 Full-time	
								小计 Subtotal	教授 Prof.
总计 Total	4	1	4372	4201	12395	866	856	520	25
北京 Beijing	2	1	865	599	2134	102	102	63	8
湖北 Hubei	1	0	918	1502	3972	244	234	165	15
四川 Sichuan	1	0	2589	2100	6289	520	520	292	2

独立函授学院

Number of Students in Independent

地区 Region	毕业生数 Graduates			招生数 Students Admitted		
	计 Total	本科 Normal Courses	专科 Short-cycle Courses	计 Total	本科 Normal Courses	专科 Short-cycle Courses
总计 Total	4372	24	4348	4201	88	4113
北京 Beijing	865	24	841	599	88	511
湖北 Hubei	918		918	1502		1502
四川 Sichuan	2589		2589	2100		2100

校基本情况
of Peasants' Colleges

单位:人

教职工数 Teachers, Staff & Workers: 本部教职工 Staff & Workers in the School Proper: 教师 Teachers: 副教授 Asso. Prof.	讲师 Lecturers	助教 Assistants	教员 Instructors	教辅人员 Supporting Staff	行政人员 Adm. Personnel	工勤人员 Workers	科研机构人员 Personnel in Affiliated Research Org.	校办厂、场职工 Employers in School-run Factories, Farms	附设机构人员 Personnel in Other Subsidiary Units	兼任教师 Part-time Teachers
10	54	58	5	7	44	27	0	1	0	9
10	54	58	5	7	44	27	0	1	0	9

院基本情况
Independent Correspondence Colleges

单位:人

教职工数 Teachers, Staff & Workers: 本部教职工 Staff & Workers in the School Proper: 教师 Teachers: 副教授 Asso. Prof.	讲师 Lecturers	助教 Assistants	教员 Instructors	教辅人员 Supporting Staff	行政人员 Adm. Personnel	工勤人员 Workers	科研机构人员 Personnel in Affiliated Research Org.	校办厂、场职工 Employees in School-run Factories, Farms	附设机构人员 Personnel in Other Subsidiary Units	兼任教师 Part-time Teachers
153	263	62	17	137	144	55	4	3	3	1131
23	29	3	0	11	17	11	0	0	0	0
61	77	12	0	24	25	20	4	3	3	325
69	157	47	17	102	102	24	0	0	0	806

本、专科学生数
Correspondence Colleges by Type of Courses

单位:人

在校学生数 Enrolment: 计 Total	本科 Normal Courses	专科 Short-cycle Courses	毕业班学生数 Graduates for Next Year: 计 Total	本科 Normal Courses	专科 Short-cycle Courses
12395	324	12071	4620	57	4563
2134	324	1810	751	57	694
3972		3972	1006		1006
6289		6289	2863		2863

教育学院

Basic Statistics of

地区 Region	学校数(所) Schools 计 Total	 其中:中央部委所属学校数 Inst. Under Central Ministries & Agencies	本专科学生数 Undergraduate Students 毕业生数 Graduates	 招生数 Students Admitted	 在校学生数 Enrolments	校 Teachers, 合计 Total	 计 Subtotal	专任 Full-time 小计 Subtotal	 教授 Prof.
总　计 Total	166	3	68624	103568	234735	32201	31298	16843	354
北　京 Beijing	1	0	1634	2630	6641	530	448	213	5
天　津 Tianjin	0	0	0	0	0	0	0	0	0
河　北 Hebei	8	1	1292	1386	4282	911	904	504	5
山　西 Shanxi	6	0	2397	4374	7999	940	869	486	2
内蒙古 Inner Mongolia	8	0	2701	2524	5450	1536	1535	862	8
辽　宁 Liaoning	2	0	493	1052	2429	786	786	442	14
吉　林 Jilin	2	0	606	865	2349	599	587	342	24
黑龙江 Heilongjiang	8	1	1719	3493	8968	1374	1335	856	23
上　海 Shanghai	0	0	0	0	0	0	0	0	0
江　苏 Jiangsu	7	0	2923	5210	10352	1763	1716	901	28
浙　江 Zhejiang	5	0	2807	4989	19107	1076	1058	597	15
安　徽 Anhui	8	0	4354	6221	13413	1322	1298	699	6
福　建 Fujian	4	0	981	2290	4800	605	556	289	1
江　西 Jiangxi	5	0	1916	2841	6229	842	842	433	18
山　东 Shandong	11	1	4988	9945	23265	2284	2236	1216	48
河　南 Henan	16	0	5439	7523	14563	2747	2725	1600	18
湖　北 Hubei	8	0	2434	3735	7101	1105	1058	523	9
湖　南 Hunan	6	0	4731	5163	13772	893	889	397	21
广　东 Guangdong	12	0	4473	6418	14754	2632	2610	1321	19
广　西 Guangxi	6	0	3406	4017	11102	1526	1386	766	9
海　南 Hainan	1	0	0	0	0	0	0	0	0
重　庆 Chongqing	3	0	1261	1792	3815	732	727	412	5
四　川 Sichuan	12	0	8498	12048	24706	2556	2525	1264	19
贵　州 Guizhou	4	0	2184	2828	6243	633	623	329	12
云　南 Yunnan	4	0	395	586	877	425	425	240	2
西　藏 Tibet	0	0	0	0	0	0	0	0	0
陕　西 Shaanxi	6	0	3094	4367	9724	1425	1403	664	17
甘　肃 Gansu	4	0	1152	1759	3289	781	757	396	11
青　海 Qinghai	0	0	0	0	0	0	0	0	0
宁　夏 Ningxia	0	0	0	0	0	0	0	0	0
新　疆 Xinjiang	9	0	2746	5512	9505	2178	2000	1091	15

基本情况

Educational Colleges

单位:人

教职工数 Teachers, Staff & Workers										兼任教师 Part－time Teachers
本部教职工 Staff & Workers in the School Proper							科研机构人员 Personnel in Affiliated Research Org.	校办厂、场职工 Employers in School－run Factories, Farms	附设机构人员 Personnel in Other Subsidiary Units	
教师 Teachers				教辅人员 Supporting Staff	行政人员 Adm. Personnel	工勤人员 Workers				
副教授 Asso. Prof.	讲师 Lecturers	助教 Assistants	教员 Instructors							
4780	7483	3409	817	3385	6779	4291	249	317	337	1167
83	80	25	20	68	132	35	6	27	49	0
0	0	0	0	0	0	0	0	0	0	0
112	191	167	29	87	162	151	0	7	0	16
120	227	113	24	95	161	127	0	67	4	0
172	484	171	27	194	235	244	1	0	0	10
263	132	31	2	83	149	112	0	0	0	0
133	157	28	0	91	91	63	12	0	0	0
410	335	68	20	162	213	104	37	2	0	43
0	0	0	0	0	0	0	0	0	0	0
248	398	170	57	173	344	298	15	19	13	0
136	279	140	27	125	195	141	3	13	2	16
194	348	103	48	155	244	200	4	18	2	40
97	148	39	4	52	164	51	0	44	5	278
123	173	88	31	110	137	162	0	0	0	0
329	518	269	52	240	499	281	2	25	21	72
415	651	412	104	215	649	261	0	22	0	21
168	213	90	43	212	197	126	47	0	0	0
154	171	40	11	90	265	137	4	0	0	22
333	653	280	36	219	751	319	14	0	8	119
158	379	192	28	123	270	227	67	9	64	149
0	0	0	0	0	0	0	0	0	0	0
97	205	82	23	80	131	104	5	0	0	97
442	530	194	79	251	667	343	14	17	0	178
103	138	66	10	44	198	52	2	3	5	49
31	119	60	28	47	70	68	0	0	0	17
0	0	0	0	0	0	0	0	0	0	0
152	317	144	34	204	284	251	0	16	6	7
78	161	127	19	70	155	136	0	0	24	18
0	0	0	0	0	0	0	0	0	0	0
0	0	0	0	0	0	0	0	0	0	0
229	476	310	61	195	416	298	16	28	134	15

教育学院本、

Number of Students in Educational

地区 Region	毕业生数 Graduates			招生数 Students Admitted		
	计 Total	本科 Normal Courses	专科 Short－cycle Courses	计 Total	本科 Normal Courses	专科 Short－cycle Courses
总计 Total	68624	15212	53412	103568	26051	77517
北京 Beijing	1634	799	835	2630	1538	1092
天津 Tianjin						
河北 Hebei	1292		1292	1386		1386
山西 Shanxi	2397	546	1851	4374	1284	3090
内蒙古 Inner Mongolia	2701	417	2284	2524	329	2195
辽宁 Liaoning	493	173	320	1052	567	485
吉林 Jilin	606	437	169	865	533	332
黑龙江 Heilongjiang	1719	64	1655	3493	707	2786
上海 Shanghai						
江苏 Jiangsu	2923	1502	1421	5210	1749	3461
浙江 Zhejiang	2807	911	1896	4989	698	4291
安徽 Anhui	4354	1019	3335	6221	1591	4630
福建 Fujian	981	381	600	2290	1298	992
江西 Jiangxi	1916	483	1433	2841	805	2036
山东 Shandong	4988	1099	3889	9945	2855	7090
河南 Henan	5439	642	4797	7523	1270	6253
湖北 Hubei	2434	350	2084	3735	1090	2645
湖南 Hunan	4731	1683	3048	5163	1750	3413
广东 Guangdong	4473	2084	2389	6418	2813	3605
广西 Guangxi	3406	147	3259	4017	302	3715
海南 Hainan	0		0	0		0
重庆 Chongqing	1261	95	1166	1792	374	1418
四川 Sichuan	8498	822	7676	12048	2293	9755
贵州 Guizhou	2184	727	1457	2828	727	2101
云南 Yunnan	395		395	586		586
西藏 Tibet						
陕西 Shaanxi	3094	500	2594	4367	881	3486
甘肃 Gansu	1152	231	921	1759	377	1382
青海 Qinghai						
宁夏 Ningxia						
新疆 Xinjiang	2746	100	2646	5512	220	5292

专科学生数

Colleges by Type of Courses

单位: 人

在校学生数 Enrolment			毕业班学生数 Graduates for Next Year		
计 Total	本科 Normal Courses	专科 Short－cycle Courses	计 Total	本科 Normal Courses	专科 Short－cycle Courses
234735	59610	175125	77278	18069	59209
6641	3385	3256	2151	1022	1129
4282		4282	1208		1208
7999	2398	5601	2306	571	1735
5450	890	4560	2018	322	1696
2429	1298	1131	817	401	416
2349	1328	1021	761	460	301
8968	1542	7426	2716	425	2291
10352	3954	6398	3435	1505	1930
19107	6031	13076	4488	1647	2841
13413	3065	10348	3952	845	3107
4800	2576	2224	1308	643	665
6229	1702	4527	2424	634	1790
23265	6472	16793	7987	1993	5994
14563	2122	12441	6156	604	5552
7101	1912	5189	2300	471	1829
13772	4678	9094	5021	1693	3328
14754	6354	8400	4546	1941	2605
11102	642	10460	3353	187	3166
0		0	0		0
3815	907	2908	1356	295	1061
24706	4010	20696	8400	922	7478
6243	1633	4610	2656	707	1949
877		877	291		291
9724	1759	7965	3571	488	3083
3289	630	2659	1417	253	1164
9505	322	9183	2640	40	2600

管理干部学

Basic Statistics of

地　区 Region	学校数(所) Schools 计 Total	学校数(所) Schools 其中:中央部委所属学校数 Inst. Under Central Ministries & Agencies	本专科学生数 Undergraduate Students 毕业生数 Graduates	本专科学生数 Undergraduate Students 招生数 Students Admitted	本专科学生数 Undergraduate Students 在校学生数 Enrolments	合　计 Total	校 Teachers, 计 Subtotal	校 Teachers, 专任 Full-time 小计 Subtotal	校 Teachers, 专任 Full-time 教授 Prof.
总　计　Total	146	41	66259	90274	189336	32135	30763	13371	493
北　京　Beijing	28	22	9105	12443	26467	5406	5227	2103	182
天　津　Tianjin	8	3	2010	2869	5405	1397	1379	525	14
河　北　Hebei	6	2	3105	4747	8796	1230	1230	552	25
山　西　Shanxi	6	1	1916	2914	5590	1158	1152	535	5
内蒙古　Inner Mongolia	2	0	960	1298	2623	398	398	186	4
辽　宁　Liaoning	5	0	4784	2584	7989	1108	1061	451	14
吉　林　Jilin	5	2	2067	1914	4499	1503	1338	467	25
黑龙江　Heilongjiang	5	0	2182	2738	5078	1344	1248	616	21
上　海　Shanghai	4	0	632	1202	2634	868	843	350	13
江　苏　Jiangsu	8	2	2467	3907	8245	1467	1412	735	15
浙　江　Zhejiang	2	1	208	296	639	634	634	257	5
安　徽　Anhui	2	0	1483	1298	3338	537	537	214	0
福　建　Fujian	4	1	2339	3434	6849	714	701	370	10
江　西　Jiangxi	2	0	1503	1437	2699	997	516	189	10
山　东　Shandong	5	0	5097	9019	17760	1400	1333	530	35
河　南　Henan	4	2	2606	3565	8336	1211	1211	548	6
湖　北　Hubei	7	2	3447	3382	8044	1492	1481	595	14
湖　南　Hunan	4	2	2625	3542	7767	883	875	411	5
广　东　Guangdong	14	1	6688	14277	27428	2964	2928	1421	27
广　西　Guangxi	4	0	2224	2978	8577	972	947	461	10
海　南　Hainan	0	0	0	0	0	0	0	0	0
重　庆　Chongqing	2	0	338	306	601	181	181	86	0
四　川　Sichuan	8	0	2780	4130	7617	1939	1839	761	34
贵　州　Guizhou	3	0	1376	2045	4425	536	525	267	1
云　南　Yunnan	0	0	0	0	0	0	0	0	0
西　藏　Tibet	0	0	0	0	0	0	0	0	0
陕　西　Shaanxi	5	0	2894	1128	2845	1011	991	408	10
甘　肃　Gansu	1	0	514	622	1280	230	230	110	2
青　海　Qinghai	0	0	0	0	0	0	0	0	0
宁　夏　Ningxia	0	0	0	0	0	0	0	0	0
新　疆　Xinjiang	2	0	909	2199	3805	555	546	223	6

院基本情况

Institutes for Administration

单位:人

教职工数 Teachers, Staff & Workers										兼任教师 Part-time Teachers
本部教职工 Staff & Workers in the School Proper							科研机构人员 Personnel in Affiliated Research Org.	校办厂、场职工 Employers in School-run Factories, Farms	附设机构人员 Personnel in Other Subsidiary Units	
教师 Teachers				教辅人员 Supporting Staff	行政人员 Adm. Personnel	工勤人员 Workers				
副教授 Asso. Prof.	讲师 Lecturers	助教 Assistants	教员 Instructors							
3840	6015	2638	385	3903	8179	5310	217	775	380	2167
681	855	330	55	690	1503	931	28	52	99	622
173	230	91	17	233	351	270	4	4	10	57
192	179	132	24	186	246	246	0	0	0	0
136	251	125	18	135	295	187	6	0	0	20
49	74	52	7	87	83	42	0	0	0	17
125	227	74	11	164	256	190	5	42	0	108
183	198	61	0	142	435	294	26	0	139	0
248	233	80	34	142	227	263	19	68	9	77
71	202	56	8	106	207	180	13	11	1	51
184	339	158	39	194	307	176	0	50	5	48
63	138	43	8	27	215	135	0	0	0	0
38	97	71	8	91	154	78	0	0	0	0
105	143	105	7	70	167	94	9	4	0	97
44	88	36	11	84	122	121	16	437	28	49
140	209	124	22	165	465	173	4	63	0	178
131	300	106	5	175	271	217	0	0	0	77
192	278	100	11	155	530	201	11	0	0	36
122	203	74	7	76	221	167	7	0	1	133
338	675	356	25	348	684	475	26	6	4	429
103	235	97	16	134	202	150	5	0	20	7
0	0	0	0	0	0	0	0	0	0	0
27	56	3	0	9	62	24	0	0	0	49
274	315	117	21	241	531	306	0	38	62	0
43	149	64	10	43	137	78	9	0	2	29
0	0	0	0	0	0	0	0	0	0	0
0	0	0	0	0	0	0	0	0	0	0
109	196	85	8	139	236	208	20	0	0	61
24	48	27	9	14	77	29	0	0	0	0
0	0	0	0	0	0	0	0	0	0	0
0	0	0	0	0	0	0	0	0	0	0
45	97	71	4	53	195	75	9	0	0	22

管理干部学院

Number of Students in Institutes for

地区 Region	毕业生数 Graduates			招生数 Students Admitted		
	计 Total	本科 Normal Courses	专科 Short-cycle Courses	计 Total	本科 Normal Courses	专科 Short-cycle Courses
总计 Total	66259	2013	64246	90274	3459	86815
北京 Beijing	9105	416	8689	12443	796	11647
天津 Tianjin	2010	51	1959	2869	27	2842
河北 Hebei	3105		3105	4747		4747
山西 Shanxi	1916		1916	2914		2914
内蒙古 Inner Mongolia	960	0	960	1298	32	1266
辽宁 Liaoning	4784	112	4672	2584	114	2470
吉林 Jilin	2067	150	1917	1914	170	1744
黑龙江 Heilongjiang	2182	96	2086	2738	161	2577
上海 Shanghai	632		632	1202		1202
江苏 Jiangsu	2467	19	2448	3907	59	3848
浙江 Zhejiang	208		208	296		296
安徽 Anhui	1483		1483	1298		1298
福建 Fujian	2339	133	2206	3434	270	3164
江西 Jiangxi	1503	27	1476	1437	118	1319
山东 Shandong	5097	165	4932	9019	302	8717
河南 Henan	2606	262	2344	3565	416	3149
湖北 Hubei	3447	68	3379	3382	107	3275
湖南 Hunan	2625	332	2293	3542	457	3085
广东 Guangdong	6688	32	6656	14277	98	14179
广西 Guangxi	2224	0	2224	2978	112	2866
海南 Hainan						
重庆 Chongqing	338		338	306		306
四川 Sichuan	2780	91	2689	4130	206	3924
贵州 Guizhou	1376		1376	2045		2045
云南 Yunnan						
西藏 Tibet						
陕西 Shaanxi	2894	59	2835	1128	14	1114
甘肃 Gansu	514	0	514	622	0	622
青海 Qinghai						
宁夏 Ningxia						
新疆 Xinjiang	909		909	2199		2199

本、专科学生数

Administration by Type of Courses

单位:人

在校学生数 Enrolment			毕业班学生数 Graduates for Next Year		
计 Total	本科 Normal Courses	专科 Short-cycle Courses	计 Total	本科 Normal Courses	专科 Short-cycle Courses
189336	7901	181435	69997	2710	67287
26467	2028	24439	10328	608	9720
5405	88	5317	2106	43	2063
8796		8796	3512		3512
5590		5590	1974		1974
2623	52	2571	1190	20	1170
7989	366	7623	4172	184	3988
4499	365	4134	2088	195	1893
5078	281	4797	2186	120	2066
2634		2634	753		753
8245	145	8100	2792	35	2757
639		639	308		308
3338		3338	1367		1367
6849	557	6292	2199	167	2032
2699	222	2477	1126	68	1058
17760	696	17064	6065	244	5821
8336	1147	7189	3330	325	3005
8044	250	7794	3101	143	2958
7767	854	6913	2871	274	2597
27428	190	27238	7953	92	7861
8577	248	8329	2471	0	2471
601		601	275		275
7617	342	7275	2866	136	2730
4425		4425	1558		1558
2845	42	2803	1682	28	1654
1280	28	1252	581	28	553
3805		3805	1143		1143

普通高等学校举办函授

Number of Students by Type of Courses in Correspondence Divisions, Evening Schools

地区 Region	函授部、夜大学 Divisions of Correspondence and Evening Schools								
	毕业生数 Graduates			招生数 Students Admitted			在校学生数 Enrolments		
	计 Total	本科 Normal Courses	专科 Short-cycle Courses	计 Total	本科 Normal Courses	专科 Short-cycle Courses	计 Total	本科 Normal Courses	专科 Short-cycle Courses
总计 Total	367825	805812	87244	5098651	45661	364204	1470727	355886	1114841
北京 Beijing	39348	9113	30235	52989	15548	37441	149499	38922	110577
天津 Tianjin	7787	2575	5212	10235	3883	6352	30000	9403	20597
河北 Hebei	15542	2915	12627	22418	6041	16377	67007	13477	53530
山西 Shanxi	7517	1260	6257	11047	2776	8271	30536	6373	24163
内蒙古 Inner Mongolia	4562	1345	3217	4813	1861	2952	14431	4396	10035
辽宁 Liaoning	24368	5884	18484	24067	7168	16899	76644	21180	55464
吉林 Jilin	15578	4858	10720	19255	6391	12864	60780	19216	41564
黑龙江 Heilongjiang	11877	3431	8446	16853	5911	10942	48009	14749	33260
上海 Shanghai	16363	5224	11139	24548	9407	15141	67736	23802	43934
江苏 Jiangsu	31719	7356	24363	40283	11784	28499	121068	25593	95475
浙江 Zhejiang	12138	4147	7991	15707	6714	8993	66670	25632	41038
安徽 Anhui	10144	1316	8828	15338	2385	12953	41010	5557	35453
福建 Fujian	5064	907	4157	7495	2074	5421	20690	4484	16206
江西 Jiangxi	6551	1524	5027	11887	3048	8839	31453	6682	24771
山东 Shandong	26529	5080	21449	37950	11245	26705	106829	26488	80341
河南 Henan	21959	3412	18547	20674	6076	14598	67129	14682	52447
湖北 Hubei	23849	5993	17856	29943	10404	19539	88955	25346	63609
湖南 Hunan	18436	2204	16232	23775	4172	19603	65177	9695	55482
广东 Guangdong	11110	1952	9158	22399	5447	16952	64081	11268	52813
广西 Guangxi	7110	1246	5864	14554	3273	11281	35035	5809	29226
海南 Hainan	2113	237	1876	2802	367	2435	6890	1301	5589
重庆 Chongqing	6437	1751	4686	10985	3302	7683	30379	7494	22885
四川 Sichuan	8492	2275	6217	15023	4942	10081	39077	10070	29007
贵州 Guizhou	916	104	812	2252	510	1742	4903	821	4082
云南 Yunnan	5196	424	4772	10116	1739	8377	26319	2766	23553
西藏 Tibet	0	0	0	151	0	151	272	0	272
陕西 Shaanxi	16188	2693	13495	21755	4856	16899	64029	12837	51192
甘肃 Gansu	6105	928	5177	7041	2173	4868	20083	4587	15496
青海 Qinghai	123	0	123	263	0	263	1118	0	1118
宁夏 Ningxia	1051	188	863	1436	338	1098	3818	637	3181
新疆 Xinjiang	3653	239	3414	11811	1826	9985	21100	2619	18481

部、夜大学、成人脱产班分本专科学生数

& Short－cycle Courses for Adults run by Regular Institutions of Higher Education

单位:人

成人脱产班 Short－cycle Courses for Adults								
毕业生数 Graduates			招生数 Students Admitted			在校学生数 Enrolments		
计 Total	本科 Normal Courses	专科 Short-cycle Courses	计 Total	本科 Normal Courses	专科 Short-cycle Courses	计 Total	本科 Normal Courses	专科 Short-cycle Courses
108717	5978	102739	157465	28819	128646	357635	52424	305211
6438	415	6023	10345	2767	7578	20707	4330	16377
809	29	780	1573	475	1098	3457	741	2716
3042	199	2843	5263	1144	4119	10752	2755	7997
1037	54	983	1674	356	1318	3676	572	3104
767	109	658	1908	369	1539	3518	611	2907
5018	377	4641	10105	3069	7036	21848	6133	15715
1706	513	1193	3603	1215	2388	8276	2398	5878
4459	122	4337	8001	1678	6323	17920	2758	15162
683	153	530	1784	391	1393	4428	782	3646
8983	155	8828	12803	1460	11343	27630	2026	25604
4236	137	4099	4028	243	3785	13040	750	12290
4525	312	4213	6889	2203	4686	15173	3980	11193
1654	17	1637	2605	141	2464	5332	169	5163
1339	0	1339	2249	169	2080	4567	224	4343
3317	68	3249	4274	741	3533	9593	1205	8388
7614	0	7614	13222	707	12515	27700	962	26738
11328	1267	10061	15074	4313	10761	35081	8756	26325
3848	479	3369	4692	755	3937	12754	1946	10808
3903	10	3893	5196	129	5067	16854	191	16663
3587	35	3552	1874	133	1741	6882	178	6704
1101	31	1070	1068	41	1027	2154	41	2113
6433	221	6212	7700	1563	6137	17863	2283	15580
9217	279	8938	11143	1349	9794	23240	2103	21137
3292	140	3152	4325	555	3770	10268	1113	9155
1963	211	1752	1986	174	1812	4109	397	3712
174	0	174	167	0	167	391	0	391
3321	373	2948	6336	1610	4726	14329	3491	10838
1332	135	1197	2618	605	2013	5144	754	4390
530	61	469	1297	231	1066	2441	370	2071
529	26	503	638	46	592	1380	103	1277
2532	50	2482	3025	187	2838	7128	302	6826

成人高等学校其

Number of Other Students in Adult Higher

地区 Region	招生数 Entrants 分专业学生总数中 高中起点本科	 高中起点专科	 专升本	 第二学历 Students for secand diploms	 预科班	 证书教育 Certificate－oriented education 单科班 Single subject courses	 专业证书班 Classes for certificate-oriented trainees	 岗位培训 Job－specific training 资格性培训 Qualification－oriented training	 适应性培训 Adaptation training	 成人中专班 Spec. Sec Classes for Adult	 电大注册视听生	 其他 Others
总计 Total	16051	469127	32842	27327	12783	90690	66465	365927	723807	89221	126899	57272
北京 Beijing	1843	22720	2859	1983	218	6649	13814	13078	10646	5466	2764	7740
天津 Tianjin	80	13449	27	1144	1672	4945	1496	7605	6739	1363	951	602
河北 Hebei	490	19947	154	7551	379	7309	6727	5878	21533	8267	11	2176
山西 Shanxi	961	9958	1404	36	178	0	695	3126	2628	676	0	296
内蒙古 Inner Mongolia	2294	3897	380	342	1	0	746	948	3587	2131	6774	443
辽宁 Liaoning	0	20462	713	64	0	0	4088	8087	4364	4849	5012	407
吉林 Jilin	198	11327	575	239	0	40	3241	2276	19124	4267	4257	545
黑龙江 Heilongjiang	0	22171	948	688	3262	0	1283	11514	5986	5438	2621	548
上海 Shanghai	850	9117	411	422	93	22646	3030	34443	461423	1276	15795	6095
江苏 Jiangsu	405	27888	2080	898	376	927	6567	17719	22508	3193	1173	2542
浙江 Zhejiang	0	22680	3168	282	1904	30057	3076	17557	12889	3324	7269	5384
安徽 Anhui	938	12734	1591	3593	651	0	2287	6698	1413	1454	13438	405
福建 Fujian	0	11710	1639	419	739	5325	1424	8825	6756	2240	7192	689
江西 Jiangxi	296	9697	142	71	92	0	328	320	893	1260	5100	472
山东 Shandong	2719	37648	3161	1276	8	1642	1406	7252	48800	5916	0	200
河南 Henan	384	19919	1219	76	140	370	2489	3866	2304	1314	12000	866
湖北 Hubei	146	24554	1434	86	543	1793	6826	11243	25253	1270	0	2947
湖南 Hunan	0	28494	2207	152	266	0	387	106001	34819	3407	5663	197
广东 Guangdong	1437	36348	3203	469	125	2737	447	30554	18909	6071	4669	2320
广西 Guangxi	12	11476	996	2000	0	0	0	401	2621	564	2449	4415
海南 Hainan	0	574	0	0	0	0	0	0	0	586	0	0
重庆 Chongqing	281	9529	447	97	266	619	1118	2000	2229	287	236	5420
四川 Sichuan	0	32677	2584	4629	1431	2657	2159	59867	2472	10449	12489	484
贵州 Guizhou	0	12955	727	124	70	509	955	361	334	123	2052	3325
云南 Yunnan	0	5705	0	5	0	33	121	387	0	4772	84	453
西藏 Tibet												
陕西 Shaanxi	1968	15195	253	131	50	2292	1120	3120	3272	7790	4544	5257
甘肃 Gansu	0	6359	377	11	0	140	199	607	371	0	5680	500
青海 Qinghai	0	1726	0	40	56	0	0	0	0	179	2203	0
宁夏 Ningxia	0	2433	0	20	0	0	40	1408	1934	695	2473	0
新疆 Xinjiang	749	5778	143	479	263	0	396	786	0	594	0	2544

他学生数(总计)

Educational Institutions (Regional Aggregates)

单位:人

在校学生数 Enrolment											
分专业学生总数中			第二学科学历 Students for secand diploma	预科班	证书教育 Certificate－oriented education		岗位培训 Job－specific training		成人中专班 Spec. Sec. Classes for Adult	电大注册视听生	其他 Others
高中起点本科	高中起点专科	专升本			单科班 Single subject courses	专业证书班 Classes for certificate-oriented trainees	资格性培训 Qualification－oriented training	适应性培训 Adaptation training			
37771	1102808	72771	56349	12151	55664	110501	175885	155724	291834	284946	99216
3811	61540	10060	4948	218	5060	12236	5617	4080	16883	6407	7588
268	32322	321	2695	1758	6405	2661	5807	3543	3049	6639	3587
955	43031	359	12549	451	8161	7965	25596	16724	34945	120	5172
1978	22692	3305	54	40	965	655	3306	2472	1455	0	296
7433	7966	1021	636	3	0	613	483	233	7747	10131	793
107	54664	1694	422	0	0	9215	731	9604	18291	9797	267
701	28703	891	946	0	51	3034	6457	19074	12400	2599	1016
0	53652	1954	1153	3262	545	2888	8765	4150	12140	11842	3228
1732	22846	1359	1179	93	7035	2698	17391	23490	5998	28490	6311
952	64155	4669	2059	416	1019	13606	19401	10813	9397	4551	5100
0	50870	6150	768	1904	1337	11568	7708	5159	11011	17258	8143
2032	31112	3092	5790	345	0	4319	5314	963	4729	24500	891
0	28624	3245	920	86	1606	5105	4909	1687	6485	16170	1181
563	22277	231	138	92	0	328	1322	3130	3752	9575	760
6842	87550	7168	3810	8	2263	4252	4265	2298	16282	109	6700
1208	48383	2798	355	457	184	4028	6399	2586	4041	21601	4910
526	54939	2658	200	488	967	7968	8020	1960	4394	0	3029
0	70012	5532	483	277	0	959	7150	3578	13137	20040	450
3054	75727	5986	1203	117	2737	5699	23950	23285	14620	11505	5181
34	32188	1650	2341	0	0	1907	235	7168	3431	3101	9203
0	1556	0	25	0	0	40	148	0	1499	273	149
590	21706	980	268	289	4304	1409	4032	2229	549	2227	7836
0	78798	4492	11292	1281	8575	3755	4818	3014	41705	48040	1633
0	26218	1633	319	70	428	1006	559	1310	416	3238	3682
0	13182	187	467	0	426	121	387	0	19112	282	1295
0	0	0	0	0	0	0	0	0	0	0	0
4081	32695	405	295	50	3483	1440	1899	2211	18931	8684	5465
0	13718	658	50	0	113	333	129	475	0	10174	531
0	3525	0	40	56	0	0	0	0	1284	3742	0
0	6441	0	99	0	0	40	19	488	1859	3816	0
904	11716	273	845	390	0	653	1068	0	2292	35	4819

成人中等专业学校基本情况

Basic Statistics of Adult Specialized
(Limited to State－planned Enrolment

地 区 Region	学校数(所) Schools	毕业生数 Graduates	招生数 Students Admitted 合计 Total	招高中毕业起点 Graduates From Senior Sec. School	招初中毕业起点 Graduates From Junior Sec. School	在校学生数 Enrolments
总 计 Total	5165	872581	697535	207253	490282	2182112
北 京 Beijing	106	25169	16388	835	15553	60919
天 津 Tianjin	103	20141	21111	2925	18186	53586
河 北 Hebei	248	47804	40349	19268	21081	126447
山 西 Shanxi	189	17320	18016	7615	10401	54523
内蒙古 Inner Mongolia	139	23799	15061	6534	8527	43212
辽 宁 Liaoning	233	28612	21253	3361	17892	76585
吉 林 Jilin	150	22567	15573	5410	10163	52270
黑龙江 Heilongjiang	333	30069	25442	3722	21720	77554
上 海 Shanghai	99	18566	22228	7307	14921	78417
江 苏 Jiangsu	245	61998	38303	14805	23498	141470
浙 江 Zhejiang	155	27426	26777	6015	20762	81633
安 徽 Anhui	158	29904	19458	6646	12812	54261
福 建 Fujian	442	44678	45716	15446	30270	124156
江 西 Jiangxi	139	12192	11548	4139	7409	34823
山 东 Shandong	300	60750	47479	20525	26954	121860
河 南 Henan	300	73855	51715	18567	33148	169387
湖 北 Hubei	227	45791	23263	5703	17560	97472
湖 南 Hunan	232	37600	24848	6592	18256	74934
广 东 Guangdong	311	65097	63685	8954	54731	179362
广 西 Guangxi	147	24650	20886	4164	16722	69760
海 南 Hainan	25	2643	836	73	763	4774
重 庆 Chongqing	100	16615	13457	703	12754	55846
四 川 Sichuan	260	41395	32452	8059	24393	106188
贵 州 Guizhou	38	11929	10880	0	10880	27088
云 南 Yunnan	141	19805	16011	1244	14767	54373
西 藏 Tibet						
陕 西 Shaanxi	125	22494	25997	16336	9661	75307
甘 肃 Gansu	96	11742	13864	7927	5937	36875
青 海 Qinghai	20	3350	2062	1541	521	8711
宁 夏 Ningxia	23	3855	3787	827	2960	10646
新 疆 Xinjiang	81	20765	9090	2010	7080	29673

注:本表未包括普通中等专业学校举办的成人中专学生。

Note: Adult student enroled in specialized secondary schools are not included.

(总计)(列入计划,学制两年以上)

Secondary Schools (Regional Aggregates) and Courses Lasting 2 Years and Over)

单位:人

毕业班学生数 Graduates for Nert Year	教职工数 Teachers, Staff & Workers					兼任教师 Part－time Teachers
	合计 Total	专任教师 Full－time Teachers	教辅人员 Supportin Staff	行政人员 Adm. Personnel	工勤人员 Workers	
857360	232255	130665	23592	43992	34006	61690
23909	7133	3277	781	1942	1133	1787
20717	4137	2078	436	984	639	1136
46551	10695	6397	1022	1860	1416	1633
19178	5410	2833	643	1200	734	1300
17899	6610	3599	789	1333	889	1224
29048	14496	8912	1051	2669	1864	3470
22634	9638	5922	1067	1694	955	653
34723	15276	8707	1416	2597	2556	1124
27522	3938	1876	573	860	629	2772
59608	13794	7259	1206	2627	2702	3180
29112	4149	2303	406	842	598	4368
22756	5976	3058	690	1249	979	1786
36482	14564	9064	1206	2508	1786	4014
13943	5641	3170	516	1169	786	1346
52485	15149	8379	1558	3004	2208	1835
78868	18247	10466	2800	2743	2238	3249
40316	12214	6934	1258	2137	1885	4616
30556	9094	5352	794	1413	1535	2080
65892	13982	8965	913	2063	2041	4097
25356	8441	4491	661	1708	1581	2085
2088	865	447	42	139	237	113
22390	3477	1798	287	824	568	2240
40776	8488	4415	914	1833	1326	2149
8984	2578	1362	304	726	186	3001
21261	4173	2160	456	894	663	1233
29090	4575	2361	563	1113	538	1267
13864	2903	1530	388	588	397	1727
3690	789	458	114	134	83	218
3917	928	512	92	173	151	217
13745	4895	2580	646	966	703	1770

广播电视中等专业学校基本

Basic Statistics of Radio/TV

(Limited to State-planned Enrolment

地　区 Region	学校数(所) Schools	毕业生数 Graduates	招生数 Students Admitted 合计 Total	招高中毕业起点 Graduates From Senior Sec. School	招初中毕业起点 Graduates From Junior Sec. School	在校学生数 Enrolments
总　计 Total	151	214152	187732	54571	133161	625419
北　京 Beijing	1	7832	5015	0	5015	15645
天　津 Tianjin	3	2343	2843	756	2087	5674
河　北 Hebei	5	16108	14405	6685	7720	46796
山　西 Shanxi	3	3397	2588	91	2497	12968
内蒙古 Inner Mongolia	2	3258	2156	491	1665	7492
辽　宁 Liaoning	8	14342	11178	3041	8137	37092
吉　林 Jilin	2	3930	3463	253	3210	10201
黑龙江 Heilongjiang	20	3058	2898	238	2660	8077
上　海 Shanghai	2	7790	12122	5420	6702	41361
江　苏 Jiangsu	3	14262	7872	242	7630	29590
浙　江 Zhejiang	16	7781	8169	1559	6610	24336
安　徽 Anhui	8	3640	1805	621	1184	7329
福　建 Fujian	10	9090	10638	3102	7536	28928
江　西 Jiangxi	3	3722	4303	2566	1737	9570
山　东 Shandong	10	7720	5841	4081	1760	13542
河　南 Henan	4	18076	15756	7555	8201	56999
湖　北 Hubei	4	7757	1725	0	1725	15752
湖　南 Hunan	12	5353	3623	958	2665	13374
广　东 Guangdong	4	5260	7204	440	6764	19429
广　西 Guangxi	3	1312	1404	404	1000	3994
海　南 Hainan	0	78	0	0	0	251
重　庆 Chongqing	2	5217	6185	0	6185	29573
四　川 Sichuan	9	15665	12607	2790	9817	45008
贵　州 Guizhou	3	3268	6376	0	6376	15818
云　南 Yunnan	4	12846	10868	786	10082	37311
西　藏 Tibet						
陕　西 Shaanxi	3	12014	13189	7551	5638	46200
甘　肃 Gansu	2	4989	6638	3505	3133	21064
青　海 Qinghai	2	993	717	680	37	3030
宁　夏 Ningxia	1	459	830	214	616	2195
新　疆 Xinjiang	2	12592	5314	542	4772	16820

情况（列入计划，学制两年以上）

Specialized Secondary Schools and Courses Lasting 2 Years and Over)

单位：人

毕业班学生数 Graduates for Next Year	教职工数 Teachers, Staff & Workers 合计 Total	专任教师 Full-time Teachers	教辅人员 Supportin Staff	行政人员 Adm. Personnel	工勤人员 Workers	兼任教师 Part-time Teachers
237347	18266	9007	3589	3780	1890	23200
6244	823	450	103	231	39	746
2603	173	88	31	29	25	341
18067	1504	810	324	266	104	1042
2343	946	542	165	162	77	972
3253	15	12	3	0	0	498
14027	933	543	139	197	54	1825
4294	0	0	0	0	0	0
3943	583	296	64	122	101	419
13174	73	19	23	25	6	17
12683	1629	758	208	324	339	1049
8725	570	310	94	133	33	1652
3077	456	205	107	101	43	448
9290	378	184	48	90	56	198
3994	799	389	113	229	68	601
6172	1035	576	123	194	142	481
25658	2069	798	769	327	175	2173
3629	100	82	2	4	12	874
5578	583	303	62	154	64	1481
6049	11	0	0	9	2	401
919	519	238	55	153	73	572
104	0	0	0	0	0	0
11899	27	15	2	6	4	1541
15043	573	273	123	127	50	567
5702	722	312	197	158	55	541
14344	679	288	193	125	73	778
19488	838	390	164	192	92	1098
8303	552	262	136	88	66	1255
1247	191	111	38	21	21	62
539	115	60	16	28	11	99
6956	1370	693	287	285	105	1469

职工中等专业学校基本情

Basic Statistics of Specialized

(Limited to State－planned Enrolment

地　区 Region	学校数(所) Schools	毕业生数 Graduates	招生数 Students Admitted 合计 Total	招高中毕业起点 Graduates From Senior Sec. School	招初中毕业起点 Graduates From Junior Sec. School	在校学生数 Enrolments
总　计　Total	2093	291295	252361	39545	212816	808863
北　京　Beijing	61	9064	6480	371	6109	25539
天　津　Tianjin	61	10631	13412	888	12524	34423
河　北　Hebei	57	10781	9767	793	8974	33381
山　西　Shanxi	56	5353	6553	238	6315	19178
内蒙古　Inner Mongolia	64	6329	5307	1055	4252	15191
辽　宁　Liaoning	105	8611	7126	0	7126	28106
吉　林　Jilin	63	8933	5197	2924	2273	18452
黑龙江　Heilongjiang	155	16259	13894	1747	12147	47116
上　海　Shanghai	86	10394	9288	1872	7416	34864
江　苏　Jiangsu	154	24815	15673	3531	12142	66572
浙　江　Zhejiang	77	15226	14246	2077	12169	44507
安　徽　Anhui	80	12591	7217	893	6324	20816
福　建　Fujian	190	15324	18420	1972	16448	50002
江　西　Jiangxi	38	4962	4814	986	3828	15256
山　东　Shandong	138	26910	21450	8687	12763	57716
河　南　Henan	83	9879	8269	353	7916	31197
湖　北　Hubei	146	18869	10513	1067	9446	41617
湖　南　Hunan	67	10329	6248	430	5818	21821
广　东　Guangdong	149	29219	34553	3334	31219	93504
广　西　Guangxi	26	2382	2741	70	2671	9268
海　南　Hainan	4	461	421	54	367	1426
重　庆　Chongqing	39	4993	5174	185	4989	16792
四　川　Sichuan	52	10299	8804	1819	6985	31592
贵　州　Guizhou	20	1394	2846	0	2846	6585
云　南　Yunnan	10	2620	2295	217	2078	7391
西　藏　Tibet						
陕　西　Shaanxi	30	3495	4313	2286	2027	13238
甘　肃　Gansu	30	2866	2571	569	2002	7333
青　海　Qinghai	14	1341	692	347	345	2909
宁　夏　Ningxia	8	2524	2195	182	2013	6518
新　疆　Xinjiang	30	4441	1882	598	1284	6553

学校基本情况

Schools for Staff & Workers

单位:人

招生数 Admitted 其中: of which 长班 A	短班 B	在校学生数 Enrolments 合计 Total	其中: of which 长班 A	短班 B	教职工数 Teachers, Staff & Workers 合计 Total	其中:专任教师 of which: Full-time Teachers	兼任教师 Part-time Teachers
1343328	4647809	3863992	866392	2997600	90019	47091	80215
56034	328323	139625	42670	96955	9099	4357	6160
12930	40775	10799	6736	4063	639	336	638
106823	242923	231297	43402	187895	7232	2578	8539
8958	32006	48139	12438	35701	1017	623	1139
7201	81734	25001	6973	18028	1496	1135	927
37192	449322	234624	34746	199878	7310	3240	5079
16791	128749	143960	17514	126446	2451	1255	1687
52242	283881	195973	33460	162513	5529	3200	6525
473041	186417	229064	122848	106216	9198	5703	8126
163172	880064	944607	189990	754617	10019	5728	8239
72443	341028	313484	67840	245644	5153	2273	6681
797	47045	10377	547	9830	660	367	673
38632	127094	165844	34900	130944	1832	904	2938
1035	2142	3113	1045	2068	100	44	290
105182	706598	472651	94296	378355	9930	5685	6519
79909	300317	147708	33840	113868	2652	1335	3583
4897	41907	49264	6017	43247	1562	622	1116
13990	80544	73584	21024	52560	4217	2162	2356
6683	27237	32439	8186	24253	852	333	573
2472	30437	32860	2498	30362	938	717	1535
1192	6628	9128	1422	7706	83	43	136
4113	32854	37197	4113	33084	407	111	334
42357	78448	124155	44026	80129	2425	1514	2430
835	983	3821	2936	885	202	151	100
5138	37415	42582	5167	37415	1188	750	812
17215	63214	68802	15434	53368	1723	815	1850
6212	28315	22946	5881	17065	1177	586	567
233	14080	14361	281	14080	65	65	9
0	6300	6302	2	6300	200	100	76
5609	21029	30285	6160	24125	663	359	578

农民技术培训

Basic Statistics of Technical

地区 Region	学校数(所) Schools	毕业生数 Graduates 合计 Total	其中: of which 长班 A	短班 B	招 Students 合计 Total
总计 Total	522889	95476543	6347022	89129521	82774157
北京 Beijing	2178	441010	12160	428850	347749
天津 Tianjin	3088	496983	43251	453732	490765
河北 Hebei	48048	7766017	415512	7350505	7592656
山西 Shanxi	29771	2484270	67032	2417238	2047921
内蒙古 Inner Mongolia	9020	1352213	46480	1305733	1121746
辽宁 Liaoning	12334	3909805	147744	3762061	3752546
吉林 Jilin	8872	3082379	136472	2945907	2606707
黑龙江 Heilongjiang	10370	2826229	87156	2739073	2746330
上海 Shanghai	172	148462	107599	40863	170877
江苏 Jiangsu	28980	6020748	559389	5461359	5058892
浙江 Zhejiang	23376	3788523	209021	3579502	4007568
安徽 Anhui	14397	4449797	108617	4341180	3708395
福建 Fujian	23310	4859464	415206	4444258	4148108
江西 Jiangxi	11991	1645445	112902	1532543	1599840
山东 Shandong	58248	9846188	290284	9555904	9150381
河南 Henan	33752	6537470	507932	6029538	6071873
湖北 Hubei	28759	2309750	69334	2240416	1797737
湖南 Hunan	34429	2361973	108179	2253794	2132265
广东 Guangdong	4480	1072169	147124	925045	704492
广西 Guangxi	13466	3778645	103839	3674806	3576910
海南 Hainan	1651	327498	808	326690	368760
重庆 Chongqing	17415	4247720	445872	3801848	3438583
四川 Sichuan	36226	7792219	1867539	5924680	5531551
贵州 Guizhou	12653	2483882	17746	2466136	2843005
云南 Yunnan	12464	5427702	88933	5338769	2342290
西藏 Tibet					
陕西 Shaanxi	26604	2504014	92753	2411261	2239128
甘肃 Gansu	11701	1818705	62478	1756227	1839631
青海 Qinghai	1458	304959	7975	296984	278117
宁夏 Ningxia	1194	139748	12805	126943	101966
新疆 Xinjiang	2482	1252556	54880	1197676	957368

学校基本情况

Training Schools for Peasants

单位:人

招生数 Admitted		在校学生数 Enrolments			教职工数 Teachers, Staff & Workers		兼任教师 Part-time Teachers
其中: of which		合计 Total	其中: of which		合计 Total	其中:专任教师 of which: Full-time Teachers	
长班 A	短班 B		长班 A	短班 B			
5534371	77239786	67502325	5197954	62304371	447109	138721	1024730
13185	334564	85545	13319	72226	2846	647	4590
44765	446000	38449	14346	24103	1671	1010	4501
386327	7206329	3995028	357765	3637263	32340	9726	78462
73948	1973973	2186076	89827	2096249	36312	7003	50396
29114	1092632	1215455	17537	1197918	9180	3896	15916
123131	3629415	2922631	139757	2782874	17856	5574	24880
149164	2457543	1715134	143393	1571741	12353	4217	19384
89967	2656363	2242125	58057	2184068	14079	8209	22507
122387	48490	46421	25630	20791	671	527	1413
522645	4536247	4721088	570266	4150822	17957	11006	55276
242850	3764718	2644265	224464	2419801	13837	4884	47416
116694	3591701	3578191	116671	3461520	11739	4228	38558
316842	3831266	3461604	207928	3253676	10156	3192	50566
106059	1493781	1649439	106630	1542809	5498	1641	28751
313073	8837308	7170130	256531	6913599	65446	22098	92553
494534	5577339	3178096	363109	2814987	7185	6283	53453
42290	1755447	1905980	52965	1853015	40866	8284	50522
89906	2042359	1826285	77585	1748700	43608	9216	61524
100875	603617	888165	148611	739554	10680	1918	10249
160709	3416201	3697137	158164	3538973	19866	5372	50674
661	368099	329886	830	329056	810	75	3814
380968	3057615	3463561	382771	3080790	4948	2243	26615
1382203	4149348	5701654	1416956	4284698	20032	7092	64915
18030	2824975	2201213	33441	2167772	9378	1216	37106
41727	2300563	2377949	48268	2329681	1618	907	35956
50800	2188328	1555543	43016	1512527	14616	5748	55643
73544	1766087	1180581	62904	1117677	18105	1033	24754
3081	275036	235557	4299	231258	70	29	2396
11079	90887	184252	11810	172442	568	236	2123
33813	923555	1104885	51104	1053781	2818	1211	9817

成人小学

Basic Statistics of

地　区 Region	学校数(所) Schools	教学班(点)(个) External Teaching Sites (Classes)	毕业生数 Graduates 合计 Total	毕业生数 Graduates 其中:女生 of which Female Students	招 Students 合计 Total
总　计 Total	180103	338963	5581463	3225131	5197010
北　京 Beijing	0	0	0	0	0
天　津 Tianjin	20	99	1028	721	797
河　北 Hebei	16660	20439	257154	134737	310344
山　西 Shanxi	10287	13137	181676	93518	182388
内蒙古 Inner Mongolia	5116	12558	136022	71361	124113
辽　宁 Liaoning	1040	2558	55547	16206	58309
吉　林 Jilin	2322	3992	57534	32238	76966
黑龙江 Heilongjiang	6154	9691	74449	44631	68150
上　海 Shanghai	55	942	11455	5570	38839
江　苏 Jiangsu	8474	9113	204690	130917	223610
浙　江 Zhejiang	3350	4917	102208	66998	84729
安　徽 Anhui	7437	16294	291035	186288	271841
福　建 Fujian	12746	18080	241104	190634	202658
江　西 Jiangxi	10434	17662	259413	181704	201629
山　东 Shandong	15431	22348	439711	251959	382594
河　南 Henan	16327	23449	493752	277738	479656
湖　北 Hubei	7420	9715	198590	90787	216323
湖　南 Hunan	10531	17611	149451	92710	149451
广　东 Guangdong	1203	4288	261753	133534	251490
广　西 Guangxi	4674	10545	199782	85026	141108
海　南 Hainan	125	339	5752	4083	4883
重　庆 Chongqing	3988	8303	107613	60076	86491
四　川 Sichuan	6326	20953	426940	224085	528376
贵　州 Guizhou	4753	20171	282869	183707	303604
云　南 Yunnan	0	20265	446625	270761	31215
西　藏 Tibet					
陕　西 Shaanxi	15012	23563	211882	134852	251531
甘　肃 Gansu	8613	17821	299886	167235	369400
青　海 Qinghai	483	1866	36124	19821	53147
宁　夏 Ningxia	729	1242	28833	16436	46034
新　疆 Xinjiang	393	7002	118585	56798	57334

基本情况

Adults Primary Schools

单位:人

生数 Admitted	在校学生数 Enrolments		教职工数 Teachers, Staff & Workers		
其中:女生 of which: Female Students	合计 Total	其中:女生 of which: Female Students	合计 Total	其中:专任教师 of which: Full-time Teachers	兼任教师 Part-time Teachers
2986260	5368296	3107534	189698	57321	486295
0	0	0	0	0	0
548	650	296	49	40	121
188237	194899	132392	12747	2077	30707
93096	190738	102446	11445	1791	15971
66479	176387	86174	7146	3678	14429
17442	56427	17183	1867	553	4161
44635	46198	25479	2582	1336	4547
38920	85129	50218	8959	5406	13834
8563	32455	5519	242	199	822
138805	240580	145392	5581	2700	14751
54228	75773	49321	3474	1630	8373
173476	299955	195770	3682	1288	22266
162698	229436	187266	3906	1090	22240
152113	236623	173756	5193	1499	31064
196816	402909	198859	20850	9075	21502
269956	344088	184173	1624	1231	23205
100624	152847	90031	8758	3658	15959
91252	162650	98610	13015	3548	22829
130928	215129	99527	2974	522	5486
64544	193856	89089	8090	1871	19155
3351	5661	3872	10	10	378
50006	97305	56241	4683	1702	11449
284131	552094	296193	10551	4223	30055
196214	311995	197728	11856	1617	44053
18770	337003	208757	651	304	23766
155419	231370	145907	14561	5047	39639
206457	267403	153131	22564	412	34325
28225	48437	25213	441	58	2913
27622	47118	27917	287	245	1605
22705	133181	61074	1910	511	6690

职工小学

Basic Statistics of

地区 Region	学校数(所) Schools	教学班(点)(个) External Teaching Sites (Classes)	毕业生数 Graduates 合计 Total	其中:女生 of which Female Students	招 Students 合计 Total
总计 Total	964	4254	155382	75840	194467
北京 Beijing	0	0	0	0	0
天津 Tianjin	1	1	50	29	16
河北 Hebei	29	45	3318	1665	3938
山西 Shanxi	21	36	1787	783	1585
内蒙古 Inner Mongolia	2	9	360	70	73
辽宁 Liaoning	10	11	1547	525	1547
吉林 Jilin	51	275	9439	4584	5640
黑龙江 Heilongjiang	77	615	4715	2801	2627
上海 Shanghai	34	872	9181	4141	36650
江苏 Jiangsu	217	601	42875	23806	54391
浙江 Zhejiang	53	76	2731	1613	3515
安徽 Anhui	0	4	120	94	83
福建 Fujian	38	80	1394	830	1116
江西 Jiangxi	5	5	328	205	413
山东 Shandong	19	68	33260	14850	37830
河南 Henan	123	274	14495	6653	19485
湖北 Hubei	46	415	5329	2678	6470
湖南 Hunan	124	433	2856	1226	4200
广东 Guangdong	13	187	7931	4742	7818
广西 Guangxi	6	28	182	94	162
海南 Hainan	0	0	0	0	0
重庆 Chongqing	0	0	0	0	0
四川 Sichuan	65	148	10406	3521	3904
贵州 Guizhou	3	28	433	61	730
云南 Yunnan	0	0	0	0	0
西藏 Tibet					
陕西 Shaanxi	18	33	1920	720	1430
甘肃 Gansu	3	3	571	86	675
青海 Qinghai	3	2	1	1	12
宁夏 Ningxia	1	1	17	8	20
新疆 Xinjiang	2	4	136	54	137

基本情况

Worker Primary Schools

单位:人

生数 Admitted	在校学生数 Enrolments		教职工数 Teachers, Staff & Workers		兼任教师 Part-time Teachers
其中:女生 of which: Female Students	合计 Total	其中:女生 of which: Female Students	合计 Total	其中:专任教师 of which: Full-time Teachers	
90287	197549	89131	3434	1752	5118
0	0	0	0	0	0
11	56	31	3	2	7
1923	1986	831	124	60	96
719	2135	1039	64	8	65
26	73	26	4	4	12
525	398	201	98	48	47
3730	5840	3830	334	178	638
1643	4922	2761	502	276	1077
7573	31907	5186	234	191	806
31973	62521	34841	472	173	734
2049	3633	2088	68	33	119
63	83	63	0	0	4
626	1080	598	8	8	82
131	350	214	12	3	10
16770	37830	16770	114	44	0
10423	13066	6501	53	22	152
3820	3941	2116	549	266	281
1960	5610	1903	269	131	171
3907	10247	5295	173	64	256
106	171	137	7	3	27
0	0	0	0	0	0
0	0	0	0	0	0
1541	6669	3146	143	72	219
224	2160	224	44	34	62
0	0	0	0	0	0
317	2338	1057	117	96	227
120	254	95	24	21	13
7	1	1	1	0	1
7	90	41	13	13	0
93	188	136	4	2	12

农民小学

Basic Statistics of

地区 Region	学校数(所) Schools	教学班(点)(个) External Teaching Sites (Classes)	毕业生数 Graduates 合计 Total	其中:女生 of which Female Students	招 Students 合计 Total
总计 Total	179139	334709	5426081	3149291	5002543
北京 Beijing	0	0	0	0	0
天津 Tianjin	19	98	978	692	781
河北 Hebei	16631	20394	253836	133072	306406
山西 Shanxi	10266	13101	179889	92735	180803
内蒙古 Inner Mongolia	5114	12549	135662	71291	124040
辽宁 Liaoning	1030	2547	54000	15681	56762
吉林 Jilin	2271	3717	48095	27654	71326
黑龙江 Heilongjiang	6077	9076	69734	41830	65523
上海 Shanghai	21	70	2274	1429	2189
江苏 Jiangsu	8257	8512	161815	107111	169219
浙江 Zhejiang	3297	4841	99477	65385	81214
安徽 Anhui	7437	16290	290915	186194	271758
福建 Fujian	12708	18000	239710	189804	201542
江西 Jiangxi	10429	17657	259085	181499	201216
山东 Shandong	15412	22280	406451	237109	344764
河南 Henan	16204	23175	479257	271085	460171
湖北 Hubei	7374	9300	193261	88109	209853
湖南 Hunan	10407	17178	146595	91484	145251
广东 Guangdong	1190	4101	253822	128792	243672
广西 Guangxi	4668	10517	199600	84932	140946
海南 Hainan	125	339	5752	4083	4883
重庆 Chongqing	3988	8303	107613	60076	86491
四川 Sichuan	6261	20805	416534	220564	524472
贵州 Guizhou	4750	20143	282436	183646	302874
云南 Yunnan	0	20265	446625	270761	31215
西藏 Tibet					
陕西 Shaanxi	14994	23530	209962	134132	250101
甘肃 Gansu	8610	17818	299315	167149	368725
青海 Qinghai	480	1864	36123	19820	53135
宁夏 Ningxia	728	1241	28816	16428	46014
新疆 Xinjiang	391	6998	118449	56744	57197

基本情况

Peasant Primary Schools

单位:人

生数 Admitted	在校学生数 Enrolments		教职工数 Teachers, Staff & Workers		兼任教师 Part-time Teachers
其中:女生 of which: Female Students	合计 Total	其中:女生 of which: Female Students	合计 Total	其中:专任教师 of which: Full-time Teachers	
2895973	5170747	3018403	186264	55569	481177
0	0	0	0	0	0
537	594	265	46	38	114
186314	192913	131561	12623	2017	30611
92377	188603	101407	11381	1783	15906
66453	176314	86148	7142	3674	14417
16917	56029	16982	1769	505	4114
40905	40358	21649	2248	1158	3909
37277	80207	47457	8457	5130	12757
990	548	333	8	8	16
106832	178059	110551	5109	2527	14017
52179	72140	47233	3406	1597	8254
173413	299872	195707	3682	1288	22262
162072	228356	186668	3898	1082	22158
151982	236273	173542	5181	1496	31054
180046	365079	182089	20736	9031	21502
259533	331022	177672	1571	1209	23053
96804	148906	87915	8209	3392	15678
89292	157040	96707	12746	3417	22658
127021	204882	94232	2801	458	5230
64438	193685	88952	8083	1868	19128
3351	5661	3872	10	10	378
50006	97305	56241	4683	1702	11449
282590	545425	293047	10408	4151	29836
195990	309835	197504	11812	1583	43991
18770	337003	208757	651	304	23766
155102	229032	144850	14444	4951	39412
206337	267149	153036	22540	391	34312
28218	48436	25212	440	58	2912
27615	47028	27876	274	232	1605
22612	132993	60938	1906	509	6678

农民小学中扫

Basic Statistics of Literacy Classes

地区 Region	学校数(所) Schools	教学班(点)(个) External Teaching Sites (Classes)	毕业生数 Graduates 合计 Total	其中:女生 of which Female Students	招 Students 合计 Total
总计 Total	128668	242867	2992728	1827695	2557784
北京 Beijing	0	0	0	0	0
天津 Tianjin	0	0	0	0	0
河北 Hebei	14399	14625	43624	27984	104786
山西 Shanxi	4575	6209	38801	20517	35474
内蒙古 Inner Mongolia	4065	8763	32334	18355	34690
辽宁 Liaoning	493	1737	23542	7444	25956
吉林 Jilin	1087	2311	8374	4827	6578
黑龙江 Heilongjiang	2706	4483	15378	9306	12951
上海 Shanghai	14	30	683	516	665
江苏 Jiangsu	2744	3470	50125	35595	31395
浙江 Zhejiang	2767	3845	66859	46735	52625
安徽 Anhui	5698	14072	209262	138456	200222
福建 Fujian	7454	10880	128748	105656	95964
江西 Jiangxi	9140	15551	216488	150872	155142
山东 Shandong	10183	14030	118543	79831	82774
河南 Henan	10618	15301	255166	138173	228410
湖北 Hubei	6371	7474	140169	58348	147122
湖南 Hunan	7162	12016	91523	58359	92253
广东 Guangdong	34	126	2475	1551	2422
广西 Guangxi	3754	7754	63472	42018	49916
海南 Hainan	89	270	5117	3653	4404
重庆 Chongqing	2410	4502	32688	19617	31796
四川 Sichuan	4630	13344	217053	115725	217802
贵州 Guizhou	4748	19959	282060	183486	301853
云南 Yunnan	0	17486	395522	243452	0
西藏 Tibet					
陕西 Shaanxi	14131	22480	198427	125667	239506
甘肃 Gansu	8263	15527	256039	138760	313140
青海 Qinghai	268	1566	29202	16634	30909
宁夏 Ningxia	601	1059	18891	10824	35949
新疆 Xinjiang	264	3997	52163	25334	23080

盲班基本情况

in Peasant Primary Schools

单位:人

生数 Admitted	在校学生数 Enrolments		教职工数 Teachers, Staff & Workers		兼任教师 Part-time Teachers
其中:女生 of which Female Students	合计 Total	其中:女生 of which Female Students	合计 Total	其中:专任教师 of which: Full-time Teachers	
1577331	2831911	1775235	136408	37434	372304
0	0	0	0	0	0
0	0	0	0	0	0
82026	103381	80215	11378	1469	25464
19401	41615	22870	5043	830	7334
20795	67964	30300	5227	2284	11200
9223	26162	9387	172	129	1931
3328	6934	3518	1631	787	2420
7499	15118	9822	3885	2451	5465
515	222	191	0	0	0
22821	30969	23650	2055	771	6868
35896	50110	33695	2849	1412	7013
129117	226851	149569	3076	1185	18966
79430	112980	95000	1792	384	14034
118071	177732	132607	3935	1261	27049
56904	96880	63907	11647	6024	13553
137222	141319	80988	1206	878	16636
61660	98076	61133	6897	2818	13020
56077	105680	65025	8114	1895	17175
1693	2364	1650	149	26	134
30715	93126	50875	6594	1150	14871
3026	5067	3466	0	0	331
19341	39164	24036	3928	1288	6817
121032	227653	126084	7758	3266	22567
195701	308843	197207	11771	1570	43916
0	295091	184169	580	240	20254
147990	219091	138213	13658	4341	36554
171015	221963	125809	21067	252	30856
17501	26210	14495	440	58	2287
20835	36963	21096	248	206	1511
8497	54383	26258	1308	459	4078

全国农业广播电视

Basic Data on National Agric.

地　区 Region	学校数(所) Schools	毕业生数 Graduates	招　生　数 Students Admitted	在校学生数 Enrolment
总　计　Total	39	149788	156237	497715
北　京　Beijing	2	1690	726	3277
天　津　Tianjin	1	1340	1745	3285
河　北　Hebei	1	13916	11326	38962
山　西　Shanxi	1	1050	3610	14051
内蒙古　Inner Mongolia	1	2038	2462	8103
辽　宁　Liaoning	1	8577	5476	19755
吉　林　Jilin	1	6373	4010	16397
黑龙江　Heilongjiang	4	9296	5665	19879
上　海　Shanghai	1	886	1883	4608
江　苏　Jiangsu	1	8961	6880	20673
浙　江　Zhejiang	1	1813	3196	6460
安　徽　Anhui	1	5370	10297	41708
福　建　Fujian	1	1574	2451	6710
江　西　Jiangxi	1	957	947	4040
山　东　Shandong	1	12268	10735	25397
河　南　Henan	1	12007	12594	42736
湖　北　Hubei	1	1522	2822	11048
湖　南　Hunan	1	7935	7257	18698
广　东　Guangdong	2	605	405	2352
广　西　Guangxi	1	3990	5047	11751
海　南　Hainan	2	1107	194	1269
重　庆　Chongqing	1	3159	4500	23152
四　川　Sichuan	1	13160	17082	55935
贵　州　Guizhou	1	1959	3314	11538
云　南　Yunnan	2	4951	6812	17680
西　藏　Tibet	1	0	0	0
陕　西　Shaanxi	1	9001	7165	29844
甘　肃　Gansu	1	3001	5927	10801
青　海　Qinghai	1	594	673	1881
宁　夏　Ningxia	1	408	650	1760
新　疆　Xinjiang	2	10280	10386	23965

学校基本情况

Broadcasting and T.V. Schools

单位：人

其他各类证书教育、技术培训毕(结)业学生数 No. of Grad. & Completers for Other Edu. Form and Tech. Traning	教职工数 Teachers, Staff & Workers					兼职教师(不在教职工数中) Part－time Teachers
	合计 Total	专任教师 Full－time Teachers	教辅人员 Supportin Staff	行政人员 Adm. Personnel	工勤人员 Workers	
3473558	21467	10416	5211	3809	2031	25857
2295	436	211	50	137	38	350
19699	96	60	21	8	7	283
457569	1555	828	380	235	112	797
375270	917	548	153	138	78	1107
9082	463	265	114	61	23	321
544447	578	333	104	109	32	1311
15614	1103	834	69	152	48	210
12807	1899	950	430	385	134	1558
10136	253	99	50	90	14	481
87028	858	326	119	139	274	810
32781	243	120	49	60	14	807
102840	826	308	313	150	55	1114
230000	685	287	208	130	60	563
0	416	127	152	95	42	473
289132	1392	688	379	184	141	1711
169264	1751	684	643	285	139	2107
50650	627	229	196	101	101	1176
201558	925	359	275	191	100	1822
14520	126	26	3	74	23	421
7000	356	190	83	59	24	297
0	285	183	18	34	50	142
0	314	166	47	64	37	1285
108371	1218	590	361	160	107	2165
145105	459	196	167	74	22	487
167671	667	302	193	106	66	778
2320	14	10	0	2	2	0
125139	838	390	164	192	92	1098
145430	539	261	145	72	61	576
4840	143	78	30	14	21	39
66071	115	60	16	28	11	99
76919	1370	708	279	280	103	1469

第二部分

Part Ⅱ

办 学 条 件

Physical Facilities

一、教育经费

Public Expenditure on Education

全国教育经费来源和支出情况

Sources of Educational Fund and Expenditure for Education

单位：万元

Unit: in 10 Thousand Yuan

年份 Year	合计 Total	国家财政性教育经费 Government Appropriation for Education	预算内教育经费 Budgetary	社会团体和公民个人办学经费 Funds of Social Organizations and Citizens for Running Schools	社会捐资和集资办学经费 Donations and Fund－raising for Running Schools	学费和杂费 Tuition and Miscellaneous Fee	其他教育经费 Other Educational Funds
1991	7315028.2	6178286.0	4597308.1		628209.7	323475.6	185056.9
1992	8670490.5	7287505.8	5387381.7		696285.2	439319.3	247380.2
1993	10599374.4	8677618.3	6443914.0	33322.7	701856.1	871476.9	315100.4
1994	14887812.6	11747395.6	8839794.7	107795.2	974487.1	1469228.1	588906.6
1995	18779501.1	14115233.3	10283930.0	203671.5	1628414.0	2012422.5	819759.8
1996	22623393.5	16717045.5	12119133.6	261998.9	1884189.5	2610391.2	1149798.4
1997	25317325.7	18625416.3	13577262.1	301746.4	1706587.6	3260792.0	1422783.4
1998	29490592.0	20324526.0	15655917.0	480314.0	1418537.0	3697474.0	3569741.0

各地区教育经费来源和支出情况(1998 年)

Sources of Educational Fund and Expenditure for Education by Region (1998)

单位：万元

Unit: in 10 Thousand Yuan

地区 Region	合计 Total	国家财政性教育经费 Government Appropriation for Education	预算内教育经费 Budgetary	社会团体和公民个人办学经费 Funds of Social Organizations and Citizens for Running Schools	社会捐资和集资办学经费 Donations and Fund－raising for Running Schools	学费和杂费 Tuition and Miscellaneous Fee	其他教育经费 Other Educational Funds
北京 Beijing	1507186.0	1086711.0	945561.0		44253.0	113436.0	262786.0
天津 Tianjin	511064.0	344212.0	287300.0	24573.0	4909.0	52473.0	84897.0
河北 Hebei	1256576.0	882622.0	632905.0	31129.0	77637.0	185109.0	80080.0
山西 Shanxi	612582.0	441510.0	334082.0	9529.0	53669.0	56976.0	50896.0
内蒙古 Inner Mongolia	470780.0	378236.0	280157.0	2254.0	11607.0	49850.0	28833.0
辽宁 Liaoning	1130355.0	855059.0	671459.0	16238.0	5102.0	120252.0	133704.0
吉林 Jilin	740020.0	566702.0	428733.0	5500.0	23626.0	80021.0	64172.0
黑龙江 Heilongjiang	868994.0	676213.0	454695.0	11757.0	9325.0	95471.0	76228.0
上海 Shanghai	1503465.0	1062297.0	871253.0	57653.0	57906.0	145021.0	180589.0
江苏 Jiangsu	2299291.0	1522469.0	1170187.0	33126.0	114370.0	266893.0	362433.0
浙江 Zhejiang	1527927.0	919749.0	620945.0	71518.0	102999.0	156678.0	276984.0
安徽 Anhui	917458.0	627896.0	483278.0	3241.0	29755.0	162743.0	93822.0
福建 Fujian	905532.0	634109.0	530652.0	13327.0	55741.0	98468.0	103886.0
江西 Jiangxi	563688.0	405836.0	321539.0	2229.0	13436.0	80182.0	62006.0
山东 Shandong	1831113.0	1342184.0	986814.0	12558.0	51707.0	245360.0	179304.0
河南 Henan	1439524.0	950190.0	693440.0	12002.0	152172.0	204201.0	120959.0
湖北 Hubei	1425359.0	798036.0	571145.0	23179.0	121549.0	247731.0	234864.0
湖南 Hunan	1222619.0	711488.0	516092.0	10415.0	72931.0	256548.0	171237.0
广东 Guangdong	2950371.0	1722525.0	1420877.0	99013.0	201067.0	544706.0	383059.0
广西 Guangxi	762311.0	534343.0	389360.0	5302.0	25059.0	96754.0	100854.0
海南 Hainan	185810.0	123483.0	93183.0	2987.0	9888.0	30271.0	19181.0
重庆 Chongqing	532976.0	357520.0	286452.0	4857.0	30943.0	50293.0	89363.0
四川 Sichuan	1216670.0	868705.0	649549.0	4616.0	41991.0	101522.0	199835.0
贵州 Guizhou	361301.0	296087.0	240600.0	1725.0	9542.0	30523.0	23424.0
云南 Yunnan	817986.0	681539.0	591791.0	1382.0	37739.0	45479.0	51847.0
西藏 Tibet	61339.0	58462.0	58012.0		2400.0	122.0	355.0
陕西 Shaanxi	732270.0	518909.0	419956.0	15189.0	36678.0	97360.0	64133.0
甘肃 Gansu	390986.0	316938.0	247926.0	2029.0	13176.0	33464.0	25379.0
青海 Qinghai	95775.0	84939.0	74756.0	469.0	2223.0	4730.0	3415.0
宁夏 Ningxia	108719.0	89451.0	72155.0	317.0	1530.0	10037.0	7384.0
新疆 Xinjiang	540545.0	466106.0	311063.0	2200.0	3607.0	34800.0	33832.0

各类学校教育经费来源和支出情况(1998年)

Sources of Educational Fund and Expenditure for Education in Various Schools (1998)

单位：万元 **Unit: in 10 Thousand Yuan**

学校类别 Type of Schools	合计 Total	国家财政性教育经费 Government Appropriation for Education	预算内教育经费 Budgetary	社会团体和公民个人办学经费 Funds of Social Organizations and Citizens for Running Schools	社会捐资和集资办学经费 Donations and Fund-raising for Running Schools	学费和杂费 Tuition and Miscellaneous Fee	其他教育经费 Other Educational Funds
全国总计 National Total	29490592	20324526	15655917	480314	1418537	3697474	3569741
中央 Gentral Government	3928264	2607645	1996666		84125	388174	848320
地方 Local Government	25562328	17716881	13659251	480314	1334412	3309300	2721421
按学校类别分组 Grouped by Type of Schools							
高等学校 Institutions of Higher Education	5981215	3837813	3551727	23854	118194	854665	1146689
普通高等学校 Regular IHEs	5493394	3567538	3350701	15577	114640	731134	1064505
成人高等学校 IHEs for Adults	487821	270275	201026	8277	3554	123531	82184
中等专业学校 Specialized Sec. Schools	2256193	1254834	1114806	14294	32564	664692	289809
中等技术学校 Technical Schools	1496470	836644	756248	5435	12854	473325	168212
中等师范学校 Teacher Training Schools	413114	224163	201548		12866	104216	71869
成人中等学校 Specialized Secondary Schools for Adults	346609	194027	157010	8859	6844	87151	49728
技工学校 Technical Schools	345673	260352	93173		1379	41192	42750
中学 Secondary Schools	8755123	6005216	4268491	260974	610617	960625	917691
普通中学 Regular Secondary Schools	8734432	5992593	4261194	259943	610427	956617	914852
高级中学 Senior Secondary Schools	1407437	777719	536050	62304	115417	213855	238142
完全中学 Complete Secondary Schools	2229101	1452398	1070978	91993	137964	244220	302526
初级中学 Junior Secondary Schools	5097894	3762476	2654166	105646	357046	498542	374184
农村 Rural	2738736	2038769	1520640		230081	297997	171889
成人中学 Secondary Schools for Adults	20692	12623	7297	1031	191	4008	2839
职业中学 Vocational Schools	1036139	624816	473254	34183	32605	206406	138129
小学 Primary Schools	9197138	7007328	5109552	147009	585676	880806	576319
普通小学 Regular Primary Schools	9188468	6999920	5104388	146702	585494	880602	575750
农村 Rular Areas	5381145	4130190	3162895		410299	588238	252418
成人小学 Primary Schools for Adults	8670	7408	5164	307	182	204	569
特殊教育学校 Special Edu. Schools	85203	74100	62582		2559	1636	6908
幼儿园 Kindergartens	399874	242177	219422		15143	77353	65201
其他 Others	1434034	1017890	762910		19800	10099	386245

二、教育基本建设投资

Capital Construction Investment in the Educational Sector

教育基本建设

Data on the Completion of Capital Construction Investment

学校类别 Type of School	投资合计 Total Investment Completed in the Current yeal (in 10 thousand Yuan)	其中:住宅 of which: Housing	本年完成投资 Investment by source of Fund Budgetary Allocation 计 Subtotal	中央 Central
总　计 **Total**	4932963	1458509	678703	199807
普通高等学校 Regular Institutions of Higher Education	1002234	358897	305426	105137
中等师范学校 Teacher Teaining Schools	117045	35771	18764	2070
普通中学 Regular Secondary Schools	2095173	570063	167821	23762
职业中学 Vocational Schools	204546	38633	16405	1701
小学 Primary Schools	1178532	246257	158041	65598
特殊教育学校 Special Education Schools	19103	3909	2315	497
幼儿园 Kindergartens	63519	7186	1774	373
其他 Other	252811	197793	8157	669

注: 1. 此表数据为 1999 年 1 月 1 日至 1999年 12 月 31 日投资完成情况。

2. 普通中等专业学校因无中等技术学校数据，所以只反映中等师范学校投资完成情况。

投资完成情况(1999年)

in the Educationral Sector (1999)

按资金来源分(万元) (in 10 Thousand Yuan)					本年新增固定资产 Fixed Assets Increased in the Current year (in 10 Thousand Yuan)	本年竣工建筑面积(平方米) Building Floor Area Completed (in m²)	
	Self-raised Fund						
		其中					
省级 Local	计 Subtotal	学校自筹 Raised by School	个人集资 Individual donations	其他 Other Sources		合计 Total	其中：教工住宅 of which: Housing for Teachers, Staff & workers
478898	3884698	1309783	977121	369562	4218064	64470998	22260619
200289	645341	392918	154251	51467	608252	7476848	4028974
16694	94455	45915	27664	3826	92762	1594981	623748
144059	1742924	519225	385050	184428	1925520	28866907	9571992
14705	169062	65305	28791	19079	184912	2666501	640493
92444	934383	221463	236244	86108	1113368	19541163	4263801
1818	15968	3297	3631	820	15583	211735	69430
1401	53640	16461	8349	8105	56010	807747	129267
7488	228925	45199	133141	15729	221657	3305116	2932914

教育基本建设

Data on the Completion of Capital Construction Investment

地区 Region		投资合计 Total Investment Completed in the Current yeal (in 10 thousand Yuan)	其中:住宅 of which: Housing	本年完成投资 Investment by source of Fund 国家预算内 Budgetary Allocation 计 Subtotal	中央 Central	省级 Local
总计	Total	4932963	1458509	678703	199807	478898
北京市	Beijing	93419	38720	12492	7167	5325
天津市	Tianjin	41609	3374	10217	1865	8352
河北省	Hebei	223805	75935	34231	6321	27910
山西省	Shanxi	66079	19840	12087	3350	8737
内蒙古	Inner Mongolia	89195	28127	19397	13604	5793
辽宁省	Liaoning	129017	46217	15965	7506	8459
大连市	Dalian	27069	2510	3815	35	3780
吉林省	Jilin	116174	39824	12145	3227	8918
黑龙江省	Heilongjiang	115716	35848	15608	5820	9788
上海市	Shanghai	240680	45763	13099	924	12175
江苏省	Jiangsu	551299	163384	26215	2531	23684
浙江省	Zhejiang	358551	29503	31941	2892	29049
宁波市	Ningbo	60366	1703	6979	0	6979
安徽省	Anhui	159261	47068	19918	7298	12621
福建省	Fujian	104971	22930	9126	523	8603
厦门市	Xiamen	8773	612	1102	15	1087
江西省	Jiangxi	92111	22942	12396	8190	4206
山东省	Shandong	287336	126805	18684	960	17724
青岛市	Qingdao	34600	2890	1910	80	1830
河南省	Henan	308382	85171	31833	9545	22288
湖北省	Hubei	217898	90947	23139	8439	14700
湖南省	Hunan	205118	62703	19833	7775	12058
广东省	Guangdong	273854	118791	69397	3714	65683
深圳市	Shenzhen	53631	1164	39724	0	39724
广西	Guangxi	130342	41695	35427	13064	22363
海南省	Hainan	29847	11020	7040	2068	4972
重庆市	Chongqing	106931	31556	12600	8683	3917
四川省	Sichuan	180685	68574	12364	3324	9040
贵州省	Guizhou	68943	19775	21508	12350	9158
云南省	Yunnan	175754	45202	50127	11102	39026
西藏	Xizang					
陕西省	Shanxi	158726	47455	30134	16163	13971
甘肃省	Gansu	96692	37054	11692	8698	2994
青海省	Qinghai	22783	7364	8621	5618	3003
宁夏	Ningxia	21415	5590	6143	5132	1011
新疆	Xinjiang	63149	27037	16133	8858	7275
新疆生产建设兵团		18782	3416	5661	2966	2695

注:同第 350 页。

投资分省完成情况(1999年)

in the Educationral Sector (Regional Aggregates) (1999)

按资金来源分(万元) (in 10 Thousand Yuan)				本年新增固定资产 Fixed Assets Increased in the Current year (in 10 Thousand Yuan)	本年竣工建筑面积(平方米) Building Floor Area Completed (in m²)	
自筹资金 Self-raised Fund			其他 Other Sources			
计 Subtotal	其中: of which: 学校自筹 Raised by School	个人集资 Individual donations			合计 Total	其中: 教工住宅 of which: Housing for Teachers, Staff & workers
3884698	1309783	977121	369562	4218064	64470998	22260619
79828	34906	21244	1099	74457	541459	292439
31392	23069	900	0	32662	334388	3744
177153	63285	53537	12421	177938	2807417	1183415
52022	15337	26883	1970	49855	896915	380449
66304	11712	25940	3494	81553	1325376	467273
104963	44362	31697	8089	101041	1130342	479675
15044	4135	2177	8210	18199	228470	23900
97235	35767	28790	6794	102418	1427242	480173
95899	32179	24554	4209	74391	1251808	493570
188085	72866	0	39496	239859	964574	23674
461293	196532	116294	63791	461726	6381462	2173408
285915	103068	28077	40695	275365	3463496	449661
47004	14207	1454	6383	55342	559729	19497
132321	47928	28569	7022	170994	2441036	890142
81572	29052	13275	14273	88169	1465109	382288
7240	698	598	431	10156	121100	11899
73881	14676	17436	5834	73460	2172092	580071
250729	120164	77224	17923	229099	3779389	1916882
32490	8607	5694	200	28551	402094	46366
271975	77346	90598	4574	288914	5647082	1590675
170617	76665	47917	24142	196532	3144642	1362246
166265	59471	49634	19020	176894	3131593	1216740
183893	37131	26874	20564	215573	3258974	1616820
12568	3648	565	1339	39594	234139	2277
88027	22421	24063	6888	107412	2321418	844068
19341	5597	4321	3466	28175	330971	142307
94331	17766	21234	0	108226	1849949	773649
161811	48438	49382	6510	166101	3370864	1510376
44027	3648	15143	3408	68449	1489040	459895
106836	18581	31920	18791	155125	2410598	754537
123067	46507	47540	5525	107873	2111696	498298
81346	9135	32114	3654	93640	1539764	564222
10737	1578	4504	3425	22610	318985	108810
14138	559	4375	1134	22022	416710	90286
42228	5677	19758	4788	59154	944429	349828
13121	3065	2836	0	16535	256646	77059

三、 仪器设备

Instrument and Equipment

教学、科研仪器设备分省情况(1998年)

Classification of Instruments and Equipment for Instruction and Scientific Research by Province (1998)

单位:万元

Unit: in 10 Thousand Yuan

地区 Region	教学科研仪器设备数 No. of Instruments and Equipment for Instruction and Scientific Research		五万元以上仪器设备数 No. of Instruments and Equipment Valued above 50 Thousand Yuan	
	台、件 Set & Piece	金额(万元) Book Value (in 10 Thousand Yuan)	台、件 Set & Piece	金额(万元) Book Value (in 10 Thousand Yuan)
合 计 Total	2893691	2257720	49523	901396
北 京 Beijing	304907	361578	9001	185119
天 津 Tianjin	81198	62570	1369	24260
河 北 Hebei	95264	58355	1111	19200
山 西 Shanxi	49413	32298	709	11083
内蒙古 Inner Mongolia	29278	15016	274	3994
辽 宁 Liaoning	144473	105269	2794	38953
吉 林 Jilin	86275	65020	1263	26914
黑龙江 Heilongjiang	98557	81199	1668	34786
上 海 Shanghai	211377	213877	4874	105562
江 苏 Jiangsu	219905	163805	3603	61341
浙 江 Zhejiang	106719	80426	1733	28638
安 徽 Anhui	85623	54014	976	18047
福 建 Fujian	65142	43117	909	15808
江 西 Jiangxi	54825	36780	768	13368
山 东 Shandong	144994	113558	2487	48450
河 南 Henan	92271	53532	1062	14879
湖 北 Hubei	188079	143278	2525	55269
湖 南 Hunan	114888	72086	1540	23973
广 东 Guangdong	173102	131681	2772	49132
广 西 Guangxi	45589	23588	467	5490
海 南 Hainan	9986	5703	102	1206
重 庆 Chongqing	63990	40222	792	11991
四 川 Sichuan	132382	92639	1849	32921
贵 州 Guizhou	26068	15391	272	3935
云 南 Yunnan	53512	32232	692	10372
西 藏 Tibet				
陕 西 Shaanxi	136492	113917	2410	46067
甘 肃 Gansu	39482	25867	481	5026
青 海 Qinghai	6410	2708	628	794
宁 夏 Ningxia	7969	4280	76	1170
新 疆 Xinjiang	25521	13714	316	3648

教学、科研仪器设备分省情况(1999年)

Classification of Instruments and Equipment for Instruction and Scientific Research by Province (1999)

单位:万元

Unit: in 10 Thousand Yuan

地 区 Region	教学科研仪器设备数 No. of Instruments and Equipment for Instruction and Scientific Research		五万元以上仪器设备数 No. of Instruments and Equipment Valued above 50 Thousand Yuan	
	台、件 Set & Piece	金额(万元) Book Value (in 10 Thousand Yuan)	台、件 Set & Piece	金额(万元) Book Value (in 10 Thousand Yuan)
合 计 Total	3245857	2620580	57642	1064065
北 京 Beijing	325393	396027	9855	202552
天 津 Tianjin	86695	70152	1557	27007
河 北 Hebei	114296	68715	2614	20888
山 西 Shanxi	55821	37272	827	12917
内蒙古 Inner Mongolia	28760	17124	335	5784
辽 宁 Liaoning	162515	119491	2583	42872
吉 林 Jilin	94936	80246	1474	36888
黑龙江 Heilongjiang	113461	94569	2039	39617
上 海 Shanghai	223363	244566	5338	125894
江 苏 Jiangsu	259979	205237	4498	80918
浙 江 Zhejiang	122947	93103	2024	34384
安 徽 Anhui	95437	61167	980	18758
福 建 Fujian	75570	54544	1160	21312
江 西 Jiangxi	64279	42772	928	15101
山 东 Shandong	154483	115058	2523	45245
河 南 Henan	106479	64981	1219	17147
湖 北 Hubei	212301	161272	3024	62143
湖 南 Hunan	133070	86182	1864	28548
广 东 Guangdong	199381	161384	3338	64099
广 西 Guangxi	48684	26211	530	6416
海 南 Hainan	13554	8150	153	1852
重 庆 Chongqing	72337	45931	814	12226
四 川 Sichuan	148334	123300	2661	54446
贵 州 Guizhou	26852	15219	452	4457
云 南 Yunnan	59036	38253	789	11799
西 藏 Tibet				
陕 西 Shaanxi	158019	134826	2985	54056
甘 肃 Gansu	45276	29986	555	10281
青 海 Qinghai	6281	2869	49	597
宁 夏 Ningxia	9995	5719	101	1432
新 疆 Xinjiang	28323	16254	373	4429

第三部分

Part Ⅲ

科学研究活动及其他

Scientific Research Activites & Other

一、自然科学与技术

Natural Science and Technology

全国普通高等学校科技人力情况(1998年)

Scientific and Technical Manpower in Regular HEIs (1998)

单位：人

	科技活动人员 Personnel Engaged in S&T Activities		研究与发展人员 R & D Personnel		研究与发展全时人员 R & D FTEs (Full－time Equivalents)	
	计 Total	其中：科学家和工程师 of Which: Scientists & Engineers	计 Total	其中：科学家和工程师 of Which: Scientists & Engineers	计 Total	其中：科学家和工程师 of Which: Scientists & Engineers
合　计: Total:	598100	530799	238404	228386	138556	132589
按学校规格分 Breakdown by category of HEIs						
重点院校 Key HEIs	167848	149196	86469	81270	57029	53677
一般院校 Ordinary Degree Level HEIs	385029	340974	140779	136186	76463	73949
高等专科学校 Short－cycle HEIs	45223	40629	11156	10930	5064	4963
按学校隶属分 Breakdown by Control						
部委院校 HEIs under Other Central Ministries	166445	146636	71750	68057	44920	42547
教育部直属院校 HEIs Under Ministry of Education	87398	78555	45851	43452	30131	28565
地方院校 HEIs under Local Governments	344257	305608	120803	116877	63505	61477
按学校类型分 Breakdown by Type of HEIs						
综合大学 Comprehensive Universities	64554	57499	29587	28736	17884	17364
工科院校 Engineering	214234	196371	101408	97259	62972	60277
农林院校 Agriculture	35983	32952	20239	19206	11971	11382
医药院校 Meclicine & Pharmacy	223639	190285	65816	62365	34835	32888
师范院校 Teachers Training	53760	48401	19707	19196	10084	9879
其他院校 Others	5930	5291	1647	1624	810	799

全国普通高等学校科技人力中科学家和工程师技术职务(职称)情况(1998年)

Statistics of Scientists and Engineer Among S & T Manpower in Regular HEIs by Level of Post (1998)

单位：人

	科技活动人员 Personnel Engaged in S&T Activities			研究与发展人员 R & D Personnel			研究与发展全时人员 R & D FTEs (Full－time Equivalents)		
	高级 Senior	中级 Middle	初级 Junior	高级 Senior	中级 Middle	初级 Junior	高级 Senior	中级 Middle	初级 Junior
合　计: Total	160195	216502	154102	98693	89700	39993	60912	50232	21445
按学校规格分 Breakdown by category of HEIs									
重点院校 Key HEIs	57331	58691	33174	39710	29001	12559	27187	18710	7780
一般院校 Ordinary Degree Level HEIs	93154	139058	108762	55332	55316	25538	31911	29142	12896
高等专科学校 Short－cycle HEIs	9710	18753	12166	3651	5383	1896	1814	2380	769
按学校隶属分 Breakdown by Control									
部委院校 HEIs under Other Central Ministries	44594	60173	41869	28797	26353	12907	18642	16250	7655
教育部直属院校 HEIs Under Ministry of Education	32605	31082	14868	22551	15224	5677	15446	9556	3563
地方院校 HEIs under Local Governments	82996	125247	97365	47345	48123	21409	26824	24426	10227
按学校类型分 Breakdown by Type of HEIs									
综合大学 Comprehensive Universities	20554	23110	13835	13826	10412	4498	8962	5936	2466
工科院校 Engineering	69233	83074	44064	45572	37274	14413	29500	22497	8280
农林院校 Agriculture	11037	13266	8649	8016	7558	3632	4982	4375	2025
医药院校 Meclicine & Pharmacy	42889	74051	73345	22218	26081	14066	12277	13394	7217
师范院校 Teachers Training	15090	20618	12693	8398	7659	3139	4848	3683	1348
其他院校 Others	1392	2383	1516	663	716	245	343	347	109

全国普通高等学校科技经费情况（1998年）

S & T Expenditure in Regular HEIs (1998)

单位：千元
Unit: in Thousand Yuan

	拨入 Revenues				支出 Expenditures				
	合计 Total	政府资金 Government Funds	企事业单位委托 Contract Research Fund	其他 Others	合计 Total	劳务费 Personnel Costs	业务费 Non－Personnel Expenses	转拨外单位经费 Expenses on External Services	其他 Others
合 计 Key HEIs Total	8198192	3894039	3645297	658856	7370661	657881	4416513	286655	2009612
按学校规格分 Breakdown by category of HEIs									
重点院校 Key HEIs	5733582	2615214	2688666	429702	5229871	489921	3296216	200544	1243190
一般院校 Ordinary Degree Level HEIs	2393822	1250987	920055	222780	2074711	162755	1103287	77783	730886
高等专科学校 Short－cycle HEIs	70788	27838	36576	6374	66079	5205	17010	8328	35536
按学校隶属分 Breakdown by Control									
部委院校 HEIs under Other Central Ministries	2966606	1658107	1053050	255449	2625481	210012	1633601	111641	670227
教育部直属院校 HEIs Under Ministry of Education	3448079	1291017	1915439	241623	3214013	335266	1999199	117374	762174
地方院校 HEIs under Local Governments	1783507	944915	676808	161784	1531167	112603	783713	57640	577211
按学校类型分 Breakdown by Type of HEIs									
综合大学 Comprehensive Universities	1056934	604123	380074	72737	944810	72696	511665	39472	320977
工科院校 Engineering	5935446	2423779	3097522	414145	5436341	493279	3373239	185279	1384544
农林院校 Agriculture	357700	286774	34375	36551	310791	20849	179457	24094	86391
医药院校 Medicine & Pharmacy	565402	407974	57033	100395	431007	42257	223096	29724	135930
师范院校 Teachers Training	272553	163718	74533	34302	239453	28328	125361	8066	77698
其他院校 Others	10157	7671	1760	726	8259	472	3695	20	4072

全国普通高等学校研究与发展课题、成果情况（1998 年）

Statistics of R & D Projects and Achievements in Regular HEIs (1998)

单位：千元

Unit: in Thousand Yuan

	科技课题 R&D Projects			出版科技专著（部）	发表学术论文（篇）	成果获奖 Achievements Awards		技术转让 Technological Transfer		专利授权数	专利出售 Income from License Arrangements	
	课题数（项） No. of Projects	投入人数 No. of Input of S&T Manpower	实际支出 Actual Exp.	No. of Monographs Published	No. of Papers Published	合计 Total	其中：国家奖 of Which: National Awards	合同数 No. of Contracts	收入 Actual Revenues	No. of Awarded	项数 No. of Items	实现金额 Income
合 计：Total	120390	137558	6034439	5869	243652	8261	2127	4225	544556	1061	371	55369
按学校规格分 Breakdown by category of HEIs												
重点院校 Key HEIs	55688	59621	4410897	2010	90556	2916	1484	2549	423674	716	344	52756
一般院校 Ordinary Degree Level HEIs	61183	73086	1570975	3690	134672	4819	628	1645	119273	312	24	2333
高等专科学校 Short－cycle HEIs	3519	4851	52567	169	18424	526	15	31	1609	33	3	280
按学校隶属分 Breakdown by Control												
部委院校 HEIs under Other Central Ministries	37341	44314	2259205	1554	70698	2496	1043	1558	220810	273	49	11773
教育部直属院校 HEIs Under Ministry of Education	33104	33293	2666199	939	52081	1512	740	1458	233374	513	283	40543
地方院校 HEIs under Local Governments	49945	59951	1109035	3376	120873	4253	344	1209	90372	275	39	3053
按学校类型分 Breakdown by Type of HEIs												
综合大学 Comprehensive Universities	15624	17300	695547	513	30685	830	229	494	92142	104	29	3264
工科院校 Engineering	64994	67592	4669202	2104	100173	3438	1414	2980	360587	797	330	50331
农林院校 Agriculture	8838	11920	221562	611	16602	590	101	264	24434	35	4	1251
医药院校 Mediicine & Pharmacy	22574	30975	287452	2266	67063	2513	297	368	59730	83	5	223
师范院校 Teachers Training	7605	9011	153941	351	26922	827	67	105	7126	41	2	0
其他院校 Others	755	760	6735	24	2207	63	19	14	537	1	1	300

二、社会科学

Social Science

全国普通高等学校人文、

Professional Manpower in Regular HEIs

		学校数(所) No. of HEIs	社会活动人员(人) Personnel Engaged in Social Science Research (in Person)				
			合计 Total	高级 Senior	中级 Middle	初级 Junior	辅助人员 Auxiliary
按学校规格分 Breakdown by category of HEIs	合计 Total	815	233079	64508	93608	66069	8894
	重点院校 Key HEIs	92	43506	16005	16586	9206	1709
	一般院校 Ordinary Degree Level HEIs	492	146591	40765	58866	41480	5480
	高等专科学校 Short-cycle HEIs	231	42982	7738	18156	15383	1705
按学校隶属关系分 Breakdown by Control	教育部直属院校 HEIs Under Ministry of Education	34	27691	12104	10416	4364	807
	其他部委院校 HEIs under Other Central Ministries	264	66324	18010	26755	18600	2959
	地方院校 HEIs under Local Governments	517	139064	34394	56437	43105	5128
按学校类型分 Breakdown by Type of HEIs	综合大学 Comprehensive Universities	74	44677	14819	17244	11030	1584
	全国重点理工农医院校 National Key HEIs Science and Technology, Agriculture and Medicine	344	62767	15804	25474	18951	2538
	师范院校 Teachers Training	226	65704	17320	26467	19666	2251
	语言院校 Languages	15	6601	2065	2654	1590	292
	财经院校 Finance and Economics	74	27772	7631	11571	7497	1073
	政法院校 Political Science & Law	25	8181	1915	3325	2525	416
	艺术院校 Art	30	7991	2481	3065	2057	388
	民族院校 Minorities	13	5149	1297	2206	1446	200
	体育院校 Physical Culture	14	4237	1176	1602	1307	152

注1:“科研活动人员”: 指高等学校职工中，在本年度内从事大专以上教学、研究与咨询工作以及直接为教学、研究与咨询工作服务的教师和其他技术职务人员、辅助人员。

注 2:“高级”:指具有副教授以上及其他相应高级技术职务(职称)的人员。

注 3:“中级”:指具有讲师及其他相应中级技术职务(职称)的人员。

注 4:“初级”:指具有助教及其他相应初级技术职务(职称)的人员,包括具有技术员任职资格或中专毕业以上学历而未评定任职资格的教师及其他技术职务系列人员。

注 5:“辅助人员”:指具有高中及以下学历未评定职称的从事与社科教学、科研活动的实施有关的工作人员,包括教学、研究秘书,办事员等一切为社科活动提供直接服务的人员。

注 6:“研究与发展人员”:指从事社科研究与发展工作时间占本人全部工作时间 10% 以上的人员,90% 以上为全时人员,10%~90% 为非全时人员,几个全时人员从事社科研究与发展工作的百分比累计达 100% 时,折合为一个全时人员。

注 7:“研究与发展全时人员”:为全时人员与非全时折合全时人员之和。

社会科学人力情况（1998 年）

in the Fields of the Humanities and Social Acience (1998)

研究与发展人员(人) R & D Personnel (in Person)					研究与发展全时人员(人年) R & D FTEs (Man/Year)				
合计 Total	高级 Senior	中级 Middle	初级 Junior	辅助人员 Auxiliary	合计 Total	高级 Senior	中级 Middle	初级 Junior	辅助人员 Auxiliary
64721	29975	24703	8094	1949	30204.4	14871.8	10638.5	3014.0	1680.1
13099	7232	4052	1019	796	6952.5	3783.7	1950.1	452.7	766.0
43757	20159	16885	5748	965	20204.3	9995.7	7283.3	2169.2	756.1
7865	2584	3766	1327	188	3047.6	1092.4	1405.1	392.1	158.0
10170	6286	2671	510	703	5559.3	3307.1	1321.0	228.2	703.0
16035	7331	6280	2047	377	7542.2	3644.8	2778.5	841.9	277.0
38516	16358	15752	5537	869	17102.9	7919.9	6539.0	1943.9	700.1
16338	8313	5652	1764	609	8308.0	4379.0	2628.7	731.3	569.0
12677	5502	5100	1735	340	6198.0	2717.4	2412.3	769.3	299.0
19801	9050	7688	2605	458	8477.3	4288.4	3029.0	791.9	368.0
1467	683	536	147	101	645.8	317.5	193.4	44.9	90.0
8074	3722	3161	952	239	3606.2	1790.1	1256.8	347.3	212.0
1931	832	744	252	103	852.9	415.0	295.2	77.7	65.0
1110	569	372	155	14	562.0	323.0	169.0	57.0	13.0
1987	703	954	280	50	901.8	325.3	427.3	111.1	38.1
1336	601	496	204	35	652.4	316.1	226.8	83.5	26.0

Note 1: "Personnel Engaged in Social Science Research":referring to HEI faculty and other employees who are engaged in teaching, research and consulting activities at subdegree level and over in the given year, as well as teachical service and auxiliary personel directly serving the needs of thd fore−going personnel.

Note 2: "Senior": referring to personnel with the rank of associate professor and higher or personnel with similar professional ranks.

Note 3: "Middle":referring to lecturers and other personnel with similar posts or professional qualifications.

Note 4: "Junior":referring to teaching assistants and other staff members with similar qualifications, and those assuming junior level technical posts, including personnel with the qualification of technicians and personnel with at least the completion of specialized technicians and personnel with at least the completion of specialized secondary education, even without formal determination of their posts or professional ranks.

Note 5: "Auxiliary":referring to personnel with the ecucational attainment of the completion of senior secondary schools or lower and without professional qualifications whose work is in one way or another related to social scienceteaching and research activities, including secretaries and clerical workers.

Note 6: "R&D Personnel":referring to all personnel employed by HEIs who devote at least 10% of their total working time to social science research and development. Those with the percentage of time over 90% are regarded as full−time personnel; those ranging from 10%−90% are regarded as part−time personnel; and several part−time personnel with the aggregate percentage reaching 100% are counted as an FTE(full−time equivalent).

Note 7: "R&D FTES":referring to the aggregate number of full−time staff members and FTES converted from part−time staff members.

全国普通高等学校人文、社会

Humanities and Social Sciences

		学校数(所) No. of HEIs	拨入 Revenues				
			合计 Total	科研事业费 Primary Research Funds	国家社科规划、基金项目经费 Funds Allocated to Projects Supported by NSSP Funds	中央其他部门社科专项经费 Earmarked SSRF Provided by Other Central Agencies	省市自治区社科专项经费 Earmarked SSRF Provided by Prov. Authorities
按学校规格分 Breakdown by category of HEIs	合计 Total	815	2974678	1591368	167608	175907	274133
	重点院校 Key HEIs	92	1142599	569311	77602	72884	74998
	一般院校 Ordinary Degree Level HEIs	492	1632974	902163	88236	100602	178379
	高等专科学校 Short-cycle HEIs	231	199105	119894	1770	2421	20756
按学校隶属分 Breakdown by Control	教育部直属院校 HEIs Under Ministry of Education	34	1004868	516213	70711	29929	52532
	其他部委院校 HEIs under Other Central Ministries	264	780899	375829	47645	99819	58918
	地方院校 HEIs under Local Governments	517	1188911	699326	49252	46159	162683
按学校类型分 Breakdown by Type of HEIs	综合大学 Comprehensive Universities	74	976319	523160	72336	41890	74009
	全国重点理工农医院校 National Key HEIs Science and Technology, Agriculture and Medicine	344	538524	139982	25252	67297	74750
	师范院校 Teachers Training	226	793542	523361	32405	23306	75774
	语言院校 Languages	15	78270	28428	1780	8120	10190
	财经院校 Finance and Economics	74	318428	197127	26519	20520	20481
	政法院校 Political Science & Law	25	58350	22840	2589	6349	3742
	艺术院校 Art	30	34174	16787	882	2050	2180
	民族院校 Minorities	13	132828	114708	3790	2715	2012
	体育院校 Physical Culture	14	44243	24975	2055	3660	10995

注1:“科研事业费”：指学校上级主管部门从科学事业费、教育事业费中通过切块和按项目戴帽下达，以及高校从教育事业费中安排的社科研究与发展经费。

注2:“国家社科规划、基金项目经费”：指国家社会科学基金委员会拨付的社会科学规划项目经费（包括全国教育科学领导小组拨付的教育科学五年一次的规划项目经费）和社会科学基金年度项目经费（包括青年基金项目经费）。

注3:“中央其他部门社科专项经费”：指中央（国务院）各部门（非学校上级主管部门）拨给学校的各种专项社科研究经费，包括中国社会科学院拨付给学校的专项科研经费。

注4:“省、市、自治区社科专项经费”：指各省、市、自治区社会科学领导机构拨付的社科研究规划（基金）项目经费，以及列入省、市、自治区党委、政府和其他委厅局（非高校上级主管部门）计划以外拨付给学校的各种专项科研经费。

注5:“自筹经费”：指学校从自有资金或其他各种收入中提取并转用于社科研究与发展的经费。

注6:“科研人员费”：指学校当年以货币或实物形式直接或间接付给从事社科研究与发展活动人员的劳动报酬及各种费用。

科学研究与发展经费情况 (1998 年)

R & D Expenditure in Regular HEIs (1998)

单位：百元 **Unit: in Hundred Yuan**

企事业单位委托项目经费 Contract Research Funds Provided by Ent.& Inst.	自筹经费 Self-raised Fubds	其他收入 Other Revenues	支出 Expenditures								
			合计 Total	内部支出 Intramural Expenditures							转拨给外单位经费 Extra-mural Exp.
				小计 Subtotal	科研人员费 Personnel Costs	业务费 Operating Expenses	仪器设备费 Instruments and Equipment	图书资料费 Books and Information	管理费 Manage-ment	其他 Other Items	
320384	224144	221134	2344453	2314198	477663	930267	268498	366905	60999	209866	30255
179923	46856	121025	832450	812067	262416	312133	56937	112825	26138	41618	20383
140076	128990	94528	1321871	1313241	191323	536765	193501	211407	32446	147799	8630
385	48298	5581	190132	188890	23924	81369	18060	42673	2415	20449	1242
157297	38804	139382	757770	740579	268585	245656	52986	109639	20381	43332	17191
107380	64673	26635	595868	589971	94998	289513	57466	95204	19500	33290	5897
55707	120667	55117	990815	983648	114080	395098	158046	162062	21118	133244	7167
105688	52971	106265	775381	760091	244727	279495	57680	108145	19790	50254	15290
135050	45393	50800	477972	470121	48309	238402	38246	96370	20733	28061	7851
34831	71195	32670	617042	611895	92962	215289	88100	101262	10921	103361	5147
10200	7032	12520	50722	50642	9108	21051	7301	10438	719	2025	80
24350	21339	8092	257546	256666	58123	88541	50763	35618	5448	18173	880
4569	16239	2022	36670	36313	5201	18290	4319	4805	989	2709	357
3000	5775	3500	29822	29822	5666	10300	8216	3378	728	1534	0
2621	2120	4862	55117	55117	7180	34908	5903	5375	467	1284	0
75	2080	403	44181	43531	6387	23991	7970	1514	1204	2465	650

Note 1: "Primary research Funds":referring to research funds allocated by the supervisory bodies of HEIs either in block grants or in grants earnarked for specific projects out of general research funds of higher education funds, including the money used for social science R&D arranged by HEIs the mselves out of higher education funds.

Note 2: "Funds Allocated to Projects Sponsored by the National Social Science Research Programme(NSSRP)Funds":referring to funds allocated to support the research projects constituting partof the National social Science Research Programme by the National social Science fund Committed (including educational research funds allocated ty the National Steering Group for Educational Sciences at 5-year intervals) and the annual allocations of the Social Science Fund (including funds for young investigators.

Note 3: "Earmarked Social Science Research Funds (SSRF)Provided by Other Central Agencies":referring to earmarked research funds provided by central agencies other than the supervisory bodies of HEIs, including funds allocated ty the Chinese Academy of Social Sciences (CASS).

Note 4: "Earmarked Social Science Research Funds (SSRF) Provided ty Provincial Authorities":referring to earmarked research funds provided by the social science leading bodies of various provinces, atutonomous regions and municipalities directly under the Central Govenment and by the subordinate departments of provincial-level governments other than the educational departments to support the conduct of research projects either incorporated into a local social science research programme or not.

Note 5: "Self-raised funds":referring to the funds drawn from institutional funds drawn from institutional funds or other revenues used to support social science R&D efforts.

Note 6: "Personnel Costs":referring to the emoluments paid in money or in kind directly paid or indirectly giver to personnel engaged in social science R&D activities.

全国普通高等学校人文、社会

Basic Statistics of Humunities and Social Sciences

		课题数（项） No.of Projects	当年投入人数（人年） Input of Man-years	其中：研究生 Of Which: Graduate Students	当年拨入经费（百元） Revenues (100 Yuan)	当年支出经费（百元） Expenditures (100 Yuan)
	合 计 Total	26917	28219.8	4227.0	1623925	1116677.0
按学校规格分 Breakdown by Category of HEIs	重点院校 Key HEIs	6960	7094.9	1449.0	690990	446265.3
	一般院校 Ordinary Degree Level HEIs	17502	18604.5	2702.8	874820	621540.0
	高等专科学校 Short-cycle HEIs	2455	2520.4	75.2	58115	48872.0
按学校隶属分 Breakdown by Control	教育部直属院校 HEIs Under Ministry of Education	6288	5591.5	1088.8	604421	380587.3
	其他部委院校 HEIs under Other Central Ministries	6144	7526.1	1445.5	449907	323806.0
	地方院校 HEIs under Local Governments	14485	15102.2	1692.7	569597	412284.0
按学校类型分 Breakdown by Type of HEIs	综合大学 Comprehensive Universities	7962	7954.3	1129.8	599299	358906.0
	全国重点理工农医院校 National Key HEIs Science and Technology, Agriculture and Medicine	5518	5970.7	967.6	442148	355888.3
	师范院校 Teachers Training	7976	7671.2	1036.5	282467	200857.0
	语言院校 Languages	614	539.2	17.3	60647	30742.0
	财经院校 Finance and Economics	2849	3257.0	444.4	147477	93999.0
	政法院校 Political Science & Law	748	1043.5	415.2	29990	16365.0
	艺术院校 Art	297	465.0	51.0	14394	20259.0
	民族院校 Minorities	456	688.7	93.0	23715	18506.0
	体育院校 Physical Culture	497	630.2	72.2	23788	21155.0

科学研究与发展课题、成果情况 (1998 年)

R & D Project and Achievements in Regular HEIs (1998)

出版专著(部) Monographs Published (Titles)	发表论文(篇) No. of Papers Published: 合计 Total	国内学术刊物 In Domestic Journals: 国内外公开发行 Published an Distributed at Home and Abroad	国内学术刊物 In Domestic Journals: 国内公开发行 Openly Distributed at Home	国外学术刊物 In Foreign Journals	应用成果(项) No. of Application-oriented Results (Items): 提交有关部门数 No. of Results Submitted to Relevant Agencies	应用成果(项) No. of Application-oriented Results (Items): 鉴定成果数 No. of Results Appraised
5981	122775	56880	64455	1440	5029	1779
2302	25662	12884	12266	512	2382	789
3290	78142	36302	40956	884	2416	879
389	18971	7694	11233	44	231	111
1935	19299	10020	8829	450	2139	706
1390	34917	15536	19010	371	1565	598
2656	68559	31324	36616	619	1325	475
1909	28758	14292	13928	538	1915	547
1096	26088	11023	14786	279	1141	236
1761	37832	18043	19431	358	924	381
169	1927	836	1041	50	54	39
449	18105	9322	8663	120	823	441
228	4408	1146	3238	24	66	36
149	1915	586	1305	24	11	7
174	2515	1190	1299	26	55	39
46	1227	442	764	21	40	53

普通高等学校

Recruitment of Student for Regular

地区 Region	总计 Total	性别 Sex 男 Male	女 Female	分类情况 Categories of Major Fields 理工类 Science and Engineering	文史类 Literature and History	外语类 Foreign Languages	艺术类 Arts	体育类 Physical Education	城镇应届高中毕业生 Urban Sec. Schools Graduates in Current Year
合计 Total	3202197	1914666	1287531	2032824	933752	98251	90590	64091	1074925
北京 Beijing	50708	23983	26725	35054	15654	0	0	0	37750
天津 Tianjin	32143	16169	15974	21559	9515	0	673	396	18821
河北 Hebei	178492	93344	85148	119744	52409	0	3749	2590	45463
山西 Shanxi	95719	53092	42627	64558	23271	3710	2012	2168	26246
内蒙古 Inner Mongolia	72378	35298	37080	47495	20075	2124	1915	769	16242
辽宁 Liaoning	122629	64014	58615	82461	32370	2	4345	3451	57499
吉林 Jilin	85862	46921	38941	57397	24192	0	2728	1545	40387
黑龙江 Heilongjiang	106626	56071	50555	66674	29822	0	6465	3665	47591
上海 Shanghai	52040	26711	25329	35521	14642	0	1323	554	38768
江苏 Jiangsu	193963	121784	72179	129929	40697	14362	4670	4305	60753
浙江 Zhejiang	125393	71766	53627	73187	47143	0	3501	1562	33585
安徽 Anhui	153330	104549	48781	87544	59865	0	3924	1997	46506
福建 Fujian	74690	52192	22498	43979	22233	5349	1702	1427	18672
江西 Jiangxi	122894	85077	37817	73230	39478	0	6252	3934	39404
山东 Shandong	296655	178169	118486	203033	63172	17068	8333	5049	64530
河南 Henan	227136	140643	86493	147945	61251	8442	5535	3963	46834
湖北 Hubei	154248	100700	53548	102716	38308	6586	4667	1971	68917
湖南 Hunan	159523	102505	57018	87908	71615	7127	6345	3839	43014
广东 Guangdong	150474	100173	50301	89196	43603	8584	4041	5050	78483
广西 Guangxi	90794	58384	32410	56110	25877	4639	1762	2406	33360
海南 Hainan	17648	12083	5565	10209	6006	752	306	375	7768
重庆 Chongqing	39886	23232	16654	24732	12489	0	1669	996	17652
四川 Sichuan	124317	74953	49364	76394	40283	0	5140	2500	45756
贵州 Guizhou	66370	44447	21923	42386	21414	0	1430	1140	21289
云南 Yunnan	81767	46540	35227	44284	29868	3514	2586	1515	19229
西藏 Tibet	2523	1753	770	945	1578	0	0	0	0
陕西 Shaanxi	129881	74816	55065	86371	33774	4698	2339	2699	38845
甘肃 Gansu	84796	52491	32305	55794	21272	3466	1719	2545	20257
青海 Qinghai	22220	10701	11519	13791	8061	0	159	209	7549
宁夏 Ningxia	24571	13173	11398	15837	6015	22440	242	233	8528
新疆 Xinjiang	62521	28932	33589	36841	17800	5584	1058	1238	25227

招生报名情况 (1998 年)

Higher Educational Institutions (1998)

单位：人

考生类别 Categories of Applicants				考生中 Among the Applicants					
农村应届高中毕业生 Rural Sec. Schools Graduates in Current Year	城镇往届高中毕业生 Urban Sec. Schools Graduates in Previous Years	农村往届高中毕业生 Rural Sec. Schools Graduates in Previous Years	其他 Others	少数民族青年 Minority Youth	港、澳台籍 Youth from HK, Taiwan & Macao	优秀干部 Outstanding Student leaders	三好学生 Three-merit-reward owners	单科优胜 Single subject superiors	残疾青年 Handicapped Youth
1135793	347261	602101	39595	160555	6325	14639	21234	8797	2166
7096	4459	1403	0	3756	142	546	1706	748	28
8037	2344	2941	0	1173	1272	275	6	220	33
82505	14290	36234	0	9575	126	365	1218	24	118
30353	14757	24363	0	316	0	84	73	141	121
24293	10212	21631	0	16798	3	301	653	263	34
45142	7774	11948	266	8610	21	1436	0	3028	24
20824	14698	9814	139	0	244	0	0	0	49
27021	18043	13789	182	0	0	0	0	0	0
10376	1811	1085	0	616	97	0	0	0	0
87488	11591	33623	508	522	19	125	523	97	13
61724	8294	21790	0	0	0	0	0	0	173
45149	27417	33511	747	1174	4	194	2832	173	135
35607	5178	14399	834	763	663	942	1304	315	0
35379	25178	22933	0	297	77	117	312	287	175
121481	24319	72480	13845	1680	137	1231	0	0	34
74987	24581	60195	20539	3371	398	1141	2287	0	213
53902	12148	17458	1823	0	0	0	0	0	0
63749	14500	38260	0	14629	0	0	0	0	120
50829	11204	9755	203	803	101	0	0	0	186
31764	10363	15307	0	34945	509	3052	6730	256	65
5271	2132	2477	0	1223	1996	90	106	13	24
13733	3119	5382	0	2397	30	78	141	450	26
49166	8849	20546	0	3211	72	363	567	1261	133
18612	10838	15631	0	28297	133	1037	1084	0	168
33232	8408	20879	19	19831	172	246	426	251	294
0	0	0	1	1462	0	0	0	0	
40422	22027	28493	94	948	43	1042	1132	1220	
25069	12730	26563	177	0	0	0	0	0	
5805	4222	4578	66	0	0	0	0	0	
6131	4210	5550	152	0	0	0	0	0	
20646	7565	9083	0	4158	66	1974	134	50	

普通高等学校

Recruitment of Student for Regular

地区 Region		报名总数 Total	性别 Sex 男 Male	女 Female	年龄分布 Age Distribution 18周岁以下 Under 18 years of age	18至25周岁 18-25 years of age	25周岁以上 Over 25 years of age
合计	Total	3404445	2022095	1382350	381507	3018109	4829
北京	Beijing	55371	26626	28745	672	54673	26
天津	Tianjin	36803	18241	18562	2386	32815	1602
河北	Hebei	194816	102784	92032	2601	192212	3
山西	Shanxi	102688	58187	44501	7341	95334	13
内蒙古	Inner Mongolia	83216	41377	41839	32344	50853	19
辽宁	Liaoning	123125	63242	59883	24829	97938	358
吉林	Jilin	86866	51459	35407	1519	85206	141
黑龙江	Heilongjiang	105639	55434	50205	2956	102637	46
上海	Shanghai	72704	35155	37549	6158	66495	51
江苏	Jiangsu	213414	132291	81123	13697	199706	11
浙江	Zhejiang	146504	81775	64729	26779	119127	598
安徽	Anhui	166347	112205	54142	33799	132522	26
福建	Fujian	83799	56593	27206	17414	66376	9
江西	Jiangxi	123755	85151	38604	37943	85097	715
山东	Shandong	312735	186940	125795	54592	257780	363
河南	Henan	235133	145789	89344	17922	217211	
湖北	Hubei	166853	106946	59907	15647	151155	51
湖南	Hunan	165395	104078	61317	26264	139091	40
广东	Guangdong	165488	108622	56866	2950	162317	221
广西	Guangxi	90901	58514	32387	1802	89084	15
海南	Hainan	16603	11378	5225	2778	13814	11
重庆	Chongqing	44655	25332	19323	1874	42779	2
四川	Sichuan	130300	77809	52491	4228	126042	30
贵州	Guizhou	68258	44682	23576	12503	55755	0
云南	Yunnan	74049	41690	32359	1660	72189	200
西藏	Tibet	3856	2152	1704	652	3201	3
陕西	Shaanxi	133188	77485	55703	3001	130037	150
甘肃	Gansu	88622	54853	33769	18765	69857	
青海	Qinghai	21840	10622	11218	2581	19150	109
宁夏	Ningxia	25019	13513	11506	2227	22792	
新疆	Xinjiang	66503	31170	35333	1623	64864	16

招生报名情况(一)(1999年)

Higher Educational Institutions (1) (1999)

单位：人

考 生 中 Among the Applicants						
少数民族青年 Minority Youth	台 籍 Youth from Taiwan prov.	优秀干部 Outstanding Student leaders	华 侨 Overseas	三好学生 Three-merit-reward owners	单科优胜 Single subject superiors	残疾青年 Handicapped Youth
218565	413	6210	20046	28202	45450	1969
4369	12	117	584	1842	734	69
1430	10	3	278	212	189	2
11516	4	56	528	1722	287	93
434	1	48	108	145	750	91
20460	2	40	285	636	354	20
21304	12	163	1701	1560	4219	41
10335	15	213			145	45
6515					0	
710					0	
545	2	9	2847	652	18	203
569					0	
1443	13	8	309	3191	4355	150
1175	97	441	847	1367	70	70
422	6	105	490	1543	9183	120
2128	9	139	1506	116	1539	121
3183					0	
6735					0	
14647	4	40	1326	2734	539	167
849	13	2188	1157	765	84	154
34365		529	3307	6108	859	84
1110	143	1560	28	49	136	29
3007	2	16	80	157	0	31
2915	6	58	983	1748	6550	102
5878	10	105	1128	1165	331	163
17757					0	
2440	1	0	45	69	447	0
911	7	14	1211	1351	4669	81
3223	4	45	536	584	182	
5509	3	10	668	332	705	17
4644	4				0	
28037	33	303	94	154	9105	116

普通高等学校
Recruitment of Student for Regular

地区 Region	分类情况 Categories of Major Fields						城镇应届高中毕业生 Urban Sec. Schools Graduates in Current Year
	理工类 Science and Engineering	文史类 Literature and History	外语类 Foreign Languages	艺术类 Arts	体育类 Physical Education	综合 Comprehensive	
合计 Total	1979155	841308	168986	98844	84260	231892	1187397
北京 Beijing	33374	12581		2488	856	6072	41974
天津 Tianjin		7654	1099	378	27672		21456
河北 Hebei	133136	54793		4262	2625		51713
山西 Shanxi	70291	24046	3546	2594	2211		29361
内蒙古 Inner Mongolia	57114	20135	2920	2248	799		21316
辽宁 Liaoning	76570	33278		5060	2784	5433	59236
吉林 Jilin	56860	25764				4242	41886
黑龙江 Heilongjiang	66346	28693		6691	3909		45939
上海 Shanghai	48275	24332		35	62		55576
江苏 Jiangsu	148550	38832	15621	5897	4514		72348
浙江 Zhejiang	79233	44854		5245	2004	15168	43564
安徽 Anhui	96899	62032		4278		3138	48626
福建 Fujian	48972	29520		1814		3493	23753
江西 Jiangxi	75320	35309		6360	4053	2713	41395
山东 Shandong	205926	54503	25040	9892	5253	12121	70245
河南 Henan	152865	71926		6292	4050		49487
湖北 Hubei	110458	43273	5641	5407	2074		70479
湖南 Hunan	96264	47724	9710	7860	3837		50650
广东 Guangdong						165488	81209
广西 Guangxi	59011	23661	3859	1987	2383		34438
海南 Hainan	9533	5445	637	253	345	390	6994
重庆 Chongqing	25676	12305		2467	1592	2615	22513
四川 Sichuan	35563	10081	74722	6860	3074		52926
贵州 Guizhou	38898	20823		1492	982	6063	23397
云南 Yunnan	40558	26394	2841	2768	1488		16987
西藏 Tibet	995	1595	61	78	92	1035	2272
陕西 Shaanxi	86312	31784	6195	2453	2703	3741	42790
甘肃 Gansu	59656	19853	4116	2121	2876		21503
青海 Qinghai	13756	7572		167	165	180	7601
宁夏 Ningxia	15156	5673	3692	234	264		8397
新疆 Xinjiang	37588	16873	9286	1163	1593		27366

招生报名情况(二) (1999 年)

Higher Educational Institutions (2) (1999)

单位：人

考生类别 Categories of Applicants			毕业类别 Categories of Graduates				
农村应届高中毕业生 Rural Sec. Schools Graduates in Current Years	城镇往届高中毕业生 Urban Sec. Schools Graduates in Previous Years	农村往届高中毕业生 Rural Sec. Schools Graduates in Previous Years	高中毕业 General Senior Sec. School Graduates	中专毕业 Specialized Sec. School Graduates	职高毕业 Vacational Senior Sec. Schools Graduates	技校毕业 Skilled Worker School Graduates	其他 Others
1149655	423019	644374	3231538	39507	80760	13879	38761
6829	5138	1430	48006	2449	4570	250	96
9217	3327	2803	33250	1432	1983	97	41
82915	17563	42625	185040	498	8944	334	
30223	17533	25571	100905	639	832	21	291
26213	11450	24237	77363	112	5579	1	161
40609	9226	14054	115772	1760	4976	284	333
18170	15734	11076	82993	1535	2216	15	107
25538	19345	14817	104282	623	478	24	232
11622	3789	1717	63097	5186	3122	1066	233
91255	14164	35647	212667	419	310	14	4
70124	9700	23116	125147	5839	14664	641	213
46717	32101	38903	165690		63		594
39563	5380	15103	80292	146	2328	49	984
33302	26154	22904	119604	309	2860	48	934
120436	47908	74146	290663	10708	36	10938	390
78416	38093	69137	202539	223	3786	19	28566
54938	16259	25177	160533	2229	3633	14	444
67756	14104	32885	151901	2423	10430		641
59274	13701	11304	165488				
31166	11009	14288	90901				
4920	2364	2325	16016	109	335		143
13323	3574	5245	41621		2889	0	145
44448	10836	22090	129769	252	179	12	88
17468	11901	15492	62248	830	4836	27	317
27193	8383	21486	73537	264	195	10	43
956	461	167	2819	972	64	0	1
38709	22547	29142	129435	12			3741
26434	13754	26931	87392	141	1089		
5092	4431	4716	21488	175	153	13	11
5949	4997	5676	25019				
20880	8093	10164	66061	222	210	2	8

附　表

Appendixes

国内生产总值

Gross Domestic Product

本表按当年价格计算。 单位：亿元

Data in value terms in this table are calculated at current prices. **Unit: in 100 Million Yuan**

年份 Year	国民生产总值 Gross National Product	国内生产总值 Gross Domestic Product								人均国内生产总值(元) Per Capita GDP (Yuan)
		合计 Total	第一产业 Primary Industry	第二产业 Secondary Industry			第三产业 Tertiary Industry			
				小计 Subtotal	工业 Industry	建筑业 Construction	小计 Subtotal	交通运输仓储邮电通信业 Transportation, Post and Telecommunications	批发和零售贸易餐饮业 Wholesale, Retail & Catering Trade	
1952	679.0	679.0	342.9	141.8	119.8	22.0	194.3	29.0	80.3	119
1953	824.0	824.0	378.0	192.5	163.5	29.0	253.5	35.0	115.5	142
1954	859.0	859.0	392.0	211.7	184.7	27.0	255.3	38.0	120.3	144
1955	910.0	910.0	421.0	222.2	191.2	31.0	266.8	39.0	119.8	150
1956	1028.0	1028.0	443.9	280.7	224.7	56.0	303.4	46.0	131.4	165
1957	1068.0	1068.0	430.0	317.0	271.0	46.0	321.0	49.0	133.0	168
1958	1307.0	1307.0	445.9	483.5	414.5	69.0	377.6	71.0	136.6	200
1959	1439.0	1439.0	383.8	615.5	538.5	77.0	439.7	94.0	145.7	216
1960	1457.0	1457.0	340.7	648.2	568.2	80.0	468.1	104.0	133.1	218
1961	1220.0	1220.0	441.1	388.9	362.1	26.8	390.0	69.2	110.8	185
1962	1149.3	1149.3	453.1	359.0	325.4	33.9	336.9	57.4	80.5	173
1963	1233.3	1233.3	497.5	407.0	365.6	42.0	328.2	55.0	76.1	181
1964	1454.0	1454.0	559.0	513.5	461.1	52.4	381.5	58.4	94.0	208
1965	1716.1	1716.1	651.1	602.2	546.5	55.7	462.8	77.4	118.3	240
1966	1868.0	1868.0	702.2	709.5	648.6	60.9	456.3	85.1	148.1	254
1967	1773.9	1773.9	714.2	602.8	544.9	57.9	456.9	72.3	153.5	235
1968	1723.1	1723.1	726.3	537.3	490.3	47.0	459.5	70.5	138.9	222
1969	1937.9	1937.9	736.2	689.1	626.1	63.0	512.6	84.9	163.6	243
1970	2252.7	2252.7	793.3	912.2	828.1	84.1	547.2	100.2	178.1	275
1971	2426.4	2426.4	826.3	1022.8	926.6	96.2	577.3	108.4	178.3	288
1972	2518.1	2518.1	827.4	1084.2	989.9	94.3	606.5	118.0	194.3	292
1973	2720.9	2720.9	907.5	1173.0	1072.5	100.5	640.4	125.5	211.0	309
1974	2789.9	2789.9	945.2	1192.0	1083.6	108.4	652.7	126.1	206.6	310
1975	2997.3	2997.3	971.1	1370.5	1244.9	125.6	655.7	141.6	175.8	327
1976	2943.7	2943.7	967.0	1337.2	1204.6	132.6	639.5	139.6	147.2	316
1977	3201.9	3201.9	942.1	1509.1	1372.4	136.7	750.7	156.9	213.8	339
1978	3624.1	3624.1	1018.4	1745.2	1607.0	138.2	860.5	172.8	265.5	379
1979	4038.2	4038.2	1258.9	1913.5	1769.7	143.8	865.8	184.2	220.2	417
1980	4517.8	4517.8	1359.4	2192.0	1996.5	195.5	966.4	205.0	213.6	460
1981	4860.3	4862.4	1545.6	2255.5	2048.4	207.1	1061.3	211.1	255.7	489
1982	5301.8	5294.7	1761.6	2383.0	2162.3	220.7	1150.1	236.7	198.6	525
1983	5957.4	5934.5	1960.8	2646.2	2375.6	270.6	1327.5	264.9	231.4	580
1984	7206.7	7171.0	2295.5	3105.7	2789.0	316.7	1769.8	327.1	412.4	692
1985	8989.1	8964.4	2541.6	3866.6	3448.7	417.9	2556.2	406.9	878.4	853
1986	10201.4	10202.2	2763.9	4492.7	3967.0	525.7	2945.6	475.6	943.2	956
1987	11954.5	11962.5	3204.3	5251.6	4585.8	665.8	3506.6	544.9	1159.3	1104
1988	14922.3	14928.3	3831.0	6587.2	5777.2	810.0	4510.1	661.0	1618.0	1355
1989	16917.8	16909.2	4228.0	7278.0	6484.0	794.0	5403.2	786.0	1687.0	1512
1990	18598.4	18547.9	5017.0	7717.4	6858.0	859.4	5813.5	1147.5	1419.7	1634
1991	21662.5	21617.8	5288.6	9102.2	8087.1	1015.1	7227.0	1409.7	2087.0	1879
1992	26651.9	26638.1	5800.0	11699.5	10284.5	1415.0	9138.6	1681.8	2735.0	2287
1993	34560.5	34634.4	6882.1	16428.5	14143.8	2284.7	11323.8	2123.2	3090.7	2939
1994	46670.0	46759.4	9457.2	22372.2	19359.6	3012.6	14930.2	2685.9	4050.4	3923
1995	57494.9	58478.1	11993.0	28537.9	24718.3	3819.6	17947.2	3054.7	4932.3	4854
1996	66850.5	67884.6	13844.2	33612.9	29082.6	4530.3	20427.5	3494.0	5560.3	5576
1997	73142.7	74462.6	14211.2	37222.7	32412.1	4810.6	23028.7	3797.2	6159.9	6053
1998	78017.8	79395.7	14599.6	38691.8	33429.8	5262.0	26104.3	5029.3	6609.6	6392

注：1980年以后一、二产业之和与国民生产总值的差额为国外净要素收入.

Since 1980, the difference between the total of primary, secondary & teriary industries and the gross national product has been the net factor income from abroad.

各地区国内生产总值(1998年)

Gross Domestic Product by Region (1998)

本表绝对数按当年价格计算,指数按可比价格计算

Absolute figures in this table are calculated at current prices while indices are calculated at comparable prices.

单位:亿元

Unit: in 100 Million Yuan

地区 Region	国内生产总值 Gross Domestic Product							人均国内生产总值(元) Per Capita GDP (Yuan)
	合计 Total	第一产业 Primary Industry	第二产业 Secondary Industry			第三产业 Tertiary Industry		
			小计 Subtotal	工业 Industry	建筑业 Construction	小计 Subtotal	教育、文化艺术和广播电影电视业 Education, Culture, Arts, Radio, Film and Television	
北京 Beijing	2011.31	86.56	786.85	610.66	176.19	1137.90	110.67	18482
天津 Tianjin	1336.38	74.03	660.00	587.83	72.17	602.35	35.70	14808
河北 Hebei	4256.01	790.60	2084.33	1822.05	262.28	1381.08	79.38	6525
山西 Shanxi	1601.11	207.26	856.13	745.47	110.66	537.72	37.28	5040
内蒙古 Inner Mongolia	1192.29	341.62	479.53	399.42	80.11	371.14	28.20	5068
辽宁 Liaoning	3881.73	531.46	1855.22	1664.05	191.17	1495.05	90.52	9333
吉林 Jilin	1557.78	429.50	597.29	504.12	93.17	530.99	44.53	5916
黑龙江 Heilongjiang	2832.84	463.05	1506.76	1332.00	174.76	863.03	58.08	7544
上海 Shanghai	3588.20	78.50	1847.20	1646.70	200.50	1762.50	89.93	28253
江苏 Jiangsu	7199.95	1016.27	3640.10	3157.69	482.41	2543.58	150.64	10021
浙江 Zhejiang	4987.50	631.31	2709.08	2445.43	263.65	1647.11	78.16	11247
安徽 Anhui	2805.45	739.70	1253.53	1112.97	140.56	812.22	63.47	4576
福建 Fujian	3330.18	610.04	1444.73	1208.75	235.98	1275.41	77.27	10369
江西 Jiangxi	1851.98	450.44	740.33	609.26	131.07	661.21	51.03	4484
山东 Shandong	7162.20	1215.81	3457.03	3052.44	404.59	2489.36	145.25	8120
河南 Henan	1356.60	1071.39	2012.74	1742.18	270.56	1272.47	84.23	4712
湖北 Hubei	3704.21	748.22	1752.91	1579.26	173.65	1203.08	80.53	6300
湖南 Hunan	3211.40	828.31	1294.17	1117.61	176.56	1088.92	97.97	4953
广东 Guangdong	7919.12	1004.92	3991.97	3463.12	528.85	2922.23	146.15	11143
广西 Guangxi	1903.04	574.25	678.19	569.90	108.29	650.60	55.27	4076
海南 Hainan	438.92	164.00	90.63	55.70	34.93	184.29	12.19	6022
重庆 Chongqing	1429.26	298.67	585.38	480.88	104.50	545.21	43.30	4684
四川 Sichuan	3580.26	941.24	1527.07	1272.41	254.66	1111.95	74.22	4339
贵州 Guizhou	841.88	264.89	326.03	273.16	52.87	250.96	26.83	2342
云南 Yunnan	1793.90	408.43	828.37	699.46	128.91	557.10	51.25	4355
西藏 Tibet	91.18	31.31	20.24	9.02	11.22	39.63	5.02	3716
陕西 Shaanxi	1381.53	283.49	567.66	445.35	122.31	530.38	56.97	3834
甘肃 Gansu	869.75	202.21	382.00	311.80	70.20	285.54	15.98	3456
青海 Qinghai	220.16	41.63	88.42	63.44	24.98	90.11	8.66	4367
宁夏 Ningxia	227.46	48.69	94.01	76.07	17.94	84.76	6.76	4270
新疆 Xinjiang	1116.67	291.05	430.73	300.00	130.73	394.89	37.95	6229

国家财政收支总额及增长速度

Total Government Revenue and Expenditures and Their Increase Rate

年 份 Year	财政收入 (亿元) Total Revenue (100 million Yuan)	财政支出 (亿元) Total Expenditures (100 million Yuan)	收支差额 (亿元) Balance (100 million Yuan)	增长速度(%) Increase Rate (%) 财政收入 Total Revenue	增长速度(%) Increase Rate (%) 财政支出 Total Expenditures
1970	662.9	649.41	13.49	25.8	23.5
1971－1975	3919.71	3917.94	1.77	4.2	4.8
1971	744.73	732.17	12.56	12.3	12.7
1972	766.56	765.86	0.70	2.9	4.6
1973	809.67	808.78	0.89	5.6	5.6
1974	783.14	790.25	－7.11	－3.3	－2.3
1975	815.61	820.88	－5.27	4.1	3.8
1976－1980	5089.61	5282.44	－192.83	7.3	8.4
1976	776.58	806.20	－29.62	－4.8	－1.8
1977	874.46	843.53	30.93	12.6	4.6
1978	1132.26	1122.09	10.17	29.5	33.0
1979	1146.38	1281.79	－135.41	1.2	14.2
1980	1159.93	1228.83	－68.90	1.2	－4.1
1981－1985	7402.75	7483.18	－80.43	11.6	10.3
1981	1175.79	1138.41	37.81	1.4	－7.5
1982	1212.33	1229.98	－17.65	3.1	8.0
1983	1366.95	1409.52	－42.57	12.8	14.6
1984	1642.86	1701.02	－58.16	20.2	20.7
1985	2004.82	2004.25	0.57	22.0	17.8
1986－1990	12280.601	12865.67	－585.07	7.9	9.0
1986	2122.01	2204.91	－82.90	5.8	10.0
1987	2199.35	2262.18	－62.83	3.6	2.6
1988	2357.24	2491.21	－133.97	7.2	10.1
1989	2664.90	2823.78	－158.88	13.1	13.3
1990	2937.10	3083.59	－146.49	10.2	9.2
1991－1995	22442.10	24387.46	－1945.36	16.3	17.2
1991	3149.48	3386.62	－237.14	7.2	9.8
1992	3483.37	3742.20	－258.83	10.6	10.5
1993	4348.95	4642.30	－293.35	24.8	24.1
1994	5218.10	5792.62	－574.52	20.0	24.8
1995	6242.20	6823.72	－581.52	19.6	17.8
1996	7407.99	7937.55	－529.56	18.7	16.3
1997	8651.14	9233.56	－582.42	16.8	16.3
1998	9875.95	10798.18	－922.23	14.2	16.9

注：1. 1985年及以前，价格补贴冲减财政收入，1985年以后改列财政支出。为统一口径，本表对1985年及以前数字做了调整。

2. 本表不包括国内外债务部分。

a) Government price subsidies ware listed as negative revenue items prior to 1986, but they have been listed as expenditure items in government accounts since 1986.

b) Domestic and foreign debts are excluded in this table.

中央财政和地方财政收支总额

Total Revenue and Expenditures of Central and Local Governments

单位:亿元

Unit: in 100 million Yuan

年份 Year	财政收入 Total Revenue			财政支出 Total Expenditures		
	合计 Total	中央 Central Government	地方 Local Government	合计 Total	中央 Central Government	地方 Local Government
1970	662.90	182.95	479.95	649.41	382.37	267.04
1971-1975	3919.71	576.43	3343.28	3919.44	2125.14	1794.30
1975	815.61	96.63	718.98	820.88	409.40	411.48
1976-1980	5089.61	904.32	4185.29	5282.44	2625.34	2657.10
1976	776.58	98.91	677.67	806.20	377.63	428.57
1977	874.46	113.85	760.61	843.53	393.70	449.83
1978	1132.26	175.77	956.49	1122.09	532.12	589.97
1979	1146.38	231.34	915.04	1281.79	655.08	626.71
1980	1159.93	284.45	875.48	1228.83	666.81	562.02
1981-1985	7402.75	2583.02	4819.73	7483.18	3725.64	3757.54
1981	1175.79	311.07	864.72	1138.41	625.65	512.76
1982	1212.33	346.84	865.49	1229.98	651.81	578.17
1983	1366.95	490.01	876.94	1409.52	759.60	649.92
1984	1642.86	665.47	977.39	1701.02	893.33	807.69
1985	2004.82	769.63	1235.19	2004.25	795.25	1209.00
1986-1990	12280.60	4104.41	8176.19	12865.67	4420.27	8445.40
1986	2122.01	778.42	1343.59	2204.91	836.36	1368.55
1987	2199.35	736.29	1463.06	2262.18	845.63	1416.55
1988	2357.24	774.76	1582.38	2491.21	845.04	1646.17
1989	2664.90	822.52	1842.38	2823.78	888.77	1935.01
1990	2937.10	992.42	1944.68	3083.59	1004.47	2079.12
1991-1995	22442.10	9038.39	13403.71	24387.46	7323.13	17064.33
1991	3149.48	938.25	2211.23	3386.62	1090.81	2295.81
1992	3483.37	979.51	2503.86	3742.20	1170.44	2571.76
1993	4348.95	957.51	3391.44	4642.30	1312.06	3330.24
1994	5218.10	2906.50	2311.60	5792.62	1754.43	4038.19
1995	6242.20	3256.62	2985.58	6823.72	1995.39	4828.33
1996	7407.99	3661.07	3746.92	7973.55	2151.27	5786.28
1997	8651.14	4226.92	4424.22	9233.56	2532.50	6701.06
1998	9875.95	4892.00	4983.95	10798.18	3125.60	7672.58

注:1. 中央财政收入和地方财政收入是各级负责组织征收的收入数。

2. 本表中不包括国内外债务收入、债务还本付息支出和利用国外借款收入安排的基本建设支出。

a) The revenue of the central and local governments refer to revenue actually collected by the central and local governments.

b) Revenue in this table does not include revenue from domestic and foreign borrowings, and expenditure does not include the payment of the principal and interestt of domestic and foreign debts and the expenditure for capital construcation using foreign loans.

人口数及构成

Population and its Composition

本表各年人口包括中国人民解放军现役军人数据，未包括香港特别行政区、台湾省和澳门特别行政区的人口数据。

Data in this table include the military personnel, but exclude the population of Hong Kong, Macao and Taiwan.

单位：万人

Unit: in 10 thousand persons

年份 Year	年底总人口 Total Population (year-end)	按性别分 By Sex 男 Male 人口数 Population	比重(%) Proportion	女 Female 人口数 Population	比重(%) Proportion	按城乡分 By Residence 市镇总人口 Urban 人口数 Population	比重(%) Proportion	乡村总人口 Rural 人口数 Population	比重(%) Proportion
1952	57482	29833	51.90	27649	48.10	7163	12.46	50319	87.54
1957	64653	33469	51.77	31184	48.23	9949	15.39	54704	84.61
1962	67295	34517	51.29	32778	48.71	11659	17.33	55636	82.67
1965	72538	37128	51.18	35410	48.82	13045	17.98	59493	82.02
1970	82992	42686	51.43	40306	48.57	14424	17.38	68568	82.62
1975	92420	47564	51.47	44856	48.53	16030	17.34	76390	82.66
1978	96259	49567	51.49	46692	48.51	17245	17.92	79014	82.08
1980	98705	50785	51.45	47920	48.55	19140	19.39	79565	80.61
1985	105851	54725	51.70	51126	48.30	25094	23.71	80757	76.29
1986	107507	55581	51.70	51926	48.30	26366	24.52	81141	75.48
1987	109300	56290	51.50	53010	48.50	27674	25.32	81626	74.68
1988	111026	57201	51.52	53825	48.48	28661	25.81	82365	74.19
1989	112704	58099	51.55	54605	48.45	29540	26.21	83164	73.79
1990	114333	58904	51.52	55429	48.48	30191	26.41	84142	73.59
1991	115823	59466	51.34	56357	48.66	30543	26.37	85280	73.63
1992	117171	59811	51.05	57360	48.95	32372	27.63	84799	72.37
1993	118517	60472	51.02	58045	48.98	33351	28.14	85166	71.86
1994	119850	61246	51.10	58604	48.90	34301	28.62	85549	71.38
1995	121121	61808	51.03	59313	48.97	35174	29.04	85947	70.96
1996	122389	62200	50.82	60189	49.18	35950	29.37	86439	70.63
1997	123626	63131	51.07	60495	48.93	36989	29.92	86637	70.08
1998	124810	63629	50.98	61181	49.02	37942	30.40	86868	69.60

注：1982－1989年数据是根据1982年、1990年两次人口普查数据调整的，1990年以后数据是人口变动抽样调查调整数，其余年份数据为户籍统计数（下表同）。

Data in 1982－1989 ware adjusted on the basis of the 1982 and 1990 National Population Censuses. Since 1990, data have been estimated on the basis of the annual National Sample Surveys on Population Changes. Data of other years were taken from the annual reports of the Minstry of Public Security. (The next table is the same.)

各地区总人口和出生率、死亡率、自然增长率(1998年)

Total Population and Birth Rate, Death Rate and Natural Growth Rate by Region(1998)

地区 Region	年底总人口(万人) Total Population (year-end) (10 000 Persons)	出生率 Birth Rate (‰)	死亡率 Death Rate (‰)	自然增长率 Natural Growth Rate (‰)
全国 **National Total or Average**	124810	16.03	6.50	9.53
北京 Beijing	1246	6.00	5.30	0.70
天津 Tianjin	957	9.89	6.49	3.40
河北 Hebei	6569	13.01	6.18	6.83
山西 Shanxi	3172	16.09	6.17	9.92
内蒙古 Inner Mongolia	2345	14.40	6.17	8.23
辽宁 Liaoning	4157	11.39	6.81	4.58
吉林 Jilin	2644	11.81	5.76	6.05
黑龙江 Heilongjiang	3773	11.68	5.32	6.36
上海 Shanghai	1464	5.20	7.00	-1.80
江苏 Jiangsu	7182	10.97	6.84	4.13
浙江 Zhejiang	4456	11.15	6.33	4.82
安徽 Anhui	6184	15.74	6.54	9.20
福建 Fujian	3299	11.53	6.20	5.33
江西 Jiangxi	4191	16.85	7.05	9.80
山东 Shandong	8838	11.58	6.12	5.46
河南 Henan	9315	14.17	6.37	7.80
湖北 Hubei	5907	12.58	6.70	5.88
湖南 Hunan	6502	12.31	7.10	5.21
广东 Guangdong	7143	16.51	5.61	10.90
广西 Guangxi	4675	15.87	6.86	9.01
海南 Hainan	753	18.48	5.56	12.92
重庆 Chongqing	3060	13.19	7.68	5.51
四川 Sichuan	8493	14.62	7.14	7.48
贵州 Guizhou	3658	22.02	7.76	14.26
云南 Yunnan	4144	20.01	7.91	12.10
西藏 Tibet	252	23.70	7.80	15.90
陕西 Shaanxi	3596	13.56	6.43	7.13
甘肃 Gansu	2519	16.45	6.41	10.04
青海 Qinghai	503	21.26	6.78	14.48
宁夏 Ningxia	538	18.19	5.11	13.08
新疆 Xinjiang	1747	19.74	6.93	12.81

注：1.全国人口中包括现役军人数，分地区数字中则未包括。

2.全国数据未包括香港特别行政区、台湾省和澳门地区的人口数据。

3.全国数据根据抽样误差和调查误差进行了修正。

a) The military personnel ware included in the national total population, but excluded in the regional total population.

b) The national total population excluded the population of Hong Kong, Macao and Taiwan.

c) The national total population was readjusted for the sampling error and investigation error.

各地区按性别和

Population by Sex,

本表是1998年人口变动抽样调查数据，抽样比为1.01‰。

Date in this table are obtained from the Sample Survey on Population Changes in 1998. The sampling fraction is 1.01‰.

地区 Region	6岁及6岁以上人口 Population Aged 6 and Over			不识字或识字很少 Illiterate			
	合计 Total	男 Male	女 Female	小计 Subtotal	男 Male	女 Female	小计 Subtotal
全　国 National Total	1150370	581911	568460	157746	47074	110672	457703
北　京 Beijing	12110	6162	5948	704	157	547	2376
天　津 Tianjin	9052	4515	4537	845	229	616	2863
河　北 Hebei	61877	31220	30657	6529	1925	4604	22925
山　西 Shanxi	28893	14793	14101	2661	911	1750	10692
内蒙古 Inner Mongolia	21992	11246	10746	3028	1016	2012	7530
辽　宁 Liaoning	39458	19698	19760	3016	844	2172	13028
吉　林 Jilin	25150	12795	12355	2012	673	1339	9099
黑龙江 Heilongjiang	35879	18353	17526	2985	1062	1923	12772
上　海 Shanghai	14208	7028	7180	1298	271	1027	3025
江　苏 Jiangsu	68018	33452	34566	11472	2922	8550	23541
浙　江 Zhejiang	42094	21493	20601	6159	1867	4292	16646
安　徽 Anhui	57065	29134	27931	9805	3230	6575	24061
福　建 Fujian	30783	15346	15436	4858	1276	3582	13609
江　西 Jiangxi	38957	19691	19265	4354	1097	3257	17898
山　东 Shandong	83863	41827	42036	15952	4386	11566	29423
河　南 Henan	87137	44269	42868	10492	3157	7335	32120
湖　北 Hubei	55536	28198	27338	7080	2173	4907	21260
湖　南 Hunan	61738	31800	29938	5685	1460	4225	27514
广　东 Guangdong	64468	32161	32307	5677	1330	4347	27257
广　西 Guangxi	43613	22281	21332	5072	1353	3719	21014
海　南 Hainan	6825	3537	3288	864	252	612	2701
重　庆 Chongqing	28251	14334	13918	3847	1170	2677	13354
四　川 Sichuan	78925	39718	39207	10890	3378	7512	36041
贵　州 Guizhou	32938	17329	15610	8227	2484	5743	14625
云　南 Yunnan	37686	18961	18726	8336	2843	5493	18431
西　藏 Tibet	2287	1132	1155	1123	463	660	975
陕　西 Shaanxi	33174	16885	16289	4468	1456	3012	13938
甘　肃 Gansu	23149	11784	11365	5714	1905	3809	8860
青　海 Qinghai	4553	2282	2271	1813	675	1138	1439
宁　夏 Ningxia	4841	2456	2386	1101	362	739	1587
新　疆 Xinjiang	15849	8031	7817	1675	745	930	7098

受教育程度分的人口

Educational Level and Region

单位:人

小学 Primary School		初中 Junior Secondary School			高中 Senior Secondary School			大专以上 College and Higher Level		
男 Male	女 Female	小计 Subtotal	男 Male	女 Female	小计 Subtotal	男 Male	女 Female	小计 Subtotal	男 Male	女 Female
228997	228707	380066	215343	164723	122741	70340	52401	32114	20158	11956
1199	1177	4060	2221	1839	3057	1510	1547	1911	1074	837
1398	1465	3284	1796	1488	1540	791	749	520	301	219
11271	11654	23806	13129	10677	6920	3879	3041	1698	1016	682
5298	5394	11634	6379	5255	3153	1733	1420	753	471	282
3793	3736	7498	4252	3246	3041	1650	1391	894	534	360
6315	6713	16598	8806	7792	4920	2623	2297	1897	1110	787
4480	4619	8758	4775	3983	4018	2126	1892	1264	742	522
6272	6500	13973	7601	6372	4778	2584	2194	1369	833	536
1499	1526	4968	2596	2372	3511	1787	1724	1406	875	531
11735	11806	22266	12460	9806	8681	4968	3713	2058	1367	691
8727	7919	13466	7537	5929	4620	2573	2047	1203	789	414
11559	12502	17944	11018	6926	4231	2642	1589	1024	686	338
6575	7034	8671	5234	3437	3019	1813	1206	625	447	178
8446	9452	12441	7376	5065	3610	2319	1291	655	454	201
14629	14794	29484	17146	12338	7707	4791	2916	1296	874	422
15755	16365	34154	19152	15002	8491	5087	3404	1879	1118	761
10422	10838	18430	10514	7916	7093	4007	3086	1671	1081	590
13791	13723	20849	11807	9042	6466	3930	2536	1223	811	412
13033	14224	21595	11763	9832	7544	4501	3043	2395	1534	861
10514	10500	13947	8187	5760	3147	1952	1195	433	275	158
1345	1356	2322	1328	994	739	467	272	201	145	56
6845	6509	8455	4867	3588	2240	1243	997	355	209	146
18628	17413	22849	12522	10327	7337	3991	3346	1807	1198	609
8336	6289	7507	4913	2594	1985	1207	778	594	389	205
9660	8771	8388	4995	3393	2108	1190	918	424	273	151
566	409	161	85	76	26	18	8	3	1	1
6997	6941	10159	5733	4426	3747	2162	1585	862	537	325
4645	4215	5845	3535	2310	2255	1380	875	476	319	157
835	604	820	511	309	340	177	163	141	85	56
854	733	1462	840	622	522	292	230	170	108	62
3574	3524	4274	2265	2009	1893	946	947	907	500	407

各地区分性别的15岁及15岁以上文盲半文盲人口

Illiterate and Semi－Literate Population Aged 15 and by Sex and Region

本表是1998年人口变动抽样调查数据，抽样比为1.01‰。

Date in this table are obtained from the Sample Survey on Population Changes in 1998. The sampling fraction is 1.01‰.

单位：人

地区 Region	15岁及15岁以上人口 Population Aged 15 and Over			文盲、半文盲人口 Illiterate and Semi－literate			文盲、半文盲占15岁及以上比例 % to population aged 15 & over		
	合计 Total	男 Male	女 Female	小计 Subtotal	男 Male	女 Female	小计 Subtotal	男 Male	女 Female
全国 National Total	941147	472749	468398	148522	42603	105918	15.78	9.01	22.61
北京 Beijing	10635	5403	5231	693	151	541	6.51	2.80	10.35
天津 Tianjin	7716	3831	3886	804	209	595	10.43	5.46	15.32
河北 Hebei	50219	25152	25066	6027	1653	4374	12.00	6.57	17.45
山西 Shanxi	23346	11899	11447	2445	795	1651	10.47	6.68	14.42
内蒙古 Inner Mongolia	18227	9288	8939	2885	949	1936	15.83	10.22	21.66
辽宁 Liaoning	34209	17052	17156	2794	735	2059	8.17	4.31	12.00
吉林 Jilin	21522	10929	10593	1814	576	1239	8.43	5.27	11.69
黑龙江 Heilongjiang	30258	15414	14844	2683	891	1793	8.87	5.78	12.08
上海 Shanghai	12635	6219	6417	1287	265	1022	10.19	4.26	15.93
江苏 Jiangsu	56947	27653	29294	11153	2784	8369	19.59	10.07	28.57
浙江 Zhejiang	36457	18494	17963	5968	1767	4200	16.37	9.56	23.38
安徽 Anhui	45911	23202	22709	9426	3035	6391	20.53	13.08	28.14
福建 Fujian	24335	12026	12309	4550	1114	3436	18.70	9.26	27.91
江西 Jiangxi	30724	15356	15368	4143	990	3153	13.48	6.45	20.52
山东 Shandong	69550	34424	35126	15337	4099	11238	22.05	11.91	31.99
河南 Henan	69248	34755	34494	9996	2929	7067	14.44	8.43	20.49
湖北 Hubei	45111	22863	22248	6840	2043	4797	15.16	8.94	21.56
湖南 Hunan	49934	25644	24290	5457	1346	4111	10.93	5.25	16.92
广东 Guangdong	51133	25163	25970	4731	857	3873	9.25	3.41	14.92
广西 Guangxi	34277	17379	16898	4565	1110	3455	13.32	6.39	20.45
海南 Hainan	5316	2726	2590	758	201	557	14.27	7.38	21.52
重庆 Chongqing	23876	12038	11838	3688	1092	2596	15.45	9.07	21.93
四川 Sichuan	66433	33208	33226	10427	3128	7300	15.70	9.42	21.97
贵州 Guizhou	26298	13781	12517	7621	2266	5355	28.98	16.44	42.78
云南 Yunnan	30648	15373	15275	7809	2589	5220	25.48	16.84	34.17
西藏 Tibet	1729	844	885	1037	423	614	59.97	50.09	69.41
陕西 Shaanxi	26183	13256	12928	4324	1385	2939	16.52	10.45	22.74
甘肃 Gansu	18544	9411	9132	5313	1744	3569	28.65	18.53	39.08
青海 Qinghai	3660	1839	1821	1571	570	1001	42.92	31.00	54.95
宁夏 Ningxia	3798	1921	1877	971	311	659	25.56	16.20	35.14
新疆 Xinjiang	12269	6206	6063	1403	596	807	11.44	9.61	13.31

注：本表"文盲、半文盲人口"指15岁及15岁以上不识字及识字很少人口。

Illiterate and semi－illiterate population in this table refers to the population aged 15 and over, who are unable or very difficult to read.

TRANSLATOR'S NOTES

Considering that many foreign readers might not be familiar with the educational system of China, it is appropriate to give some explanations to part of the English terms used in this book.

1. "Secondary school" is used throughout instead of the conventional "middle school" to indicate Zhongxue(中学), in view of the fact that in the United States and the United Kingdom, "middle school" means quite different things from Zhongxue in China, the upper stage of which leads to higher education directly.

2. "Putong gaodeng xuexiao" (普通高等学校) is rendered into "regular higher educational institutions" so as to distinguish them from institutions for adult. But "Putong zhongxue" (普通中学) is rendered into "general secondary schools" so as to distinguish them from schools for adults as well as from vocational－technical schools.

3. "Zhiye jishu xueyuan" (职业技术学院) is rendered into "short－cycle vocational colleges".

4. "Zhuanke xuexiao" (专科学校) is rendered into "short－cycle colleges".

5. "Guangbo dianshi daxue" (广播电视大学), "Zhigong gaodeng xuexiao" (职工高等学校), "Nongmin gaodeng xuexiao" (农民高等学校), "Guanli ganbu xueyuan" (管理干部学院), and "Jiaoyu xueyuan" (教育学院) are rendered into radio/TV universities, workers' colleges, peasants' colleges, institutes for administration, and educational colleges respectively.

6. In summary tables showing the number of schools and enrolments and the number of staff and workers, the number of schools is always given in an absolute number, while the other figures are given in 10 thousand.

7. In the statistical tables the translator has freely used the device of English letters to indicate the more clumsy terms or phrases, with the full translations given at the bottom of the table.